Introduction to Sicilian Grammar

Introduction to
Sicilian Grammar

by

J. K. "Kirk" Bonner
Edited by Gaetano Cipolla

LEGAS

Library of Congress Cataloging-in-Publication Data

Bonner, J.K., (J. Kirk), 1939-
   Introduction to Sicilian grammar/J.K. "Kirk" Bonner; edited by Gaetano Cipolla.
      p.cm.
   Includes bibliographical references and index.
   ISBN 1-881901-25-4
      1. Italian language-Dialects--Italy--Sicily--Grammar. 2. Italian language--
   Dialects--Italy--Sicily--Textbooks for foreign speakers--English.
      I. Cipolla, Gaetano, 1937- II. Title.

PC18091 .B66 2001
457'.8--dc21   2001029837

Printed and bound in Canada

Acknowledgments
   The publisher gratefully acknowledges a generous grant from Arba Sicula that made it possible, in part, to publish this book.

For information and for orders, write to:
LEGAS

P.O. Box 040328	3 Wood Aster Bay	2908 Dufferin Ave
Brooklyn, NY 11204	Ottawa, Ontario	Toronto, Ontario
USA	K2R 1B3 Canada	M6B 3S8 Canada

A me mugghieri
a l'amici dâ lingua siciliana,
e a tutti chiddi chi â vonnu sarvari

Contents

Preface

Background

Who am I and why have I written this book? My background is not Sicilian; my heritage is not Sicilian. So why bother to write a book dealing with the grammar of a language that doesn't form part of my cultural heritage? To answer that question, I can say I have an abiding interest in different languages and different peoples. Ever since I studied Italian, I was intrigued by Sicilian. It is a truly marvelous and expressive tongue, very well suited for poetry, lyrics, and song. It would break my heart to see it disappear, but unless more interest is taken in it, it could very well do just that. All educated Sicilians speak, read, and write Italian. In Sicily Italian is the language heard in the schools, on television; it is the language in which Sicilians today write novels and stories. Italian is what is used in the newspapers, and Italian will eventually replace Sicilian unless a concerted effort is made to keep it a living language.

In the eighteenth century Giuvanni Meli (1740-1815) and several others attempted to form a standard literary Sicilian which would enjoy the same prestige as Tuscan enjoyed on the Italian mainland. Unfortunately in the case of Sicilian, attempts to create a literary Sicilian were inconsequential. Lacking the support of Sicilian intellectuals and the political power structure in Sicily, a true Sicilian literary language never formed around which acceptable grammatical, lexical, and syntactic forms could coalesce. The Spaniards controlled Sicily for almost five centuries, up to the late eighteenth century, and the Italians controlled it beginning in the latter half of the nineteenth century and up to the present day. Consequently Sicilian remained, and remains to this day, chiefly a spoken language used in the home and among close friends. There is no common, shared Sicilian language used among all Sicilians; there is simply no common language that they can all call Sicilian. Each Sicilian dialect (see below in the **Introduction**) expresses itself through slightly different linguistic norms. I'm excluding the Albanian and Northern Italian, or so-called Gallo-Italian (or Gallo-Italic), dialects that are still spoken in parts of Sicily. Albanian isn't even a Romance language, and the Gallo-Italian dialects, although Romance, are just too divergent from the Sicilian dialects.

All this means that the dialect situation in Sicily is very complex. Putting aside the complicating issue of the incursion of Standard Italian in Sicily, the various dialectical differences in Sicily depend on several things, among which are:

- Geographical area of the speaker;
- Coastal area versus inland area (predominantly agricultural);
- City/town versus village/countryside;
- Socioeconomic level of the speaker;
- Sex and/or age of the speaker;
- Speaker's level of formal education;
- Speaker's exposure to other *parrati* (Sicilian dialects);
- Speaker's exposure to Standard Italian.

Given that the linguistic situation today in Sicily is difficult to describe adequately, what I'm attempting to present here is a language that most Sicilians would recognize as being distinctly Sicilian. One of the problems in doing this is that there are generally several ways that a word may be presented. For example, it's perfectly feasible to write the word "cat" in Sicilian as: gattu, iattu, attu; and the word "rooster" can realistically be represented as: gaddu, addu, addru, iaddu, iạddru. Which one is correct depends on which *parrata* is being spoken. A person who speaks a dialect of Sicilian may look at this work and exclaim, "Well, it's a form of Sicilian, I guess, but it's not the Sicilian I speak." or "it's not the Sicilian my parents (or grandparents) spoke." Since there never was a true literary Sicilian that could function as the basis for a common language, it seems a good idea to set forth something that can at least be considered a start. Since I'm not of Sicilian origin, a few Sicilians may be unhappy with my effort. I say to this, "That's fine. I've made an honest effort for preserving the Sicilian language." Hopefully, you, the reader, will agree.

Just a note on the spelling of Sicilian found in this book. It is to a considerable extent modelled on the suggestions in Giorgio Piccitto's *Elementi di Ortografia siciliana* (1947). The spelling conventions found in the poetry of Gnaziu Buttitta (1899-1998), one of the greatest Sicilian poets of the twentieth century, and in Giuseppi Cavallaru's translation of some of the cantos of Homer's *Iliad* (*Iliadi*, Palermu: Nuova Tavolozza, 1997) are to some extent also employed. Where practical, I've also tried adhering to the spelling conventions found in the very comprehensive *Vocabolario Siciliano* dictionaries (sometimes referred to as the *Piccitto* dictionaries since Giorgio Piccitto was the original editor). It is certainly possible to employ Sicilian to compose works of the highest literary order. Hopefully, this book will help promote such efforts being undertaken.

Goal of This Book
The goal of this book is to introduce you, the reader, to the Sicilian language. To do this, it concentrates heavily on practicing. There are numerous examples in the book illustrating the use of each principle as it is taken up. Emphasis is strong on learning how to construct simple, but clear, sentences in Sicilian. This book also introduces a number of Sicilian proverbs. Since one of the goals is to be able to read and understand Sicilian proverbs and since Sicilian is an earthy language replete with pithy sayings, I've included some words in the vocabulary that might seem a bit off-color. I don't wish to offend anyone, but knowledge of these words is necessary to capture the authentic flavor of the language.

References and Resources
Of course, I didn't make it this far without considerable help. Anyone who speaks English and who is sincere in her/his effort to learn Sicilian should acquire Mr. Joseph Bellestri's dictionaries. These are the *Basic Sicilian-English Dictionary* (Ann Arbor, MI: 1985) and the *English-Sicilian Dictionary* (Ann Arbor, MI: 1988). These represent the best Sicilian-English and English-Sicilian dictionaries available; the other dictionaries cited in the **References** require a working knowledge of Italian. For a more extensive list, consult the **References** in the back of the book.

Acknowledgements
First and foremost I must give my sincerest thanks and appreciation to Dr. Gaetano Cipolla, President of Arba Sicula, the well-known and renowned Sicilian-American organization. Dr. Cipolla has done a tremendous amount and expended a lot of energy to keeping Sicilian alive as a language and in promoting Sicilian culture. Arba Sicula publishes numerous books on Sicily and Sicilian culture, and many of these books are in Sicilian. Dr. Cipolla, in addition to encouraging me and helping me master the Sicilian language, took it on himself to edit this

entire work. He made many cogent suggestions and recommendations that greatly improved the presentation of materials in this book, and he edited all the examples of Sicilian to ensure that they ring true. He far exceeded his role as editor in improving this book and ensuring that it would make a lasting contribution to the Sicilian language and its preservation.

I also extend my sincerest thanks to Dr. Joseph Siracusa of the State University of New York, College at Brockport, who gave me considerable encouragement and made many useful suggestions on how to improve my Sicilian. My deepest thanks also to Mr. Joseph Bellestri who kindly read my entire book and made a number of important corrections and suggestions. I would also like to thank Mr. Art Dieli. Mr. Dieli has given me considerable encouragement to continue in my effort to produce this work.

My warmest thanks also go to Ms. Emma Sorrentino of the Foreign Language Center of the Defense Language Institute (DLIFLC). Ms. Sorrentino was good enough to review my entire initial effort (at that time called *A Sicilian Grammar*) and pointed out errors or ways to say things more correctly in Sicilian. I also extend my appreciation to Dr. Karl Nicholas for his support and encouragement. Finally, I must thank my wife, Mary, for her support and for putting up with me while I wrote this book.

I'm sure there are still errors remaining in this work, and I alone am responsible for them. I would highly appreciate all positive criticisms and/or comments. If you want to contact me to point out any errors and/or to make any comments, you can send them to Dr. Cipolla at Arba Sicula who will forward them to me, or if you have access to a computer, you can email me if you wish. My email address is: jkbonner@gte.net

1   Introduction

Purpose of the Chapter

The chief purpose of this chapter is to discuss some of the history and background of the Sicilian language. Although Sicilian is a Romance language, that is, it is derived from Latin, it is a language in its own right. It should not be considered a dialect of Italian. It has its own vocabulary, grammar, and syntax. Since there are several dialects of Sicilian, this book sets forth a common Sicilian.

Historical Development of Sicilian

Sicily. Land of blazing sun and wind-swept coasts. The jewel in the Mediterranean that looks like a triangle. The land of three points often symbolized by the Trinacria, like the one on the cover of this book. Sicily's a mysterious and enchanted land. Its prehistoric inhabitants carry the names Siculi and Sicani. No one knows who these people were or where they came from. They will forever remain shrouded in the mists that envelop so many people before recorded history. But we do know that the Carthaginians and the Greeks colonized Sicily. At one time Syracuse in southeastern Sicily was the most populous Greek city in the world. The philosopher Plato (429 BCE-347 BCE) visited it several times trying to talk its ruler, Dionysios, into creating Plato's dream republic ruled by philosophers. And that city also gave rise to the greatest physical scientist of the ancient world, the great Archimedes of Syracuse (287? BCE-212 BCE).

But the world of the Carthaginians and the Greeks was not destined to last. In three protracted wars called the Punic Wars, Rome succeeded in totally crushing its powerful rival, the Carthaginians, and by so doing gained the hegemony of the Mediterranean world. By the beginning of the second century BCE, Sicily had been reduced to a Roman province. Besides conquering Sicily, the Romans also brought their Latin language to the island, which largely replaced the other languages spoken there. The long Roman occupation of Sicily (almost 700 years) was sufficient to ensure that the inhabitants of the island learned a form of Latin.

So it is that Sicilian is a Latin language. Much of its vocabulary, its grammar, and its syntax (how sentences are put together from words) come from Latin. In addition, most of the languages of Southern and Western Europe also emanate from Latin, including of course Italian, French, Spanish, Portuguese, and Romanian. As the Vulgar Latin spoken in Central Italy was evolving into Tuscan, which forms the basis of the Standard Italian spoken today and which is the official language of the Italian state, the Vulgar Latin spoken in Sicily was evolving into Sicilian. Subsequently Sicilian was exposed to Greek, Germanic, Arabic, Norman and French influences, and also Aragonese and Spanish, which didn't affect Tuscan (except possibly Germanic and French). These influences on Sicilian mainly affected the vocabulary, but in the case of the French and Spanish, also some of the grammar.

To sum up, Sicilian is a distinct language from Italian. It has a separate history, and it evolved in parallel with Italian. Both experienced different influences. Sicilian is not a slightly different version of Italian as is widely held. Although both Italian and Sicilian are based on Latin, they are separated by a different history, and they lack mutual intelligibility. That these two criteria are sufficient can be ascertained by comparing Spanish and Portuguese. These latter two languages are also based on Latin and have more of a shared history than do Italian and Sicilian, yet they are considered separate languages.

As you study Sicilian, you will note that there are many words that are different in the two languages (assuming that you have a working knowledge of Italian). Sicilian has certain grammatical features that are nearer to Spanish. Two prominent examples are the use of the *personal a* and the use and meaning of the *preterite* tense. The latter is used like the *preterite* in Spanish, not like the *passato remoto* in Italian. Sicilian also has certain sentence structures (syntactical features) that are different from Italian. Sicilian is a language in its own right.

However, today Sicily is part of Italy (just as for almost five centuries it was part of Spain). It is politically part of the Italian state, whose capital is in Rome. The same may be said of Sardinia, the language of which is a Romance language distinct from both Italian and Sicilian. But because Sicily is not an independent country (and I'm certainly not advocating that it should strive for political independence), it is not expedient to consider Sicilian as a separate language from Italian, even though historically it is. For political reasons, all of the various regional languages of Italy are considered to be dialects of Italian, even though in reality many have separate histories and are, linguistically speaking, separate languages. For political reasons, they are today considered dialects.

Sicilian Dialects – the Parrati siciliani

End of story? Not quite. Remember that Sicilian is, historically speaking, a true language. Different villages and regions in Sicily developed divergent ways of speaking. In most cases not greatly divergent, but divergent nonetheless, so that Sicilian has its own dialects (*parrati*). Most of these dialects are mutually intelligible, that is, a person speaking the dialect of Catania would be able to understand someone speaking the dialect of Palermu, but he/she would also be conscious of some distinctive differences.

For convenience, the various Sicilian dialects can be divided into three broad regions. The separation of these three regions is shown in the map (see page 3) by the two broad bands.

- Western Sicilian (WS)
- Central Sicilian (CS)
- Eastern Sicilian (ES).

The dialects in these regions can be further subdivided into several distinctive subdialects.

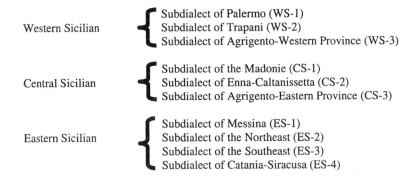

Western Sicilian
{
Subdialect of Palermo (WS-1)
Subdialect of Trapani (WS-2)
Subdialect of Agrigento-Western Province (WS-3)

Central Sicilian
{
Subdialect of the Madonie (CS-1)
Subdialect of Enna-Caltanissetta (CS-2)
Subdialect of Agrigento-Eastern Province (CS-3)

Eastern Sicilian
{
Subdialect of Messina (ES-1)
Subdialect of the Northeast (ES-2)
Subdialect of the Southeast (ES-3)
Subdialect of Catania-Siracusa (ES-4)

There are two major exceptions to this classification. In the fourteenth century, groups of Albanians, fleeing Turkish encroachment in the Balkans, fled across the Adriatic Sea, settling in Southern Italy and also in Sicily. Although Albanian is an Indo-European language, it is, in general, not very similar either to Standard Italian, Sicilian, or any of the other various regional languages of Italy. So the regional Albanian dialects of Sicily were never understandable by local Sicilians. Sicilian, and for that matter, Italian, is just too divergent from Albanian.

The other exception is that during the Norman occupation of Sicily (1061-1194 CE) and after them the French (until the great Sicilian Vespers massacre of the French on Easter Monday, 1282 CE), various peoples from Northern Italy came to Sicily as colonists. In general, the towns where Gallo-Italian (sometimes referred to as Gallo-Italic) and French influence were the strongest are found in the provinces of Messina and Enna. Although their language (Gallo-Italian, actually several different Gallo-Italian dialects) was nowhere nearly as divergent from Sicilian as was Albanian, still Gallo-Italian and Sicilian were not mutually intelligible, and so the dialects formed from Gallo-Italian are not mutually intelligible with the other Sicilian dialects.

The above sets forth a very brief history of how the Sicilian language came to be. Now it's necessary to propose common conventions and acceptable forms so that communication, especially written communication, can more easily take place. With this in mind, let's move to the next chapter, which discusses the sounds used in Sicilian and their generally accepted spelling conventions. Howevever, there is a caveat here. Regarding the spelling of Sicilian, there are few standard norms covering usage for the entire language. What is common in Eastern Sicilian may not be common in Western Sicilian. Even the pronunciation is not uniform. The word "river" can realistically be written as *ciumi* (soft c), *sciumi* (soft sc), **or** *xiumi* (x = an aspirated consonant like the Spanish *j*); the word for "flame" as *ciamma*, *sciamma*, **or** *xiamma*. The pronunciation depends on the particular *parrata* being spoken. In the next chapter, we'll make compromises in order to set forth normal spelling rules so that some agreement can be reached as to how to spell the words of the language.

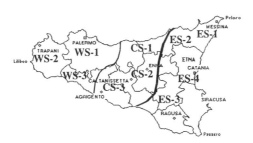

Figure 1 Map of Sicily (courtesy of A. Dieli) showing the distribution of the ten subdialects

2   Pronunciation and Spelling

Purpose of the Chapter
The chief purpose of this chapter is to discuss how Sicilian words are pronounced, and it also discusses the recommended way to spell them. In general, the spelling conventions used will be similar to those of Italian since Sicilian has a similar phonology. However, it is necessary to impart to Sicilian to some extent its own distinctive spelling conventions so that the language doesn't too slavishly follow other Romance languages. The conventions unique to Sicilian are pointed out at the end of the chapter (see **Spelling Conventions for Sicilian** below). You must be willing to read this chapter carefully since Sicilian is more difficult to pronounce than Italian, or for that matter, Spanish. By the time you finish, however, you should have a very good idea of how to pronounce and spell Sicilian words. If you still have trouble with this, then try to locate someone who speaks Sicilian and have that person help you with the pronunciation.

Note: As an aid to the student, at times the simulated pronunciation will be given between two forward slashes, / /. This is done merely to help the student attain the correct pronunciation. It is not intended to indicate the spelling. **Examples:** Chi canta idda? /kikkanta id'd'a?/ What's she singing?; di vui /dibbui/ of you; emu /yemu/, we go; nun dormi /nun normi/, he doesn't sleep.

Introduction
Like any language, Sicilian has both vowels and consonants. Although many of the sounds in Sicilian are similar to sounds in English, there are some subtle differences. To learn how to pronounce Sicilian correctly, carefully read the descriptions of how to pronounce each letter. Don't be shy about trying to make these sounds. Sicilian proverbs and Sicilian poetry sound more authentic if you try to say it the way a Sicilian would. Let's look at the vowels first.

Vowels
Sicilian has only five principal vowel sounds. These are:

a has the sound of *a* in the English word "father". **Example:** sapi, he/she knows.

e has the sound of *e* in the English word "bed". This is an open sound. **Example:** e, and.

i has the sound of *i* in the English word "machine". **Example:** mi, me.

o has the sound of *o* in the English word "odd" or the aw in the English word "law" but more rounded. This is an open sound. **Example:** pò, he/she can.

u has the sound of *oo* in the English word "mood". **Example:** cu, with.

For these five vowels, the spelling symbols in Sicilian are: a, e, i, o, u; unless one of these vowels ends a word and also receives the stress, in which case by convention they're written with a grave accent: à, è, ì, ò, ù. It is also important to distinguish the back vowels, *a*, *o*, and *u*, from the front vowels, *e* and *i*. This distinction will occur in some of the discussions below.

A few words need be said about the vowels. Unlike Italian, which maintains a distinction between *close e* and *open e*, and *close o* and *open o*, Sicilian has only an *open e* sound and an *open o* sound. In many cases in which Italian has a *close e*, Sicilian has an *i*; in many cases in which Italian has a *close o*, Sicilian has a *u*. This is an important point to remember. In unstressed syllables, generally only *a*, *i*, and *u* appear although there are some exceptions. In summary, as opposed to Italian, which maintains seven distinct vowel sounds, Sicilian maintains only five. These five vowel sounds are commonly referred to as the Sicilian vowel system.

Vowels in Unstressed Positions

In Sicilian, vowels in unstressed positions are not particularly tense although they are more tense than vowels in unstressed positions in English. This has three effects.

(1) The vowel sound is shorter and less well formed in unstressed syllables, thus changing the quality. So in *unstressed syllables* the vowels sound more like these:

a has the sound of *a* in the English word "tall". **Example:** portanu, they carry.

e has (1) the sound of *i* in the English word "bid" or (2) the sound of *a* in the English word "tall". **Examples of (1):** esami, examination; eleganti, elegant. Very often this sound will appear in the spelling as an *i* instead of an *e*. **Examples:** divuzzioni, devotion; liganti, elegant. At times, *unstressed e* has the sound indicated in (2), and such words may be written with an *a* instead of an *e*. **Examples of (2):** esempiu/asempiu, example; esercitu/asercitu, army.

i has the sound of *i* in the English word "bid". **Example:** sicilianu, Sicilian.

o has (1) either the sound of *u* in the English word "put" or (2) the sound of *a* in the English word "tall". Some *parrati* favor one pronunciation; some favor the other. In this book the first sound (1) will often appear in the spelling simply as a *u* instead of an *o*. **Examples of (1):** divuzzioni, devotion; prucissioni, procession.* When *unstressed o* appears in a word, assume it has the second sound (2). Words containing this vowel may often be spelled with either an *o* or an *a*. **Examples of (2):** oduri/aduri, odor (not pejorative); oliva/aliva, olive; occupari/accupari, to occupy. **Note:** Although *stressed o* (see above) and *unstressed o* (as in (oduri, oliva, etc.) have similar sounds, i.e., both are open sounds, *stressed o* is a more rounded sound.

u has the sound of u in the English word "put". **Example:** miricanu, American.

* Alternative ways of spelling these words are: devozzioni, processioni. This practice will not be followed in this book.

(2) Very often at the beginning of words, the initial vowel, if not stressed, simply disappears. This is especially true of *initial i; initial e* also often disappears, especially in the spoken language.

Examples

nzignari, to teach (*initial i* disappears)
mparari, to learn (*initial i* disappears)
nnuccenti, innocent (*initial i* disappears)
talianu, Italian (*initial i* disappears)
miricanu, American (*initial a* disappears)
liganti, elegant (*initial e* disappears)

(3) In the situation where the third syllable from the end (the antepenult) is stressed, the vowel in the following syllable often tends to elide, regardless of what vowel it is. This has the effect of reducing these words to two syllables in the spoken language. The accent then ends up on the second to the last syllable (the penult). This is common in rapid speech, and you should be aware of this. Note that this tendency also affects the pronunciation of the infinitives of Conjugation 2 verbs that receive their stress on the antepenult.

Examples

debbuli, weak – rapid pronunciation debb'li (**don't spell it like this!**)
pussibbili, possible – rapid pronunciation pussibb'li (**don't spell it like this!**)
commodu, commode – rapid pronunciation comm'du (**don't spell it like this!**)
debbitu, debt – rapid pronunciation debb'tu (**don't spell it like this!**)
mettiri, to place – rapid pronunciation mett'ri (**don't spell it like this!**)

The three points made above regarding the pronunciation of vowels in unstressed syllables has an impact on the spelling. Variation in the spelling is especially the case if the accent falls on the antepenult. In that case, there is a great deal of variability in the pronunciation of the unstressed vowel in the penult, which is another way of saying that the vowel in the penult is a rather indeterminate sound that can sound like an *a*, an *i*, or a *u* depending on the particular *parrata*. For example, in the *Piccitto* dictionaries under the entry for "monk" (Vol. II, p. 818), one finds the following entries: monacu, monicu, monucu. In similar fashion, we'll see in Chapter 5 on verbs that the 3rd person plural, which normally receives the stress on the antepenult, admits several different spellings: portanu, portunu; ripetinu, ripetunu; finiscinu, finisciunu (see Chapter 5). **Caution:** This doesn't mean that unstressed vowels in the penult all sound exactly the same. The sounds are those pointed out above in (1) above.

Semivowels

Like Italian, Sicilian has two semivowels. These sounds are also called glides. The semivowels occur in semi-diphthongs. See below.

i has the sound of *y* as in English "yes", but more faintly enunciated; the sound is not quite as strong as a full *y*. This sound is also called *semivowel i*. It occurs between two vowels, the first of which is a front vowel, and the second of which is a back vowel. Generally, this sound is not written. It can be represented phonetically as a superscript *y*. Also see *consonantal i* below. **Examples:** dia /ddi^{y}a/, goddess; schiavu /ski^{y}avu/, slave; eu /ye^{y}u/, I.

u has the sound of *w* as in English "we", but more faintly enunciated; the sound is not quite as strong as a full *w*. This sound is also called *semivowel u*. It occurs between two vowels, the first of which is the back vowel *u*, and the second is another vowel.

Generally, this sound is not written. It can be represented phonetically as a superscript *w*. Also see *consonantal u* below. **Examples:** tua /tuᵂa/, yours; vui /vuᵂi/, you.

Diphthongs

A diphthong is a set of two vowels pronounced as one sound. There are several diphthongs in Sicilian. These are they.

ai has the sound of *ie* as in English "pie" **or** *uy* as in Eng. "buy". **Examples:** ai, you have (2^(nd) person singular familiar); ass**ai**, much, many, a lot of

au has the sound of *ou* as in the interjection "ouch". **Examples:** tauru, bull; fausu, false.

ei has the sound of *ai* as in English "rain". **Example:** dei, gods. This is a literary form of the plural. The form *dii* is also very common.

oi has the sound of *oy* as in English "toy". **Example:** voi, ox (**or** oxen since the plural of *voi* is the same as the singular in Sicilian).

Semi-diphthongs

A semi-diphthong is a set of two vowels pronounced almost as one sound. However, in a semi-diphthong the two vowels are separated by a semivowel, or glide. See **Semivowels** above. There are several semi-diphthongs in Sicilian. These are they.

eu has the sound of *e-u* as if one were pronouncing these two vowel sounds quickly. If done properly, *semivowel i* occurs between the two vowels. **Examples:** seu /seᵞu/, his; meu /mmeᵞu/, my; meusa /mmeᵞusa **or** mmeᵞuza/, spleen.

ia has the sound of *i-a* as if one were pronouncing these two vowel sounds quickly. If done properly, *semivowel i* occurs between the two vowels. **Examples:** via /viᵞa/, way; dia /diᵞa/, goddess.

iu has the sound of *i-u* as if one were pronouncing these two vowels quickly. If done properly, *semivowel i* occurs between the two vowels. **Example:** diu /ddiᵞu/, god.

ua has the sound of *u-a* as if one were pronouncing these two vowels quickly. If done properly, *semivowel u* occurs between the two vowels. **Example:** tua /tuᵂa/, your, yours.

ui has the sound of *u-i* as if one were pronouncing these two vowels quickly. If done properly, *semivowel u* occurs between the two vowels. **Example:** vui /vuᵂi/, you.

Consonants

Sicilian shares many of the same consonants as Standard Italian. In many instances, the spelling conventions are also the same. However, there are some exceptions, and these will be pointed out below. It is also important to distinguish the voiceless consonants, *c* (hard c), *f*, *p*, *s*, *t*, and *z* from the voiced consonants, *b*, *d*, *g* (hard g), *l*, *m*, *n*, *r*, *s*, *v*, and *z*. This distinction will occur in some of the discussions below. Note that *s* can be voiceless or voiced, and the same is true of *z*. See below under *s* and *z*.

b has the sound of *b* as in the English word "boy". **Example:** bonu, good.

c (hard) has the sound of *c* as in the English word "scare", that is, with no aspiration. Note that *hard c* occurs before the back vowels *a, o,* and *u*. If it occurs before *e* or *i*, it is written with an *h* following the *c*. See *h* below. **Examples:** capu, chief; chi, what; cu, who. This sound is written as *cc* (before the back vowels) or *cch* (before the front vowels) in certain word initial situations, chiefly in the case of commonly appearing monosyllabic words. **Examples:** ccà, here; cchiù, more. The same is generally true within the interior of words, that is, the sound is doubled. **Examples:** chiacchira, gossip, chatter; acchianari, to climb; picca, few. See **Double Consonants (Gemination)** below.

c (soft) has a sound intermediate between *sy* and the *sh* as in the English word "shut". Note that *soft c* before *e* or *i* is written as *ce* or *ci*. If it occurs before the back vowels, *a, o,* and *u*, the *c* is followed by an *i* first. **Examples:** cena, supper, dinner; ciacca, crack; ciumi, river. **Note:** In some of the *parrati*, *soft c* has the sound of *ch* in the English word "chat" but slightly more emphatic. If *soft c* is doubled in the spelling **or** if *soft c* follows a consonant such as *n* or *r*, it explicitly has the sound of *ch* in the word "chat". **Examples:** cci, to him/to her/to them/to you; duccia, shower; sacciu, I know; cancia, he/she changes; torcia, he/she twists. A *cc* before a front vowel or *cci* before a back vowel to indicate a definite *ch* sound (*ch* as in "chat") is a spelling convention that will be adopted in this book.

d has a similar sound of the *d* as in the English word "dog". However, Sicilian *d* is a dental sound. The tongue strikes the upper front teeth in producing this sound, not the alveolar ridge (English *d*). **Example:** dumanna, question.

f has the sound of *f* as in the English word "fun". **Example:** fama, fame.

g (hard) has the sound of *g* as in the English word "gate". Note that *hard g* occurs before the back vowels *a, o,* and *u*. If it occurs before *e* or *i*, it is written with an *h* following the *g*. See *h* below. **Examples:** gattu, cat; godi, he/she enjoys; ghettu, ghetto. This sound is generally doubled within the interior of words. If this is the case, it is written as *gg* (before the back vowels) or *ggh* (before the front vowels) within the interior of words. **Example:** agghicari, to arrive. See **Double Consonants (Gemination)** below.

g (soft) before an *e* or an *i*, has the sound of *g* as in the English word "gem". If it occurs before the back vowels, *a, o,* and *u*, the *g* is followed by an *i* first. **Examples:** gemma, gem; giarra, jar. In the interior of words, *soft g* is often doubled, and this is also reflected in the spelling. **Example:** raggiuni, reason.

gn has the sound very similar to *ni* in English "onion". **Example:** vagnu, bath.

h isn't really a true consonant because it has no sound of its own. It is used between *g, c,* and *sc* and the front vowels *e* and *i* to harden the sound. That is, *ghe* sounds like *ge* in the English "get"; *ghi* sounds like English "ghee"; *che* sounds like *ke* and *chi* sounds similar to English "key"; *sche* sounds like *ske* and *schi* sounds like English "ski". Other than this use to harden *c* and *g*, *h* isn't required in the Sicilian alphabet.

i has the sound of *y* as in English "yes" (1) when it occurs at the beginning of a word or (2) when it occurs between two vowels. This sound is often called *consonantal i*. It differs from *semivowel i* in being more forcefully made, but don't overdo the *y* sound. It is represented in writing as an *i*, **Examples:** aiu, I have; annoiu, boredom. **Note:** In certain words, the initial *i* functions both as *consonantal i* and as *vocalic i*, as in ittari /yittaři/, to throw. In Sicilian words it sometimes occurs where *soft g* occurs in Italian words. **Examples:** Sic. iustu/It. giusto, right; Sic. iornu/It. giorno, day. Today in Sicilian, the use of *soft g* is increasing, and one also finds *giustu* and *giornu*.

Note: In certain verb forms, an initial *e* has a *consonantal i* preceding it even though this *consonantal i* isn't written. This is particularly the case in certain verb forms of the verb *iri* /yiři/, to go. **Examples:** emu /yemu/, we go; eru /yeřu/, they went; ettu /yettu/, I throw. It is also acceptable to spell such words with an *i* preceding the *e*. **Examples:** iemu, we go; ieru, they went; iettu, I throw. Either spelling practice is permissible.

j is sometimes used in the Sicilian alphabet to indicate *consonantal i*. This practice will not be followed in this book; an *i* (*consonantal i*) will be used instead. **Examples:** aiu, **not** aju; staiu, **not** staju, etc.

k does not exist in the Sicilian alphabet and is used only in foreign words.

l has two sounds. At the beginning of words and standing alone between two vowels, *l* has the sound of *l* as in English "lie". That is, the tongue moves toward the hard palate, touching the alveolar ridge, in making the sound. This *l* is sometimes referred to as *light l*. **Examples:** liggi, law; lassari, to leave; pilu, body hair.

l following a vowel in the same syllable has the sound of *l* as in English "bile". In this case, the tongue doesn't push much against the palate, and this sound resembles the *w* in English "paw". This latter *l* is sometimes called *dark l*. In Sicilian, *dark l* often changes into an *r* or into a true *u* sound. This *dark l* is really a semivowel (*semivowel u*). See **Semivowels** above. **Examples:** balsamu, balm; calmu, calm. The pronunciation of such words is very close to /ba^wsamu/ and /ka^wmu/.

m has the same sound as *m* in English. **Example:** manu, hand.

n has the same sound as *n* in English. **Example:** nanna, grandmother.

ng has the sound as *ng* as in English "long", never the *ng* of the English word "finger". **Examples:** sangu /saŋu/, blood; rungulu /řřuŋulu/, snarl. **Caution:** Unlike English, in Sicilian the *ng* sound can begin a word. **Examples:** ngratu /ŋřatu/, ungrateful; ngagghiari /ŋaggi^yaři/, to grab hold of.

nz **or** ns is made by first an *n* followed by a sharp *dz* sound (or *ts* in some of the *parrati*). In the vocabulary, words with this digraph (two letters used together to represent a sound) are written with an *nz*. **Examples:** pinzari, to think; nzignari, to instruct. In some books, the digraph *ns* is used instead. **Examples:** pinsari, nsignari. **Note:** The digraph *nz* will be used in this book rather than *ns*.

p has the sound of *p* as in English "spin", that is, with no aspiration. **Example:** pani, bread.

q always followed by a *u* (same as in English), and *qu* has the sound of *qu* as in English "queen". Essentially this digraph sounds like *kw*. See *consonantal u*. **Example:** quinnici, fifteen.

r in Sicilian has several distinct sounds. The first is to make it by a single flap of the tongue on the alveolar ridge, much like the *t* in certain American pronunciations of "water", when it begins a word or when it falls between two vowels. Often, this single flap will sound like a kind of *d* sound to Americans, especially because American *d*s are made with the tongue on the alveolar ridge and not against the upper teeth (dental stop) as in Sicilian and Italian. This sound of *r* is also the normal one when *r* either precedes or follows a consonant. **Examples:** rota /řota/ (word-initial), wheel; puru /puřu/ (between two vowels), pure; grassu /gřassu/ (follows a consonant), fat; cuncertu /kunčeřtu/ (precedes a consonant), concert.

r is strongly trilled when word initial or doubled (*rr*). **Note:** There are, therefore, two acceptable pronunciations of *word-initial r*. Either pronounce it as a single flap or strongly trill it. When *r* is doubled, it must be strongly trilled. **Examples:** rota /řřota **or** řota/ (word-initial *r*), wheel; parru /parřu/ (double *r*), I speak; barra /barřa/ (double *r*), barrier.

In some of the Sicilian *parrati*, when *r* precedes a consonant, it may have a retroflex sound. In retroflex (also called cacuminal) combinations (see **Cacuminal Consonants** below), *r* sounds like the *r* in Standard American English (Midwestern variety). **Examples:** cuncertu /kunčeᶉtu/, concert; sparti /spaᶉti **or** špaᶉti/, he/she divides. There's an alternative way to make the *rr* (double r) sound if it occurs within a word. Instead of trilling, you can make a retroflex *r* following by the *z* in the English word "azure" although this latter sound is somewhat faint. **Examples:** parru /paᶉ^{ž}u/ (double *r*), I speak; barra /baᶉ^{ž}a/ (double *r*), barrier. **Note:** The trilled double *r* is the recommended pronunciation. There are other variations of *r* in several of the *parrati*. It is beyond the scope of this work to discuss every nuance. In particular, see the paper by Bonner (1998) cited in the **References** in the back.

s has the sound of *s* as in English "see" (voiceless) or *z* in English "zero" (voiced). At the beginning of a word, it sounds like an *s*, either before a vowel or a voiceless consonant. **Examples:** sanu, healthy; siti, thirst; stari /staři/, to dwell. When doubled, it sounds like a prolonged *s*. **Example:** dissi /dissi/, he/she said. When *s* falls between two vowels, it can be voiceless as the *s* in English "see" or voiced as the *z* in English "zero". Some *parrati* pronoun it voiceless and some voice it. **Examples:** casa /kasa **or** kaza/, house; rosa /řřosa **or** řřoza/, rose. However, *s* before a voiced consonant is voiced. **Examples:** sgangu /zgaŋu/, bunch (e.g., of grapes); sgarbatu /zgařbatu/, rude. **Note:** In some of the Sicilian *parrati*, *s* before a voiceless consonant has the sound of *sh* in the English word "shut", and before a voiced consonant has the sound of *z* as in English "azure". **Examples:** stari /štaři/, to dwell; spisa /špisa **or** špiza/, expense; festa /fešta/, party; sgarbatu /žgařbatu/, rude.

sc (hard) has the sound of *sk* as in English "sky" or like *šk* in some of the *parrati*. See *s* directly above. Note that *hard sc* occurs before the back vowels *a, o,* and *u.* If it occurs before *e* or *i*, it is written with an *h* following the *c*. See h above. **Examples:** scanciu, exchange; schiavu, slave; scupa, broom.

sc (soft) has the sound of *sh* as in English "shut" but distinctly more emphatic. In actuality, the sound is doubled. Note that *soft sc* before *e* or *i* is written as *sce* or *sci*. If it occurs before the back vowels, *a, o,* and *u*, the *c* is followed by an *i* first. **Examples:** sciotu /ššotu/, loose; scrusciu /skřuššu **or** škřuššu /, noise; finisciu /finiššu/, I finish.

t has a similar sound of the *t* as in English "stay", that is, with no aspiration. However, Sicilian *t* is a dental sound. The tongue strikes the upper front teeth in producing this sound, not the alveolar ridge (English *t*). **Examples:** teni, he/she has; tema, theme.

u has the sound of *w* as in English "we" when it follows a *q* or a *g*. This sound is also called *consonantal u*. The *qu* sounds like *kw* and *gu* sounds like *gw*. **Examples:** quannu, when; guerra, war.

v has the sound of *v* as in English "vow". A note must be said about this sound. In some of the *parrati*, *initial b* replaces the *v*. In others, the *v* has the sound of *w*, or it simply disappears altogether. The pronunciation of *v* as in English "vow" is the recommended one. **Examples:** vasari, to kiss; vagnu, bath. **Note:** After gemination-causing words (see **Gemination-Causing Words** below), the *v* sound becomes a *b* sound although it is still spelled with a *v*.

w does not exist in the Sicilian alphabet and is used only in foreign words.

x does not exist in the Sicilian alphabet and is used only in foreign words. **Note:** Some of the *parrati* employ an *x* to indicate an aspirated sound similar to Spanish *j*. This practice will not be followed in this book. Such words will be written with a *soft c* **or** *soft sc* instead. **Examples:** ciumi **or** sciumi **instead of** xiumi, river; ciuri **or** sciuri **instead of** xiuri, flower.

y does not exist in the Sicilian alphabet and is used only in foreign words.

z has two sounds. When voiced, *z* sounds like a sharp *d* (dental *d*) sound rapidly followed by a *z* sound (*z* as in English "zero"). This *z* is known as *hard z*. When voiceless, it sounds like a sharp *t* (dental *t*) sound rapidly followed by an *s* sound (*s* as in English "see"). This *z* is known as *soft z*. If *hard z* is intended, it will be indicated in the vocabularies as [dz]. Otherwise assume the *z* is soft. **Examples:** zia, aunt; zebbra [dz], zebra. In the interior of words, both *hard z* and *soft z* are often doubled, and this is also reflected in the spelling. **Examples:** divuzzioni, devotion; azzolu [dzdz], blue.

Cacuminal Consonants

There are a series of sounds peculiar to Sicilian represented by a combination of two letters (digraph) or three letters (trigraph). These sounds are called retroflex sounds, or cacuminals, and they differ markedly from the corresponding digraphs and trigraphs as found in Italian.

dd is made very much like a prolonged, or double, *d*, much like the double *dd* in the American word "daddy" except that the tongue pushes even more against the roof of the mouth while making this sound. It sounds somewhat like the *j* in the English word "jam", but more flattened against the roof of the mouth. This *dd* sound is a characteristic Sicilian sound occurring where *ll* is found in Italian. **Example:** Sic. beddu/It. bello, beautiful. In certain cases, this sound will be written as a double *d* in word initial situations. **Example:** ddocu, over there.

Caution: Not every *dd* is a cacuminal sound. In certain cases, *dd* merely represents a double dental *d*. Assume it is cacuminal unless indicated otherwise. If *double d* is truly intended, it will be indicated in the vocabularies as [dd]. **Example:** addittari [dd], to dictate.

nt sounds similar to *nt* as in English "ant", but this sound is also made by the tongue pushing against the roof of the mouth. Because it is a retroflex sound and not a dental (like normal Sicilian *t*) the *t* in *nt* sounds intermediate between a *t* and a *d*. **Examples:** nta, in, into; ntontaru, foolish.

dr sounds much like the *dr* in Midwestern American "dry" except that the tongue should push even more against the roof of the mouth while making this sound. It's like the sound of *dd* above combined with a Standard American English (Midwestern variety) *r*. **Example:** drittu, straight. Within the interior of words, this sound is doubled and written as *ddr*. **Example:** addrizzari, to adjust. See **Double Consonants (Gemination)** below.

tr sounds much like the *tr* in Midwestern American "try" except that the tongue should push even more against the roof of the mouth while making this sound. It sounds somewhat like a *ch* in the English word "chum" but more flattened against the roof of the mouth and combined with a Standard American English (Midwestern variety) *r*. **Examples:** truvari, to find; ntricari, to plot. Within the interior of words, this sound is doubled and written as *ttr*. **Example:** attrassari, to delay. See **Double Consonants (Gemination)** below.

str sounds much like the *shr* in Midwestern American "shrill" except that the tongue should push even more against the roof of the mouth while making this sound. It's like the sound of *sh* combined with a Standard American English (Midwestern variety) *r*. **Examples:** strata, street; stranutari, to sneeze.

To make these sounds properly, it would be a good idea to listen to a native Sicilian speaker pronouncing them carefully.

Double Consonants (Gemination)
Double consonant sounds occur very frequently in Sicilian. In the interior of words, they are written as double consonants. **Examples:** accattari, to buy; unni, where; picca, few. Although such sounds occur even at the beginning of a word, normally they are not written as such. **Examples:** bonu /bbonu/, good; diu /ddiᵛu/, god. The consonants that are generally doubled at the beginning of a word in the pronunciation are the voiced sounds.

It is important in pronouncing double consonants to prolong the sound. Speakers of English must be careful since double consonants don't normally exist as distinct sounds in English. There are some words in Sicilian differing only in the length of the consonant found in the word, so it is important to distinguish a single consonant from a double consonant. Here are some examples of words that are spelled the same except that one word has a double consonant and the other has a single consonant. Linguists call these contrastive pairs.

Examples

cc/c	picca, few	pica, spear, pike
cc/c	loccu, stupid	locu, place
dd/d	peddi, skin	pedi, foot
mm/m	addummari, to tame	addumari, to light (e.g., a fire)
nn/n	sonnu, sleep, dream	sonu, sound
nn/n	canni, reeds	cani, dog
pp/p	cappi, cloaks	capi, chiefs
rr/r	carru, cart, car	caru, dear, expensive
rr/r	parru, I speak	paru, pair
ss/s	cassa, he/she cancels, annuls	casa, house
tt/t	notti, night	noti, you note
tt/t	cottu, cooked	cotu, picked

Gemination-Causing Words

There are several words, including many simple prepositions, that cause consonant doubling in the pronunciation, although generally not in the spelling. Such words are called gemination-causing since they cause consonants following them to double in pronouncing them. These will be indicated in the book by placing a superscript plus ($^+$) after such a word. **Note:** This plus is **not** to appear in the spelling. It is added in this book solely as an aid in the proper pronunciation.

Examples

è$^+$, it is
ma$^+$, but
e$^+$, and
a$^+$, to
di$^+$, of
pi$^+$, for
chi$^+$, what

Examples in phrases

È bonu. /ebbonu./ It's good.
Ma picchì? /mappikki?/ But why?
a Palermu /appaleřmu/ to Palermo
Chi canta idda? /kikkanta id'd'a?/ What's she singing?
di vui /dibbui/ of you

Gemination-causing words have another effect. They cause several consonants to mutate, changing their quality. The consonants affected are *v*, *soft c*, and *consonantal i*. Sometimes these changes are reflected in the spelling.

13

Examples in phrases

È veru. /ebbeřu/ It's true. **Sometimes written as:** È bberu.

e cincu /eččiŋku/ and five. **Sometimes written as:** e ccincu.

pi iri /piggyiři/ in order to go. **Sometimes written as:** pi gghiri.

Note: These spelling changes as indicated here in most cases will not be followed in this book, but be aware that the pronunciation is affected. Where direct speech is being indicated however, at times such changes may be indicated. **Example:** Si voli affittari na machina pi gghiri a Catania. He wants to rent a car to go to Catania.

Consonant Assimilation

This is a linguistic term used to refer to the tendency of two, or more, different consonants to become reduced to a double consonant of the same consonantal value. Assimilation is widespread in Sicilian, and the student must be aware of this since it has a definite effect on pronunciation. Assimilation is also found in Italian, but it is even more common in Sicilian.

Examples

Italian: accettare (from Latin adceptare), to accept

Sicilian: accattari (from Latin adcaptare), to buy

Most of the Sicilian dialects carry assimilation further than Italian does. This is especially true if a nasal (*n*, *m*, *ng*) precedes a voiced stop or fricative (especially *b*, *d*, *g*, *v*). In Sicilian, the stop is assimilated (changes into) the preceding nasal.

Examples

Italian: condurre (older Italian conducere)/Sicilian: cunnuciri, to lead

Italian: combattere/Sicilian: cummattiri, to fight

Italian: in bocca/Sicilian: in + vucca = nvucca = mmucca, in the mouth

The following consonant clusters (two consonants side by side) do not occur in most of the Sicilian dialects. They are transmuted into the geminated consonant pair following the arrow:

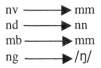

nv ⟶ mm
nd ⟶ nn
mb ⟶ mm
ng ⟶ /ŋ/

Note: In the dialect of Messina (ES-1), the first three assimilations above don't take place.

Examples

Standard Sicilian: cummintu, convinced; Messinese: cunvintu

Standard Sicilian: cunnuciri, to lead; Messinese: cunduciri

Standard Sicilian: cummattiri, to fight; Messinese: cumbattiri

There are sentences where this assimilation takes place, but it isn't indicated in the written form.

Examples
Nun dormu mai nni nu lettu. /nunnormu mai nni nu lettu./ I never sleep in a bed.
Nun batti a so frati cu vastuni. /nummatti a so frati ku bbastuni./ She isn't beating her brother with a cane.
Un gattu veni e si vivi u latti. /uŋ ŋattu veni e ssi bbivi u latti./ A cat comes and drinks the milk. **But note:** Nu gattu veni e si vivi u latti. /nu gattu veni e ssi bbivi u latti./

Stress
In general, in a word of two or more syllables, the stress falls on the second from the last syllable (called the *penult*). In some cases, the last syllable (called the *ultima*), receives the accent. In this case the vowel is marked (almost all Sicilian words end in a vowel): à, è, ì, ò, ù. In some cases, the third from the last syllable (called the *antepenult*) receives the stress. Although this is not marked in the written word, it will be so indicated in this book for ease of pronunciation by bolding the vowel in the antepenult syllable. **Example:** mu**z**zicu, I bite. In the case of words ending in two vowels, if the stress falls on the first of the two vowels, this too will be indicated by bolding the stressed vowel. **Examples:** farma**c**ia, pharmacy; dis**i**u, desire.

If you do not see a bolded vowel in a word of two or more syllables, assume that the stress is on the penult. **Example:** pettu (pettu). In this book, stress on the penult will not be indicated by a bolded letter. Nor will stress on the ultima be indicated since it is already marked using an accent mark: à, è, ì, ò, ù. **Remember:** When writing Sicilian, stress is only indicated in the case of a stressed vowel on the last syllable: à, è, ì, ò, ù. However, note that accents are often used for certain monosyllabic words to distinguish them clearly in writing. Of course, they are pronounced the same. **Examples:** è (is) versus e (and); sì (yes; you are) versus si (if).

A circumflex accent mark is used in Sicilian to denote a contraction, for example, as in the contraction of a preposition with one of the articles. **Note:** The circumflex accent does **not** denote stress. **Examples:** nnâ (in the, feminine singular) versus nna (in). However, the vowel sound having the circumflex accent is slightly prolonged in sound. That is, *nnâ* sounds as long in articulation as the uncontracted form, *nna la*.

Syllables
Syllables in Sicilian follow the rule that an internal syllable should begin with a consonant. The first syllable may begin with a vowel or a consonant. If two consonants occur within a word, the first consonant ends the first syllable and the following consonant forms the beginning of the second syllable.

Examples
a-li-va	di-na-ru	n-ciu-ria	pir-su-na
ac-cus-sì	let-tu	od-dia-ri	ro-ta
bo-nu	mer-da	pa-ni	sim-pa-ti-cu

However, note that the following consonant clusters act as a single consonant when applying this rule: dd; s + consonant; gn; ng; ggh; cch; consonant + r, for example, tr **or** ttr, dr **or** ddr, pr, str.

Examples

a-ddriz-za-ri	fe-sta	no-stru	scun-tra-ri
be-ddu	fi-gghiu	o-gni	sem-pri
chia-cchi-ra	lo-ngu	pu-gnu	spe-cchiu
e-sta-ti	ma-tri	sa-ngu	tra-va-gghia-ri

Spelling Conventions for Sicilian

Establishing adequate orthographic norms for Sicilian is a goal that is very important. The spelling conventions found in this book to a considerable extent are those suggested by Giorgio Piccitto in his *Elementi di Ortografia siciliana* (Catania: 1947). Unfortunately however, Piccitto's book is very short on concrete examples. In general, these conventions are also to be found in the poetry of Gnaziu Buttitta (1899-1998) and in Giuseppi Cavallaru's translation of some of the cantos of Homer's *Iliad* (*Iliadi*, Palermo: Nuova Tavolozza, 1997). The Sicilian as rendered by these two authors is elegant looking and streamlined without making Sicilian resemble Italian too greatly. Where practical, the spelling conventions found in the *Vocabolario Siciliano* dictionaries are also adhered to (sometimes referred to the *Piccitto* dictionaries since Giorgio Piccitto was the original editor). A real effort is made to set forth conventions useful in writing Sicilian.

In addition, regarding the orthography, it seems best to adhere to the generally accepted orthography which is chiefly that of Italian also. See the discussion above under **Consonants**. However, in addition to the conventions used in Italian and also employed in Sicilian, there are some that are unique to Sicilian. These unique conventions used in this book for writing standard Sicilian are summarized here.

- Elimination of *h* except to harden *c* and *g*. **Example:** aiu, **not** haiu, etc.
- Elimination of *j* entirely. **Example:** vaiu, **not** vaju, etc.
- Elimination of an initial apostrophe indicating the disappearance of an initial vowel, e.g., an *i*. This is done to avoid using too many apostrophes. **Examples:** mmucca, nzignari, talianu, etc. **not** 'mmucca, 'nzignari, 'talianu, etc. See **Use of the Apostrophe** below. See also **Disappearance of Initial *i*** below.
- Doubling a consonant based on linguistic evidence that the consonant cluster is truly geminate. **Examples:** libbru, possibbili, ntroduzzioni, nni, cci, etc. **not** libru, possibili, ntroduzioni, ni, ci, etc. The doubling is also shown at the beginning of a word if the word is monosyllabic. **Examples:** nni, cci, cchiù, etc. In the case of polysyllabic words, the doubling generally isn't shown in the spelling at the beginning of a word. **Examples:** miscari, **not** mmiscari; diu, **not** ddiu; bonu, **not** bbonu, etc. In pronounciation though, such consonants are doubled. The exception is with words where the *initial i* has disappeared. **Examples:** (i)nnamuratu, (i)mmitari, (i)nnuccenti, etc.
- Use of *z* instead of *s* following an *n*. **Examples:** nzignari, cunzigghiari, etc. **not** nsignari, cunsigghiari, etc.
- Use of *initial g*. **Examples:** granni, gattu, etc. **not** ranni, attu (**or** iattu), etc.
- Use of *double c* before *e* or *i* to indicate the sound of *ch*. **Examples:** cci, ccippu, etc.

- Disappearance of *l* before another consonant. In Sicilian, *l* is rarely found in front of or following another consonant. In general, it changes into either an *r* or into a *u*. **Examples of l changing to an r:** sordi (from the older soldi), money; arma (from alma), soul; quarchi (**also** qualchi, some). **Examples of l changing to a u:** fausu (**not** falsu), false; autu (**not** altu), tall; caudu (**not** caldu), hot.
- Use of *u* and *i* for *o* and *e* in unstressed syllables. Although there are exceptions, in general Sicilian prefers the use of of *u* and *i* for *o* and *e* in unstressed syllables. **Examples:** divuzzioni, prucissioni, etc. instead of devozzioni, processioni, etc.
- If an article, preposition, or conjunctive pronoun ends in an unstressed vowel and the following word is one where the initial *i* is lost, it is common to elide the vowel of the article, preposition, or pronoun, replace it with an apostrophe, and write the *i* on the following word. **Examples:** l'immigranti **instead of** li mmigranti, the immigrants; t'inzignu **instead of** ti nzignu, I teach you; un casu d'incendiu **instead of** un casu di ncendiu, a case of fire; l'incigneri **instead of** lu ncigneri, the engineer; m'innamuru **instead of** mi nnamuru, I fall in love, etc. See **Loss of Initial *i*** below.

Use of the Apostrophe

Like any other language, Sicilian uses the apostrophe to indicate the disappearance of a letter. However, in Sicilian initial vowels are very often elided, and this will not be indicated using an apostrophe. This is done to reduce the number of apostrophes used in writing the language. The use of too many apostrophes gives the resulting written sentence a very unappealing appearance.

Examples
in vucca = 'nvucca = mmucca, in the mouth
inzignari = 'nzignari = nzignari, to teach
italianu = 'talianu = talianu, Italian

Loss of Initial i

The loss of initial *i* must be mentioned in particular since the tendency in Literary Sicilian was, and still is, to include it in the spelling. It's clear that to the Sicilian ear, this vowel disappears in the spoken language, but retaining it in writing is a legitimate option, of course. In addition, because of the influence of Italian, in which initial *i* does not disappear, the tendency has grown in Sicilian to retain it. Here are a few examples.

Examples

Written without the initial *i*	Written with the initial *i*
n (before a noun without an article)	in
ntilliggenti	intilliggenti
nnuccenti	innuccenti
nzignari	inzignari
talianu	italianu

The reason why we speak of the disappearance of initial *i* is that, etymologically speaking, the above words are derived from Latin and the Latin words from which they are derived did contain an initial *i*, but in Sicilian this *i* disappeared from the pronunciation. The Latin words from which the above five words are derived are: in, intellegentem, innocentem, insignāre (Late Latin), ītalicus **or** ītaliānus (Late Latin).

Many more examples could be given. Piccitto in his book clearly favors writing such words without the *i* (see *Elementi di Ortografia siciliana*, especially pp. 44-45). Note that the practice of omitting it will be followed in this book. However, the trend today seems to be to write words containing double consonants without the double consonants and in addition to retain the initial *i*. For illustrations of the above examples written with the *i* and without the double consonants, see **Influence of Italian on Sicilian** below.

Note: To indicate that writing such words with the initial *i* is a legitimate option, the attempt is made to list such words in the vocabularies with the initial *i* given in parenthesis. For example, the five words listed above will appear as follows: (i)n, (i)ntilliggenti, (i)nnuccenti, (i)nzignari, (i)talianu. It is up to the discretion of the user whether he/she wishes to include this *i* in writing Sicilian.

Written Language versus Spoken Language

The user of this book should be aware that through much of its history Sicilian has remained largely a spoken language. Although Giuvanni Meli (1740-1815) and some other notable Sicilian intellectuals attempted to establish a Sicilian literary tradition in the eighteenth century, they were thwarted in this effort by the reactionary climate existing in Sicily at that time. It is unfortunate also that too few of Sicily's great writers chose Sicilian as a medium in which to write. Lacking a common literary Sicilian idiom, Sicilian has remained largely a spoken language with strong oral traditions. There is, of course, nothing wrong with this, except that the lack of a good literary standard has allowed each Sicilian dialect (*parrata*) to express itself through slightly different linguistic norms. This book will endeavor to use a more literary form of the language, but at certain points different forms will be given for what is essentially the same thing.

The user of this book should also be aware that there are differences between the written forms of a language and its spoken forms. This is true of any language. The written forms of a language are normally more formal and tend to use fewer abbreviations and contractions. The written forms of a language also generally employ an enlarged vocabulary and more precise grammatical constructions. Spoken forms of a language can range all the way from a formal acceptance speech to a person talking with someone with whom he/she is on intimate terms. Also, it must be born in mind that the use of dictionaries and commonly accepted spelling and punctuation is of fairly recent origin. All of these points are pertinent to Sicilian. Here are several examples drawn from American English.

   Spoken level (very colloquial and substandard)
   Whatcha doin' now?
   I dunno. Whatcha want?
   You crazy or somethin'?
   Who you talkin' to anyway?
   Between you and I I gotta know whatcha doin' right now.

We all recognize what's being expressed in these sentences, but unless one were an author trying to illustrate very informal speech, no one in his or her right mind would ever write this way. If they did, we'd immediately suppose that they had very poor spelling habits and poor grammar.

<u>**Spoken level (colloquial but more standard)**</u>
What are you doin' now?
I don't know. What do ya want?
Are you crazy or something?
Who are you talking to anyway?
Between you and me I gotta know what you're doin' right now.

<u>**Written level (formal)**</u>
What are you doing now?
I don't know. What do you want?
Are you crazy or something?
Who are you talking to anyway?
Between you and me I've got to know what you're doing right now.

<u>**Written level (very formal)**</u>
What are you doing now?
I do not know. What do you want?
Are you crazy or something?
To whom are you talking anyway?
Between you and me I must know what you are doing right now.

The above sentences illustrate that every language shows some discrepancies between its written and spoken forms. In some languages, this discrepancy can be quite large. For example, in Modern Greek the discrepancy is very noticeable. The written language utilizes certain grammatical forms drawn from Classical Greek, whereas the spoken language has long ago lost these forms. Because of the immense prestige of Classical Greek, the forms in question are still preserved in the written form of the modern language. Although Modern Greek is possibly an extreme case, every language displays some differences between its spoken and written forms.

What was said above applies to Sicilian. Therefore, as various forms are set forth, several different levels may be noted. Here are several examples drawn from Sicilian.

<u>**Written level**</u>
(1) Mi vaiu a accattari nu pocu di libbra pri studiari pri l'esami dumani.
(2) Si tu fai sta cosa nautra vota, t'ammazzu.
(3) Comu aiu a fari?
(4) Dda fimmina canta beni.
(5) Qualchidunu tuppulia a la porta.
(6) Aiu vistu lu libbru, la pinna, e li vanca.
(7) Pigghiu la petra n pugnu (**or** in pugnu) e la ettu (**or** iettu) luntanu.

<u>**Spoken level (more formal)**</u>
(1) Mi vaiu a accattu nu pocu di (**or** i) libbra pi studiari pi l'esami dumani.
(2) Si tu fai sta cosa nautra vota, t'ammazzu.
(3) Comu aiu a fari?
(4) Dda fimmina canta bonu.

(5) Quarchidunu tuppulia â porta.
(6) Aiu vistu u libbru, a pinna, e i vanca.
(7) Pigghiu a petra mpugnu e â iettu luntanu.

Spoken level (less formal/more intimate)
(1) Mi vâ 'ccattu nu pochê libbra pi studiari pi l'esami dumani.
(2) Si tu fa' sta cosa nautra vota, t'ammazzu.
(3) Com'ê fari?
(4) Dda fimmina canta bonu.
(5) Cacchidunu tuppulia â porta.
(6) A vistu u libbru, a pinna, ê vanca.
(7) Pigghiu a petra mpugnu e â iettu luntanu.

Translation of the above seven sentences
(1) I'm going to buy some books to study for the exam tomorrow.
(2) If you do that one more time, I'm going to kill you.
(3) How should I do (it)?
(4) That woman sings well.
(5) Someone's knocking at the door.
(6) He/she's seen the book, the pen, and the benches.
(7) I take the stone in my fist and throw it far.

Don't concentrate on the particulars of these Sicilian sentences since you will understand them better later after you've studied the language in more detail. Which sentence is correct? The answer, of course, depends on the context. Sicilian, like any other language, including English, can differ significantly depending on the particular social context. In general, in this book a standard written Sicilian will be employed. At times though, more informal spoken forms will be indicated where appropriate since they do occur in the literature.

Dialectical Differences
It isn't the purpose of this introduction to delve deeply into the dialectical differences existing within Sicilian itself. However, it is appropriate to mention two very prominent differences since you will definitely encounter them as soon as you start to read or listen to Spoken Sicilian. For further details on dialectical differences, see the paper by Bonner (1998).

(1) In many Sicilian dialects, one finds the substitution of *r* for *d*. The substitution of *r* for *d* is commonly found in both Eastern Sicilian (ES) and Western Sicilian (WS). It can occur internally, or it can affect initial *d*, a phenomenon characterizing some of the subdialects of Eastern Sicilian. At first glance, this substitution may seem odd, but *r* is made by a single flap of the tongue against the upper alveolar ridge, and this actually sounds like a kind of *d* sound. This is a linguistic phenomenon known as *rhotacism*, the substitution of *r* for another consonant.

Examples
pedi ⟶ peri, foot (or feet)
cuda ⟶ cura, tail
ridiri ⟶ ririri **or** rirri, to laugh

diri ———▶riri, to say
dari ———▶rari, to give

Note: The changes following the arrows will **not** be followed in this book.

(2) The disappearance of *hard g*, either initially before *r* or before a vowel, is also very widespread.

The disappearance of *hard g* initially before an *r* is given in the following examples.

Examples
granni ———▶ranni
gravi ———▶ravi
gridari ———▶ridari & rirari

Note: The changes following the arrows will **not** be followed in this book.

The disappearance of *hard g* before a vowel is given in the following examples.

Examples
gattu ———————▶attu; iattu, cat
gaddu ———————▶addu; addru; iaddu; iaddru, rooster
gaddina ———————▶addina; addrina; iaddina; iaddrina, hen
pagari ———————▶paiari, paari, to pay
prigari ———————▶priari, to beseech

Note: The changes following the arrows will **not** be followed in this book.

Influence of Italian on Sicilian

Since Italian has been impressed upon the Sicilians, various Italianisms have entered the language. For example, many Sicilians today are familiar with Italian and find no special problem pronouncing *l* in front of a consonant or pronouncing the consonant cluster *nv* so that today *qualchi* is found alongside of *quarchi* and *cunvinciri* is found alongside of *cumminciri*. Regarding Sicilian vocabulary, one notes in more recent Sicilian literature the use of certain words that have either changed in form to more closely resemble a corresponding Italian word or that have been completely replaced by a different Italian word altogether. The following are some examples.

Examples

Sicilian	Italian	More recent Sicilian
abbitutini, habit, custom	abitudine	abitudini
accuminzari, to begin	cominciare	cuminciari
aviri a + inf., to have to, ought to	dovere	duviri*
assai, much, many	molto	moltu
carzari (**or** carziri), prison	carcere	carciri
chiazza, plaza, (town) square	piazza	piazza
cumpritari, to complete	completare	completari
cummintu	convinto	cunvintu

21

Sicilian	Italian	More recent Sicilian
distrubbari, to disturb	disturbare	disturbari
distrudiri (**or** strudiri), to destroy	distruggere	distruggiri
disiari (**or** addisiari), to desire	desiderare	disiddirari
facci, face	faccia	faccia
mmitari	invitare	invitari
mpurtanti, important	importante	importanti
n (before a noun), in	in	in
nomu, name	nome	nomi
ntilliggenti, intelligent	intelligente	intelligenti
nnuccenti, innocent	innocente	innocenti
nzignari, to teach	insignare	insignari
mparari, to learn	imparare	imparari
palora, word	parola	parola
praia, beech	spiaggia	spiaggia
praciri, to please	piacere	piaciri
raggia, anger	rabbia	rabbia
sonnu, dream	sogno	sognu
vrancu (**or** iancu), white	bianco	biancu

* Literary Sicilian such as the works of G. Meli sometimes used *duviri*.

This list could be extended, of course. Are the changes in the words noted above important? All languages are subject to change, that is, as long as they're still living. This is a linguistic fact and has been well documented. In fact, the relation between Sicilian and Italian in Sicily has been under serious investigation by a number of scholars because of the unique linguistic situation between the two languages. In reference to this issue, see in particular the poem by Gnaziu Buttitta entitled *Lingua e Dialettu* (Language and Dialect, that is, Italian and Sicilian) in Chapter 14, **Exercise (Sicilian Poem)**. Although the poem is given in its original Sicilian, a full translation is rendered in English in the Key to the Exercises, **Key to Chapter 14**. It's important for Sicilian to maintain its own unique vocabulary and to distinguish itself from Italian. If Sicilian simply degenerates into a slightly different version of Italian (that is, a form of Regional Italian), then it seems to me, Why bother? One may as well just learn to speak proper Italian.

The Sicilian in this book will attempt to set forth the language more or less as it existed before the onslaught of Standard Italian on the Sicilian language. This latter movement can generally be traced back to Mussolini's attempt to impose Italian throughout the Italian peninsula and the islands belonging to Italy, and this movement has only accelerated after the Second World War (1939-1945).

Punctuation in Sicilian

The chief symbols used in the punctuation of Sicilian are the comma (la virgula) and the period (lu puntu). The period is used for a full stop, just as in English. Unlike English, a comma is normally not required for two clauses connected by a coordinating conjunction. A comma is not required for a sentence having an independent clause and a dependent clause connected by a subordinating conjunction if the dependent clause follows the independent clause. If the dependent clause precedes the independent clause, a comma is generally used to separate them.

Examples
(1) L'omu sta liggennu u giurnali e so mogghi sta cucennu (**or** cucinannu) a carni. The man's reading the newspaper, and his wife is cooking the meat. (two independent clauses connected by a coordinating conjunction)
(2) Aiu a studiari assai ma non vogghiu. I have a lot to study, but I don't want to. (two independent clauses connected by a coordinating conjunction)
(3) U giuvinottu canta mentri a so nnamurata sona u pianu. The young man's sings while his girl friend plays the piano. (independent clause followed by a dependent clause)
(4) Aiu a studiari assai picchì vulissi essiri prumossu. I've got to study a lot so because I want to pass. (independent clause followed by a dependent clause)
(5) Sebbeni aiu iu i sordi, non vogghiu accattarimi a casa. Although I have the money, I don't want to buy the house. (dependent clause preceding an independent clause)
(6) Si tu non fai zoccu disiddiru, non sarò cuntenta. If you don't do what I want, I won't be happy. (dependent clause preceding an independent clause)

Commas are used to separate a noun or noun phrase in apposition.

Examples
(1) Carru, nu patri bonu, voli beni ê figghi. Charles, a good father, loves his children.
(2) Maria, chiamata a bedda, abbitava nnôn paisi nicu dâ pruvincia di Caltanissetta. Maria, called the beautiful, lived in a tiny village in the province of Caltanissetta.

To indicate direct discourse, the long dash (linietta longa) is used. It only occurs before and after a quotation if the quotation is directly followed by indirect discourse in the same paragraph.

Examples
— Chi voi? — L'omu cci dumannau a lu picciutteddu e chistu cci rispunniu.
— Vegnu ccà p'accattari ova.
L'omu si sinteva ncagnatu ddu iornu e cci dissi.
— Bonu! Non ti nni vogghiu vinniri!
"What do you want?" The man asked the lad, and the latter answered him.
"I've come to buy some eggs."
The man was feeling cranky that day and so he said, "Well, I don't want to sell you any!"

As noted, the question mark (lu puntu nterrugativu) and the exclamation point (lu puntu esclamativu) are used as in English.

If a minor quotation occurs within a sentence, small arrows (virguletti), «...», can be used to indicate this to make it clear that something's being said.

Example
(1) Ogni matina Anna cci dicia «bon giornu» a so patri. Every morning Anne would say "good morning" to her father.

3   Nouns and Adjectives

Purpose of the Chapter

The chief purpose of this chapter is to discuss nouns, adjectives, and grammatical gender. Nouns are the things we talk about. A noun is a name of a person, place, or thing, and adjectives describe, modify, or limit a noun. They characterize the noun in more detail or specify it. It's no longer just any thing; it's this thing or that thing with such-and-such attributes. The chapter also discusses the definite and indefinite articles and how to form the plurals of nouns.

Gender

A word should be said about gender since it is an important classification scheme in the Romance languages. It is an important classificatory scheme in many other languages too, but not in English. Although Latin has three genders, masculine, feminine, and neuter, almost all the Romance languages, including Sicilian, have only two: masculine and feminine. Gender in this sense is called grammatical gender; it must be stressed that it has nothing to do with natural gender. **Examples**: libbru (book) is masculine gender in Sicilian; porta (door) is feminine. As we clearly know, books don't have what we'd call masculine characteristics, and doors don't have what we'd call feminine characteristics. Gender just happens to be a convenient classificatory scheme in Sicilian, as it is in the other Romance languages. Since the term "gender" has been used for centuries to express this particular grammatical concept, it will be retained in this book. It must be stressed that there are absolutely no sexist implications whatsoever regarding its usage.

Endings in the Singular

In Sicilian, nouns ending in -*u* in the singular are generally masculine (there are only a few exceptions), and nouns ending in -*a* in the singular are generally feminine (there are some exceptions). Nouns ending in -*i* in the singular can be masculine or feminine. In most cases, the accompanying article also identifies the gender. The following endings are feminine:

- -zzioni;
- -tà (older form: -tati).

Definite Articles

In English, there is one, and only one, definite article, "the". It is used with all nouns, singular and plural, and of course, English doesn't use grammatical gender as a classificatory scheme, but Sicilian does. In Sicilian, there is a masculine singular definite article, there is a feminine singular definite article, and there is one common plural article. There are both long forms and short forms of the definite article. The long forms are the original forms of the definite articles; the short forms are formed from the long forms by dropping the initial *l*.

Long Forms of the Definite Article

Definite articles
lu (masculine singular), the
la (feminine singular), the
li (common plural), the

Short Forms of the Definite Article
In some of the Sicilian dialects, the forms of the definite articles are slightly different. These forms are often found in speech, and can also be found at times in Written Sicilian. The forms below will be referred to as the short forms of the definite article.

Definite articles (often used in speech)
u (masculine singular), the
a (feminine singular), the
i (common plural), the

In this book, the *lu/la/li* forms of the articles will generally be used, but the user should also be aware that the *u/a/i* forms are also very common (see examples in the **Written Language versus Spoken Language** in Chapter 2). In front of the singular form of nouns beginning with vowels, the *lu/la/li* forms are used, but the vowel of the article is elided (disappears) before the vowel of the noun and is replaced by an apostrophe. The elision of the vowel is optional in the plural.

Examples
lu capu, the boss	li capi, the bosses
la porta, the door	li porti, the doors
lu patri, the father	li patri, the fathers
la matri, the mother	li matri, the mothers
l'amicu, the friend	l'amici, the friends **or** li amici
l'unna, the wave	l'unni, the waves **or** li unni

Gender of Nouns
The gender of a noun in the vocabularies will be indicated in this book by the use of the long form of the definite article unless it's not obvious. The only case where the gender is not obvious is for nouns beginning with a vowel and ending neither in *-u* (masculine) nor in *-a* (feminine). **Note:** Please note that these abbreviations will be employed throughout this book. For gender ambiguous nouns, an M will be used to indicate a masculine noun, and F a feminine noun. In addition, an s will be used to indicate singular, and p will be used to indicate plural.

Examples of masculine nouns	Examples of feminine nouns
lu patri, the father	la matri, the mother
lu suli, the sun	la luna, the moon
lu libbru, the book	la pinna, the feather; the pen
l'amicu, the friend	l'ala, the wing
l'amuri (M), the love	l'estati (F), the summer

Indefinite Articles
In English, there is one, and only one, indefinite article, "a" (for euphony before a vowel, "an"). It is used with all singular nouns. In Sicilian, there is a masculine singular indefinite article, and there is a feminine singular indefinite article. There is no plural form of the indefinite article.

Indefinite articles
nu* **or** un (masculine singular), a, an
na (feminine singular), a, an

Before a *z* or *s* followed by a consonant, *nu* is the correct form to be used. In some of the Sicilian *parrati*, *nu* is used as the only masculine indefinite article. The form *un* is more frequently used in this book, except before a *z* or *s* followed by a consonant. However, because of assimilation, it is also advisable to use *nu* before words beginning with *d* and *g*. See **Consonant Assimilation** in Chapter 2.

In front of nouns beginning with vowels, the form *n'* is used. If the form *un* is used, it sometimes loses its *u* and coalesces with the following noun. This is especially true in the spoken language (see **Written Language versus Spoken Language** in Chapter 2).

Examples of masculine nouns	Examples of feminine nouns
un **or** nu libbru, a book	na matri, a mother
un **or** nu patri, a father	na porta, a door
nu studenti, a student	n'amica, a friend (F)
nu donu, a gift	n'oliva, an olive
n'amicu, a friend (M)	

Plural of Common Nouns
Plural nouns, both masculine and feminine, end in -*i* except for the exceptions given below.

Examples
capu, boss	capi, bosses
porta, door	porti, doors
gattu, cat	gatti, cats
matri, mother	matri, mothers

A few masculine nouns end in -*a* in the singular; these are normally nouns referring to male subjects. The plurals still end in -*i*.

Examples
pueta (Ms), poet	pueti (p), poets
socialista (Ms **or** Fs) socialist	socialisti (p) socialists

Nouns in -*gghiu/-gghia* and -*cchiu/-cchia* change to -*gghi* and -*cchi* respectively in the plural.

Examples
figghiu, son	figghi, sons
figghia, daughter	figghi, daughters
stinnicchiu, stretching	stinnicchi, stretchings
oricchia, ear	oricchi, ears

Note: Because *figghi* can mean either "sons" or "daughters", it's common to find *figghi masculi* (Mp) and *figghi fimmini* (Fp).

Some nouns in *-cu* change to a *soft c* if the accent is on the antipenult. If it's on the penult, the *c* normally remains hard, but there are a few noted exceptions.

Examples of accent on the antipenult

monacu, monk   monaci, monks
medicu, physician   medici, physicians
fisicu, physicist   fisici, physicists
Note: monaca (F), nun   monachi (Fp), nuns

Examples of accent on the penult

parcu, park   parchi, parks
sceccu, donkey   scecchi, donkeys
beccu, beak   becchi, beaks

Exceptions to the accent on the penult

amicu, friend   amici, friends
grecu, Greek   greci, Greeks (*grechi* is also found)
porcu, pig   porci, pigs
nimicu, enemy   nimici, enemies
Note: amica (F), friend   amichi (Fp), friends

However, there are some nouns, and most adjectives, ending in *-cu* in which the antepenult is accented and whose plural ends either in *-ci* or in *-chi*. If the noun or the adjective is masculine, the ending *-ci* should be used. Sometimes for a masculine noun, the plural can be found either in *-ci* or in *-chi*. **Example:** sinnacu/sinnaci **or** sinnachi, mayor/mayors. If the noun or the adjective is feminine, the ending *-chi* should be used.

Examples

dizziunari giugrafici **versus** mappi giugrafichi
amici simpatici **versus** amichi simpatichi
fatti pubblici **versus** cosi pubblichi
spittaculi fantastici **versus** visti fantastichi

Vocabulary: lu dizziunariu, dictionary; la mappa, map; giugraficu/a, geographic; l'amicu, l'amica, friend; simpaticu/a, nice; lu fattu, fact; la cosa, thing; pubblicu/a, public; lu spittaculu, show (e.g., at the theater); la vista, sight; fantasticu/a, fantastic.

Plural of Nouns Ending in -iu and -ia

Nouns ending in *-iu* and *-ia* follow a certain pattern. For nouns ending in *-gghiu/-gghia* and *-cchiu/-cchia*, see above. Masculine nouns ending in *-iu* change to *-ii* in the plural, and masculine nouns ending in *-iu* change to *-ii* in the plural. Feminine nouns ending in *-ia* change to *-ii* in the plural; feminine nouns ending in *-ia* change to *-ii* in the plural.

Examples

studiu, study   studii, studies
disiu, desire   disii, desires
grazzia, grace, charm   grazzii, charms; thank you
farmacia, pharmacy   farmacii, pharmacies

Invariable Plurals

A noun having an invariable plural means that the plural form is identical to the singular form. There are five classes of invariable plurals. They are given below.

(1) By far the largest class of invariable nouns are those ending in -*i* in the singular. They can be either masculine or feminine.

Examples

l'azzioni (F), the action	l'azzioni, the actions **or** li azzioni
lu brinnisi, the (drinking) toast	li brinnisi, the toasts
la facci, the face	li facci, the faces
la matri, the mother	li matri, the mothers
lu patri, the father	li patri, the fathers
lu pedi, the foot	li pedi, the feet
lu voi, the ox	li voi, the oxen

(2) Feminine nouns ending in -*u* in the singular are invariable. There are three common ones.

la ficu, the fig	li ficu, the figs
la manu, the hand	li manu, the hands
la soru, the sister	li soru, the sisters

(3) Nouns ending in a stressed accented vowel are invariable in the plural.

Examples

lu cafè, the coffee, the café	li cafè, the coffees, the cafés
la cità, the city	li cità, the cities
lu tassì, the taxi	li tassì, the taxis
la tribbù, the tribe	li tribbù, the tribes
la virtù, the force; virtue	li virtù, the forces; virtues

(4) A few nouns are monosyllabic (one syllable). These are invariable in the plural.

Examples

la ci, the C (letter of the alphabet)	li ci, the Cs
lu re, the king	li re, the kings

(5) A few nouns in Sicilian are contractions. These are invariable in the plural.

Examples

lu cinima, the movie theater; the movies*	li cinima, the movie theaters; the movies
la fotu, the photo†	li fotu, the photos

* Contraction of *cinimatografu*
† Contraction of *fotografia*

Nouns with an Irregular Plural in -a

In Sicilian there is a very large group of masculine nouns generally ending in -*u* in the singular (there are some ending in -*i* in the singular) but ending in -*a* in the plural. This plural ending is most probably a remnant of the Latin neuter plural in -*a*. In some cases, a plural in -*i* is also found, and this has been indicated below. These masculine nouns ending in -*a* in the plural can be considered to remain masculine in the plural. Only with certain types of adjectives (see **Adjectives with Four Different Endings** below) does this fact make any difference.

This category of noun is quite common. Only the most important are given below, but you should be on the lookout for them since such nouns frequently occur in Sicilian. Also, a plural in -*a* can sometimes be predicted, and this is shown below by classifying these nouns into several subclasses. In the vocabularies, such nouns will be indicated using the notation (p -a).

General nouns with a plural in -a

lu cannolu, the pipe	li cannola **or** li cannoli, the pipes
lu celu, the sky, heavens	li cela **or** li celi, the skies, heavens
lu chilu, the kilo (kilogram)	li chila, the kilos
lu chiovu, the nail (for building)	li chiova **or** li chiovi, the nails
lu cocciu, the berry	li coccia, the berries
lu cornu, the horn	li corna, the horns
lu corpu, the blow	li corpa, the blows
lu filu, the thread	li fila, the threads
lu focu, fire	li foca **or** li fochi, the fires
lu fruttu, the fruit	li frutta **or** li frutti, the fruits
lu gigghiu, the lily; the eyebrow	li gigghia, the lilies; the eyebrows
lu iardinu, the garden	li iardina **or** li iardini, the gardens
lu iornu, the day	li iorna, the days
lu libbru, the book	li libbra, the books
lu lignu, the piece of wood	li ligna, the pieces of wood
lu linzolu, the sheet	li linzola, the sheets
lu migghiu, the mile	li migghia, the miles
lu muru, the wall	li mura **or** li muri, the walls
lu numiru, the number	li numira, the numbers
l'ogghiu, the oil	l'ogghia, the oils
l'ovu, the egg	l'ova, the eggs
lu piattu	li piatta **or** li piatti, the plates
lu pizzu, point, tip	li pizza **or** li pizzi, the points, tips
lu piru, the pear	li pira, the pears
lu pregu, the joy	li prega, the joys
lu prunu, the plum	li pruna, the plumes
lu pumu, the apple	li puma, the apples
lu sirvizzu, the task, the service	li sirvizza, the tasks, the services
lu solu, the soil, the ground	li sola, the soils
lu spicchiu, the fruitstone	li spicchia **or** li spicchi, the fruitstones
lu trenu, the train	li trena **or** li treni, the trains

29

Nouns relating to the body with a plural in -a

lu ciriveddu, the brain	li cirivedda, the brains
lu ficatu, the liver	li ficata, the livers
lu iditu, the finger	li idita, the fingers
lu inocchiu **or** lu ginocchiu, the knee	li inocchia **or** li ginocchia, the knees
lu labbru, the lip	li labbra, the lips
l'ossu, the bone	l'ossa, the bones (articulated) **or** l'ossi (disarticulated)
lu piditu, the fart	li pidita, the farts
lu pilu, the body hair	li pila, the body hairs
lu pugnu, the fist	li pugna, the fists
l'ugnu, the nail (as in "fingernail")	l'ugna, the nails
lu vrazzu, the arm	li vrazza, the arms
lu vudeddu, the gut	li vudedda, the guts

Caution: Not all masculine nouns relating to the body have a plural in -*a*. **Examples:** lu nasu/li nasi, the nose/noses; l'occhiu/l'occhi, the eye/eyes.

Nouns ending in -eddu with a plural in -a

l'agneddu, the lamb	l'agnedda **or** l'agneddi, the lambs
l'aneddu, the ring	l'anedda **or** l'aneddi, the rings
lu casteddu, the castle	li castedda **or** li casteddi, the castles
lu cuteddu, the knife	li cutedda **or** li cuteddi, the knifes
lu marteddu, the hammer	li martedda **or** li marteddi, the hammers
lu panareddu, the little basket*	li panaredda **or** li panareddi, the little baskets
lu piatticeddu, the little plate*	li piatticedda **or** li piatticeddi, the little plates

* This noun is a diminutive. See Chapter 15 for a treatment of diminutives.

Note: Many of the nouns in this subclass can also be found with regular plurals.

Nouns ending in -aru with a plural in -a

lu buttunaru, the button-maker*	li buttunara, the button-makers
lu cintinaru, the hundred	li cintinara, the hundreds
lu firraru, the blacksmith*	li firrara, the blacksmiths
lu fucularu, the hearth	li fuculara, the hearths
lu furmicularu, the anthill	li furmiculara, the anthills
lu migghiaru, the thousand	li migghiara, the thousands
lu pagghiaru, the haystack	li pagghiara, the haystacks
lu panaru, the basket	li panara, the baskets
lu paru, the pair	li para, the pairs
lu picuraru, the shepherd*	li picurara, the shepherds
lu scarparu, the shoemaker*	li scarpara, the shoemakers
lu sularu, the attic	li sulara, the attics
lu tabbaccaru, the tobacconist*	li tabbaccara, the tobacconists

* There are a number of trades/professions ending in -*aru* with a plural in -*a*.

Nouns ending in -uni with a plural in –a

lu baruni, the baron	li baruna, the barons
lu buttuni, the button	li buttuna, the buttons
lu campiuni, the champion	li campiuna, the champions
lu cugghiuni, the testicle	li cugghiuna, the testicles
lu liuni, the lion	li liuna, the lions
lu patruni, the owner, master	li patruna, the owners, masters
lu scagghiuni, the canine tooth	li scagghiuna, the canine teeth
lu scaluni, the step (of stairs)	li scaluna, the steps
lu turruni, the large tower*	li turruna, the large towers
lu vasuni, the kiss	li vasuna, the kisses
lu vastuni, the club, stick	li vastuna, the clubs, sticks

* This noun is an augmentative. See Chapter 15 for a treatment of augmentatives.

Nouns ending in -uri with a plural in -a

lu cumpusituri, the composer	li cumpusitura, the composers
lu dutturi, the doctor	li duttura, the doctors
lu prufissuri, the professor	li prufissura, the professors
lu tradituri, the traitor	li traditura, the traitors
lu piccaturi, the sinner	li piccatura, the sinners

You can see that this broad class of nouns having a plural in -a includes a large number of masculine nouns. **Note:** The list above is not exhaustive so be on the alert for them.

Nouns with an Irregular Plural in -ura

There are a few nouns having a plural in -ura. Note the placement of the accent in the plural. In the vocabularies, such nouns will be indicated using the notation (p -ura). **Note:** In some of the Sicilian dialects (*parrati*), these have regular plurals.

lu corpu, the body	li corpura **or** li corpi, the bodies
lu iocu, the game	li iocura **or** li iochi, the games
lu tempu, the time	li tempura **or** li tempi, the times
lu voscu, the forest	li voscura **or** li voschi, the forests

Noun with an Irregular Plural in -ini

There is one very common noun in Sicilian with an irregular plural ending in -ini.

l'omu, the man	l'omini, the men

Feminine Forms of Nouns

Certain masculine nouns have corresponding feminine nouns. The feminine forms vary. In some cases, the same word is used, and in other cases, when the masculine form ends in -u, the feminine form ends in -a. In some nouns, there is no clear relationship, and for other nouns, the corresponding feminine form ends in -issa (sometimes also given as -essa). If the masculine noun ends in -turi, the corresponding feminine form typically ends in -tura or sometimes -trici.

Examples

l'artista, the artist (M)	l'artista, the artist (F)
lu gattu, the cat (M)	la gatta, the cat (F)
lu re, the king	la riggina, the queen
lu cani, the dog (M)	la cagna, the bitch
lu liuni, the lion	la liunissa, the lioness
l'atturi, the actor	l'attrici, the attress
lu cumpusituri, the composer (M)	la cumpusitura, the composer (F)
lu duca, the duke	la duchissa, the duchess
lu principi, the prince	la principissa, the princess
lu prufissuri, the teacher, professor	la prufissurissa, the teacher, professor
lu pueta, the poet	la puitissa, the poetess
lu studenti, the student (M)	la studintissa, the student (F)
lu tissituri, the weaver (M)	la tissitura **or** la tissitrici, the weaver (F)

Adjectives

In general, adjectives follow the same rules given above for nouns. Furthermore, adjectives can often function as nouns. In fact, both classes are often referred to as substantives (things having substance with definitive characteristics).

Adjectives with Four Endings

As noted above, there are some adjectives accented on the antepenult that have four terminations: -cu (Ms), -ca (Fs), -ci (Mp), -chi (Fp). This category of adjective is small.

Examples

catolicu	catolica	catolici	catolichi, catholic
fantasticu	fantastica	fantastici	fantastichi, fantastic

Adjectives with Three Endings

There are adjectives having three terminations: -u (Ms), -a (Fs), -i (p). This category of adjective is very large.

Examples

bonu	bona	boni, good
beddu	bedda	beddi, beautiful
pricisu	pricisa	pricisi, precise

Adjectives with Two Endings

There are a few adjectives (generally formed from nouns) having two terminations: -a (Ms and Fs), -i (p).

Examples

socialista	socialista	socialisti, socialist
cumunista	cumunista	cumunisti, communist

Adjectives with One Ending

There are adjectives with one termination, -*i* (Ms, Fs, p). This category of adjective and the adjectives with three different endings make up the great bulk of adjectives in Sicilian.

Examples
granni	granni	granni, large; old
filici	filici	filici, happy

Note: Adjectives ending in -*i* but referring to nationalities take a feminine singular in -*a*, not -*i*. The plural of such adjectives still ends in -*i*. **Examples:** francisi (Ms)/francisa (Fs), French; nglisi (Ms)/nglisa (Fs), English. Some other adjectives the masculine of which ends in -*i* also follow this pattern. **Example:** giuvini (Ms)/giuvina (Fs), young.

Adjectives Used as Nouns

In Sicilian, as in all the Romance languages, it's very common for an adjective to function as a noun.

Examples
chiddu granni, the great one (male)
chidda cuntenti, the happy one (female)
chidda bedda, the beautiful one (female)
chiddi poviri, the poor (plural)

Note: The demonstative pronouns, *chiddu/chidda/chiddi*, are used in place of the definite articles in this case. See **Demonstrative Pronouns and Adjectives** in Chapter 7.

Position of Adjectives

As in the other Romance languages, descriptive adjectives generally follow nouns, especially adjectives denoting religion, nationality, color, etc. There are some exceptions to this rule. Possessive adjectives and demonstrative adjectives generally precede the noun they govern. Here are some examples of adjectives that follow the noun they describe.

Examples
l'omu nglisi **or** lu nglisi **or** l'inglisi, the Englishman
la fimmina nglisa **or** la nglisa **or** l'inglisa, the Englishwoman
li re catolici, the Catholic kings **or** the Catholic king and queen
la fimmina cuntenti, the happy woman
li libbra grossi, the big books
l'omu grossu, the large man
l'omu vecchiu, the old man
la figghia cchiù granni, the oldest daughter
lu figghiu cchiù nicu, the youngest son
la vistina niura, the black dress
l'erba virdi, the green grass
l'occhiu azzolu, the blue eye

Certain descriptive adjectives sometimes precede the noun. These are:

autru, other	megghiu (invariable), better
beddu, handsome, beautiful	nicu, little; young
bonu, good, pretty, nice	peiu **or** peggiu (invariable), worse
bruttu, ugly, bad (weather)	picciulu, small
granni, great; older; adult	poviru, poor; unfortunate
giuvini, young	stissu, same
malu, bad, wicked	tintu, bad
ladiu **or** lariu, ugly	vecchiu, old

Examples

nautru omu, another man*	nautra fimmina, another woman
beddu tempu, good weather	la bedda fimmina, the beautiful woman
lu bon senzu, the good sense	la bona cosa, the good thing
bruttu tempu, bad weather	na brutta vista, an ugly view
nu **or** un giuvini omu, a young man[†]	la giuvina fimmina, the young woman[†]
lu gran omu, the great man	na granni vittoria, a great victory
lu ladiu fattu, the ugly deed	la ladia picciotta, the ugly young woman
lu malu omu, the wicked man	la mala ntinzioni, the bad intention
nu megghiu locu, a better place	la megghiu cosa, the best thing
lu nicu surci, the tiny mouse[‡]	na nica cosa, a little thing, a trifle
nu **or** un peiu avviniri, a worse future	na peggiu situazzioni, a worse situation
lu picciulu nuddu, the little nobody[‡]	la picciula casa, the little house
lu stissu libbru, the same book[††]	la pirsuna stissa, the very person
lu vecchiu gaddu, the old rooster	la vecchia casa, the old house

* "Another" in the sense of a refill is "di cchiù". **Example:** Pi favuri, portami nu gottu di birra di cchiù. Please bring me another mug of beer. **Note:** *bucali* also means "mug".

† *Picciottu* means "boy" (adolescent) **or** "young man", and *giuvinottu* means "young man"; ditto for *picciotta* and *giuvinotta*. When a young man marries, the term *omu* is generally applied to him. In the case of a woman, the term *fimmina* applies. **Note:** Today, the term *picciottu* often refers to someone in the Mafia.

‡ Often a diminutive ending would be used rather than the adjective *nicu* or *picciulu*.

†† Note *stissu* before a noun may mean "own", as in *ntra lu so stissu ogghiu*, "in his own oil".

Some of these adjectives have a different meaning if they follow the noun. In general, placing an adjective after the noun renders it more objective, whereas if it precedes the noun, the meaning is more subjective (or figurative), that is, it expresses the opinion of the speaker as opposed to the fact being common knowledge (objective meaning). In Sicilian an adjective is more likely to follow its noun than in some of the other Romance languages.

Exercises

Exercise #1: Sicilian words for practicing pronunciation.

b	**p**	**d**
bonu, good	pani, bread	dinari, money
abbaiari, to bark	pesti, pest	diri, to say
banna, place	pirsuna, person	dari, to give
bannera, flag	paisi, town	deci, ten
fibbia, buckle	pastu, food	doppu, after

t	**hard g**	**hard c**
tempu, time	gattu, cat	cani, dog
teniri, to hold	gula, throat	chiaru, clear
testa, head	godiri, to enjoy	cui, who
tali, such	ghiacciu, ice	culuri, color
tu, you	grassu, fat	chi, what

hard sc	**soft g**	**soft c**
scarpa, shoe	già, already	cecu, blind
scola, school	giru, tour	città, city
schiavu, slave	giustu, fair; right	cincu, five
scopu, effect	giuvini, young	citari, to quote
scurriri, to flow	gergu, slang	celu, heaven

soft sc	**f**	**v**
scrusciu, noise	facci, face	vuci, voice
scinniri, to go down	funnu, bottom	vita, life
scena, scene	fumu, smoke	vasu, vase
sceccu, donkey	facili, easy	veru, true
scioccu, stupid	fami, hunger	veniri, to come

z (voiceless)	**z (voiced) [dz]**	**s**
ziu, uncle	zeru, zero	sali, salt
zitu, fiancé	zona, zone	casa, house
zampa, paw	zagara, orange blossom	sutta, under
zingaru, gypsy	zainu, knapsack	cosa, thing
azzaru, steel	zefiru, breeze	risu, rice

m	**n**	**ng**
ma, but	novi, nine	longu, long
magru, thin	nasu, nose	sangu, blood
mettiri, to put	nutari, to record; note	lunghizza, length
amuri, love	nivi, snow	nglisi, English
amicu, friend	niputi, nephew/niece; grandchild	ngannari, to cheat

gn
ogni, every
signuri, sir
pugnu, fist
dugnu, I give
sugnu, I am

consonantal i
inchiri, to fill
iditu, finger
iri, to go
aiu, I have
aiutu, help

qu
quannu, when
quarchi, some
qualità, quality
quali, which
quartu, fourth

r (initial)
riccu, rich
rosa, rose
russu, red
rubbari, to rob
rumpiri, to break

rr
ferru, iron
sciarra **or** scerra, quarrel
arreri, behind, again
arrassu, far off
parrari, to speak

r (intervocalic)
parola, word
dari, to give
cura, care
fari, to do
raru, unusual

r (before a C)*
arba dawn
garzuni [dz], helper; apprentice
barbaru, barbarian
marmu, marble
pardu, leopard

l (light)
lacu, lake
luna, moon
lingua, tongue
lettu, bed
lista, list

l (dark)
palmu, palm
calmu, calm
altaru, alter
cultu, cultured
fulmini, lightening

dd
beddu, beautiful
fedda, slice
stidda, star
fudda, crowd
cuteddu, knife

tr
truvari, to find
trasiri, to enter
patri, father
ncuntrari, to meet
tristu, sad

nt
nta, in
tintu, evil
tantu, so much
puntu, dot
vinti, twenty

nz
pinzari, to think
nzemi, together
nzignari, to teach
cunziddirari [dd], to consider
cunzigghiari, to advise

str
strata, street
struzzu, ostrich
stranu, strange
lustru, shiny; bright
finestra, window

gghi
pagghia, straw
figghiu, son
fogghia, leaf
ogghiu, oil
agghiu, garlic

cchi
occhiu, eye
spicchiu, fruitstone
cucchiaru, spoon
chiacchiariari, to chatter
acchianari, to climb

mC*
mparari, to learn
mpastari, to knead dough
mpidiri, to hinder
mmitari, to invite
mmriacu, drunk

nC*
nchiudiri, enclose
ncigneri, engineer
nfacci, facing
nfatti, in fact
ncagna, grimace

* C = a consonant

4   Prepositions

Purpose of the Chapter
The chief purpose of this chapter is to discuss prepositions. Prepositions are indispensible words in any language since they give the relationship of words to other words. Every language has them. In some languages they are placed after the noun (and so are called postpositions), but in the Indo-European languages, including English, Sicilian, and Italian they are placed before the noun. Prepositions can either be simple (stand-alone) or compound.

Simple Prepositions
These are prepositions that can stand by themselves. As is noted, many simple prepositions are gemination-causing words. Don't use the $^+$ in spelling. The most common in Sicilian are:

a$^+$, at, to, for, by means of, from, in
circa, about, approximately
comu, like, as
contra, against, opposite, versus
cu$^+$, with, by means of
darreri **or** darrè, behind*
davanti, before, in front of
di$^+$, of, from, by, about†
doppu, after (time)
duranti, during
eccettu, except, save for, but for

ncapu, on, on top of
nni **or** nna, in, at the place of **or** at the house of
ntra, within, into
pi$^+$ **or** pri$^+$, for, by, to, through, for the sake of, in order to
scancia, instead of
secunnu, according to
senza, without
sparti, besides, not including
supra, on, on top of, over
sutta, under
tranni, except for, save for, but for

* Also *arreri*, *arrè*, *nnarrè*, and *nnarreri* are found. **Note:** *arreri* and *arrè* also commonly mean "again".
† In literary Sicilian, *da* is sometimes used for *di* with the meaning "from" or "by". This is an Italianism. Use *di* in Sicilian.

Comments on the Prepositions
The following comments are made regarding the simple prepositions.

1. The preposition *nni* (**or** *nna*), when standing alone without an article, is written *n* before a noun, that is, *n + noun*. **Examples:** n tempu, in time; n casa, at home; n puntu di fattu, in point of fact; n Sicilia, in Sicily. If the *n* changes to an *m* (the *n* changes to *m* when a word beginning with an *m* or *v* follows), it will be directly attached to the noun. **Examples:**   mmenzu, in the midst of; mmucca, in the mouth. As this practice is widespread, it will be followed in this book although *n menzu* and *n vucca* are also acceptable.
2. The forms *nni* and *nna* are alternate forms of the same word, and usage of each depends as much on euphony, that is, how the phrase sounds to the ear, as on strict conformity to grammar.
   Examples
   (1) ...e nna sta terra nun si campa assai. ...and in this land a person can't live long.
   (2) ...ristamu nni sta terra marturiati. ...we remain tormented in this land.
   (3) Cantavi sulu tu nni lu silenziu... .Only you were singing in the silence....

(4) ...vistuti e senza cuda nna lu fangu. ... dressed and without a tail in the mud.

The first two examples, (1) and (2), were taken from Vincenzo Ancona, *Malidittu La Lingua* (New York: Legas, 1990), p. 78. The second two, (3) and (4), were taken from the poem of Lina La Mattina, "A 'Gnaziu Buttitta" in *Na Vuci a la Scurata* (Edizioni ARCI SICILIA), pp. 18-19. You'll note that each author uses both forms.

3. In Literary Sicilian, the convention also exists of writing the preposition *nni* (or *nna*), when standing alone without an article, as *in*, that is, *in + noun*. This is a writing convention. See in particular **Disappearance of Initial *i*** in Chapter 2. The *i* in the *in* is not pronounced in spoken Sicilian.

4. The preposition *nta* is sometimes used in place of *nni* or *nna*.

5. In some of the *parrati*, *nta* and *pri* are more common forms than *nni/nna* and *pi*.

6. The preposition *nni* and *nta* is also frequently used to indicate location, especially within a country. **Example:** ntâ Sicilia, nnâ Sicilia, **or** n Sicilia, in Sicily.

7. If a pronoun follows one of the simple prepositions, *di* is inserted between the preposition and the pronoun. The pronoun must be a object disjunctive pronoun. See Chapter 7, **Pronouns**, for a discussion of disjunctive pronouns. Actually, almost all prepositions are simple before nouns (and noun phrases) and compound before pronouns.

8. The *d* of the preposition *di* often elides in speech when it is found before a consonant. Sometimes this is found in the written language also. **Examples:** lu libbru i Maria (lu libbru di Maria), Mary's book; la figghia i Cuncetta (la figghia di Cuncetta), Cuncetta's daughter. **Note:** This practice will not be followed in this book.

9. The preposition *a* is frequently combined with the *l* of the article before a vowel or a word in which the initial *i* is lost, thus restoring the *i*. The *l* of the article is doubled. **Examples:** all'improvisu, suddenly; all'università, at the university.

10. Standing alone without an article and before a word beginning with a vowel, these prepositions are often written in a contracted form: di (d'), nni (nn'), nta (nt'), pi (p').

11. The use of *su* in place of *supra* is on the increase due to the influence of Italian.

12. The following prepositions don't form contractions with the definite articles under any circumstances: circa, comu, contra, darreri, davanti, doppu, duranti, eccettu, ncapu, scancia, secunnu, senza, supra, sutta, tranni.

Contractions of the Simple Prepositions with Definite Articles

Several of the simple propositions form contractions with the short forms of the definite article, *u/a/i*. The contractions don't take place with the long forms. **Note:** For nouns beginning with a vowel, the articles retain the *l*, so no contractions. The other prepositions forming contractions with the *u/a/i* forms of the definite articles are: nna, nta, ntra, pi, and pri. They follow the same patterns as given below for *a*, *cu*, *di*, and *nni*.

Examples

a lu patri, to the father
or ô patri, to the father
a l'omu, to the man
a la matri, to the mother
or â matri, to the mother
a l'unna, to the wave
a li patri, to the fathers
or ê patri, to the fathers
a l'omini, to the men

cu lu patri, with the father
or cû patri, with the father
cu l'omu, with the man
cu la matri, with the mother
or câ matri, with the mother
cu l'unna, with the wave
cu li patri, with the fathers
or chî patri, with the fathers
cu l'omini, with the men

di lu patri, of the father
or dû patri, of the father
di l'omu, of the man
di la matri, of the mother
or dâ matri, of the mother
di l'unna, of the wave
di li patri, of the fathers
or dî patri, of the fathers
di l'omini, of the men

nni lu patri, in the father
or nnû patri, in the father
nni l'omu, in the man
nni la matri, in the mother
or nnâ matri, in the mother
nni l'unna, in the wave
nni li patri, in the fathers
or nnî patri, in the fathers
nni l'omini, in the men

Contractions of the Simple Prepositions with the Indefinite Article

A few of the simple propositions form contractions with the indefinite masculine article *un* (not *nu*). These contractions are optional. No contraction takes place with the indefinite feminine article *na*.

cu un patri, with a father
or cûn patri, with a father
cu na matri, with a mother

di un patri, of a father
or dûn patri, of a father
di na matri, of a mother

nta un patri, in a father
or ntôn patri, in a father
nta na matri, in a mother

nni (or nna) un patri, in a father
or nnôn patri, in a father
nni (or nna) na matri, in a mother

Compound Prepositions

There are a number of propositions that are compounds of an adverb with a simple preposition. They also function as true prepositions. As was pointed out, both *a* (a[+]) and *di* (di[+]) are gemination-causing words. However, so as not to clutter the following lists, the [+] will be left off these words.

Compound Prepositions Formed with a

accantu a, near, close by, besides, along side of
allatu a, at the side of , beside
appressu a, near, close to
avanti a, in front of
fina a **or** affina a **or** finu a, up to, as far as, until
iuntu a, next to
nfacci a, facing
ntornu a, around, about
ntunnu a, around, about
ntunnu ntunnu a **or** ntornu ntornu a, all around
oltri a **or** noltri a, besides
pi quantu riguardu a, regarding, in regard to, on the subject of
quantu a, for, as to, regarding
vicinu a, near
sinu a **or** nzinu a **or** nzina a **or** sina a, up to, as far as, until

Note: The *a* isn't always used, that is, they are often used as simple prepositions. See Note 7 above in **Comments on the Prepositions**.

Other Compound Prepositions

a causa di, because of, on account of
a prupositu di **or** a propositu di, as for, as to, regarding, on the subject of
a riguardu di, regarding, with regard to, about
a rispettu di, regarding, with respect to, about
dintra di, inside of
fora di, outside of
luntanu di, far from
ncugnuntu di, in conjunction with
mmeci di, instead of
mmenzu di **or** mmezzu di, in the midst of
pi menzu di **or** pi mezzu di, by means of
pi via di, by means of
prima di, before (time)
sarvu di **or** salvu di, except for, save for
versu di, near, to, towards, in the direction of

Note: The above prepositions are often used as simple prepositions. See Note 7 above in **Comments on the Prepositions**.

Vocabulary

Try to learn the meanings of the prepositions given in this chapter as the given vocabulary along with the words introduced in Chapters 2 and 3. If you can't find a word, look it up in the Sicilian-English Vocabulary in the back or consult the words listed in Chapters 2 and 3.

Exercises

Exercise #1: Review the following words and make sure you understand them. Look them up in a dictionary if you need to.

Parts of Speech

Adjective	Predicate
Adverb	Preposition
Articles-definite and indefinite	Prepositional phrase
Conjunction	Pronoun
Noun and Noun phrase	Subject
Object	Verb and Verb phrase

Exercise #2: Translate these phrases into English.

(1) ogghia di Sicilia (2) vicinu â città (3) ô principiu (4) iuntu â scrivania (5) luntanu dâ città (6) sutta u lettu (7) supra a tavula (8) duranti a simana (9) doppu a cena (10) arré â porta **or** darreri (**or** *darrè*) â porta (11) davanti â seggia (12) sinu ô ciumi (**or** sinu ô sciumi) (13) avanti ê picciriddi (14) dintra dâ scatula (15) pi l'amuri (16) ntâ Sicilia **or** nnâ Sicilia **or** n Sicilia (17) versu â casa (18) fora dâ casa (19) cu l'ogghiu (20) a riguardu dû cuntu (21) ntê rivisti (22) comu u prisidenti (23) ntra i populi dû munnu (24) mmeci dû frati (25) nna l'angulu dâ cammara (26) cû marteddu (27) a causa di l'acqua (28) cu l'isca nta l'amu (29) contra l'elementi dâ natura (30) pi menzu dû telefunu (31) prima dû pranzu (32) a propositu dâ lizzioni di sta grammatica (33) ntornu a l'arvulu (34) a l'ariuportu (35) sarvu dû picciottu (36) eccettu a picciotta (37) nfacci ô prufissuri (38) pû gattu (39) mmenzu dî voscura sarvaggi (40) pi via dâ littra dâ prufissurissa (41) pi menzu dî littri dî prufissura (42) sparti Giuvanni (43) ô muru (44) a pruposìtu dû prubblema gravi (45) appressu â cabbina dû telefunu (46) nnâ littra (47) vicinu â chiazza (48) i taliani contra i tideschi (49) u russu contra u virdi (50) nnê celi

5   Verbs: Present and Imperative

Purpose of the Chapter
The chief purpose of this chapter is to discuss verbs. Verbs are among the most important words of any language. They typically express actions, processes, conditions, or states of affairs. In particular, the chapter sets forth the present indicative of verbs and the imperative, or command forms. Subject pronouns are also introduced.

Verbal Conjugations
In Sicilian there are only two conjugations. A conjugation is a verb class, and the endings that are attached to the verb stem depend on the verb's conjugation. The two conjugations are normally indicated by the infinitive.

Conjugation 1
Infinitive ends in -ari

Conjugation 2
Infinitive ends in –iri

Verbs of Conjugation 2 can accent either the antepenult (third from the last syllable) or the penult (second from the last syllable). Some *parrati* favor one pronunciation; some favor the other. In this book the stress on the antepenult is favored, but there are some exceptions. This stressed antepenult will be indicated by a bolded theme vowel, but this is only a convention used in this book. It is not part of normal Sicilian spelling conventions. **Examples:** rispunniri (Conjugation 2), to reply, respond; scinniri (Conjugation 2), to descend, climb down.

Within Conjugation 2 are found certain verbs that accent the penult of the infinitive and, in addition, insert -sc- between the verb stem and the verbal endings in the present (except for the 1st person plural and 2nd person plural) and also in the imperative. These special Conjugation 2 verbs will be indicated in the vocabularies by adding an (sc) after the verb in the infinitive form. **Examples:** finiri (sc), to finish; capiri (sc), to understand, etc.

Subject Pronouns
Pronouns are discussed in detail in Chapter 7, but the subject pronouns are introduced here in connection with the verb forms of the present tense. In this book, to simplify the presentation, only one pronoun from each category will be used with a given verb form.

I, 1st person singular	iu, eu, io (pronouned /yŏ or iʸŏ/)
you, 2nd person singular familiar	tu
you, 3rd person singular polite	vossìa, vussìa, vassa, assa*
he, 3rd person singular masculine	iddu
she, 3rd person singular feminine	idda
it, 3rd person singular neuter	iddu **or** idda
we, 1st person plural	nuiatri, nuiautri, niatri, nuatri, nui
you, 2nd person plural	vuiatri, vuiautri, vuatri, vui†
they, 3rd person plural	iddi

* Note that *vossìa* is a 3rd person singular form in Sicilian. See Chapter 7 for the explanation. In English, of course, "you" is a 2nd person singular pronoun.

† Note that *vui* also can be used as a 2nd person singular pronoun. See Chapter 7.

Although English no longer uses a 2nd person singular familiar form (the form is "thou"), Sicilian, like the other Romance languages, does. The word "it" in Sicilian depends on the gender of the corresponding noun. If the noun is masculine, say *libbru*, the "it" is *iddu*. If the noun is feminine, say *porta*, the "it" is *idda*. Normally though, the "it" won't be expressed by any pronoun.

The 1st and 2nd person plural subject pronouns are combinations of *nui* and *vui* with *atri* **or** *autri* (others). In essence, they mean "we others" and "you others". Although subject pronouns will be used in conjunction with the various verb forms to illustrate the present tense of verbs, their use is optional since the verb endings alone are sufficient to indicate the meaning involved. This usage parallels Italian and Spanish, but not French.

Present Indicative

This is a very common tense in all of the Romance languages, including Sicilian, and it absolutely must be mastered. The paradigms (patterns) of three verbs are given here. These verbs are: parrari (Conjugation 1), rispunniri (Conjugation 2), and finiri (Conjugation 2 sc verb). The paradigms below cover the conjugations in the present indicative tense and in the imperative. The verb stem is obtained by dropping the ending of the infinitive. The accented vowel in the verb stem is known as the theme vowel. **Note:** For both conjugations, there are two slightly different, but acceptable, endings for the 3rd person plural.

The paradigm for verbs of whatever tense will always be given in this format:

- 1st person singular – the *I* or *iu* form;
- 2nd person singular familiar – the familiar *you* or *tu* form;
- 3rd person singular polite – the polite *you* or *vossìa* **or** *lei* form* (as indicated above, this form requires a 3rd person singular ending);
- 3rd person singular – the *he/she/it* or *iddu/idda* form;
- 1st person plural – the *we* or *nuiatri* form;
- 2nd person plural – the *you* or *vuiatri* form;
- 3rd person plural – the *they* or *iddi* form.

* Note that *lei* is now a 3rd person singular polite pronoun that has become more acceptable. The use of *lei* is increasing, especially among the younger generation, due to the influence of Italian.

To conjugate a verb, first drop the infinitive ending to obtain the verb stem. Then add the personal endings to the stem. The personal pronouns will be used to indicate the person and number. For the 3rd person singular, only *iddu* will be shown to conserve space. In the three examples below, the three verb stems are: parr-, rispunn-, and fin- respectively. **Note:** To make them more easily recognizable, the personal endings are given in italics.

Conjugation 1	**Conjugation 2**	**Conjugation 2 (sc)**
parrari, to speak	rispunniri, to reply	finiri, to finish
iu parr*u*, I speak	iu rispunn*u*, I reply	iu finisci*u*, I finish
tu parr*i*, you (fam.) speak	tu rispunn*i*, you (fam.) reply	tu finisc*i*, you (fam.) finish
vossìa parr*a*, you (pol.) speak	vossìa rispunn*i*, you (pol.) reply	vossìa finisc*i*, you (pol.) finish
iddu parr*a*, he speaks	iddu rispunn*i*, he replies	iddu finisc*i*, he finishes
nuiatri parr*amu*, we speak	nuiatri rispunn*emu*, we reply	nuiatri fin*emu*, we finish
vuiatri parr*ati*, you speak	vuiatri rispunn*iti*, you reply	vuiatri fin*iti*, you finish
iddi parr*anu*, they speak	iddi rispunn*inu*, they reply	iddi finisc*inu*, they finish
or iddi parr*unu*, they speak	**or** iddi rispunn*unu*, they reply	**or** iddi finisci*unu*, they finish

Note: The 3rd person plural verbal ending in -*unu* is found chiefly in central and eastern Sicily, whereas the verbal endings in -*anu* and -*inu* tend to be found in western Sicily.

Uses of the Present Indicative

There are three chief uses of the present indicative. These are:

- Simple present;
- Emphatic present;
- Simple future.

In addition to the simple present, the present indicative forms can also be translated as emphatic verb forms since Sicilian doesn't have an emphatic tense as English does, that is, *parru* can be translated as "I do speak", *rispunnu* as "I do reply", and *finisciu* as "I do finish", etc.

The present indicative in Sicilian can also be used to express the future tense, a practice common to all the Romance languages. Examples are given in the Exercises of the use of the present tense to indicate the future. Although Sicilian has a true simple future tense, it is not common in the spoken language. It is used in the written language, so it is important to know it. See **Simple Future** in Chapter 6.

In Sicilian two or more singular subjects take a plural verb. The appropriate article is also used.

Examples
(1) L'omu e lu so cani sunnu sempri nzeparabbili. Man and his dog are always inseparable.
(2) L'amuri e l'oddiu sunnu dui lati di la stissa munita. Love and hatred are two sides of the same coin.
(3) Quarchi vota lu gattu e lu surci abballanu nzemi. Sometimes cat and mouse dance together.

Note: In some Sicilian proverbs, two or more subjects connected with *e* (and) are followed by a singular verb, especially if they are viewed psychologically as a unit. The use of the articles is also often dispensed with in proverbs. See the Exercises; generally Exercise #1 contains proverbs.

Examples from proverbs

(1) Acqua e terra fa rimarra. Rain and earth make mud. (*fa* is 3rd person singular)
(2) Omu e cani è sempri nzeparabbili. Man and dog are always inseparable. (*è* is 3rd person singular)
(3) La fimmina, lu ventu e la vintura pocu dura. A woman, the wind and fortune last only a short while. (*dura* is 3rd person singular)

Imperative

The imperative of the three verbs given above is set forth here. The paradigm for each verb in the imperative is given below, which is slightly different from the one for normal tenses. See above.

- 2nd person singular familiar – the familiar *you* or *tu* form;
- 3rd person singular polite – the polite *you* or *vossìa* **or** *lei* form
- 3rd person singular – the *he/she/it* or *iddu/idda* form;
- 1st person plural – the *we* or *nuiatri* form;
- 2nd person plural – the *you* or *vuiatri* form;
- 3rd person plural – the *they* or *iddi* form.

Normally the subject pronouns are not given with the imperative since it is a command form, but often *vossìa* is used with its imperative. **Example:** vossìa parrassi, (you) speak.

Conjugation 1	Conjugation 2	Conjugation 2 (sc)
parrari, to speak	rispunniri, to reply	finiri, to finish
(tu) parr*a*, speak*	(tu) rispunn*i*, reply*	(tu) finis*ci*, finish*
(vossìa) parr*assi*, speak	(vossìa) rispunn*issi*, reply	(vossìa) fin*issi*, finish
(iddu) parr*assi*, let him speak	(iddu) rispunn*issi*, let him reply	(iddu) fin*issi*, let him finish
(nuiatri) parr*amu*, let us speak	(nuiatri) rispunn*emu*, let us reply	(nuiatri) fin*emu*, let us finish
(vuiatri) parr*ati*, speak	(vuiatri) rispunn*iti*, reply	(vuiatri) fin*iti*, finish
(iddi) parr*assiru*, let them speak	(iddi) rispunn*issiru*, let them reply	(iddi) fin*issiru*, let them finish

* Sometimes *vossìa* is used with this form.

Note: The verb endings *-assi* and *-issi* are subjunctive endings as are the *-assiru* and *-issiru* endings. See Chapter 13.

Note: In the province of Messina, the following polite imperative forms are found: Vossìa mi + 3rd person singular form of the verb. **Examples:** Vossìa mi veni, please come; Vossìa mi mancia, please eat.

Negative Imperative

To form the negative imperative, place *non* **or** *nun* before the appropriate form. The only exception to this is in the 2nd person singular form. There add *non* **or** *nun* before the infinitive.

Examples

Non fumari. Don't smoke. (2nd person singular)
Non ripetiri. Don't repeat. (2nd person singular)
Non parrassi. **or** Vossìa non parrassi. Don't speak. (3rd person singular polite)
Non finissi. **or** Vossìa non finissi. Don't finish. (3rd person singular polite)
Non ripitemu. Let's not repeat. (1st person plural)
Non ripititi. Don't repeat. (2nd person plural)
Non parrassiru. Let them not speak. (3rd person plural)
Non finissiru. Let them not finish. (3rd person plural)

Stem-Changing Verbs

Certain Sicilian verbs exhibit an internal change depending on whether the theme vowel is stressed or unstressed. In particular, the patterns *i* (unstressed)/*e* (stressed) and *u* (unstressed)/*o* (stressed) are observed in various verbs. If the unstressed principal theme vowel in a verb is *i* or *u*, when stressed it is generally *e* or *o*. The two verbs used to illustrate this principal are: purtari, to carry (Conjugation 1); ripetiri, to repeat (Conjugation 2).

Conjugation 1	**Conjugation 2**
purtari, to carry	ripetiri, to repeat
iu port*u*, I carry	iu ripet*u*, I repeat
tu port*i*, you (fam.) carry	tu ripet*i*, you (fam.) repeat
vossìa port*a*, you (pol.) carry	vossìa ripet*i*, you (pol.) repeat
iddu port*a*, he carries	iddu ripet*i*, he repeats
nuiatri purt*amu*, we carry	nuiatri ripit*emu*, we repeat
vuiatri purt*ati*, you carry	vuiatri ripit*iti*, you repeat
iddi port*anu*, they carry	iddi ripet*inu*, they repeat
or iddi port*unu*, they carry	**or** iddi ripet*unu*, they repeat

Note that the stress moves to the verb endings in the 1st person plural and 2nd person plural, so the theme vowel reverts to its unstressed value. **Note:** These changes only occur in the present tense and the imperative forms. In all other tenses, the verb endings bear the stress, so the theme vowel always maintains its unstressed value.

Several other verbs exhibiting these changes are: accuminciari (accumenciu), to begin; moriri (moru), to die; rubbari (robbu), to rob; truvari (trovu), to find; vulari (volu), to fly; vestiri (vestu), to dress. **Note:** Many verbs in the vocabularies have the 1st person singular of the verb in parentheses after the infinitive unless the verb is completely regular. This practice will help identify stem-changing verbs and verbs displaying other irregularities. **Examples:** mpristari (mprestu), to loan; offriri (offru), to offer; rimpruvirari (rimproviru), to scold.

Spelling Changes in Verbs

Certain verbs have stems ending either in *soft c, soft g, hard c, hard g*. It's only necessary to remember that the sound must be preserved whether soft or hard, and to remember also that *h* is used after a *c* or a *g* and before *e* and *i* to keep the sound hard. For Conjugation 1 this affects only the 2nd person singular. For Conjugation 2 this affects all persons singular and plural. The four verbs used to illustrate this principal are: circari, to search for; manciari, to eat; cogghiri, to gather; danniggiari, to injure. Three out of the four are also stem-changing verbs: circari, cogghiri, and danniggiari. Since you know the pattern by now, only the English meanings of the infinitives will be given, and the endings will no longer be italicized since you should be able to recognize them.

Conjugation 1 - hard c
circari, to look for, to try (to)
iu cercu
tu cerchi
vossìa cerca
iddu cerca
nuiatri circamu
vuiatri circati
iddi cercanu
or iddi cercunu

Conjugation 1 - soft c
manciari, to eat
iu manciu
tu manci
vossìa mancia
iddu mancia
nuiatri manciamu
vuiatri manciati
iddi mancianu
or iddi manciunu

Conjugation 2 - hard g
cogghiri, to pick, to gather
iu cogghiu
tu cogghi
vossìa cogghi
iddu cogghi
nuiatri cugghiemu
vuiatri cugghiti
iddi cogghinu
or iddi cogghiunu

Conjugation 1 - soft g
danniggiari, to injure, harm
iu danneggiu
tu danneggi
vossìa danneggia
iddu danneggia
nuiatri danniggiamu
vuiatri danniggiati
iddi danneggianu
or iddi danneggiunu

The same principles apply to verbs whose stems end in -*sc*, which can either be hard or soft. **Examples:** asciari, to find (Conjugation 1 - soft sc); vuscari, to earn a living (Conjugation 1 - hard sc). As noted, many verbs in the vocabularies have the 1st person singular of the verb in parentheses after the infinitive. This will help identify verbs displaying spelling changes. **Examples:** sciogghiri (sciogghiu), to loosen; ammuccari (ammuccu), to put in the mouth; ammucciari (ammucciu), to hide.

One other type of verb needs to be mentioned here. These are Conjugation 1 verbs having a stressed *i* in all persons and numbers except 1st person plural and 2nd person plural. This type of verb is fairly common in Sicilian. Two verbs used to illustrate this type are: taliari, to look at; passiari, to take a stroll. Since you know the pattern by now, only the English meanings of the infinitives will be given, and the endings will no longer be italicized since you should be able to recognize them.

Conjugation 1 - stressed i
taliari, to look at
iu taliu
tu talii
vossìa talia
iddu talia
nuiatri taliamu
vuiatri taliati
iddi talianu **or** iddi taliunu

Conjugation 1 - stressed i
passiari, to take a stroll
iu passiu
tu passii
vossìa passia
iddu passia
nuiatri passiamu
vuiatri passiati
iddi passianu **or** iddi passiunu

Note: Although the 2nd person singular imperative of *taliari* is *talia*, *talè* is also very common. **Examples:** Eh, talè ccà, Look here!; Talè, Just look!

Again, such verbs will be indicated in the vocabularies by displaying the 1st person singular (1s) of the verb in parentheses after the infinitive. **Examples:** maniari (maniu), to handle (with the hand), to drive; arricriari (arricriu), to please, amuse. For impersonal verbs, the 3rd person singular (3s) will be given, and the abbreviation 3s will be used. **Example:** agghiurnari (3s agghiorna).

Vocabulary

Nouns

l'annu, year
l'amuri (M), love
la biancaria, laundry; linens
la camula, moth
la casa, house
lu celu, sky, heavens (p -a **or** -i)
la chiazza, square (e.g., of a town), piazza
lu cori, heart
lu difettu, defect
lu dinaru **or** dinari, money (p more common)
lu diu, god (p li dei **or** li dii)
la donna, lady*
lu donu, gift (p -a)
lu feli, bile; hatred
lu figghiu, son
la fimmina, woman
lu focu, fire (p -a or -i)
lu frati, brother
lu gaddu, rooster
la gilusia, jealousy
la iamma **or** l'amma, leg
lu iornu, day (p -a)
lu libbru, book (p -a)
lu lignu, piece of wood (p -a)
la luna, moon
la manu, hand (p manu)
la mamma, mother; momma
la matina, morning
la matri, mother
lu millipedi, millipede (poisonous)
lu nervu, nerve; strength; switch (to whip with)
l'occhiu, eye
l'ovu, egg (p -a)
l'omu, man (p omini)
lu parmu, span, breath of hand (lit. palm)**
la parola **or** la palora, word
la picciridda **or** piccilidda, baby; child; little girl
lu picciriddu **or** picciliddu, baby; child; little boy
lu tempu, time (p -ura)
la scala, ladder; stairs

Verbs

acchianari (nna), to climb; climb into (e.g., a car)
addrizzari (addrizzu), to straighten
amari, to love (*vuliri beni* is more common)
ammucciari (ammucciu), to hide
avvilinari (avvilenu) **or** abbilinari (abbilenu), to poison
cantari, to sing; crow
chianciri (chianciu) **or** cianciri, to cry, weep
è, he/she is
fa, he/she makes; he/she does
finiri (sc), to finish
guardari, to notice; to look out for; look at
lavari, to wash
misurari (misuru), to measure; gauge
(i)mpristari (mprestu), to loan, lend
passari, to pass (time, etc.); pass over to
purtari (portu), to carry
riciviri (ricivu), to receive
ripetiri (ripetu), to repeat
rimpruvirari (rimproviru), to scold
rispunniri (rispunnu), to reply, answer, respond
spanniri, to spill; leak
supirari (supiru), to surpass; exceed
teniri (tegnu) d'occhiu (a), to keep an eye (on)
travagghiari (travagghiu), to work
vinniri (vinnu), to sell
vulari (volu), to fly; disappear

Adjectives

beddu, beautiful, good-looking[†]
bonu, good
duci, sweet
debbuli, weak; feeble
forti, strong; heavy; intense; severe
ogni, each, every (precedes noun - invariable)
simplici, simple; common
stortu, twisted
veru, true

Nouns (cont.)

lu scurpiuni **or** lu scorpiuni, scorpion
lu sirpenti, serpent
la soru, sister (p soru)
lu studiu, study
lu suli, sun
lu travagghiu, work; job
la vasca, basin, tub
lu viddanu, peasant; for-hire farm laborer

Adverbs

non **or** nun **or** 'un **or** nn' (before a vowel), not[‡]
sempri, always
spissu, often

Conjunctions

e, and

* The term *donna* is, strictly speaking, a title of address of an upper class woman and is always used in conjunction with her first name, e.g., Donna Tresa. The corresponding male term is *don*, and it is used in conjunction with the first name of a man, e.g., Don Pippinu. The use of *donna* with the meaning of "woman" is an Italianism, but it can be used alone to mean "lady".
† *Bellu/bella/belli* are also found for "handsome, beautiful". However, these forms are more impersonal and don't convey the same warmth of feeling as *beddu/bedda/beddi*.
‡ All forms are found. However, you are advised to use either *non* **or** *nun*.
** Also an old standard of length equal to about 25.7 cm (10.1 in.).

Exercises

Exercise #1: Translate these proverbs into English and discuss what they mean. Note that in some cases the use of the definite article is dispensed with although if you were writing Sicilian, it should be used. As pointed out above, proverbs sometimes display certain features that should not be followed, such as using a singular verb for compound subjects and dispensing with the definite article.

(1) Amuri ammuccia ogni difettu. (2) Lu tempu è dinaru. (3) Passanu li anni e volanu li iorna. (4) La gilusia è camula di l'amuri. (5) L'omu nun si misura* a parmu. (6) La gilusia avvilena lu cori, spanni lu feli ntra lu duci amuri. (7) Cu gaddu o senza gaddu, Diu fa iornu. (8) La casa non s'acchiana* senza scala. (9) Tinemu d'occhiu û scurpiuni e û sirpenti, ma nun nni[†] guardamu dû millipedi. (10) Lu lignu stortu s'addrizza* a lu focu.

* Translate as a passive, that is, (5) "is measured", (8) "is climbed", (10) "is straightened". Of course, the *non* before the word creates a negative sentence, that is, "is not measured", etc.
† *nni* = don't try to translate this word.

Exercise #2: Translate these sentences into English. Some of these sentences employ the long forms of the definite article, *lu/la/li*, and some the short forms, *u/a/i*.

(1) L'omu porta li libbra nta lu studiu. (2) Lu picciriddu ripeti li paroli di so [his] mamma. (3) U viddanu vinni l'ova nnâ chiazza. (4) L'amuri veru è nu donu di Diu. (5) A fimmina lava a biancaria nnâ vasca. (6) Li picciriddi finiscinu (**or** finisciunu) lu travagghiu. (7) A mamma rimprovira a* so figghiu e u picciriddu chianci. (8) Lu suli è nta lu celu. (9) La luna è bedda; amu la luna. (10) A matina u gaddu canta sempri.

* Example of *personal a*. Do not translate. See **Personal a** in Chapter 6.

49

Exercise #3: Translate these Sentences into Sicilian. Use the long forms of the definite article, *lu/la/li*, or the short forms, *u/a/l*, or try writing each sentence using both.

(1) The son loves his (use *a so*) mother. (2) The peasant carries a rooster. (3) In the middle of the piazza the woman cries (weeps). (4) The men measure the pieces of wood. (5) The gift of the man is beautiful. (6) The son of the man climbs* the ladder. (7) The scorpion poisons the rooster. (8) The little boys don't keep an eye out for serpents. (9) The man always hides the eggs with a[†] defect. (10) The lady of the house notices the books in the study.

* Use *si* before the correct form of the verb.
† Translate as "the".

Exercise #4: Say these sentences aloud. Don't worry about translating them at this point.

(1) Sugnu ccà. (2) Accussì si fa. (3) Aiu na soru. (4) Chista è la casa di Vanni. (5) È pisanti comu lu chiummu. (6) Non cadiri! (7) U latti ccà è pû gattu. (8) Ascuta! Tuppulianu â porta. (9) Dunami na guccia d'acqua. Moru di siti. (10) Bonu! Bedda matri!

6   Common Verbs

Purpose of the Chapter

The chief purpose of this chapter is to set forth the most common verbs of the Sicilian language. Like almost all other languages, Sicilian has a number of verbs that are very commonly used, and many of these verbs have irregular present tenses. The verbs will be listed in their infinitive form, then the present tense of each verb will be given following the scheme set forth in the last chapter. Ways of forming the future are also given, and numerous expressions of several of the common verbs are listed with examples. The *personal a* is also taken up in this chapter.

Common Verbs

Probably the most important and frequently used verbs of the Sicilian language are these.

(1) essiri **or** siri, to be
(2) aviri, to have
(3) dari, to give
(4) stari, to stay, dwell, be
(5) fari, to make, do
(6) diri, to say, tell
(7) putiri, to be able
(8) iri, to go

(9) vuliri, to wish, want
(10) sapiri, to know (a fact); know how
(11) veniri, to come
(12) teniri, to hold, keep
(13) poniri, to place, set*
(14) vidiri, to see
(15) duviri, to owe, to ought to

* Its use is confined more frequently to compounds. **Examples:** pruponiri, to propose; supponiri, to suppose.

Present Indicative of the Common Verbs

You'll note that some of these verbs belong to Conjugation 1 and some of them to Conjugation 2. Regardless of which conjugation they belong to, they all have irregular features in the present tense. It's especially important to know these verbs thoroughly since they occur with great frequency in Sicilian. Almost all of these verbs have highly irregular forms in the 1st person singular. Note that the 3rd person singular is often regular, and the 1st person and 2nd person plurals are always regular (except for *essiri, diri,* and *fari*). Since you know the pattern by now, only the English meanings of the infinitives will be given, and the endings will no longer be italicized since you should be able to recognize them. **Note:** The forms of the verb *aviri* are sometimes written as: haiu, hai, havi, avemu, aviti, hannu.

(1) **essiri**, to be	(2) aviri, to have	(3) dari, to give	(4) stari, to stay
iu sugnu	iu aiu	iu dugnu	iu staiu
tu sì+	tu ai **or** a'	tu duni **or** dai	tu stai **or** sta'
vossìa è+	vossìa avi	vossìa duna **or** da	vossìa sta
iddu è+	iddu avi	iddu duna **or** da	iddu sta
nuiatri semu	nuiatri avemu	nuiatri damu	nuiatri stamu
vuiatri siti	vuiatri aviti	vuiatri dati	vuiatri stati
iddi sunnu	iddi annu	iddi **dunanu or** dannu	iddi stannu

51

(5) fari, to make*
  iu fazzu
  tu fai **or** fa'
  vossìa fa⁺ **or** faci
  iddu fa⁺ **or** faci
  nuiatri facemu
  vuiatri faciti
  iddi fannu

(6) diri, to say[†]
  iu dicu
  tu dici
  vossìa dici
  iddu dici
  nuiatri dicemu
  vuiatri diciti
  iddi dicinu
  or iddi dicunu

(7) putiri, to be able
  iu pozzu
  tu poi **or** po'
  vossìa pò
  iddu pò
  nuiatri putemu
  vuiatri putiti
  iddi ponnu

(8) iri, to go
  iu vaiu
  tu vai **or** va'
  vossìa va
  iddu va
  nuiatri emu **or** iemu
  vuiatri iti
  iddi vannu

(9) vuliri, to wish
  iu vogghiu
  tu voi **or** vo'
  vossìa voli
  iddu fa voli
  nuiatri vulemu
  vuiatri vuliti
  iddi vonnu

(10) sapiri, to know
  iu sacciu
  tu sai **or** sa'
  vossìa sapi **or** sa
  iddu sapi **or** sa
  nuiatri sapemu
  vuiatri sapiti
  iddi sannu

(11) veniri, to come
  iu vegnu
  tu veni
  vossìa veni
  iddu veni
  nuiatri vinemu
  vuiatri viniti
  iddi veninu
  or iddi venunu
  or iddi vennu

(12) teniri, to hold
  iu tegnu
  tu teni
  vossìa teni
  iddu teni
  nuiatri tinemu
  vuiatri tiniti
  iddi teninu
  or iddi tenunu
  or iddi tennu

(13) poniri, to place
  iu pognu
  tu poni
  vossìa poni
  iddu poni
  nuiatri punemu
  vuiatri puniti
  iddi poninu
  or iddi ponunu
  or iddi ponnu

(14) vidiri, to see
  iu viu **or** vidu
  tu vidi
  vossìa vidi
  iddu vidi
  nuiatri videmu
  vuiatri viditi
  iddi vidinu
  or iddi vidunu

(15) duviri, to owe, ought to[‡]
  iu devu **or** divu
  tu devi **or** divi
  vossìa devi **or** divi
  iddu devi **or** divi
  nuiatri duvemu
  vuiatri duviti
  iddi devinu **or** divinu
  or iddi devunu **or** divunu

* The infinitive used to be *faciri*. The 1st person and 2nd person plurals are regular for this form. As will be revealed later, the imperfect, imperfect subjunctive, and the two regular forms of the preterite (2nd person singular and 2nd person plural) are formed from *faciri*.

† The infinitive used to be *diciri*. All of the forms of the present tense are regular for this form. As will be revealed later, the imperfect, imperfect subjunctive, and the two regular forms of the preterite (2nd person singular and 2nd person plural) are formed from *diciri*.

‡ This is not the common way to express obligation in Sicilian. However, the use of *duviri* has increased, probably due to the influence of Italian.

Imperative of the Common Verbs

Almost all the commonly occuring verbs have regular imperative forms. The forms of *essiri*, *aviri*, *stari* and *iri* can be either regular or irregular. The irregular forms are related to the present subjunctive forms, but the regular forms are more common. In colloquial Sicilian, the corresponding indicative forms are generally used for the imperatives, except for *iamu*–let us go).

(1) **e**ssiri, to be
(tu) sia
(vossìa) fussi
(iddu) fussi
(nuiatri) semu
(vuiatri) siti **or** s**i**ati
(iddi) f**u**ssiru

(2) aviri, to have
(tu) ai, a', **or** aia
(vossìa) avissi
(iddu) avissi
(nuiatri) avemu
(vuiatri) aviti
(iddi) av**i**ssiru

(3) dari, to give
(tu) duna **or** dugna
(vossìa) dassi
(iddu) dassi
(nuiatri) damu
(vuiatri) dati
(iddi) d**a**ssiru

(4) stari, to stay
(tu) sta' **or** staia
(vossìa) stassi
(iddu) stassi
(nuiatri) stamu
(vuiatri) stati
(iddi) stassiru

(5) fari, to make
(tu) fa' **or** fazza
(vossìa) facissi
(iddu) facissi
(nuiatri) facemu
(vuiatri) faciti
(iddi) facissiru

(6) diri, to say
(tu) dici **or** dica
(vossìa) dicissi
(iddu) dicissi
(nuiatri) dicemu
(vuiatri) diciti
(iddi) dicissiru

(7) putiri, to be able
(tu) po' **or** pozza
(vossìa) putissi
(iddu) putissi
(nuiatri) putemu
(vuiatri) pututi
(iddi) putissiru

(8) iri, to go
(tu) va' **or** vaia
(vossìa) issi
(iddu) issi
(nuiatri) iamu **or** emu
(vuiatri) iti
(iddi) **i**ssiru

(9) vuliri, to wish
(tu) voi **or** vo' **or** vogghia
(vossìa) vulissi
(iddu) vulissi
(nuiatri) vulemu
(vuiatri) vuliti
(iddi) vulissiru

(10) sapiri, to know
(tu) sa' **or** saccia
(vossìa) sapissi
(iddu) sapissi
(nuiatri) sapemu
(vuiatri) sapiti
(iddi) sap**i**ssiru

(11) v**e**niri, to come
(tu) veni **or** vegna
(vossìa) vinissi
(iddu) vinissi
(nuiatri) vinemu
(vuiatri) viniti
(iddi) vinissiru

(12) t**e**niri, to hold
(tu) teni **or** tegna
(vossìa) tinissi
(iddu) tinissi
(nuiatri) tinemu
(vuiatri) tiniti
(iddi) tinissiru

(13) p**o**niri, to place
(tu) poni **or** pogna
(vossìa) punissi
(iddu) punissi
(nuiatri) punemu
(vuiatri) puniti
(iddi) pun**i**ssiru

(14) vidiri, to see
(tu) vidi
(vossìa) vidissi
(iddu) vidissi
(nuiatri) videmu
(vuiatri) viditi
(iddi) vidissiru

(15) duviri, to owe, ought to
(tu) devi **or** divi
(vossìa) duvissi
(iddu) duvissi
(nuiatri) duvemu
(vuiatri) duviti
(iddi) duvissiru

Common Verbs Governing the Infinitive

These verbs directly govern infinitives or govern infinitives with an intervening preposition.

Examples

essiri: Nun è facili mparari lu sicilianu. It's not easy to learn Sicilian.

aviri a: Aiu a purtari (**or** ê purtari) li libbra. I've got to carry the books.

stari: L'ariupranu sta pi partiri pi Roma. The airplane's ready to depart for Rome.

fari: La matri cci fa purtari li libbra a so figghiu. The mother makes her son carry the books.

putiri: Pozzu teniri d'occhiu a lu picciriddu. I can keep an eye out for the boy.

iri: La fimmina va a mparari lu sicilianu. The woman's going to learn Sicilian.

vuliri: Vogghiu vinniri la casa a li me amici. I want to sell the case to my friends.

sapiri: Sacciu maniari bonu la machina. I know how to drive a car well.

veniri: Veninu a vidiri a so matri. They come to see their mother.

vidiri: Viu a la matri rimpruvirari a so figghiu. I see the mother scolding her son.

duviri: Cci devu dari li libbra a Maria. I ought to give the books to Mary.

Future Time

Sicilian very frequently expresses future time using the present indicative. Actually, there are four very common ways in the spoken language to express futurity in Sicilian, all of which possess different shades of meaning, and none of which involves the simple future grammatical forms. You should thoroughly understand and master these uses.

> **Use #1: Present indicative:** Vinnu la casa. This can mean either "I sell the house" or also "I'll sell the house". Intent directed towards the future.
>
> **Use #2: Use with *vuliri + infinitive*:** Vogghiu vinniri la casa. "I want to sell the house." Strong intent directed towards the future.
>
> **Use #3: Use with *iri a + verb*:** Vaiu a vinniri (**or** vaiu a vinnu) la casa. "I'm going to sell the house." The act, in this case "selling the house" will soon take place.
>
> **Use #4: Use with *aviri a + infinitive*:** Aiu a vinniri (**or** ê vinniri) la casa. "I've got to sell the house." **or** "I should sell the house." **or** "I will sell the house." Obligation to accomplish the act in question – it is directed towards a future activity. This method of expressing the future is very characteristic of Sicilian, and it is very common.

Abbreviated Forms of iri a + verb

The use of *iri a* followed by a verb form is common in Sicilian. In Literary Sicilian, the verb form is the infinitive as indicated in Use #3 above, but the colloquial forms (abbreviated forms) are simply the verb forms corresponding to the form of *iri* (same person and number). Although colloquial, these forms are also found in the literature. They are a unique Sicilian construction. In rapid colloquial speech, these forms are contracted even further. **Note:** Remember that the circumflex accent is not a stress accent.

Present indicative of iri a + verb

iri a accattari, to go to buy

Literary	Literary and spoken	Spoken
iu vaiu a accattari	vaiu a accattu **or** vaiu e accattu	vâ 'ccattu
tu vai a accattari	vai a accatti **or** vai e accatti	vâ 'ccatti
vossìa va a accattari	va a accatta **or** va e accatta	vâ 'ccatta
iddu va a accattari	va a accatta **or** va e accatta	vâ 'ccatta

Similar constructions can be found with other verbs of motion, especially *veniri*. The abbreviated forms are not just limited to the present; they can be used with other tenses as well. In particular, see Leone (1995), especially pp. 44-45. **Note:** The plural forms are theoretically possible, but are *de facto* never used. The abbreviated forms are restricted to the 1st, 2nd, and 3rd person singular. In the plural the infinitive is used.

Examples
(1) Û vegnu a pigghiu. I'll come to pick him up.
(2) Û vinemu a pigghiari. We'll come to pick him up.
(3) Iddu ti veni a vidi. He'll come to see you.
(4) Torni a cerchi a to scarpa pirduta. You're looking for your missing shoe again.
(5) Emu a acchianari e taliamu a città di ccassusu. We're going to climb up, and we'll look at the city from up here.

(6) Ti vegnu a trovu. I'll come to get (find) you.
(7) Iddu va a gghioca ê carti. **or** Iddu vâ gghioca ê carti. He's going to play cards. **Note:** Recall that when an *i* follows a gemination-causing word, the *i* ofter changes to *gghi*.
(8) Mi vaiu a curcu. **or** Mi vâ curcu. I'm going to bed. **Literal meaning:** I'm going to lie down.
(9) Iddu va a vidi a so matri. He's going to see his mother.
(10) Iddi vannu a vidiri a so matri. They're going to see their mother.

Simple Future

The simple future was at one time rare in spoken Sicilian, its use being restricted chiefly to literature. This has changed somewhat, again probably due to the influence of Italian. So you should at least familiarize yourself with these forms because you will encounter them. The endings are very regular for the two conjugations. Several verbs show irregular futures.

Conjugation 1	**Conjugation 2**
parrari, to speak	rispunniri, to reply
iu parr*irò*, I will speak	iu rispunn*irò*, I will reply
tu parr*irai*, you (fam.) will speak	tu rispunn*irai*, you (fam.) will reply
vossìa parr*irà*, you (pol.) will speak	vossìa rispunn*irà*, you (pol.) will reply
iddu parr*irà*, he will speak	iddu rispunn*irà*, he will reply
nuiatri parr*iremu*, we will speak	nuiatri rispunn*iremu*, we will reply
vuiatri parr*iriti*, you will speak	vuiatri rispunn*iriti*, you will reply
iddi parr*irannu*, they will speak	iddi rispunn*irannu*, they will reply

The following verbs have an irregular future.

Verbs Having an Irregular Future	**Future Forms**
essiri, to be	**Singular forms:** iu sarò, tu sar**ai**, vossìa sarà, iddu sarà
	Plural forms: nuiatri saremu, vuiatri sariti, iddi sarannu
fari, to do, make*	**Singular forms:** iu farò, tu farai, vossìa farà, iddu farà
	Plural forms: nuiatri faremu, vuiatri fariti, iddi farannu
vuliri, to want, wish	**Singular forms:** iu vurrò, tu vurr**ai**, vossìa vurrà, iddu vurrà
	Plural forms: nuiatri vurremu, vuiatri vurriti, iddi vurrannu

* The verbs *dari* and *stari* follow exactly the same pattern as *fari*.

Simple Future Used as a Dubitative

The simple future is sometimes employed to indicate a doubt whether something will occur in the future. In this use, it's often accompanied by the adverb *forsi*, "perhaps", or some other adverb having a similar force.

Examples

(1) Dumani forsi cantirò. Maybe I'll sing tomorrow (and then again, maybe I won't).
(2) Forsi nn'accattiremu dda machina nova. Maybe we'll buy that new car (and then again, maybe we won't).

(3) Pussibbilmenti lu farà iddu. Possibly he'll do it (and then again, possibly he won't).

Abbreviated Forms of aviri a + infinitive
This construction is often translated into English as "have got to (do something)" or "should (do something)". As in the case of *iri*, *aviri* also has more colloquial forms that are commonly found in the spoken language. These colloquial forms of *aviri a* are called its abbreviated forms.

Present of aviri a + infinitive

aviri a accattari, to have to buy (future, often with sense of obligation)

Literary	Literary and spoken	Spoken
iu aiu a accattari	ê accattari	ê 'ccattari
tu ai a accattari	â accattari	â 'ccattari
vossìa avi a accattari	â ccattari	â 'ccattari
iddu avi a accattari	â accattari	â 'ccattari
nuiatri avemu a accattari	amâ (amu a) accattari	amâ 'ccattari
vuiatri aviti a accattari	atâ (ati a) accattari	atâ 'ccattari
iddi annu a accattari	annâ (annu a) accattari	annâ 'ccattari

Note: All the abbreviated forms are gemination-causing words: ê⁺, â⁺, amâ⁺, atâ⁺, annâ⁺.

Examples
(1) Aiu a parrari cu me patri. **or** Ê parrari cu me patri. I've got to speak with my father.
(2) Comu aiu a fari? **or** Com' ê fari? What should I do? **or** How should I do it?
(3) Aiu a finiri a lizzioni. **or** Ê finiri a lizzioni. I've got to finish the lesson.
(4) Pi favuri, tu ai a accattari l'ova culurati. **or** Pi favuri, tu â accattari l'ova culurati. Please, you've got to buy the colored eggs.
(5) Dumani avemu a gghiri (a) Catania. **or** Dumani amâ gghiri (a) Catania. Tomorrow we've got to go to Catania. **or** Tomorrow we're going to Catania. **Note:** In formal literary style, the *gghi-* probably wouldn't be shown even though it would be spoken that way: Dumani avemu a iri (a) Catania. See **Written Language versus Spoken Language** in Chapter 2. Also, before the name of a geographical location, the preposition *a* often disappears after another preposition. **Examples:** (1) Me zia abbita vicinu Londra. My aunt lives near London. (2) Vai pagghiri Catania? Mû duni un passaggiu? Are you going in the direction of Catania? Can you give me a ride?

Personal a
Sicilian employs what is known as the *personal a*, like Spanish. This *a* is untranslatable; its function is to mark a human as a direct object in a sentence. It is obligatory before proper nouns, nouns modified by a possessive, and pronouns (disjunctive, indefinite, or interrogative) referring to one person or more than one. Its use is optional before a person noun preceded by a definite or indefinite article. It is not used after the verb *aviri*, to have. Its use can sometimes be extended to animate beings, for example, a dog or donkey, towards which a human feels affinity. **Caution:** One must be careful since the preposition *a* is also often used to indicate an indirect object. In most cases the context and the sense of the verb will distinguish the usage.

Examples of direct object
Viu a Giorgiu. I see George.
A matri vidi a so figghiu. The mother sees her son.
Rimproviru a iddu. I reproach him.

Examples of indirect object
Parru a Giorgiu. I speak to George.
A matri parra a so figghiu. The mother speaks to her son.
Fazzu na dimanna a iddu. I ask him a question.

Expressions with Common Verbs: esseri, aviri, dari, fari, stari
Probably the most common verbs in Sicilian, as in the other Romance languages, are:

- essiri **or** siri, to be
- aviri, to have
- dari, to give
- fari, to make; do
- stari, to stay; to dwell

These verbs are used in numerous common constructions. Some of the more frequent ones are given here, but the lists below are by no means exhaustive. In some of these constructions, a preposition is also required.

Expressions with essiri
The following are expressions using the verb *essiri*. All of the words used in conjunction with *essiri* which are adjectives behave like adjectives and agree with the subject in both gender and number, e.g., bonu (masculine singular), bona (feminine singular), boni (common plural), etc.

- essiri affittatu, to be rented
- essiri bonu, to be well (i.e., one's state of well being)
- essiri n casa, to be at home
- essiri capaci (di), to be able, have the capacity (to)
- essiri d'accordu (cu), to agree (with)
- essiri energicu, to be bouncy, have a lot of energy
- essiri garanti, to answer for
- essiri (i)ncazzatu (cu), to be angry (at)
- essiri n'erruri (di), to be in error (about), be wrong (see *aviri tortu* below)
- essiri (i)nfurmatu, to be informed, be in the know
- essiri (i)nnamuratu (di), to be in love (with)
- essiri (i)n ciuri **or** (i)n sciuri, to be in flower, be blossoming
- essiri patruni, to be master
- essiri prumossu, to be promoted, pass
- essiri raggiatu (cu) **or** arraggiatu (cu), to be angry (at), upset (at)
- essiri vivu, to be alive
- essiri vizziusu, to have vices **or** to be spoiled

<u>Examples</u>
(1) La bedda casuzza gianna è già affittata. The pretty little yellow house is already rented.
(2) Iu sugnu bonu, e lei? I'm well, and you?
(3) Lu studenti è prumossu. The student is promoted.
(4) Iddi non sunnu n casa a sta ura. They're not home at this time.
(5) Tutti li pedi di pumu sunnu n ciuri. All the apple trees are blossoming. **Note:** In Sicilian *lu pedi di* + name of a fruit signifies the tree of that fruit.
(6) Marta è nnamurata di lu figghiu di lu dutturi. Martha's in love with the doctor's son.
(7) Idda è ncazzata cu so mamma. She's angry at her mother.
(8) Iu sugnu studenti. I'm a student. **Note:** If the noun is not modified by an adjective, an indefinite article is not required.
(9) Iddu è un prufissuri univirsitariu. He's a university professor.
(10) Chi cc'è? What's the matter? Nun cc'è nenti. There's nothing the matter.
(11) Maria è energica assai e fa tanti cosi. Mary's very energetic and does a lot of things.
(12) Iddu è capaci d'imparari tanti cosi. He's capable of learning many things.
(13) I me ginituri non sunnu cchiù vivi. My parents are no longer living.

Expressions with aviri
The following are expressions using the verb *aviri*.

- aviri la trimulina, to shiver
- aviri di bisognu (di) **or** aviri bisognu (di), to need something
- aviri caudu, to be hot (refers to a person, not the weather)
- aviri chiffari, to be busy
- aviri chiffari (cu), to have business (with someone – can have a sexual connotation)
- aviri disidderiu (di), to have a desire (for), have an urge (to)
- aviri fami, to be hungry
- aviri fiducia (di), to trust (in)
- aviri fretta, to be in a hurry
- aviri friddu, to be cold (refers to a person, not the weather)
- aviri lu bon senzu, to have good sense
- aviri na bona mimoria, to have a good memory
- aviri n testa (di), to be thinking (about)
- aviri ntinzioni (di), to intend (to)
- aviri pacenza **or** pacenzia (cu), to have patience (with)
- aviri paura (di), to be afraid (of)
- aviri prescia, to be in a hurry
- aviri na raggia (cu) **or** n'arraggia (cu), to be angry (at)
- aviri raggiuni, to be right
- aviri rilazzioni sissuali (cu), to have sex (with)
- aviri siti, to be thirsty
- aviri spinnu (di), to have a desire (to), feel like (doing something)
- aviri sonnu, to be sleepy
- aviri successu, to be successful
- aviri tortu, to be wrong
- aviri vrigogna (di), to be ashamed (of)
- aviri vogghia (di), to have an urge (to), feel like (doing something)

- aviri X anni, to be X years old
- aviri, to have a particular physical characteristic

<u>Examples</u>
(1) Me matri avi na raggia cu mia. My mother's angry at me.
(2) Fa friddu e la picciridda avi la trimulina. It's cold, and the little girl's shivering.
(3) Vogghiu fari a me lizzioni e aiu bisognu di na pinna pi scriviri. I want to do the lesson, and I need a pen to write with.
(4) Ora li picciriddi annu sonnu. The children are sleepy now.
(5) L'omini travagghianu assai e ora annu siti. The men are working a lot, and now they're thirsty.
(6) Vossìa avi raggiuni. Non aiu nenti mmanu (**or** in manu). You're right. I don't have anything in my hand.
(7) La picciotta bedda avi l'occhi azzoli. The pretty girl has blue eyes.
(8) Li picciotti annu vogghia di iri a lu cinima. The boys feel like going to the movies.
(9) Francu avi ntinzioni di iri a la bibbliuteca stasira pi studiari. Frank intends to go to the library this evening to study.
(10) Giorgiu è vecchiu ma tuttavia avi na bona mimoria. George is old, but he still has a good memory.
(11) Giuvanni avi successu comu chimicu. John enjoys success as a chemist.
(12) La picciridda avi paura di lu so cani. The little girl's afraid of your dog.
(13) Lu dutturi avi a vidiri tanti pirsuni oggi e avi prescia. The doctor's got to see many people today, and he's in a hurry.
(14) Bisogna aviri pacenzia cu tutti e spicialmenti chî picciriddi. It's necessary to have patience with everybody and especially with children.
(15) Lei non avi vrigogna di zoccu fici? Aren't you ashamed of what you did?
(16) Chi ai? What's wrong with you? Nun aiu nenti. Nothing's wrong with me.
(17) Chi cci ai? What do you have (there)? Nun cci aiu nenti. I don't have anything (there).
(18) Aiu cinquanta anni. I'm fifty years old.

Expressions with dari
The following are expressions using the verb *dari*.

- dari a, to look out (on)
- dari accura (a), pay attention (to)
- dari a nenti, to come to nothing
- dari attinzioni **or** attenzioni (a), to pay attention (to)
- dari beni (a), to do good (to)
- dari carti, to deal cards
- dari cuntu (a), to pay attention (to); heed (someone **or** something); take notice (of)
- dari cuntu (di), to give an account (of)
- dari di pedi, to run away
- dari di tu, dari di vossìa, to use *tu* or *vossìa* with a person
- dari fini (a), to put an end (to)
- dari la risposta (a), to answer (to)
- dari lizzioni (a), to give instruction (to), instruct

- dari l'ura, to strike the hour; to tell time
- dari mali (a), to make a bad time (for)
- dari mmastu (a), to face (something or a group of people)
- dari na botta (a), to hit (someone)
- dari na manu (a), to give a hand (to)
- dari na taliata (a), to glance (at)
- dari nfluenza, to influence
- dari mpurtanza (a), to give importance (to); to think important
- dari la palora **or** la parola (a), to promise
- dari passi (a), to take steps (to)
- dari scannulu, to create a scene
- dari scantu (a), to scare (someone)

Examples
(1) Lu prufissuri duna a lizzioni a li studenti. The teacher instructs the students.
(2) La fimmina duna accura (**or** duna attinzioni) a so figghia. The woman pays attention to her daughter.
(3) Cercu di parrari sicilianu cu li me amici e iddi mi dunanu la risposta n nglisi. I try to speak Sicilian with my friends, and they answer me in English.
(4) Li miricani dû Norti dunanu picca mpurtanza ê genti di l'America dû Sud. North Americans give little importance to the peoples of South America.
(5) Duna mmastu iddu sulu a tutti. He alone faces everyone.
(6) Duna accura! Non ti bruciari. Be careful! Don't burn yourself.
(7) Vâ duna u culu! Go to hell!
(8) L'omu duna na taliata a la picciotta bedda. The man glances at the pretty girl.
(9) A mamma diventa raggiata cu so figghiu e cci duna na botta n testa. The mother becomes angry with her son and smacks him on the head.
(10) L'affari duna a nenti. The affair comes to nothing.
(11) Ni damu di tu. Let's use the *tu* form.
(12) Cci dugnu na manu a Petru. I give a hand to Peter.
(13) Turiddu cci duna carti a l'amici e iddi iocanu. Salvatore deals cards to his friends, and they play.
(14) Lu picciriddu cci duna la risposta giusta a la prufissurissa. The little boy gives the correct answer to the teacher.
(15) Cci dugnu la risposta chi merita a Carru. I'm answering Charles as he deserves.
(16) So figghia duna scannulu cu dda gonna accussì curta. His daughter's creating a scene with her short skirt.
(17) U patri cci duna a so palora a so figghiu ca cci va a accattari na bicicletta nova. The father promises his son that he's buy him a new bicycle.
(18) Luigi cci resta a dari cincumila liri. Louis owes him 5,000 lire.
(19) La statua non cci duna cuntu. The statue doesn't pay any attention to him.
(20) Li latri dunanu di pedi comu vidunu ô patruni dâ casa. The thieves scamper away when they see the owner of the house.
(21) A finestra dâ cammara duna ô mari. The window of the room looks out on the sea.

Expressions with fari

The following are expressions using the verb *fari*.

- fari attinzioni **or** attenzioni (a), to pay attention (to)
- fari la varva (a), to give a shave (to)
- farisi la varva, to shave oneself
- fari beddu tempu, to be good weather
- fari bruttu tempu **or** malu tempu, to be bad weather
- farisi canusciri (a), to make oneself known (to)
- farisi capiri, to make oneself understood
- fari caudu, to be hot (weather)
- fari cena, to have supper
- fari na chiacchiariata (cu), to chat (with)
- fari comu tutti li iorna, to go about business as usual
- fari culazzioni, to have breakfast
- fari di, to act as
- fari friddu, to be cold (weather)
- fari friscu, to be cool (weather)
- fari esercizii, to exercise (e.g., at a gym)
- fari l'esperienza, to experience
- fari li corna (a), to cuckold (someone)
- fari l'effettu (di), to give the impression (of)
- fari lizzioni (a), to lecture (to)
- fari mali (a), to hurt
- farisi mali, to hurt oneself
- fari na dumanna (a), to ask (someone) a question
- farisi un pinzeri, to imagine
- fari na passiata, to take a walk
- fari un pannemoniu **or** pandemoniu, to raise a ruckus
- fari na pinzata, have an idea
- fari prugressu, to make progress
- farisi riccu, to become rich
- fari la spisa **or** fari spisi, to go shopping
- fari tortu (a), to do harm (to)
- fari un piaciri (a), to do a favor (for)
- farisi nu vagnu, to take a bath
- fari nu viaggiu, to take a trip
- farisi + profession, to be training to be (that particular profession)
- fari lu + profession, to be (that particular profession)
- fari X anni, to be X years old on a particular day
- fari l'anni, to have a birthday
- fari a + infinitive, to make someone + verb; let someone + verb

Examples

(1) Oggi fa caudu e aiu siti. It's hot today and I'm thirsty.
(2) Chi fa lei? What do you do (as a profession)? Fazzu l'avvucatu. I'm a lawyer.
(3) Chi sta facennu ora? What are you doing now? See **Progressive Tenses** in Chapter 12.

(4) Chi si fa lei? What are you training to become? Mi fazzu lu chimicu. I'm studying to be a chemist.

(5) Ora fazzu iu di patruni e di cammareri. Now I'll act as owner and waiter.

(6) Cci fazzu un piaciri a Marcu. I'll do a favor for Mark.

(7) Li studenti cci fannu na dumanna â prufissurissa. The students ask the teacher a question.

(8) Facemu cena sempri prestu. We always eat supper early.

(9) La matina iddi fannu sempri na passiata nni lu parcu quannu fa beddu tempu. In the morning they always take a walk in the park when it's nice weather.

(10) Lu varveri cci fa la varva a l'avvucatu. The barber shaves the lawyer.

(11) Oggi fazzu trenta anni. I turn thirty today.

(12) Dumani Catarina fa l'anni. Tomorrow's Catherine's birthday.

(13) Tresa fa a stissa pinzata dû so nnamuratu. Teresa has the same idea as her boyfriend.

(14) La genti dû paisi fa comu tutti i iorna. The people of the town go about their usual business.

(15) Mi fa veniri lu lanzu. He makes me want to puke.

(16) Mi fa scantari. He scares me.

(17) Mi fa pena. I feel sorry for him.

(18) Nun fa nenti. Everything's OK **or** It doesn't matter.

(19) La nora fa sempri la spisa e so soggira s'arraggia cu idda. The daughter-in-law always goes shopping, and her mother-in-law becomes exasperated with her.

Expressions with stari

The following are expressions using the verb *stari*.

- stari a marteddu, to fulfill a difficult duty
- starisi bonu (cu), to get along well with (someone)
- stari friscu, to wait in vain
- stari n casa, to live at home
- stari n spiranza, to hope
- stari cu pinzeri, to worry
- stari zittu, to be silent, be quiet
- stari pi + infinitive, to be about to + verb
- stari, to live (in a particular place)

Examples

(1) La mamma sta cu pinzeri picchì lu picciriddu non rispunni a la so vuci. The mother's worried because the child doesn't respond to her voice.

(2) Dda picciotta sta ancora n casa cu li so ginituri. That girl still lives at home with her parents.

(3) Avi tri anni ca me zia sta nna dda casa. It's been three years that my aunt's been living in that house (and she's still living there).

(4) Stamu n spiranza ca veni dumani. We hope he'll come tomorrow.

(5) Mi staiu bonu cû me capu. I get along well with my boss.

(6) Iu staiu. I'm staying.

(7) Dda picciotta pò stari frisca si aspetta un maritu pirfettu. That girl'll wait in vain if she's waiting for the perfect husband.

(8) L'omini stannu n pedi e li fimmini sunnu assittati. The men are standing, and the women are sitting.

(9) I picciriddi stannu zitti. The children are silent.

(10) Zittiti! U diritturi sta pi parrari. Be quiet! The director's about to speak.

(11) U surdatu avi a stari a marteddu. The soldier must fulfill a difficult duty.

(12) L'ariupranu sta pi partiri pi li Stati Uniti. The airplane's about to depart for the United States.

Word Order with essiri and aviri

It was fairly common in Sicilian to place these two verbs at the end of a sentence, especially in short sentences. Probably because of the influence of Italian, this isn't done as much as formerly.

Examples

(1) Vossìa cuntenti è? **or** Vossìa è cuntenti? Are you happy?

(2) Veru è. **or** È veru. It's true.

(3) A suppa bona è. **or** A suppa è bona. The soup is good.

(4) A picciridda vattiata è? **or** A picciridda è vattiata? Is the child baptized?

(5) Raggiuni aiu. **or** Aiu raggiuni. I'm right.

(6) Fami avi. **or** Avi fami. He's hungry.

(7) Finiri aiu. **or** Aiu a finiri. I'll finish. **Note:** When forms of *aviri* follow the infinitive, the *a* is dropped. Also, this form has more of a true future meaning.

(8) Veniri aviti. **or** Aviti a veniri. You'll come. **or** You should come.

Vocabulary

Nouns

l'acqua, water; rain
l'ala, wing
l'amica, friend (p amichi)
l'amicu, friend (p amici)
la bistecca, beefsteak, meat
la carni, meat
la cena, supper, dinner, evening meal
la chesa **or** la chiesa **or** la cresia, church
lu citrolu, cucumber
lu ciumi **or** lu sciumi, river
lu ciuri **or** lu sciuri, flower
lu denti, tooth
lu discursu, discourse, talk
lu duluri, pain; sorrow; affliction
la duminica, Sunday
l'energia, energy
la famigghia, family
la fami, hunger
la finestra, window
lu iditu, finger (p -a)
la lingua, tongue; language
la luci, light (natural)
lu lumi, lamp; light (artificial)

Verbs

accuminzari (accumenzu) **or**
   (i)ncuminzari (ncumenzu) **or**
   accuminciari (accuminciu **or** accumenciu) **or**
   cuminciari (cuminciu **or** cumenciu), to begin
battiri, to beat, strike, hit
cunnuciri (cunnuciu), to conduct*
doliri **or** duliri (mi doli), to hurt (impersonal)
fumari (fumu), to smoke (e.g., a cigarette)
godiri **or** gudiri (godu), to enjoy
(i)mparari, to learn
macinari (macinu), to crush, grind
maniari (maniu), to handle (e.g., by hand);
   touch; manage; drive (e.g., a car)
moriri **or** muriri (moru), to die
offriri **or** uffriri (offru), to offer
sciarriarisi (mi sciarriu) (cu), to argue (with),
   fight (with)
stari pi, to be ready to + infinitive
vidiri **or** vidiri (viu **or** vidu), to see
vuliri beni, to love

Nouns (cont.)

la machina, machine; car
la manu, hand (p manu)
lu mazzu, bouquet; bunch (p -a)
l'impiegu (mpiegu), employment, employment
l'oduri **or** l'aduri, odor, smell (not pejorative)
l'ossu, bone (p -a)
la pagghia, straw
lu patri, father
la petra, stone
lu pumu, apple (p -a)
la rosa, rose
la sciarra **or** la scerra, quarrel, argument
la sicaretta, cigarette
la scola, school
la terra, earth, land

Conjunctions

ma, but

Adjectives

amaru, bitter
assenti, absent
grassu, fat
mortu, dead
russu, red; Russian
offertu **or** uffrutu, offered
prisenti, present
vecchiu, old
vivu, living, alive

Adverbs

aieri, yesterday
dumani, tomorrow
cchiù, more
menu, less
oi **or** oggi, today
poi, then, afterwards
unni, where

* cunnuciri (cunduciri) with the *nd* replaced by *nn*.

Exercises

Exercise #1: Translate these proverbs into English and discuss what they mean. Note that in some cases the use of the definite article is dispensed with although if you were writing Sicilian, it should be used.

(1) Vidi Palermu e godi, vidi Napoli e poi mori. (2) Acqua passata non macina cchiù. (3) L'amuri è comu lu citrolu, accumenza duci e poi finisci amaru. (4) La lingua batti unni lu denti doli. (5) Vuliri è putiri. (6) Donna senza amuri è rosa senza oduri. (7) U vivu assenti è comu u mortu. (8) Non si pò aviri la carni senza l'ossa. (9) A petra offerta di n'amicu è comu un pumu. (10) Sciarri nâ famigghia sunnu comu focu di pagghia.

Exercise #2: Translate these sentences into English. Some of these sentences employ the long forms of the definite article, *lu/la/li*, and some the short forms, *u/a/i*.

(1) L'amicu di l'omu voli vinniri a la so* machina. (2) U picciriddu sta pi gghiri a scola. (3) U vecchiu fuma sempri na sicaretta doppu a cena. (4) A duminica iemu a chesa. (5) Viu a n'omu grassu a la finestra. (6) Ê dari a me† matri un mazzu di beddi ciuri. (7) Dumani portu i libbra di Vanna â scola. (8) U suli duna l'energia e a luci â terra. (9) A matri voli beni ê so figghi. (10) Dina va a mparari (**or** vâ mpara) a maniari la machina.

* Translate *so* as "his".
† Translate *me* as "my".

64

Exercise #3: Translate these sentences into Sicilian. Use the long forms of the definite article, *lu/la/li*, or the short forms, *u/a/i*, or try writing each sentence using both.

(1) Today the son gives the red apples to his* mother. (2) Tomorrow I'm selling the car to the friend. (3) In the middle of the house the little boy begins to† cry (weep) for his* mother. (4) The woman beats the man and hurts him‡. (5) The smell of the flowers is good. (6) The little boy offers his* hand to the little girl. (7) The hand has five (cincu) fingers, and the two (dui) hands have ten (deci) fingers. (8) The windows of the house are large and old. (9) The little boy wants to know where his* mother is. (10) The old woman** crushes the tooth in a pestle (pistuni).

* Translate "his" as *so*.
† Translate "to" as *a*.
‡ Translate as *cci fa mali*.
** Don't translate "woman". Use the adjective as a noun.

Exercise #4. Say these sentences aloud. Don't worry about translating them at this point.

(1) Stamatina u vecchiu nesci dâ casa. (2) Na fimmina bedda nni fa na visita a simana chi trasi. (3) Nuiatri parramu accussì ma ddà parranu accuddì. (4) Mi vaiu a curcari. **or** Mi vaiu a curcu. **or** Mi vâ curcu. (5) U picciriddu granni è. (6) Raggiuni avi. (7) U cani arrusica l'ossu. (8) Pigghia tempu e campa. (Sicilian proverb) (9) — Sugnu raggiatu cu tia e ti dugnu un pugnu ntâ facci. — Petru dici a Carru. (10) Cchiù tardu chiancennu* Carru cci dici a so mamma. — Petru mi fici curriri sangu dû nasu.

* *chiancennu* = "crying". See Chapter 12, **Verbs: Nonfinite Forms**.

65

7   Pronouns

Purpose of the Chapter
The chief purpose of this chapter is to discuss the various kinds of pronouns in the Sicilian language. A pronoun is a word that takes the place of a noun or stands for a noun in a sentence. Sicilian, like all the other Romance languages, has several kinds of pronouns. In addition, with the introduction of pronouns, it's then possible to discuss reflexive verbs.

The types of pronouns are:

- Personal pronouns;
- Demonstrative pronouns;
- Possessive pronouns;
- Indefinite pronouns;
- Relative pronouns;
- Interrogative pronouns.

Personal Pronouns
In addition, the class of personal pronouns can be subdivided into several subclasses. These are:

- Disjunctive personal pronouns;
- Conjunctive personal pronouns;
- Reflexive pronouns.

Disjunctive Personal Pronouns
These pronouns are called "disjunctive" because they are "dis-joined" from the verb. They can be subject pronouns or objects of prepositions, and in some cases the same form functions as both. Some are singular only; some are plural only; some function as singular and plural.

Disjunctive Pronoun Table	1st Person	2nd Person (fam.)	2nd Person (pol.)	3rd Person
Singular; subject only	iu **or** io **or** eu, I	tu, you	vossìa **or** vussìa **or** lei, you[†]	iddu, he, it idda, she, it
Singular; object only	mia, me	tia, you	vossìa **or** vussìa **or** lei, you[†]	iddu, him, it idda, she, it
Plural; subject only	nuiatri **or** niatri **or** nuiautri **or** niautri **or** nui, we*	vuiatri **or** vuatri **or** vuiautri **or** vuautri, you[†]	vuiatri **or** vuatri **or** vuiautri **or** vuautri, you[†]	iddi, they
Plural; object only	nuiatri **or** niatri **or** nuiautri **or** niautri **or** nui, us*	vuiatri **or** vuatri **or** vuiautri **or** vuautri, you[†]	vuiatri **or** vuatri **or** vuiautri **or** vuautri, you[†]	iddi, them

* The form *nui* for "we" **or** "us" is sometimes used, but *nuiatri* **or** *niatri* is far more common.
† The pronoun *vui* is also used, but see the Note on the following page.

It is difficult to convey to someone in the contemporary U.S. the implications and subtleties inherent in the different words for "you" which exist in most of the other European languages. We use one simple word, "you", in all social situations from the most intimate family relations, the relations between two lovers, between friends, casual acquaintances, strangers, even enemies, and for one or more than one. Plural forms as "yous", "ya'll" and "yousins" can sometimes be found in local speech, but such forms are not condoned in Standard English. They are considered substandard, and as such frowned upon in all the better circles of society. In addition, the English familiar pronoun, "thou" (subject) and its other forms "thy" (possessive adjective), "thine" (possessive pronoun), and "thee" (object) disappeared in the eighteenth century (except for their continued use among several minority religious sects). Have you recently heard anyone express himself using English like this, "Hast thou spoken well of all thy brethren? Shame on thee if thou hast not." I thought not. Perhaps all of this betokens democracy triumphant, but it doesn't prepare us for understanding the subtle, but real, social distinctions conveyed by such words as *tu*, *vui*, *vossìa* and *vuiatri*.

Another problem is that the Sicilian pronouns have different usages in different parts of Sicily. However, we'll try to present a simplified usage pattern for the purposes of this book:

- *tu* – *Tu* is used among family and close friends and connotes intimacy. It takes the 2nd person singular form of the verb, e.g., tu parri.
- *vossìa* – *Vossìa* is used when addressing a person one doesn't know well or someone much older and connotes respect. It takes the 3rd person singular form of the verb, e.g., vossìa parra. Since *vossìa* takes the 3rd person singular form of the verb, its conjunctive pronouns (see below) are third person singular also.
- *lei* – *Lei* is now also used when addressing a person one doesn't know well, especially a contemporary of about the same age. Its usage is growing significantly, whereas the use of *vossìa* is now often restricted to addressing older people. *Lei* takes the 3rd person singular form of the verb, e.g., lei parra.
- *vuiatri* – *Vuiatri* (*vuatri* **or** *vuiautri* **or** *vuautri*) is the plural form of *tu*. It takes the 2nd person plural form of the verb, e.g., vuiatri parrati.
- *vui* – *Vui* is used among acquaintances of the same social level, strangers (sometimes contemptuously), used in addressing God and individual saints (using *tu* is an Italianism although it's now very common). Although *vui* is singular in meaning, it was originally a plural pronoun, so it takes the 2nd person plural form of the verb, e.g., vui parrati.

Note: The use of *vui* is tricky; it is best simply to avoid its use if possible and employ either *tu* (familiarity with person addressed) or *lei* or *vossìa* (respect for person addressed). With family and acquaintances, use *tu* (familiar *you* singular) if one person is being addressed. With strangers, casual acquaintances, colleagues you know on a formal basis, someone you don't know well, use *lei* or *vossìa*. To someone you wish to show respect, e.g., an older person, use *vossìa*. In the plural use *vuiatri* **or** *vuiautri*, which is the correct plural form of *tu*, *lei* and *vossìa*. However, note that the 2nd person plural form of the verb with a singular meaning often occurs in Sicilian. **Example:** Canusciti beni a cità? Sì, iu â canusciu beni. Do you know the city well? Yes, I know it well.

Note: *Vossìa* takes the 3rd person singular form of the verb because it is a contraction of *vostra signuria* **or** *vossignuria* **or** *vussignuria*, that is, "your lordship". It is directly akin to Spanish *usted* and Portuguese *você*. A very, very polite form of "you" is *vostra eccelenza* **or** *voscenza*, "your excellency". It was formerly used when addressing a member of the nobility or a high dignitary of the Roman Catholic Church. It too takes the 3rd person singular form of the verb. If you perchance ever encounter the Archbishop of Palermo, you would probably find *voscenza* useful. Otherwise, you probably wouldn't have any occasion to use it.

Sicilian doesn't normally require the use of the subject pronouns. A subject pronoun may be used under the following circumstances:

- To emphasize the subject or to clarify the subject;
- In compound sentences where the subject of the first sentence is different from the second;
- With verbs sharing the same form, e.g., tu rispunni **versus** iddu rispunni.

Examples
(1) Iu vogghiu offriri un pumu a vuiatri. I want to offer you an apple.
(2) Porta tu i libbra! **You** carry the books!
(3) Lei parra sicilianu cu n'accentu. You speak Sicilian with an accent.
(4) Idda canta e iddu sona u pianu. She sings, and he plays the piano.
(5) Iddu mi chiama. He calls me.
(6) Idda mi vidi. She sees me.
(7) Iddu accatta i libbra a nuiatri e idda duna i puma duci a vuiatri. He buys the books for **us**, and she gives the sweet apples to **you**.
(8) Vossìa sapi maniari a machina. You know how to drive the car.
(9) Lei avi na bona testa pi l'affari. You have a good head for business.

Personal a with Disjunctive Pronouns
Disjunctive pronouns can be used as direct or indirect objects. Again, like their usage as subject pronouns, they're often used for emphasis. The *personal a* is used with a direct object disjunctive pronoun if the disjunctive pronoun refers to a human being.

Examples
(1) Dumani viu a idda. Tomorrow I'll see **her**. (a = personal a)
(2) Lu picciriddu veni a mia. The child comes to **me**.
(3) La mamma va a rimpruvirari a tia. Mom is going to scold **you**. (a = personal a)

Conjunctive Personal Pronouns
These pronouns are called "conjunctive" because they are "con-joined" to the verb. They can function as direct object, indirect object, or reflexively. Unlike disjunctive pronouns, which always receive stress, the conjunctive pronouns never take stress. They are **never** used as either subject pronouns or as objects of a preposition. They generally precede the verb, but see **Spelling Rules – Conjunctive Pronouns Added to Verb Forms** below.

Conjunctive Pronoun Table	1st Person	2nd Person (fam.)	2nd Person (pol.)	3rd Person
Singular; direct object	mi, me	ti, you	lu (**or** û), you la (**or** â), you	lu (**or** û), him/it la (**or** â), her/it
Singular; indirect object	mi, to me, for me	ti, to you, for you	cci*, to you, for you	cci, to him/her/it, for him/her/it
Singular; reflexive	mi, myself	ti, yourself	si, yourself	si, himself/herself/itself
Plural; direct object	ni*, us	vi, you	vi, you	li (**or** î), them
Plural; indirect object	ni, to us, for us	vi, to you, for you	vi, to you, for you	cci, to them, for them
Plural; reflexive	ni, ourselves	vi, yourselves	vi, yourselves	si, themselves

* *nni* and *cci* are also used as adverbs of place; *nni* = of here, of there and *cci* = here, there. Note also that *nni* = of him/her/it/them. Spell *nni* with two *n*s when it is a conjunctive adverb. These particles occur often in Sicilian sentences.

Note: A translation "from" can at times be demanded for indirect objects. **Example:** Cci arrob-banu i sordi. They rob his money. **Literal translation:** From him they rob the money. Context determines the meaning of *cci* since it also means "from her", "from you", or "from them".

Note: The forms, *lu/la/li* are always found before vowels. Their own vowel, that is, the *u, a,* or *i* elides (disappears). **Example:** l'ammazzu, I'll kill him. If the short form of the pronoun is used, the initial vowel of the verb disappears. An apostrophe is used to mark the disappearance of the vowel. **Example:** Û 'mmazzu, I'll kill him.

Note: Rather than use the rather clumsy designations of indirect object conjunctive pronoun and direct object conjunctive pronoun, we'll simply call them indirect conjunctive pronoun and direct conjunctive pronoun. If the context is clear that we're talking about conjunctive pronouns, we'll simply call them indirect pronoun and direct pronoun.

Position of the Conjunctive Pronouns with Verbs
The conjunctive pronouns generally precede the verb. If both a direct pronoun and an indirect pronoun are used, the indirect precedes the direct pronoun. A reflexive pronoun comes before both an indirect and a direct pronoun. The mnemonic RID (reflexive, indirect, direct) is useful in remembering the order of pronouns. They also generally precede the verb with verbs governing infinitives, e.g., vuliri, putiri, etc. Numerous examples are given below. In the case of the infinitive, imperative forms, and the gerund, they are directly attached at the end of the verb form. See **Spelling Rules – Conjunctive Pronouns Added to Verb Forms** below.

Conjunctive Pronoun Contractions

When two conjunctive pronouns occur together, they often form contractions if the short forms of the pronoun are used, that is, if the forms *û*, *â*, and *î* are used. If *lu*, *la*, and *li* are used, the contractions don't take place. **Note:** To preserve simplicity, in the examples below *cci* will be translated as "to/for him." Bear in mind that it may also mean "to/for her", "to/for you", "to/for them". Again, the context determines the meaning. All 3rd person singular verbs unaccompanied by a personal pronoun will also be translated as "he". They may also mean "she", "you", or "it".

mi lu	ni lu
or mû	**or** nû
mi la	ni la
or mâ	**or** nâ
mi li	ni li
or mî	**or** nî
ti lu	vi lu
or tû	**or** vû
ti la	vi la
or tâ	**or** vâ
ti li	vi li
or tî	**or** vî
cci lu	si lu
or cciû	**or** sû
cci la	si la
or cciâ	**or** sâ
cci li	si li
or ccî	**or** sî

Examples

(1) Cci dugnu un pumu. I give him an apple.
(2) Cciû dugnu. **or** Cciô dugnu. I give it (e.g., an apple) to him.
(3) Iddu mi vidi nnâ chiazza. He sees me in the piazza.
(4) L'omu ti offri la rosa. The man offers the rose to you.
(5) L'omu ti l'offri. The man offers it (e.g., the rose) to you.
(6) L'omini ni dunanu i rosi. The men give the roses to us.
(7) L'omini nî dunanu. The men give them (e.g., the roses) to us.
(8) A fimmina vecchia â lava. The old woman washes it (e.g., the laundry).
(9) A fimmina vecchia cciâ lava. The old woman washes it (e.g., the laundry) for him.
(10) Mi lavu. I wash myself.
(11) Mi lavu i manu. I wash my hands.
(12) Mî lavu. **or** Mi li lavu. I wash them (e.g., my shirts).
(13) Mi nni lavu na pocu. I wash some of them.
(14) Aiutami! Mi arrobbanu i sordi. Help me! They're robbing my money.
(15) Pippinu ti duna un ciuri beddu. Joe gives you a pretty flower.
(16) Ti pozzu vidiri ddà. I can see you over there.
(17) Ti vogghiu dari un bon libbru a leggiri. I want to give you a good book to read.

(18) Portali. Carry them!

(19) Pigghiatillu! Take it!

(20) Oggi û vogghiu vidiri. **or** Oggi vogghiu vidillu. **or** Oggi vogghiu vidirlu. I want to see him today.

(21) Va a scanciallu â banca. **or** Va a scanciarlu â banca. Go to cash it at the bank.

(22) Dumani î vaiu a vidiri (**or** î vâ viu). I'm going to see them tomorrow.

(23) Dunamilli! Give them to me.

(24) Li purtamu n casa. **or** Î purtamu n casa. We'll take them home. **or** Let's take them home.

Conjunctive Pronouns Added to Verb Forms – Spelling Rules

Rules must be given for the cases where conjunctive pronouns are attached directly to the end of various verb forms. These verb forms are the imperative, the infinitive, and the gerund. The case where conjunctive pronouns are attached to gerunds will be discussed in Chapter 12, but the same rules are followed that are set forth here. If both an indirect conjunctive pronoun and a direct pronoun are added to one of these verb forms, the indirect pronoun always precedes the direct pronoun form. If the pronoun begins with a single consonant, double the consonant of the pronoun if the verb form is monosyllabic. These are illustrated in the examples below. To simplify the presentation, only the masculine translation of pronouns will be given.

The situation involving *lu/la/li* can be stated this way:

- If *lu/la/li* is added directly to an imperative (or gerund), don't double the *l*.
- (1) If *lu/la/li* is added to an infinitive after dropping the final *i* of the infinitive, the *l* is doubled if the *r* of the infinitive disappears by assimilation. (2) If the *r* doesn't disappear, the *l* is not doubled. (3) Also *lu/la/li* can be added directly to the infinitive. Some *parrati* do it following (1), some (2), and some (3). See the examples below.
- If *lu/la/li* is added after an indirect pronoun attached to a verb form, double the *l*.

If *ni* is attached to one of these forms, double the *n* unless *ni* + *nni*. **Example:** Iamuninni.

Examples using the familiar form of the imperative
- ripetilu, repeat it
- ripeticcillu, repeat it to (**or** for) him
- mustrala, show it
- mustraccilla, show it to him
- portali, carry them
- portaccilli, carry them for him
- dunamillu, give it to me
- dimmi, tell me
- scancialu, cash it
- vaittinni **or** vattinni, go! get out of here!

Examples using plural forms of the imperative
- ripititilu, repeat it
- ripititimillu, repeat it to me
- mustratila, show it
- mustraticcilla, show it to him

- purtatili, carry them
- purtatinnilli, carry them for us
- daticcilli, give them to him
- dicitimi, tell me
- dicitimillu, tell it to me
- scanciatilu, cash it
- scanciatimillu, cash it for me
- iamuninni, let's go

Examples using the infinitive
- ripitirlu **or** ripitillu **or** ripitirilu, to repeat it
- ripitirimillu, to repeat it to me
- mustrarlu **or** mustrallu **or** mustrarilu, to show it
- mustrariccilla, to show it to him
- purtarli **or** purtalli **or** purtarili, to carry them
- purtarinnilli, to carry them for us
- liggirli **or** liggilli **or** liggirili, to read them
- daricci, to give to him
- dariccillu, to give it to him
- dirla **or** dilla **or** dirila, to say it
- irisinni, to go away, to leave

Repetition of Conjunctive Pronouns with Noun Objects

In Sicilian, it is common practice to place a direct pronoun before the verb corresponding to a noun or noun phrase especially if the noun/noun phrase proceeds the verb. This is sometimes done if the if the noun/noun phrase follows the verb. This is illustrated in Examples 1, 3, and 5 below. The regular order of these sentences is shown in Examples 2, 4, and 6. It is common practice to place an indirect pronoun before the verb corresponding to a noun or noun phrase if the noun/noun phrase either precedes or follows the verb. This is illustrated in Examples 7-9 below.

Examples
(1) A la me zita la viu nna la chiazza cu nautru omu. I see my fiancée in the town square with another man. (**Literal translation:** My fiancée her I see in the town square with another man.) **Remember:** *Personal a* before nouns modified by a possessive adjective, but the corresponding conjunctive pronoun does not take the *personal a*.
(2) Viu a la me zita nna la chiazza cu nautru omu. I see my fiancée in the town square with another man.
(3) A me frati û taliu chi è assittatu nnâ seggia. I'm looking at my brother sitting in the chair. (**Literal translation:** My brother him I look at who is seated in the chair.)
(4) Taliu a me frati chi è assittatu nnâ seggia. I'm looking at my brother sitting in the chair.
(5) U me libbru di francisi û taliu chi è supra a tavula. I'm looking at my French book lying on the table.
(6) Taliu u me libbru di francisi chi è supra a tavula. I'm looking at my French book lying on the table.

(7) Un iornu l'omu cci dici a so mugghieri ca la (**or** cci) voli beni assai. One day the man says to his wife that he loves her a lot. (**Literal translation:** One day the man to her says to his wife that he loves her a lot.)

(8) Ê me amici nun cci dicu minzogni. I don't tell my friends lies. (**Literal translation:** To my friends to them I don't tell lies.)

(9) Cci arrobbanu la vurza a la signura. **or** A la signura cci arrobbanu la vurza. They rob the lady's purse. (**Literal translation:** From her they rob the purse from the lady.)

(10) Mi lavu i manu. I wash my hands **or** I'll wash my hands. (**Literal translation:** For me I wash my hands.)

(11) La criata mi pulizzia la cammara. The maid's cleaning my bedroom **or** The maid'll clean my bedroom. (**Literal translation:** For me the maid cleans my bedroom.)

Disjunctive Pronouns Used for Contrast

Disjunctive pronouns may be used for contrast or for emphasis. The examples give a conjunctive pronoun use followed in the next sentence by disjunctive pronoun use. Sometimes both a conjunctive and a disjunctive pronoun are used in the same sentence. See Examples 6-8 below.

Examples

(1) Iu vi vogghiu offriri un pumu. I want to offer you (plural) an apple.

(2) Iu vogghiu offriri un pumu a vuiatri, non a iddi. I want to offer you (plural) an apple, not to them.

(3) U picciriddu mi vidi. The little boy sees me.

(4) U picciriddu vidi a mia, non a tia. The little boy sees me, not you.

(5) Iddu accatta i libbra a nuiatri e non a vuiatri. He buys the books for us, not for you. **Note:** The *a* in this sentence indicates an indirect object.

(6) Brasi mi canusci a mia. Brasi knows me.

(7) M'importa a mia. It's important to me.

(8) La bilici cci la dugnu iu a iddu di manu mmanu (**or** in manu). I give the suitcase to him from my hand into his.

Impersonal Construction with Conjunctive Pronouns

There are a fair number of verbs utilizing an impersonal construction employing either the 3rd person singular or the 3rd person plural with one of the appropriate indirect object conjunctive pronouns (mi, ti, cci, nni, vi). This form of construction is common in Sicilian. If a noun is used, it must be preceded by *a*. Some verbs taking this construction are:

- piaciri, to be pleasing to, to like
- dispiaciri, to be sorry
- pariri, to seem to
- rincrisciri, to regret
- mancari, to lack, not to have
- manciari, to itch
- bisugnari, to need

Examples in Sentences
(1) Chi ti pari? What do you think? Ti piaci lu libbru? **or** Lu libbru tû piaci? Do you like the book?
(2) Duminica a mia e a me famigghia ni piaci passiari nnô parcu. On Sundays my family and I like to take a stroll in the park.
(3) Â fimmina cci piaciunu libbra boni. The woman likes good books.
(4) Ô vecchiu non cci piacinu i custumi di ssa genti. The old man dislikes the habits of that people.
(5) Mi dispiaci. Nun lu sacciu. I'm sorry. I don't know.
(6) Mi pari ca cc'è troppa genti ccà. I think there are too many people here.
(7) Cci parinu ca sunnu quatri brutti. He thinks they're bad pictures.
(8) Mi mancanu i sordi p'accattari dda bedda machina russa. I don't have the money to buy that beautiful red car.
(9) Mi mancianu li iammi. My legs itch.
(10) Mi bisognanu sti cosi pi scriviri a carta. I need these things to write the letter.
(11) Mi rincrisci ca non pozzu veniri. I regret that I can't come.

Partitive Construction
The partitive construction is sometimes difficult for an English speaker to grasp because it seems superfluous to us. In Sicilian, however, it is often necessary to use the pronoun *nni* (of it, of them) to complete the meaning of the sentence, which is generally left understood in English. **Caution:** Of course *nni* also means "us, to us".

Examples
(1) Aiu un pumu. I have an apple. Nni aiu unu. **or** Nn'aiu unu. I have one (of them).
(2) Ti dugnu na vistina. I'll give you a dress. Ti nni dugnu una. I'll give you one (of them).
(3) Pigghia n'aranciu. Take an orange. Mi nni pigghiu unu. I'll take one. Mi nni pigghiu quattru. I'll take four. **or** I'll take several. Pigghianni na pocu (**or** un pocu). Take some.
(4) Cci nni parru. I'll speak to him about it.
(5) Cci parru di so patri. I'll speak to him about his father. Cci nni parru. I'll speak to him about him (i.e., his father).
(6) Si cci nni parra. One speaks to him about it. **Note:** Notice the order of the pronouns.

Reflexive Verbs
Reflexive conjunctive pronouns have a reflexive meaning, that is, the action of the subject is reflected back on the subject. **Example:** Mi lavu. I wash myself. You'll note that a reflexive verb in Sicilian doesn't necessarily have a reflexive meaning in English. Several examples of reflexive verbs in the present tense are given. These are: lavarisi, to wash; scurdarisi, to forget; vistirisi, to dress (oneself); scantarisi, to be frightened. Again, exactly the same scheme is followed as in Chapter 5. Two of the four verbs presented in the patterns are also stem-changing verbs: scurdarisi and vistirisi.

Present indicatives of lavarisi, scurdarisi, vistirisi, and scantarisi

lavarisi, to wash oneself
iu mi lavu
tu ti lavi
vossìa si lava
iddu si lava
nuiatri ni lavamu
vuiatri vi lavati
iddi si **lavanu or** iddi si lavunu

scurdarisi, to forget
iu mi scordu
tu ti scordi
vossìa si scorda
iddu si scorda
nuiatri ni scurdamu
vuiatri vi scurdati
iddi si scordanu **or** iddi si scordunu

vistirisi, to dress oneself
iu mi vestu
tu ti vesti
vossìa si vesti
iddu si vesti
nuiatri ni vistemu
vuiatri vi vistiti
iddi si vestinu **or** iddi si vestunu

scantarisi, to be afraid
iu mi scantu
tu ti scanti
vossìa si scanta
iddu si scanta
nuiatri ni scantamu
vuiatri vi scantati
iddi si scantanu **or** iddi si scantunu

Use of Reflexive Verbs

Reflexive verbs are very common in Sicilian. Verbs having to do with one's body or that pertain directly to the speaker's welfare are almost always reflexive when they are followed by an object. Even if they aren't followed by an object, many of them are reflexive. If the verb governs the preposition *di*, the particle *nni* will often be required as a pronoun meaning "of him/her/it/them".

Examples

(1) Mi ricordu dû so nomu. I remember his name.
(2) Mi nni ricordu. I remember it.
(3) Nun mi scantu dî palori soi. I'm not afraid of his words.
(4) Ti sciarrii cû patruni di l'autra machina. You argue with the owner of the other car.
(5) Nuiatri n'addunamu ora ora di chidda. We just now notice that.
(6) Nuiatri ni nn'addunamu ora ora. We just now notice it.
(7) Si leva a cammisa e si lava i manu. He takes off his shirt, and he washes his hands.
(8) Doppu cena mi fumu na sicaretta e m'assettu nna na pultrona e mi mettu a leggiri u giurnali. After dinner I smoke a cigarette, sit down in an armchair and start to read the newspaper.
(9) A sira vi spugghiati e vi mittiti u piggiama e vi curcati nnô lettu. In the evening you undress, put on your pijamas and get in bed.
(10) S'addurmiscinu subbitu picchì annu sonnu assai. They fall asleep immediately because they are very sleepy.
(11) M'accattu na machina nova e â maniu strati strati. I buy a new car and I drive it around (i.e., through the streets).
(12) M'assettu n tavula e mi manciu i maccarruna cu caciu supra e mi vivu nu bicchireddu di vinu russu. I sit down at the table, I eat maccaroni with cheese on top and I drink a small glass of red wine.

(13) Prima chi idda va ô cuncertu, si nni va a casa e si cancia i robbi e si vesti bedda bedda. Before going to the concert she goes home, she changes her clothes, and she dresses really nicely.

Impersonal Reflexive Passive

In Sicilian, as in the other Romance languages, it's very common to use a 3rd person singular or 3rd person plural reflexive verb in an impersonal sense. This meaning is often translated as a passive in English. When used in 3rd person singular, the *si* is sometimes translated as *one*. As will be seen in the Examples 4-5 below, plural nouns cause the verb to be in the plural, indicating that using *one* (singular) is only a translation convenience. The first three examples are drawn from Chapter 5, **Exercise #1**.

Examples
(1) L'omu non si misura a parmu. One doesn't measure a man by the span of his hand. (*one* construction) **or** A man isn't measured by the span of his hand. (*passive* construction)
(2) La casa non s'acchiana senza scala. One doesn't climb a house without a ladder. (*one* construction) **or** A house isn't climbed without a ladder. (*passive* construction)
(3) Lu lignu stortu s'addrizza a lu focu. One straightens the piece of wood in the fire. (*one* construction) **or** The piece of wood is straightened in the fire. (*passive* construction)
(4) Libbra si vinninu nnâ chiazza. One sells books in the square. (*one* construction) **or** Books are sold in the square. (*passive* construction)
(5) Na pocu d'omini si vidunu nnô campu. One sees a few men in the field. (*one* construction) or A few men are seen in the field. (*passive* construction)

Demonstrative Pronouns and Adjectives

Demonstrative Pronouns
A demonstrative points out, that is, it's this or it's that. In Sicilian, there are three demonstrative pronouns. Each has a masculine form, a feminine form, and a common plural form.

chistu, this one (near the speaker)
| chistu | chista | chisti |

chissu, this one/that one (intermediate – near the person spoken to)
| chissu | chissa | chissi |

chiddu, that one (over there – away from the speaker and the person spoken to)
| chiddu | chidda | chiddi |

Examples
(1) Aiu chistu. I have this one.
(2) Chissa è bedda. That one (near you) is beautiful.
(3) Mi vogghiu pigghiari chiddu. I want to take that one (over there).

(4) Iddu si voli pigghiari chista e idda si voli pigghiari chidda. He wants to take this one, and she wants that one.

Adverbs of Place
The three adverbs of place corresponding to the demontratives are:

- ccà, here (near the speaker);
- ddocu, there (intermediate – near the person spoken to);
- ddà, there **or** over there (over there – away from the speaker and the person spoken to).

Demonstrative Adjectives
Just as there are demonstrative pronouns, there are also demonstrative adjectives. A demonstrative adjective is never used alone. It is always used to modify a noun, and it's placed before the noun. Various nouns are used to illustrate this.

stu, this (near the speaker)
stu libbru, this book   sta casa, this house   sti cosi, these things

ssu, this/that (intermediate – near the person spoken to)
ssu libbru, that book   ssa casa, that house   ssi cosi, those things

ddu, that (over there – away from the speaker and the person spoken to)
ddu libbru, that book   dda casa, that house   ddi cosi, those things

Examples
(1) Vogghiu ssu libbru. I want that book there (near you).
(2) Vogghiu ddi libbra. I want those books over there.
(3) Ssa machina è bedda. That car is beautiful.
(4) Ssi machini sunnu veramenti beddi (**or** beddi beddi). These cars are really pretty.
(5) I cosi ca mi piaciunu sunna ddà. Those things that I like are over there.

Possessive Pronouns and Adjectives
Possessive pronouns are related to personal pronouns, but they indicate possession.

Possessive Pronoun/Adjective Table	1st Person	2nd Person (fam.)	2nd Person (pol.)	3rd Person
Used with either a singular or plural noun	me (invariable), my, mine	to (invariable), your, yours	so (invariable), your, yours	so (invariable), his, her/hers, its
Used with either a singular or plural noun	nostru/nostra /nostri, our, ours	vostru/vostra /vostri, your, yours	vostru/vostra /vostri, your, yours	so (invariable), theirs

77

The pronouns are normally used in conjunction with the definite articles, but there are exceptions. They can also be used as adjectives. A possessive adjective is never used alone. It is always used to modify a noun, and it is generally placed before the noun. In the examples below, the long forms of the definite article are used, but the short forms are acceptable too. However, with singular kinship nouns or a part of one's body, the definite article is not used. When referring to plural kinship nouns, the definite article is used. **Note:** To preserve simplicity, in the examples below *so* will be translated as "his." Bear in mind that it may also mean "her/hers", "its" and "their/theirs".

Examples

È lu me libbru. It's my book.	È lu nostru libbru. It's our book.
È me figghiu. It's my son.	È nostru figghiu. It's our son.
È lu me. It's mine. He's mine.	È lu nostru. It's ours. He's ours.
È la me casa. It's my house.	È la nostra casa. It's our house.
È me mugghieri. It's my wife.	È nostra nora. It's our daughter-in-law.
È la me. It's mine. She's mine.	È la nostra. It's ours. She's ours.
Sunnu li me panara. They're my baskets.	Sunnu li nostri panara. They're our baskets.
Sunnu li me figghi. They're my children.	Sunnu li nostri figghi. They're our children.
Sunnu li me. They're mine.	Sunnu li nostri. They're ours.
È lu to quaternu. It's your notebook.	È lu vostru quaternu. It's your (p) notebook.
È to ziu. It's your uncle.	È vostru ziu. It's your (p) uncle.
È lu to. It's yours.	È lu vostru. It's yours (p).
È la to matita. It's your pencil.	È la vostra matita. It's your (p) pencil.
È ta zia. It's your aunt.	È vostra zia. It's your (p) aunt.
È la to. It's yours.	È la vostra. It's yours (p).
Sunnu li to puma. They're your apples.	Sunnu li vostri puma. They're your (p) apples.
Sunnu li to figghi. They're your children.	Sunnu li vostri figghi. They're your (p) children.
Sunnu li to. They're yours.	Sunnu li vostri. They're They're yours (p).
È lu so iardinu. It's his garden.	È lu so iardinu. It's their garden.
È so patri. It's his father.	È so patri. It's their father.
È lu so. It's his.	È lu so. It's theirs.
È la so machina. It's his car.	È la so machina. It's their car.
È so matri. It's his mother.	È so matri. It's their mother.
È la so. It's his.	È la so. It's theirs.
Sunnu li so machini. They're his cars.	Sunnu li so machini. They're their cars.
Sunnu li so ginituri. They're his parents.	Sunnu li so ginituri. They're their parents.
Sunnu li so. They're his.	Sunnu li so. They're theirs.

Disjunctive Pronouns to Express Possession

Because *so* can mean his/her/its/their, *d'iddu* (of him = his), *d'idda* (of her = her), *d'iddi* (of them = their) are sometimes used if the context doesn't make *so* clear. Of the three, *d'iddi* is the most common.

Examples

lu libbru d'iddu, his book	lu libbru d'idda, her book	lu libbru d'iddi, their books
la matri d'iddu, his mother	la matri d'idda, her mother	la matri d'iddi, their mother
li machini d'iddu, his cars	li machini d'idda, her cars	li machini d'iddi, their cars

Of course, *d'iddu* and *d'idda* can also mean "its" when referring to an animate thing, e.g., a cat. These are rarely used for inanimate objects.

Possessive Adjectives Following the Noun

Sometimes the following possessive pronouns/adjectives are used. If they are used as an adjective, they follow the noun. It is more common, however, for the possessive adjective to precede its noun.

Possessive Pronoun/Adjective Table	1st Person	2nd Person (fam.)	2nd Person (pol.)	3rd Person
Used with either a singular or plural noun (follows the noun)	miu **or** meu/ mia/mei, my, mine	to (invariable)/toi, your, yours	so (invariable)/soi, your, yours	so (invariable)/soi, his, her/hers, its

Examples
È lu libbru miu. **or** È lu libbru me. It's my book.
È lu quaternu to. It's your notebook.
È lu iardinu so. It's his garden.
È lu frati miu. **or** È lu frati me. It's my brother.
È la soru to.   It's your sister.
È lu patri so. It's his father.
È la casa mia. **or** È la casa me. It's my house.
È la machina so. It's his/her/their car.
È la mugghieri mia. **or** È la mugghieri me. It's my wife.
È la matri so. It's his mother.
Sunnu li panara mei. They're my baskets.
Sunnu li palori toi. They're your words.
Sunnu li machini soi. They're his cars. **or** They're their cars.
Sunnu li figghi mei. They're my children.
Sunnu li ginituri soi. They're their parents. **or** They're his parents.

General Examples of the Use of Possessive Pronouns and Adjectives
Some general examples of the use of possessive pronouns and adjectives are given.

Examples
(1) U me libbru è supra a tavula. My book's on the table. Unni è u to? Where's yours?
(2) Me ziu si chiama Vanni. My uncle's name is John. Comu si chiama u so? What's yours called?
(3) A so machina è nova. Their car is new. È nova a vostra? Is yours?
(4) I so ginituri abbitanu n Sicilia. His parents live in Sicily. Unni abbitanu i so? Where do yours live?
(5) Non pozzu truvari a me pinna. I can't find my pen. Malidittu! Pozzu usari a to? Damn! Can I use yours.
(6) To patri parra câ me prufissurissa. Your father's speaking with my teacher.
(7) Non mi scantu di palori soi. Mi scantu di zoccu è capaci di fari. I'm not afraid of his words. I'm afráid of what he can do.

Indefinite Pronouns and Adjectives

There are a number of indefinite pronouns and adjectives in Sicilian. The most common are these.

anticchia **or** tanticchia **or** nanticchia, a little bit, a small amount (pronoun)
anticchia di **or** tanticchia di **or** nanticchia di, a little bit of, a small amount of (adjective) –
   used with uncountable nouns
ass**ai**, much, many (pronoun **or** invariable adjective) – used with countable nouns
arcunu **or** alcunu, anyone (pronoun); any (adjective)
l'autru...l'autru, the one...the other
l'unu...l'autru, the one...the other
cchiù, more (pronoun **or** invariable adjective)
cui[+], he who, she who, they who, whoever, whosoever (masculine/feminine/plural)
cu[+], he who, she who, they who, whoever, whosoever – abbreviated version of *cui*
chiddu chi[+] **or** chiddu ca[+], the one who, he who, that which, what, whoever, whosoever
   (masculine singular)
chidda chi[+] **or** chidda ca[+], the one who, she who, that which, what, whoever, whosoever
   (feminine singular)
chiddi chi[+] **or** chiddi ca[+], the ones who, they who, that which, what, whoever, whosoever
   (plural)
l'unu e l'autru, each other (pronoun)
mancu, not even (negative adjective and also an adverb – See **Adverbs** in Chapter 8)
menu, less (pronoun **or** invariable adjective)
nautru, another (pronoun **or** adjective)
nè[+]...nè[+] **or** ni[+]...ni[+], neither...nor/either...or (negative adjective **or** a coordinating
   conjunction)
nenti, nothing/anything (negative pronoun)
nuddu, nobody, no one (negative pronoun); no (negative adjective)
ogni, each, every (invariable adjective)
ognunu **or** ognidunu **or** ognirunu, everyone, everybody (pronoun)
picca, few; little (pronoun **or** invariable adjective) – used with countable nouns
pocu few; little (pronoun **or** adjective)
na pocu **or** un pocu, some (pronoun) – used in place of countable nouns
na pocu di **or** un pocu di, several, some (adjective) – used with countable nouns
quarchi **or** qualchi, some (invariable adjective – takes a singular noun)
quarcunu **or** qualcunu, someone, somebody; anyone, anybody (pronoun)
quarchidunu **or** qualchidunu **or** quarchirunu, someone, somebody; anyone, anybody (pronoun)
quarchiccosa **or** qualchiccosa, something; anything (pronoun)
qualunqui **or** qualunchi, whatever (invariable adjective)
quantu, so much, so many (pronoun **or** invariable adjective)
quattru (**Literal meaning:** four), several
tali, such a, such
tantu, much, as much, so much (pronoun **or** adjective)
tanti, many, as many, so many (pronoun **or** adjective)
tuttu, all, everything (pronoun); all (adjective)
zoccu, that which, what (doesn't refer to people or animals) – can stand for
   chiddu/chidda/chiddi chi when the latter means "that which" or "those which"

Note: If a negative word follows the verb, *non* **or** *nun* must precede the verb. The *nun* negates the verb, and the negative pronoun (or adjective) takes on its nonnegative meaning when translated into English since Standard English does not tolerate double negatives in the same sentence. Sicilian, like the other Romance languages, admits a double, or even a triple, negative in the same sentence. Note carefully the examples below.

Examples

(1) Mi manciu anticchia di pani e mi vivu anticchia di vinu. I eat a little bread and I drink a little wine.

(2) Manciu anticchia e vivu anticchia. I eat a little and I drink a little.

(3) Mi mancianu assai li manu. My hands itch a lot.

(4) L'omu grassu avi tantu e so zia avi menu. The fat man has a lot (much) and his aunt has less.

(5) Vogghiu qualchiccosa (**or** quarchiccosa) di manciari. I want something to eat.

(6) Cui parra prima sempri otteni chiddu ca voli. He who speaks first always gets what he wants.

(7) Cu disia troppu finisci cu nenti. Whoever desires too much ends up with nothing.

(8) Cu dormi non pigghia pisci. He who sleeps doesn't catch any fish.

(9) Idda avi puma assai e cci nni duna unu a Carrinu. She has many apples and gives one to Charlie.

(10) Mi manciu quattru pira, ma pi diri la virità mi nni manciu sulu dui. I'm eating several pears, but actually I'm eating only two.

(11) Avemu picca sordi (**or** pochi sordi) e nun ti li putemu mpristari (**or** nun ti putemu mpristalli). We have little money, and we can't lend it to you.

(12) Fa beni a cui ti voli mali. **or** Fa beni a chiddu chi ti voli mali. Do good to him who hates you.

(13) Stu omu sapi pricisu chiddu chi voli fari. This man knows precisely what he wants to do.

(14) Qualunqui libbru voi, pigghiatillu. Whatever book you want, take it.

(15) Zoccu avi iddu è na cosa prizziusa. What he has is a precious thing.

(16) Nuddu vidi a mia. No one sees me.

(17) Nun viu a nuddu. I see no one.

(18) Nun ai nenti. There's nothing wrong with you.

(19) Nun cci ai nenti. You have nothing (there).

(20) Nun ai nenti di diri. You have nothing to say.

(21) Nun ai a diri (â diri) nenti. You don't have to say anything.

(22) Non aiu nuddu libbru. I have no book. **or** I don't have a book.

(23) Nun sapi nenti di chissu. He knows nothing about that.

(24) Quarcunu (**or** quarchidunu) tuppulia â porta. Someone's knocking at the door.

(25) Tuttu lu munnu sapi chissu **or** Tutti sannu chissu. Everybody knows that.

(26) Ognunu voli guadagnari cchiù sordi. Everyone wants to earn more money.

(27) Amativi comu frati. Love each other like brothers.

(28) Cci aiu a dari (cc'ê dari) quarchi libbru a Maria. I've got to give Mary some books.

(29) Cci aiu a dari (cc'ê dari) libbra a Maria. I've got to give Mary some books (none in particular).

(30) Cci aiu a dari (cc'ê dari) certi libbra a Maria. I've got to give Mary some (particular) books.

(31) Na pocu di giuvinotti talianu a na pocu di picciotti beddi. Several young men are looking at several pretty girls.

(32) Picca (**or** pochi) studenti studianu assai. Few students study much.

(33) Nni pigghiu quattru. I'll take four (of them).

(34) Fa zoccu ti dicu e non fari zoccu fazzu. Do what I tell you; don't do what I do.

(35) Zoccu vogghiu iu, tu nun l'ai. What I want, you don't have.

(36) Zoccu a fimmina avi, l'omu û disia. What the woman has, the man wants.

Whoever and Whatever

Although *whoever* and *whatever* are indefinite pronouns, they are handled a bit differently in Sicilian. In both cases, the verb is repeated with the appropriate pronoun, namely, *cu* and *zoccu*.

cu (**or** cui) + verb + verb = whoever + verb
zoccu + verb + verb = whatever + verb

Examples
(1) Cu offri offri, non nni pigghiu nenti. Whoever offers, I don't take any.
(2) Cu mi voli voli vidiri, fallu aspittari. Whoever wants to see me, let him wait.
(3) Zoccu ti piaci piaci, ti nni poi pigghiari. Whatever you like, you can take some.
(4) Zoccu vi dici dici iddu, nun facitilu. Whatever he says to you, don't do it.

Relative Pronouns

Relative pronouns introduce subordinate clauses. Basically a subordinate clause is a sentence within the main sentence. The relative pronoun refers back to someone or something (the antecedent) in the main sentence. By so doing, the relative pronoun takes the place of its antecedent in the subordinate clause. The relative pronouns in Sicilian are given below. **Note:** Using *chi* versus *ca* depends on the preference of the speaker and the speaker's *parrata*. If a subject pronoun is used in a subordinate clause, it follows the verb.

chi[+], who, whom, which, that – refers to a person, animal, or thing
ca[+], who, whom, which, that – refers to a person, animal, or thing
cui[+] **or** cu[+], whom, which, that (*cu* is an abbreviated version of *cui*) – used with a preposition
(l)u/(l)a/(l)i quari **or** (l)u/(l)a/(l)i quali, who, which – found more often in the written language than in the spoken language.

Note: Some of the examples below employ past tense verb forms to make the sentence more realistic. Don't worry too much about these forms at this point. They'll be explained in Chapter 11 in more detail.

Examples
(1) Viu a l'omu chi è u me amicu nnâ chiazza. I see the man who is my friend in the square.
(2) Chiddu chi sapi tuttu è l'unu chi vinci u premiu. He who knows everything is the one who'll win the prize.
(3) La vecchia, la quali (**or** chi) chiacchiaria cu dd'omu, è me zia. The old woman who's chatting with that man is my aunt.

(4) A fimmina a cui detti iu (**or** chi cci detti iu) u libbru abbita nautra città. The woman to whom I gave the book lives in another city.

(5) L'omu di cui m'**accattai** u ritrattu dû papa è un bon amicu di me patri. The man from whom I bought the portrait of the pope is a good friend of my father.

(6) A fimmina di cui vi parru iu è siciliana. The woman whom I'm talking about to you is Sicilian.

(7) U cani chi acchiana ntô palazzu vidi ô patruni e cci abbaia. The dog that climbs into the mansion sees the owner and barks at him.

(8) Sugnu nnamurata di ddu beddu picciottu chi viu ogni iornu vicinu u puzzu. I'm in love with the handsome youth whom I see every day at the well.

(9) Tu sì u Diu chi sai tuttu. You are the God who knows all. **Note:** In this construction, the verb in the relative clause is in the 2nd person singular rather than the 3rd person singular. This is occasionally done in English, especially in very formal address. **Examples:** (1) Thou art the God who knowest all. (2) Our Father, who art in heaven.

(10) Vui siti lu Diu chi sapiti tuttu. **Note:** Same sentence as above using *vui* to address God; the use of *tu* is an Italianism.

Interrogative Pronouns and Adjectives

Interrogative pronouns and adjectives are used in asking questions. The interrogative pronouns and adjectives in Sicilian are given here. One must carefully distinguish their use versus that of relative pronouns. However, in some constructions an intervening phrase such as *è chi...* is used. In such a phrase this latter *chi* is a relative pronoun. Carefully note the word order when the phrase *è chi...* is used. Examples are given below. **Note:** Both *cui* and *cu* take a *personal a* when used as direct objects.

chi$^+$?, what?
cui$^+$?, who? **or** cu$^+$?, who? (*cu* is an abbreviated version of *cui*)
di cui$^+$?, whose? **or** di cu$^+$?, whose?
a cui$^+$?, who? **or** a cu$^+$?, whom? to whom?
quali? which? which one? which ones? what?
quantu? how much? how many? (invariable)

Examples

(1) Cu veni? Who's coming?
(2) Cu ti cridi ca sì? Who do you think you are?
(3) Cu lu (**or** C'û) sapi? Who knows?
(4) Cu è â porta? Who's at the door?
(5) A cu vidi? Whom do you see?
(6) A cu sta parrannu iddu? To whom is he speaking? Who is he speaking to?
(7) Di cu è stu libbru? Whose book is this? È di Petru. It's Peter's.
(8) Di cu sunnu ssi quaterna? Whose notebooks are those (near you)? Sunnu di Maria. They're Mary's.
(9) Chi voi? What do you want?
(10) Chi è ca iddu mi voli diri? What does he want to tell me?
(11) Chi vogghiu iu? **or** Chi è chi iu vogghiu? What do I want?
(12) Tu sai chi vogghiu iu. You know what I want.
(13) Chi dici iddu? **or** Chi è chi iddu dici? What is he saying?
(14) Chi è? What is it?

(15) Lei sapi chi dici iddu? Do you know what he's saying?

(16) Cu è? Who is he?

(17) Sai cu è. You know who he is.

(18) Cu sugnu iu? Who am I?

(19) Lei sapi cu sugnu iu? Do you know who I am?

(20) Lei sapi cu sugnu iu. You know who I am.

(21) Chi voli? What does he want?

(22) Nun sacciu chi è. I don't know what it is.

(23) Tu sai chi è chi iu vogghiu? Do you know what I want?

(24) Chi m'ai a diri (m'â diri)? What do you have to tell me? **or** What will you tell me?

(25) Chi è l'elettricità? What is electricity?

(26) Quantu costa? How much is it?

(27) Quantu mi costa? What is the cost to me?

(28) Quantu latti voli? How much milk do you want?

(29) Quantu libbra avi? How many books do you have?

(30) Quali omu è u prisidenti? Which man (out of a group of men) is the president?

(31) Quali libbru vai a leggiri? What book (out of a group of books) are you going to read?

(32) Chi libbru avi vossìa? What (kind of) book do you have?

(33) Fici u travagghiu. I did the job. Chi usasti? What did you use (to do it)?

Note: *Chi* is used in many simple questions as an interrogative particle. Its presence indicates that a question's being asked. Depending on the meaning of the sentence, it may or may not have a translational meaning. Very often *ma* precedes the *chi*. At times *chi* also starts a declarative sentence. The correct use of *chi* in sentences will make your Sicilian sound much more authentic.

Examples
(1) Chi sì pazzu? Are you crazy?

(2) Ma chi cci pozzu fari? What can I do about it?

(3) Ma chi m'accattai na casa o un purcili? Did I buy a house or a pigsty?

(4) Chi mi nni futtu di sti cosi. I don't give a rap about these things.

Zoccu and Chiddu chi/ca
The meaning of *chiddu chi/ca* is more broad than *zoccu*. *Chiddu chi/ca* can refer to people or to a more indefinite thing. In the latter case, it is best simply to translate it as "that which" **or** "what". The indefinite pronoun *zoccu* also means "that which" **or** "what", but it never refers to people. When both have the meaning "that which" **or** "what", they are for all practical purposes interchangeable. Several examples are given to illustrate their usage. Note that both *chiddu chi/ca* and *zoccu* function as indefinite pronouns in these examples, not as adjectives, nor as interrogative pronouns. **Note:** The interrogative pronoun "what" is, of course, *chi*.

Examples
(1) Zoccu vogghiu, nun pozzu aviri. What I want, I can't have.

(2) Zoccu aiu, nun vogghiu. What I have, I don't want.

(3) Chiddu chi (not *zoccu*) disìa troppu nun avi a filicitati nâ vita. He who wants too much will not be happy in life.

(4) Chiddu ca dissi u prufissuri fu ntirissanti assai. What the professor said was really interesting.

(5) Zoccu mi piaci è beddu. What I like is beautiful.

(6) Mi piaci chiddu ca è beddu. I like what is beautiful.

(7) Nun sacciu chi dici. I don't know what he's saying (he seems to be speaking in some foreign language and I haven't a clue).

(8) Nun sacciu zoccu dici. I don't know what he's saying (I understand the language allright but the subject matter's way over my head).

(9) Viu quarchi cosa nnâ strata ma nun sacciu zoccu è. I see something on the street, but I don't know what it is.

(10) Viu a iddu nnâ strata ma nun sacciu cu è. I see him on the street, but I don't know who he is. (contains a personal referent = a iddu nnâ strata)

(11) Non mi scordu mai chiddu ca dissi. I'll never forget what he said.

(12) Non mi scordu mai zoccu dissi. I'll never forget what he said.

Vocabulary

Nouns

l'arvulu or l'arburu, tree (p -a)
la cammara, bedroom
lu cani, dog
la chiacchiara or la chiacchira, chatter, gossip
la facci, face
la gatta, cat
lu gattu, cat
lu gattareddu, kitten
la nanna or la nonna, grandmother
lu nannu or lu nonnu, grandfather
lu nimicu, enemy (p nimici)
la pacenza or la pacenzia, patience; forbearance
li picciuli, money; small change
lu scaluni, step (p -a) (e.g., of a staircase)
lu scrusciu, noise
lu senzu, sense, feeling
lu signu, sign; proof (p -a)
la tavula, table
lu vastuni, cane; stick (p -a)
la vicina, neighbor
lu vicinu, neighbor
la vista, sight, view
la vistina, dress
la zampa, paw
la zappa, hoe
lu zappuni, mattock (p -a)

Adjectives

biatu or beatu, blessed; happy; fortunate
fausu, false
furtunatu, fortunate
malu, bad, wicked, evil
(i)ntricanti, scheming, plotting

Verbs

accattari, to buy
accumulari (accumulu), to accumulate
arraspari, to scratch, grate
arricogghiri (arricogghiu), to gather up, reap
arrusicari (arrusicu), to gnaw
canusciri (canusciu), to know (a person)
capiri (sc), to understand
chiacchiariari (chiacchiariu), to chatter, gossip
chioviri (3s chiovi), to rain
cridiri (criu or cridu), to believe, think
cc'è, there is
cci sunnu or cci su', there are
diri (dicu), to say, to tell
dormiri or durmiri (dormu), to sleep
guadagnari, to earn
icari (icu), to bend
ittari (ettu or iettu), to throw
leggiri (leggiu), to read
manciari, to eat; itch (e.g., from an irritation)
nesciri (nesciu) (di), to go out (of)
pariri (mi pari), to seem to; think
parrari, to speak
perdiri (perdu), to lose
piaciri (mi piaci), to please
pigghiari (pigghiu), to take; seize; catch
ringrazziari (ringrazziu), to thank
scantarisi (mi scantu), to be frightened
scappari, to run away, flee; run off
scinniri (scinnu) (di), to go down (from); climb out of (e.g., a car)
scuncicari (sconcicu or scuncicu), to provoke; incite; vex
scurdarisi (mi scordu), to forget

Adjectives (cont.)

sfurtunatu, unfortunate
vicinu, living nearby

Adverbs

accussì, thus, so
ccà, here
unni, where

Interjections

bonu! well! just imagine!
caspita! good heavens! wow!

Verbs (cont.)

sentiri (sentu), to hear
sintirisi (mi sentu), to feel
siminari (siminu **or** seminu), to sow
sparrari, to talk poorly about
spidiri (sc), to send; dispatch
taliari (taliu), to look at
talia **or** talè, look (familiar imperative)
truvari (trovu), to find
vestiri (vestu), to dress
vistirisi (mi vestu), to dress oneself
vuscari (vuscu), to earn (e.g., a living)

Exercises

Exercise #1: Translate these proverbs into English and discuss what they mean. The same applies to these proverbs as was said of those in **Exercise 1** in Chapters 5 and 6.

(1) Chiddu chi si simina s'arricogghi. (2) Di chiddu chi vidi nni cridi pocu, di chiddu chi senti nun cridiri nenti. (3) Nun scuncicari lu cani chi dormi. (4) Quannu la gatta si lava la facci è signu c'avi a chioviri. (5) Ogni amicu chi si perdi è nu scaluni chi si scinni. (6) Lu veru amicu è chiddu chi* nun ti sparra. (7) L'arvulu vecchiu non si ica. (8) La terra si fa pi lu viddanu. (9) Arraspa a lu to amicu unni cci mancia. (10) Amicu fausu è malu vicinu, etta la petra e ammuccia la manu.

* Why can't *zoccu* be used here in place of *chiddu chi*?

Exercise #2: Translate these sentences into English.

(1) Dugnu dinari ê me amici e feli ê me nimici. (2) Dda fimmina granni chi mi talia nnâ strata è me zia. (3) Chiddu chi mi voli beni biatu è. (4) Nun capisciu nudda cosa di zoccu tu mi dici. (5) Nun diri nenti a nuddu. (6) Iddu si nni pò pigghiari di zoccu trova trova ccà. (7) A fimmina fa na chiacchiariata câ so vicina chi porta na vistina russa. (8) Ti ringrazziu dâ to gran pacenza chi ai. (9) Dunaminni una e tu ai a essiri cuntenti c'â facisti.* (10) A finestra è aperta e pozzu sentiri i scrusci dî machini nnâ strata.

* *facisti* = "did".

Exercise #3: Translate these sentences into Sicilian.

(1) The little boy takes his mother's hand. (2) Tomorrow I must go to my friend's house and give him a present from my sister. (3) I'll keep an eye on your money which is on the table. (4) My hand hurts; my hands hurt. (5) Anyone who wishes to act like that can leave. (6) Today I'll take two that the old woman is selling. (7) I'll buy it and give it to him. (8) I see him; he's coming out of the house right now. (9) Well! What do you (plural) want to do today? (10) Don't hit me with your cane!

Exercise #4: Say these sentences aloud. Don't worry about translating them at this point.

(1) Vinnemu ddu ritrattu. (2) Lei si pigghia chissa e iu mi pigghiu chista. (3) Dimmilla. (4) 'Un vidi chi sì vecchiu quantu a mia? (5) Non ciusciaricci ntâ facci! (6) Non pozzu truvari i to scarpi. (7) Stu iornu vâ chioviri. (8) Raggiuni aiu. Nun cci sunnu chi ducentu scuti sutta u me cappeddu. (9) Dumani spidisciu i picciuli e pagu stu debbitu finarmenti. (10) Sugnu to patri chi ti voli beni assai.

8   Adverbs

Purpose of the Chapter

The chief purpose of this chapter is to discuss the various kinds of adverbs in the Sicilian language. Adverbs are an essential part of sentences. On the one hand, just as adjectives describe, modify, or limit nouns; on the other hand, adverbs describe, modify, or limit verbs, adjectives, and other adverbs. The proper use of adverbs, like prepositions, can impart a flavor of authenticity to discourse in a language. There are numerous adverbs in Sicilian; this chapter can't set forth all of them. The best way to learn them is by reading and listening to spoken Sicilian. Only the most important adverbs of each category will be given. In addition, forming the comparison of adjectives and adverbs will be treated as well as the absolute superlative.

There's another way to describe adverbs. Adverbs are involved in answering the following questions.

- Where
- When
- How
- To what degree, to what extent, or how much
- How many times

Adverbs of Place

There are a number of adverbs of place answering the question, Where?

abbasciu, below
a nuddabbanna, nowhere (negative adverb)
appressu **or** pressu, nearby, close at hand
a tutti banni **or** dappirtuttu, everywhere
arrassu, away, far off
avanti, in front of, forward
ccà, here
cci, here, in this place; there, at that place – always precedes the verb; a conjunctive adverb
darreri **or** darrè **or** arreri **or** arrè, behind (arreri **or** arrè also means "again")
davanti, in front of
dintra, inside, within
ddocu, there (near the person spoken to)
ddà, there (over there away from both speaker and person spoken to)
iusu, down
luntanu, far away
nni, of there, of that place – always precedes the verb; a conjunctive adverb
susu, up
supra, on, on top, over
sutta, underneath, at the bottom, under
unni **or** dunni, where (also used in questions – see **Interrogative Adverbs** below)
vicinu, nearby

Note: Many adverbs of place are closely related to prepositions, and it seems highly likely that prepositions developed from adverbs of place or in some cases adverbs of time. The difference is that a preposition governs a noun of a noun phrase whereas an adverb does not. An adverb of place often modifies a verb.

Examples
(1) Unni û viu? Where do I see him? Û viu ddà. I see him over there.
(2) Unni sunnu i picciriddi? Where are the children? Iddi sunnu ddassusu. They're up there. Iddi sunnu ccà. They're here.
(3) Unni vai? Where are you going? Vaiu luntanu. I'm going far away.
(4) Di unni veni? Where are you coming from? Vegnu di luntanu. I'm coming from far away.
(5) Vaiu ddocu. I'm going over there.
(6) Unni sì? Where are you? Sugnu propiu ccà. I'm right here.
(7) Nun û viu a nuddabbanna. I don't see him anywhere.
(8) A nuddabbanna û viu. Nowhere do I see him.
(9) Nun viu a nuddu a nuddabbanna. I don't see anyone anywhere.

Adverbs of Time
There are a number of adverbs of time answering the question, When?

accamora **or** camora **or** accamodora, right now, at present, presently
a manu a manu, right away; quickly; expeditiously (See *manu manu*)
aieri, yesterday
aieri avanti **or** aieri l'autru, the day before yesterday
aieri sira **or** arsira **or** assira, last evening
allura, then, in that case
ancura **or** ancora, still, yet
period of time + arrè, ago (see Examples 13 and 14 in **Examples** below)
avi + period of time + ca (see Example 15 in **Examples** below)
di iornu, during the day, in the daytime
di notti, during the night, at night
dumani, tomorrow
doppu, afterwards
doppu dumani, the day after tomorrow
period of time + fa, ago (see Example 13 in **Examples** below)
già, already
la sira avanti, the evening before last
manu manu, little by little, gradually (sometimes has the same meaning as *a manu a manu*)
ntantu, meanwhile
oggi **or** oi, today
ora, now **Note:** *ora* is often used in sentences where we'd use "listen" or "look".
oramai, by now, by this time
ora ora **or** ora stissu, right now
ottu iorna oi, a week from now
pirtempu, earlier
poi, then; afterwards
prestu, soon, early

prima, first; before
propiu ora **or** propriu ora, right now
quinnici iorna oi, two weeks from now
sempri, always
pi sempri, forever
spissu, often
stamatina, this morning
stasira, this evening
stanotti, tonight
stu iornu, today
subbitu, quickly; right now
tannu, then, at that time, just then
tardu, late
tra pocu, soon
quannu, when (also used in questions – see **Interrogative Adverbs** below)
quantu tempu, how long (also used in questions – see **Interrogative Adverbs** below)

Examples

(1) Quannu vai? When are you going? Vaiu dumani. I'm going tomorrow. Vaiu dumani matina. I'm going tomorrow morning.
(2) Quantu tempu resti ddà? How long will you be there? Quattru iorna restu ddà. I'll be there four days.
(3) Oggi m'accattu u giurnali e stasira û leggiu. Today I'll buy the newspaper, and this evening I'll read it.
(4) Vanni veni prestu ma Carruzzu veni ora ora (**or** ora stissu). Johnny's coming soon, but Charlie's coming right now.
(5) Iddu vidi spissu ê so soru. He often sees his sisters.
(6) Stamatina aiu a iri a la bibbliuteca. **or** Stamatina ê gghiri â bibbliuteca. (This would be found more in the spoken language.) This morning I've got to go to the library.
(7) Nenti dura pi sempri. **or** Nun cc'è nenti chi dura pi sempri. Nothing lasts forever.
(8) Quannu veni to patri n casa (**or** in casa)? Veni prestu. When will your father come home? He's coming soon.
(9) Accamora sugnu senza travagghiu. Right now I don't have a job.
(10) Turiddu arriva sempri tardu tardu. Salvatore always comes very late.
(11) Fallu ora ora. Do it right now.
(12) Già è ura di iri a casa. It's already time to go home.
(13) Tri iorna fa (**or** tri iorna arrè) vitti ô me bon amicu ô mircatu nnâ chiazza. Three days ago I saw my good friend at the market in the piazza.
(14) So matri muriu tri iorna arrè. His mother died three days ago.
(15) Avi tri iorna ca semu ccà. We've been here three days (and we're still here).

Adverbs of Manner

There are a number of adverbs of manner answering the question, How? In what manner?

accussì **or** cussì (spoken), as, thus, like this
accuddì **or** cuddì (spoken), as, thus, like that
adaciu, slowly, in a whispered manner
a l'improvvisu, suddenly

beni, well

comu, how (also used in exclamations **and** questions – see Interrogative Adverbs below)

dirittu **or** drittu, right; directly

di prupositu **or** di propositu, on purpose, intentionally

di quarchi manera **or** di qualchi manera, in what way (used in questions)

lestu, fast, quickly

mai, never/ever; no (negative adverb)

masinnò **or** vasinnò, otherwise (also used as a conjunction)

mancu, not even; not at all; no longer/even; hardly, scarcely (negative adverb)

nippuru, not even

nzemi **or** nzemmula, together

macari, perhaps; maybe; of course; also

mali, poorly

nè già, not even/even (negative adverb)

non **or** nun **or** 'un, not (negative adverb)

oramai, almost, nearly

propiu **or** propriu, exactly; just; right

puru, also, likewise, too

quasi, almost

subbitu, suddenly

veru, really, truly

vivu, lively

Adverbs of manner are very common. In colloquial Spoken Sicilian an adjective itself may function as an adverb. Only the masculine singular form of the adjective is used as an adverb, and of course it is invariable when used in this fashion. The use of adjectives functioning as adverbs of manner is the norm in German, and is often done in spoken English. **Examples:** (German) Er spricht gut. He speaks well.; You did it good.

Examples of adjectives functioning as adverbs of manner
(1) Iddu scrivi bonu. He writes well.
(2) Idda scrivi bonu. She writes well.
(3) Iddi scrivinu bonu. They write well.
(4) L'omu parra chiaru. The man speaks clearly.
(5) La fimmina parra chiaru. The woman speaks clearly.
(6) Li picciotti parranu chiaru. The boys speak clearly.

Caution: Watch out for verbs taking a predicate adjective because with such verbs the adjective is truly an adjective, not an adverb.

Examples
(1) Iddu si senti bonu. He feels good.
(2) Idda non si senti bona. She doesn't feel good.
(3) Iddi si sentunu boni. They feel good.

Using an invariable adjective as an adverb is at variance with the literary language in English and also in Sicilian, which recognizes the proper use of adverbs formed from adjectives. Although the above examples are found in speech, the student is not advised to speak or write in this fashion. In **Examples of adjectives functioning as adverbs of manner** Sentences 1-3, the adverb *beni* should be used and in Sentences 4-6 the adverb *chiaramenti* should be used. In the examples below, adverbs proper are used. In Literary Sicilian, adverbs of manner are formed by adding the ending *-menti* to the feminine singular form of an adjective. Adjectives ending in *-i* generally retain the *i* before adding the ending *-menti*. Of course, for adjectives ending in *i*, the masculine, feminine, and plural forms are identical. However, if the adjective ends in *-li* or *-ri*, the *i* is dropped before the *–menti*; often the *l* changes into an *r*.

Examples of adverbs of manner formed from adjectives
- chiara (feminine), clear; chiaramenti, clearly
- ricca (feminine), rich; riccamenti, richly
- vera (feminine) true; veramenti, truly
- cuntenti, happy, content; cuntentimenti, happily, contentedly
- facili, easy; facilmenti, easily
- populari, popular; popularmenti, popularly
- finali, final; finarmenti, finally

In certain cases, adverbs of manner, although related to their adjectives, are not formed by adding the ending *-menti*. Two very common ones are: beni, well; mali, badly, poorly.

Examples
(1) È propriu accussì. It's just like that.
(2) L'omu fa accussì e a fimmina fa accuddì. A man does it this way, and a woman does it that way.
(3) Accussì fannu tutti. They're all like that. **Literal meaning:** They do (it) thus.
(4) Accussì si fa. That's the way it's done.
(5) Mancu aiu u tempu a fari chiddu ca vogghiu. I hardly have the time to do what I want.
(6) Nun û viu mai. I never see him. **or** I don't ever see him.
(7) Mai û viu. Never do I see him. **or** I never see him.
(8) A l'improvvisu â sentu nnâ strata. Suddenly, I hear her on the street.
(9) Dda vecchia cucina beni. That old woman cooks well.
(10) U vecchiu parra accussì gintilmenti. The old man speaks so politely.
(11) Mancu ni veninu a vidiri nè Vanni nè Petru. **or** Nè Vanni nè Petru quasi mai ni veninu a vidiri. Neither Johnny nor Peter hardly ever comes to see us.
(12) Nun viu nè a Vanni nè a Petru. I don't see either Johnny or Peter. **or** I see neither Johnny nor Peter.
(13) Capisciu abbastanza ma nun cumpletamenti. I understand enough but not completely.
(14) Chistu non basta pi livari tutti i suspetti. This doesn't suffice to remove all suspicions.
(15) Comu pulizzia idda a casa? Idda â pulizzia assai beni. How does she clean the house? She cleans very well.
(16) Comu si cumporta u picciriddu? Si cumporta mali. How does the child behave? He's misbehaving.
(17) Dda picciotta è veramenti bedda. That girl is really beautiful.

Adverbs of Degree or Quantity

There are a number of adverbs of degree answering the question, To what degree? To what extent? How much? How many? How often? Of course, many of these adverbs can also function as adjectives or pronouns. If they modify a noun, they're adjectives. If they modify a verb, adjective, or another adverb, they're adverbs. Examples of both uses are given here in examples.

anchi, also, too (*puru* is more common)
anticchia **or** tanticchia **or** nanticchia, a little
arrè **or** arreri **or** di novu, again
ass**ai**, a lot
cchiù, more (*cchiui* is sometimes used if a comparative/superlative formation isn't called for)
cchiuttostu, rather; somewhat; kind of
granni, a lot, very
macari, even, also
menu, less
na pocu **or** un pocu, some
non **or** nun … chi, only
picca, a little, less
puru, also, too
na vota, once
du voti, twice
tanti voti, many times
quarchi vota **or** qualchi vota, sometimes
sparti, besides, moreover
sulu, only **Note:** As an adjective, *sulu* means "alone".
tantu, so much, much **Note:** Also used as an adjective.
troppu, too much

Examples
(1) Ora û fa ass**ai**. Now he does it a lot.
(2) Stu omu nun avi chi tri figghi. This man has only three children.
(3) Giorgiu non avi chi a cammisa (i)ncoddu e nenti di cchiù. George has only the shirt on his back and nothing more.
(4) A fimmina camina cchioss**ai** di prima. The woman walks much more than she used to.
(5) Marta è cchiuttostu laria. Martha is kind of ugly.
(6) Ti vogghiu ben' ass**ai**. I love you a lot.
(7) È ntilliggenti ass**ai**. He's very intelligent.
(8) È fissa. He's a fool. Sapi picca e nenti. He knows next to nothing.
(9) Iddu mancia troppu ma idda mancia pocu. He eats too much, but she eats only a little.
(10) Avi pocu. He has little.
(11) 'Un û sacciu quali mi piaci cchioss**ai**. I don't know which one (e.g., a dress) I like the most.
(12) A fimmina parra puru. The woman also speaks.
(13) Quarchi vota mi sentu di chianciri. Sometimes I feel like crying.

(14) Tri voti a matri chiama a so figghiu ma nuddu rispunni. Three times the mother calls her boy, but no one answers.

(15) Cc'era na vota na picciridda c'avia na gattaredda. Once upon a time there was a little girl who had a cute little kitten.

(16) Comu è bedda dda picciotta! How beautiful that girl (is)! Chi biddizza avi! What beauty she has!

Interrogative Adverbs

There are a number of interrogative adverbs. Some of these are the following.

comu, how? **Note:** *comu* is often used in response when one doesn't understand something.
  Example: Comu? What?
quannu, when?
unni **or** dunni, where?
picchì **or** pirchì? why?
pi quali raggiuni, why?
quantu, how? how much?
di chi manera, how? in what manner?

Examples
(1) Comu è? Tuttu va beni? How are you. Everything OK?
(2) Quannu ni veni a vidiri? When are you coming to visit us?
(3) Unni abbiti tu? **or** Unni abbita lei? **or** Unni abbitati? Pagghiri di ccà o luntanu di ccà? Where do you live? Around here or far away from here?
(4) Picchì mi taliati? Nun mi piaci. Why are you looking at me? I don't like it.
(5) Quantu costanu sti libbra? How much do these books cost?
(6) Di chi manera vai a cucinari (**or** vâ cucina) l'agneddu? How are you going to cook the lamb?

Whenever, Wherever, However, and However Much

Whenever, wherever, however, and *however much* are indefinite adverbs; they are handled the same way as *whoever* and *whatever* (see Chapter 7). The verb is simply repeated following the appropriate adverb, namely, *quannu, unni, comu,* and *quantu.*

quannu + verb + verb = whenever + verb
unni + verb + verb = wherever + verb
comu + verb + verb = however + verb
quantu + verb + verb = however much + verb

Examples
(1) Quannu me mugghieri fa fa a spisa, spenni sempri sordi assai. Whenever my wife goes shopping, she always spends a lot of money.
(2) Unni vannu vannu, vidunu sempri i stissi pirsuni. Wherever they go, they always see the same people.
(3) Comu û fazzu fazzu, sarà un bonu travagghiu. However I do it, it'll be a good job.
(4) Quantu si pigghia pigghia idda, pagu iu. However much she takes, I'll pay.

Comparison of Adjectives

Adjectives are compared using the adverbs of degree, *cchiù* and *menu*. To form the comparative, *cchiù* and *menu* are used. To form the superlative, *cchiù* and *menu* are used in conjunction with the definite articles. The word "than" is translated by *chi* unless a proper noun, a noun modified by a possessive, or a pronoun (disjunctive, indefinite, or interrogative) follows. In these cases, *di* is used instead of *chi*. If a pronoun follows *di*, it is a disjunctive pronoun in the direct object case, not a subject pronoun. The disjunctive pronouns in the direct object case can be found in Rows 2 and 4 in the **Disjunctive Pronoun Table** in Chapter 7.

Of course, *cchiù* and *menu* can be used as adjectives also, as the examples below show. When they are used as adjectives, they are invariable. They can also be used as adverbs modifying a verb (see below) rather than an adjective. See Examples 18 and 19. **Note:** Modern English grammar is followed, namely, object pronouns are used after "than", not subject pronouns as was done formerly. **Example:** My sister is prettier than her. **Not:** My sister is prettier than she.

Examples

(1) Me soru è cchiù bedda d'idda. My sister is prettier than her.
(2) I me soru sunnu cchiù beddi chi ddi picciotti fimmini. My sisters are prettier than those girls.
(3) Vanni è cchiù spertu chi ntilliggenti. Johnny's more clever than intelligent.
(4) Vogghiu cchiù acqua. I want more water. Nni vogghiu cchiù. I want some more.
(5) Petru avi cchiù dinari di mia. Peter has more money than I.
(6) Avi cchiù di deci libbra. He has more than ten books.
(7) Lei avi menu sordi di Rubertu. You have less money than Robert.
(8) Rubertu avi cchiù sordi di lei. Robert has more money than you.
(9) Petru avi cchiù libbra di chiddu. Peter has more books than that one (over there).
(10) Idda è menu bedda di so soru. She's less pretty than her sister.
(11) A fimmina è menu filici nnâ so secunna casa chi nnâ prima. The woman's less happy in her second house than in her former house.
(12) Sugnu menu malatu di tia. I'm less sick than you.
(13) Iddu è cchiù spertu di cui? He's smarter than whom?
(14) Tresa è a cchiù ntirissanti dâ classi. Teresa's the most interesting in the class. **Note:** English uses "in" with the superlative.
(15) Luigi è u carusu cchiù stupitu dû munnu. Louis is the stupidest boy in the world.
(16) Palermu è a cità cchiù bedda dâ Sicilia. Palermo's the prettiest city in Sicily.
(17) Iddu è u menu spertu di tutti. He's the least clever of all.
(18) Lei avi menu dinari di tutti. You have the least money of all.
(19) Ddi omini sunnu cchiù ricchi chi onesti. Those men are richer than (they are) honest.
(20) Sta cosa è sicuramenti cchiù bona chi mala. This thing's certainly more good than bad.
(21) Cchiù si travagghia cchiù si guadagna. The more one works the more one earns.
(22) Cchiù leggiu stu libbru menu capisciu. The more I read this book the less I understand.

As...As

Suppose we're not comparing something; rather, we're pointing out that it's of equal value. In this case use *tantu...comu* or *tantu...quantu*. The *tantu* is often left understood. Since *comu* or *quantu* are adverbs, they are invariable, but *tantu* can function as either an adjective or an adverb. If it is an adjective, it must agree with the following noun. If a pronoun follows, it is generally a disjunctive pronoun in the direct object case. In the examples *tantu* is placed in parenthesis to indicate its use is optional. Note that *comu* requires the *personal a* if a proper noun, a noun modified by a possessive, or a pronoun (disjunctive, indefinite, or interrogative) follows.

Examples
(1) Iddu è (tantu) longu comu a so patri. He's as tall as his father.
(2) Petru avi (tanti) sordi comu a so amicu. Peter has as much money as his friend.
(3) Petru avi (tanti) sordi comu a chiddu. Peter has as much money as that one (over there).
(4) A picciotta è (tantu) gintili quantu bedda. The young woman is as kind as she's beautiful.
(5) L'omu è riccu quantu avaru. The man's as rich as he's stingy.
(6) Nun vidi chi sì vecchiu quantu a mia? Don't you see that you're as old as me?
(7) Studiu quantu a iddu. I study as much as him.

Irregular Comparatives and Superlatives

There are a few adjectives in Sicilian having irregular comparative and superlative forms. These are:

Adjective	Comparative	Superlative
bonu, good	megghiu, better	lu megghiu, best
malu, bad	peiu **or** peggiu, worse	lu peiu **or** lu peggiu, worst
picciulu, small	minuri **or** cchiù picciulu, smaller	lu minuri **or** lu cchiù picciulu, the smallest
nicu, small	minuri **or** cchiù nicu, smaller	lu minuri **or** lu cchiù nicu, the smallest
granni, large	maiuri **or** maggiuri **or** cchiù granni, the larger	lu maiuri **or** lu maggiuri **or** lu cchiù granni, the largest

All the irregular comparative and superlative forms are sometimes combined with *cchiù* in colloquial speech. Do not follow this practice. **Example:** Chista è cchiù megghiu di chissa. This one's better than that one. **Note:** When talking about the oldest and youngest in a family, use the regular forms.

Examples
(1) Chista è megghiu di chissa. This one's better than that one.
(2) Ma chidda è a megghiu di tutti. But that one over there is the best of all.
(3) Luigi è u peggiu studenti dâ classi. Louis is the worst student in the class.
(4) Carruzzu è u cchiù nicu dî figghi masculi. Chuck's the youngest of the sons.
(5) Teresa è a cchiù granni dî figghi fimmini. Teresa's the oldest of the daughters.

Absolute Superlative

The absolute superlative is a construction common to all the Romance languages. It's called "absolute" because the substantive in question isn't being directly compared to anything else. It's a stand-alone assessment. It's common to form the absolute superative by taking the feminine singular adjective, dropping the -a, and adding -issimu (masculine singular)/-issima (feminine singular)/-issimi (common plural). Translate the absolute superlative into English using "very" + the adjective or "really" + the adjective, etc.

The following techniques having the same effect as the absolute superlative are also used in Sicilian.

- Use a special adjective or adverb such as *beddu, granni, assai, veramenti*, etc. in place of the absolute superlative;
- The adjective itself is simply repeated (reduplicated);
- The ending -*uni* is added to the adjective to form a superlative;
- Use of a simile.

Note: Reduplication's common with mono- or disyllabic adjectives in Spoken Sicilian. Even in colloquial English, reduplication is commonly used. **Example:** Boy, he's really, really nice.

Examples
(1) Dda picciotta è veramenti bedda. **or** Dda picciotta è bedda bedda. **or** Dda picciotta è bellissima. That girl's very pretty.
(2) L'omu è assai malatu. **or** L'omu è malatissimu. The man's very sick.
(3) Sti studenti sunnu spertissimi. These students are really smart.
(4) U meli è duci duci. **or** U meli è ducissimu. The honey's very sweet.
(5) A casa d'iddu è granni assai. His house is very large.
(6) N'omu riccuni è. **or** Iddu è ricchissimu. He's a very rich man.
(7) Iddu è riccu n funnu. He's really rich.
(8) Iddu ti voli assaiuni. He loves you very much.
(9) Iddu è riccu comu a Crisu. He's rich as Croesus (that is, very rich).
(10) Lei parra u sicilianu beni assai. You speak Sicilian really well.
(11) È brutta quantu na malanova. It's as unpleasant as a bad piece of news.
(12) È bedda comu a luna. She's as pretty as the moon.
(13) Sapi duci comu u meli. It tastes as sweet as honey.

Comparison of Adverbs

Since *cchiù* and *menu* are adverbs (most of the time), in addition to modifying adjectives (as in the comparative and superlative forms), and verbs, they can also modify other adverbs.

Examples
(1) Lu vecchiu parra cchiù gintilmenti dâ signura. The old man speaks more politely than the lady.
(2) Lu picciottu capisci menu chiaramenti chiddu ca avi a fari. The boy understands less clearly what he must do.

Reflexive Verbs with the Conjunctive Adverb nni

This combination is often used with verbs of motion to indicate either motion towards or motion away. One of the most common reflexive verbs with *nni* is *irisinni*, to go there, to leave (a place). Another example is *vinirisinni*, to come here, to return (to a place). These are the present indicative and imperative forms. Note the orthographic changes in the imperative forms.

Present Indicative

irisinni, to go away, leave	vinirisinni, to come from (a place), climax *
iu mi nni vaiu	iu mi nni vegnu
tu ti nni vai	tu ti nni veni
vossìa si nni va	vossìa si nni veni
iddu si nni va	iddu si nni veni
nuiatri ni nni emu **or** ni nni iemu	nuiatri ni nni vinemu
vuiatri vi nni iti	vuiatri vi nni viniti
iddi si nni vannu	iddi si nni veninu **or** iddi si nni venunu

Imperative

vattinni	venitinni
si nni va	si nni veni
si nni issi	si nni vinissi
iamuninni	vinemuninni
itivinni	vinitivinni
si nni issiru	si nni vinissiru

* Means "have an orgasm, climax (sexually)."

In fact, *verb + si nni* can be used with potentially any verb implying coming and going either in the direction of or away from. **Examples:** acchianarisinni, to climb towards **or** away; scinnirisinni, to climb up or down. The direction intended depends on the context.

Examples
(1) Avanti. Ni nni emu di ccà. Come on. We're leaving here.
(2) Itivinni vuiatri. Go away (you).
(3) Ni nni vinemu cchiù tardu. We'll come back later.
(4) Ora viu a l'omini chi si nni scinnunu dâ muntagna. Now I see the men who are climbing down the mountain.

Singular Noun as a Collective Plural

It's common in Sicilian to use a noun in the singular when it refers to a collective plural. In this case, the noun is seen as applying to what pertains to the matter at hand or in question.

Examples
(1) Davanti u prisidenti l'omini si levanu u cappeddu. Before the president the men remove their hats.

(2) Fabbricanu li pazzi la casa, li savii l'accattanu. Fools build their houses; prudent people buy them. (Sicilian proverb)

Common Meanings of mettiri

The verb *mettiri* or its reflexive form, *mittirisi*, has many useful meanings. Some of these are given below in the examples for reference.

Examples

(1) Mi mettu la giacca. I put on my jacket.
(2) Si metti a leggiri u giurnali. He starts to read the newspaper.
(3) Si metti a chioviri. It's starting to rain.
(4) Ni mittemu d'accordu. We'll reach an agreement.
(5) Mi la (**or** mâ) mettu supra li iammi. I'll put it on my legs.
(6) Iddu metti i libbra ncapu a tavula. He puts the books on top of the table.
(7) A mia mi piaci a pinzata e poi mi mettu sta putia. I like the idea, and so I'll set myself up in this shop.

Vocabulary

Nouns

lu bottu, explosion; noise
lu carciri, jail
lu culu, rear end, ass
la cucchiara, (large) spoon; ladle
la cucchiaredda, teaspoon
lu cucchiaru, spoon (p -a)
la festa, party; festival
la genti, people (collective noun)
lu gottu, goblet, mug
la gula, throat (also i cannarozza)
la guccia, drop
lu lettu, bed
la littra, letter
la mà, mother; momma, mom
lu mali, evil; trouble; illness, disease
la malatia, illness
la mugghieri **or** la mogghi, wife
lu munnu, world
la natura, nature
la nicissità **or** la nicissitati, necessity
l'ogghiu, oil (p -a)
lu pà, father; dad, pop
la padedda, frying pan
lu **or** la parenti (M **or** F), relative
la pesta **or** la pesti, pest; disease; plague
lu piaciri, pleasure
la picciotta, girl (adolescent), young woman
lu picciottu, boy (adolescent), young man
la pignata, pot, sauce pan
la pignatedda, little pot, little sauce pan
la pipa, pipe

Verbs

abbitari (abbitu), to live (in a place), inhabit
accabbari (accabbu), to finish, end
addisiari (addisiu) **or** disiari (disiu), to desire
addisiddirari (addisiddiru) **or**
    disiddirari (disiddiru), to desire
addumannari **or** dumannari, to ask
addumari (addumu), to light up, start (e.g., a car)
affumari (affumu), to smoke (e.g., meat)
agghiurnari (3s agghiorna), to dawn; start a new day
ammuccari (ammuccu), to put in the mouth; bite
assittarisi (m'assettu), to sit down
campari, to live
chiamari, to call out
chiamarisi, to be called, be named
circari (cercu), to seek, look for
circari (cercu) di, to try to
cociri **or** cuciri (cociu), to cook (takes an object)
cucchiariari (cucchiariu), to serve; ladle
cucinari (cucinu), to cook (in a general sense)
cummigghiari (cummogghiu), to cover; protect; hide
cungratulari (cungratulu), to congratulate
cuntari (cuntu), to count; tell (e.g., a story)
friiri, to fry
fuiri, to flee
iri (vaiu), to go
irisinni (mi nni vaiu), to go away; leave (e.g., a place)
isari (isu), to lift up, raise
lassari, to allow, let; leave (alone)
ligari (legu), to tie, bind; connect
limitari (limitu), to limit
livari (levu), to take away, carry away

Nouns (cont.)

la pirsuna, person
la prudenza **or** la prudenzia, prudence, caution
lu quaternu **or** quadernu, notebook (p -a **or** -i)
lu quatratu, square (geometric form)
lu quatru, picture; painting
li quattrini, money
la radica, root; origin; source
lu scantu, fear; freight
la scatula, box
la seggia, chair
li sordi, money (very common)
la spiranza, hope
lu spiritu, spirit; mind; wit
la stanza, room
lu tata, dad
lu tema, theme, subject; topic
la vasciurata, afternoon
la viggilia, vigil, watch
la vigna, vineyard
lu vilenu, poison
la vota, turn; time (common in time expressions)

Adjectives

chiaru, clear
commudu, comfortable; convenient
cunfurtibbili, comfortable
cutiddianu, daily
difficili, difficult, hard
facili, easy
gintili, polite, courteous, kind
(i)mmriacu **or** (i)mpriacu, drunk
(i)ntilliggenti **or** (i)ntelliggenti, intelligent
(i)ntirissanti **or** (i)ntrissanti, interesting
prizziusu, precious
propiu **or** propriu, proper; exact; accurate; own
scantusu, frightened, scared
simpaticu, nice
stissu, same; very; own
tintu, bad, wicked, evil; dyed
vasciu, low, soft (e.g., voice)
vigurusu, vigorous; hard (e.g., by exertion)

Verbs (cont.)

livarisi (mi levu), to take off (e.g., a shirt)
(i)ncuntrari (ncontru), to encounter; meet
(i)nzignari (nzignu), to teach
proiri (proiu) (a), to hand (to), hand over (to), give (to)
pulizziari (pulizziu), to clean
sapiri, to taste, have a determinate taste
sbattiri, to bang; bump
scriviri (scrivu), to write
scummigghiari (scummogghiu), to uncover; reveal
scuntrari (scontru), to encounter; meet; run into; collide head on
scusari (scusu), to excuse
spiari (spiu), to ask, inquire
spugghiari (spogghiu), to deprive, strip
spugghiarisi (mi spogghiu), to undress
stuiari, to wipe
tagghiari (tagghiu), to cut
tastari, to taste
tinciri (tinciu), to dye; cheat
timpuliari (timpuliu), to slap, smack
togghiri, to take away, remove
trasiri (trasu) (ntra **or** nna), to enter
turmintari (turmentu), to torment; torture
tussiri (sc), to cough
viaggiari, to travel
viggilari (viggilu), to watch over, keep watch
vinirisinni (mi nni vegnu), to come from (a place)
viviri, to drink
vuliri mali, to hate
vutari (votu), to vote; turn

Adverbs

a prupositu **or** a propositu, by the way
macari, also, even
mai cchiù, never again
puru, also, even
na vota, once
du voti, twice
propiu **or** propriu, exactly; just; right
tuttavia, still; yet; nevertheless; however

Exercises

Exercise #1: Translate these proverbs into English and discuss what they mean.

(1) Parenti chi nun ti duna, amicu chi nun ti mpresta, fuili comu la pesta. (2) Cu s'assetta ntra du seggi sbatti lu culu n terra. (3) Cu avi mugghieri bedda sempri canta, cu avi dinari picca sempri cunta. (4) Chiddu ca fai a l'autri lu fai a tia. (5) Carciri, malatii e nicissitati scummogghianu lu cori di l'amici. (6) Amicu di gottu ti lassa ntra un bottu. (7) A to amicu veru parracci (parra a iddu) chiaru. (8) Cu campa tuttu l'annu tutti li festi vidi. (9) Arvulu chi nun fa fruttu, tagghialu di li radichi. (10) Lassalu friiri lu tintu omu ntra lu so stissu ogghiu.

Exercise #2: Translate these sentences into English.

(1) Dimmi chiddu ca voi e subbitu tû dugnu. (2) Oggi m'accattu dui libbra e dumani mî leggiu tutti dui. **Note:** *tutti i dui* is peculiar to the dialect of Messina. (3) Mi nni vaiu dumani e tu nun mi vidi mai cchiù. (4) Zoccu vuiatri vuliti fari, vuiatri putiti fari. (5) A vecchia si pigghia l'ogghiu e cciû metti nnâ padedda pi friiri u pisci. (6) I picciotti travagghianu (tantu) vigurusi comu ponnu. (7) A picciridda si scanta dû cani chi cci abbaia forti e chiama a so mamma câ vuci scantusa. (8) Pigghiati l'assegnu e scancialu. (9) Unni abbitanu ora? Nun î viu c'avi assai tempu. (10) Mi piaci leggiri libbra ntrissanti e canusciri pirsuni chi viaggianu pû munnu.

Exercise #3: Translate these sentences into Sicilian.

(1) You're the best one, and I'll never see you again. (2) Let me see you one more* time and I'll be happy. (3) Do you think that this is a comfortable bed? (4) This woman is small and old, and she can't see well. (5) Buy it now or tomorrow or someone else (qualchi autru cristianu) will buy it. (6) Tell me clearly what you want me to do, and I'll do it right away. (7) The peasant's family live in a small house near us. (8) I believe that he's a rich man, but George is richer than he. (9) I'll just sit down right here and light my pipe. (10) The polite old man enters the room, and I leave it.

* Put "more" before "one" in the Sicilian. **Hint:** Don't use "tempu".

Exercise #4: Say these sentences aloud. Don't worry about translating them at this point.

(1) Vattinni a cacciari. (2) U vinu mi fa doliri a testa. (3) Mi vaiu a curcari picchì aiu sonnu. (4) Ssu cappeddu so è grossu. (5) Quannu me matri cumanna, û fazzu. (6) Chista è a casa chi mi voli vinniri. (7) Mi dispiaci ma 'un pozzu manciari sta fedda di carni bruciata. Levala. (8) A picciridda s'ammuccia sutta u lettu e u picciriddu nun â pò truvari (**or** non pò truvalla). (9) Dumani partemu dû paisi pî Stati Uniti unni avemu parenti chi abbitanu a Nova York. (10) U vecchiu tussisci e parra accussì vasciu ca nun û putemu capiri (**or** nun putemu capillu) chiaramenti.

9   Numbers and Time Relations

Purpose of the Chapter

The chief purpose of this chapter is to give the cardinal and ordinal numbers in Sicilian. It also gives the days of the week, the months of the year, and the four seasons. Numbers consist of cardinal numbers (counting numbers) and ordinal numbers (telling the order of a thing).

Numbers

Cardinal numbers

unu (M), una (F)	1	trentacincu	35
dui (often abbreviated *du*)	2	trentasei	36
tri	3	trentasetti	37
quattru	4	trentottu	38
cincu	5	trentanovi	39
sei	6	quaranta	40
setti	7	cinquanta	50
ottu	8	sissanta	60
novi	9	sittanta	70
deci	10	ottanta	80
unnici	11	novanta	90
dudici	12	centu	100
tridici	13	centuunu (M), centuuna (F)	101
quattordici	14	centuunnici	111
quinnici **or** chinnici	15	centu vintidui	122
sidici	16	centu trentatri	133
diciassetti	17	centu quarantaquattru	144
diciottu (**or** diciadottu **or** diciarottu)	18	centu cinquantacincu	155
diciannovi	19	centu sissantasei	166
vinti	20	centu sittantasetti	177
vintunu (M), vintuna (F)	21	centu ottantottu	188
vintidui	22	centu novantanovi	199
vintitri	23	ducentu	200
vintiquattru	24	triccentu	300
vinticincu	25	quattrucentu	400
vintisei	26	cincucentu	500
vintisetti	27	seicentu	600
vintottu	28	setticentu	700
vintinovi	29	ottucentu	800
trenta	30	novicentu	900
trentunu (M), trentuna (F)	31	milli **or** middi	1,000
trentadui	32	dumila	2,000
trentatri	33	centumila	100,000
trentaquattru	34	un miliuni	1,000,000
		un miliardu	1,000,000,000

In the rest of the world, which uses the metric system, the use of commas and periods in writing numbers is just the reverse of our usage; la virgula, comma **versus** lu puntu, the point **or** period.

Examples
- un miliuni ottucentu sittantatrimila cincucentu trentunu 1.873.531 (Sicily); 1,873,531 (U.S.)
- triccentu cinquantadumila novicentuunnici 352.911 (Sicily); 352,911 (U.S.)
- dui virgula cinquantadui 2,52 (Sicily); 2.52 (U.S.)

Ordinal Numbers
The ordinal numbers are just like any other adjectives. Below only the masculine singular form is given. Since they are regular, the feminine singular, and common plural are formed in a regular fashion. Normally the ordinal number precedes the noun.

Example
primu (masculine singular)/prima (feminine singular)/primi (common plural), first

primu	first
secunnu	second
terzu	third
quartu	fourth
quintu	fifth
sestu	sixth
settimu	seventh
ottavu	eighth
nonu	ninth
decimu	tenth

Beyond *decimu*, the ordinal numbers are formed by taking the corresponding cardinal number, dropping the final vowel, and adding *-esimu*.

vintesimu	twentieth
trentesimu	thirtieth
quarantesimu	fourtieth
cinquantesimu	fiftieth
sissantesimu	sixtieth
sittantesimu	seventieth
ottantesimu	eightieth
novantesimu	ninetieth
centesimu	hundredth

and so on.

In most cases, the ordinal number precedes the noun it modifies. However, if used to denote a king, pope, etc., it's placed after the name (using a Roman numeral with the name). In this case, only the ordinals up to *decimu* are used. Past that, use the corresponding cardinal number. This is true of other situations as well. Actually, it's rare to find ordinals used past *decimu*.

Examples
- la prima classi, the first class
- la secunna lizzioni, the second lesson
- la terza stanza, the third room
- lu quartu omu, the fourth man
- lu quintu gottu, the fifth mug
- la vintunesima lizzioni, the twenty-first lesson **or** a lezzioni vintunu (more common)
- Enricu Ottavu, Henry VIII
- Piu Nonu, Pius IX
- Giuvanni Vintitriesimu, John XXIII

Ordinal numbers can be used as fractions.

Examples
- dui terzi, 2/3 = 0,667 (Sicily); 0.667 (U.S.)
- novi decimi, 9/10 = 0,9 (Sicily); 0.9 (U.S.)

Note: a mità (F), half; menzu, half (adjective **or** adverb).

Examples
- Usa menza porzioni di burru, un quartu d'ogghiu, Use a half portion of butter, quarter (portion) of oil
- menzu litru di vinu russu, half a liter of red wine
- tri quarti di litru di vinu, three quarters of a liter of wine

Approximate Numbers
Approximate numbers are sometimes used when an exact number isn't known.

na vintina, about twenty*
na trentina, about thirty
na quarantina, about forty
na cinquantina, about fifty
na sissantina, about sixty
na sittantina, about seventy
na ottantina, about eighty
na novantina, about ninety
un cintinaru, about a hundred (p -a)
un migghiaru, about a thousand (p -a)

Examples
(1) A fimmina avi na quarantina d'anni. The woman's about forty years old.
(2) Cc'è un cintinaru di pirsuni nna sta stanza. There's about a hundred people in this room.

Note: It's possible to express one's age in terms of *vintina* (twenty). Quant'anni avi? How old are you? Aiu du vintini e deci. I'm fifty. The use of *vintina* sounds as antiquated to a Sicilian today as the use of "score" for "twenty years" in English. What would you think of someone who replied to your question, "How old are you?" with "I'm two score and ten." If one wishes to say that he's about fifty, say: Aiu na cinquantina.

Arithmetic Calculations
cchiù, plus (+)
menu, minus (–)
pi, by (x)
divisu, divided by (÷)
fa, makes, equals

Examples
2 cchiù 3 fa 5 (2 + 3 = 5)
10 menu 8 fa 2 (10 – 8 = 2)
3 pi 5 fa 15 (3 x 5 = 15)
21 divisu 3 fa 7 (21 ÷ 3 = 7)

Time relations

Days of the Week
All of the days of the week are masculine except *duminica*, Sunday. They are not capitalized.

duminica **or** duminicaddì **or** duminicaddìa, Sunday
luneddì **or** luniddì **or** luniddìa **or** lunidi, Monday
marteddì **or** martiddì **or** martiddìa **or** martidi, Tuesday
mercoleddì **or** merculiddì **or** merculiddìa **or** mercuddì **or** mercuddìa **or** mercudi, Wednesday
gioveddì **or** giuviddì **or** giuviddìa **or** iuviddì **or** iuviddìa **or** iovidi, Thursday
venneddì **or** vinniddì **or** vinniddìa **or** vennadi, Friday
sabbatu **or** sabbatuddì **or** sabbatuddìa, Saturday

Examples
(1) Sabbatu vaiu a vidiri a me soru. On Saturday I'm going to see my sister.
(2) La duminica vaiu a vidiri a me frati. On Sundays I go to see my brother.
(3) Ogni lunidi vaiu a vidiri ê me zii. Every Monday I go to see my uncle and aunt.
(4) Tutti i sabbati tutta a famigghia s'arricogghiunu e mamma pripara nu bonu manciari pi niatri. Every Saturday the entire family gathers together, and mama prepares a good meal for us.
(5) Na vota â simana u prufissuri scrivi na littra a so soru. Once a week the professor writes a letter to his sister.
(6) Na vota ô misi u picciriddu cci porta un pumu â so prufissurissa. Once a month the little boy brings his teacher an apple.

Months of the Year
All of the months of the year are masculine. They are not capitalized.

innaru **or** ginnaru, January

frivaru, February
marzu, March
aprili, April
maiu **or** maggiu, May
giugnu, June
lugliu **or** giugnettu, July
austu **or** agustu, August
settembri **or** sittemmiru, Semtember
ottubri **or** utturu **or** uttuviru, October
novembri **or** nuvemmiru, November
dicembri **or** dicemmiru, December

Note: Older Sicilian used the ordinal *prima* when referring to the first day of the month. This is no longer done. Now *primu* is used. After that use a cardinal number.

Examples
- lu primu d'aprili **or** la prima d'aprili, the first of April, April 1
- lu dui di giugnu, the second of June, June 2
- l'ottu d'austu, the eighth of August, August 8
- l'urtimu di settembri **or** l'**urtima di sittemmiru**, the last (day) of September

Seasons of the Year
Two of the seasons of the year are masculine, and two are feminine.

la primavera, spring
la stati **or** l'estati (F), summer
l'autunnu, autumn
l'immernu (mmernu) **or** l'invernu (nvernu), winter

Vocabulary

Nouns
l'agneddu, lamb (p -a or -i)
l'amu, hook
l'annu, year
l'asciuttu, dryness, drought
l'avvucatu **or** abbucatu, lawyer
la biddizza, beauty
bunazza, calm (of the sea), tranquility (of the sea)
la buttigghia, bottle
la canigghia, bran, chaff (worthless outer husk)
lu caudu, heat
lu chiummu, lead (the metal)
la cuda, tail
la dieta, diet
la disgrazzia, misfortune, bad luck
la fami, hunger
la farina, flour
lu ferru, iron
la fini, end

Verbs
abbaiari, to bark
abbannunari (abbannunu), to abandon, leave
arrifarisi (m'arrifazzu), to make oneself over
  again; recover (e.g., one's health)
arrinesciri, to succeed at (arrinesciu)
arristari (arrestu) **or** ristari (restu), to remain, stay
ascutari (ascutu), to listen to (takes direct object)
avanzari, to advance; surpass
cacari, to defecate, shit
cadiri, to fall
chiantari, to plant
ciuriri **or** sciuriri (sc), to flower
cogghiri (cogghiu), to pick; gather
curriri (curru), to run
duminari (dominu), to dominate
fabbricari (fabbricu) **or** frabbicari (frabbicu), to build
ficcari (ficcu), to thrust; push
ficcarisi (mi ficcu), to insinuate oneself

106

Nouns (cont.)

la fini di la (**or** dâ) simana, end of the week
lu fini, purpose, goal, aim
la furtuna, fortune
lu fruttu, fruit (p -a **or** -i)
la gaddina, hen
lu gaddinaru, chicken coop (p -a)
lu guaiu, woe, misfortune (p guai)
l'isca, bait
lu iudici, judge
la lana, wool
lu latti, milk
lu meli, honey
lu misi, month
lu mortu, dead man
la muddica, crumb; soft part of bread
lu munnizzaru, dung heap; rubbish pile (p –a)
lu murticeddu, present given on November 2*
lu mustu, must (juice extracted from grapes)
l'oddiu, hatred
l'oricchia **or** l'aricchia, ear
la paci, peace
lu paradisu, paradise
lu pazzu, fool (**Literal meaning:** crazy man)
la pecura, sheep
la peddi, skin; hide (of an animal)
lu plausu, applause; thanks
la porta, door
lu poviru, poor man
lu prisidenti, president
lu pugnu, fist (p -a)
lu puvireddu, poor little one (diminutive)
la raggia, anger, rage; rabies
la raggiuni, reason (e.g., man's reason)
la rama, branch
la rota, wheel
lu sangu, blood
lu saviu, wise person
lu sbagghiu, mistake, error
lu seculu, century
la simenza, seed
la siti, thirst
la spata, sword
la staciuni **or** la stagiuni, season
la testa, head
l'ura, hour
la vintura, fortune, destiny, fate
lu voscu, woods, forest (p –ura **or** -i)
lu vrazzu, arm (p -a)

Verbs (cont.)

finciri (finciu), to pretend, feign
maturari (maturu), to mature, ripen
migghiurari (migghiuru), to improve, better
(i)mmagginarisi (m'immagginu), to imagine
murmuriari (murmuriu), to murmur
(i)ngarzari [dz], to take a mistress
(i)nnamurarisi (m'innamuru) (di), to fall in love
    (with), be in love (with)
nasciri (nasciu), to be born
priparari (priparu), to prepare
prividiri, to foresee (like vidiri)
ridiri (riu **or** ridu), to laugh
risparmiari (risparmiu), to save, economize
scanzari, to avoid, shun; save, rescue
scippari (scippu), to extract, pull out
sfragari, to waste, to squander
siccari (siccu), to dry up, wither away
sparagnari, to save up, spare (e.g., a life)
stirari (stiru), to flatten, stretch out; iron
taciri (taciu), to be silent, remain silent
tuppuliari (tuppuliu), to knock
veniri a vidiri, to come to see, visit
vinciri (vinciu) to conquer, win
visitari (visitu), to visit, call on

Adjectives

arrinisciutu (past participle of *arrinesciri*),
    successful
asciuttu, dry; skinny
bastibbili, enough, sufficient
caudu, hot
curtu, short
longu, long; tall
mortu, dead
niuru **or** niru, black; dark; gloomy
orvu **or** orbu, blind
pazzu, crazy; foolish
pisanti, heavy
prividutu (past participle of *prividiri*), foreseen
poviru, poor
riccu, rich
saviu, wise, prudent
scioccu, silly, foolish
siccu, thin, skinny; weak
stupennu, stupendous
tirribbili, terrible
tinaci, stubborn, tenacious
vivu, alive; alert

---

* *murticedda* = presents given to children and exchanged between sweethearts on All Souls Day, November 2. **Literal meaning:** Little dead ones. All Souls Day is an important feast day in Sicily.

Exercises

Exercise #1: Translate these proverbs into English and discuss what they mean. Also say these sentences aloud.

(1) Ogni santu avi a so festa. (2) Ogni gaddu canta ntra lu so munnizzaru. (3) L'acqua di austu fa ogghiu, meli, e mustu. (4) Innaru è menzu duci e menzu amaru. (5) Quannu n sittemmiru caudu e asciuttu domina, la terra si pripara pi la simenza. (6) Nuvembri è lu misi di li murticeddi. (7) Un sittemmiru caudu e asciuttu fa maturari ogni fruttu. **Note:** See (5) which also refers to September. (8) Frivaru lu curtu è lu peiu di tutti. (9) Aprili fa li ciuri e li biddizzi e nn'avi plausu lu misi di maiu. (10) Finu a l'autunnu dura la bunazza. (11) L'unu nun dici mai chiddu chi fa e l'autru nun fa mai chiddu chi dici. (12) Quannu lu mmernu non avi testa, avi cuda. (13) I iardina siccanu e i munnizzara ciurisciunu. (14) Lu mercudi è mmenzu la simana. (15) Cu sapi finciri sapi vinciri. (16) Furtuna è rota e va e veni. (17) Annu a veniri li me iorna. (18) Chianta arvuli ntra la vigna, si nun cogghi frutta, cogghi ligna. (19) L'arvulu chi d'aprili nun fa ciuri, mancu nni fa ntra l'autra staciuni. (20) A picca a picca l'amuri si ficca. (21) Casa senza suli, trasi lu medicu a tutti l'uri. (22) Mentri lu ferru è caudu si stira. (23) Disgrazzia prividuta menu si senti. (24) Amara la pecura ca duna la lana. (25) Cu ti voli beni ti fa chianciri e cu ti voli mali ti fa ridiri. (26) Fabbricanu li pazzi la casa, li savii l'accattanu. (27) Li dinari di lu sagristanu cantannu veninu e cantannu si nni vannu. (28) Amuri si sapi comu nasci e nun si sapi comu finisci. (29) Cu amuri ti pigghiu e cu raggia ti lassu. (30) Cu avi manu friddi è nnamuratu e cu avi manu caudi è ngarzatu. (31) Cani ca abbaia ettacci n'ossu. (32) Guai a dda casa unni a gaddina canta e u gaddu taci. (33) Sparagnari la canigghia e sfragari la farina. (34) Manciari l'isca e cacari l'amu. (35) Iddu avi un vrazzu longu e unu curtu. (36) Iddu parra quantu un iudici. (37) Lu iudici avi ad aviri dui oricchi. (38) Iudici, prisidenti e avvucati, ntô paradisu nun cci sunnu truvati. (39) Cu mancia fa muddichi. (40) A cu avi furtuna ogni cosa cci va bona.

Exercise #2: Make up some sentences in Sicilian. Try your skill and see if you can compose some proverbs on your own. If you are taking Sicilian in a classroom setting, have your instructor check them. Here are some sample sentences. Translate them into English.

(1) Cu avi prescia, fa sbagghi. (2) Mi doli arristari cu tia però mi doli di cchiù lassariti. (3) U vintesimu seculu fu tirribbili. U vintunesimu seculu sarà megghiu pi l'umanità? (4) L'amuri è megghiu di l'oddiu. (5) Nna na manu tegnu a spata e nna l'autra tegnu a rama di paci.

10   Conjunctions

Purpose of the Chapter
The chief purpose of this chapter is to discuss clauses and conjunctions. A clause is a part of a sentence containing a noun phrase and a verb phrase. In the case of simple sentences, the clause is the sentence itself. However, for compound sentences (two independent clauses joined together) and for complex sentences (an independent clause joined with a dependent clause whose meaning depends on the independent clause), some sort of conjunction (joining word) is normally required.

Coordinating Conjunctions
Coordinating conjunctions (coordinators) combine two independent clauses to create a compound sentence. The most important coordinating conjunctions in Sicilian are:

e[+], and
ma[+], but
però **or** parò, however; but
o[+]...o[+], either...or
nè[+]...nè[+] **or** ni[+] ...ni[+], neither...nor

Note: Recall that the superscript plus ([+]) indicates a gemination-causing word. Don't use the [+] in spelling.

Examples
(1) A fimmina va a fari a spisa e so maritu è n casa. The woman is going shopping, and her husband is at home.
(1) Viu a l'omu nnô parcu e poi m'avvicinu. I see the man in the park, and I approach.
(2) Aiu a vogghia di fallu ma non pozzu. I have the urge to do it, but I can't.
(3) Iu dissi ca cci ieva però ora non cci vogghiu iri. I said that I'd go; however, now I don't want to.
(4) Mi vogghiu accattari stu libbru però nun aiu abbastanza sordi. I want to buy this book, but I don't have enough money.
(5) O û dici Vanni o û dici chiddu (**or** l'autru). Either John'll say it or the other fellow will.
(6) Nè so cugnatu nè so ziu diciunu nenti. **or** Non diciunu nenti nè so cugnatu nè so ziu. Neither his brother-in-law nor his uncle says anything.

Subordinating Conjunctions
Subordinating conjunctions (subordinators) combine an independent clause (main clause) with a subordinate clause (dependent clause) to create a complex sentence. The correct punctuation is if the subordinate clause comes first, a comma is placed after the end of the clause, especially if the clause is long. If the subordinate clause follows the main clause, in general a comma isn't needed. The most important subordinating conjunctions in Sicilian are the ones listed here. In some cases one of the coordinators precedes the subordinator. See the examples below.

Note: Almost all the subordinating conjunctions utilize *chi* or alternatively *ca*. To simplify the list, only the form of the conjunction with *chi* will be listed. **Example:** finu chi (*finu ca* is also acceptable). Both *chi* and *ca* are gemination-causing, but since you know this by now, the superscript plus (⁺) indicating this fact will be left off. If *chi* is combined to form one word, it carries a grave accent. **Example:** picchì, because.

Some of the subordinating conjunctions are followed by the verb in the subjunctive mood if the verb in the subordinate clause refers to or is felt to imply past time. These conjunctions are noted by using the notation (subjunctive) after the conjunction. Examples of conjunctions triggering the subjunctive in the subordinate clause will be covered in more detail in Chapter 13. In the sentences below, to make them more realistic, some of the verb forms utilize one of the past tense forms. See Chapter 11, **Verbs: Past Time**. Don't worry too much about this at this point. Just observe the forms. After studying Chapter 11, the various distinctions will become clearer.

(a) menu chi, unless (subjunctive)
a pattu chi, provided that (subjunctive)
ancorchì, even though, although (subjunctive)
benchì **or** binchì, although (subjunctive)
ca (in some of the *parrati*, also *chi*), that, because, so that (subjunctive if the meaning is "so that") **Note:** Remember that English doesn't always require the conjunction "that", but Sicilian does.
comu, as, when, how
comu si, as if (subjunctive)
cu tuttu chi, although (subjunctive)
datu chi, given that
doppu **or** doppu chi, after (time)
dunca **or** nca, thus, therefore, for this reason (strictly speaking an adverb)
eccettu chi non, except that, unless (subjunctive)
finu chi **or** fina chi **or** sinu chi **or** sina chi, until (sometimes requires the subjunctive)
giacchì **or** già ca, now that, since
masinnò **or** vasinnò, otherwise (strictly speaking an adverb)
nnô modu chi **or** (i)n modu chi, so that, in order that (subjunctive)
ntantu, meanwhile (strictly speaking an adverb)
mentri **or** mentri chi, while
nostanti chi **or** nustanti chi, notwithstanding that; although (subjunctive)
nnô casu chi, in case that (subjunctive)
nunnimenu, nevertheless; however (strictly speaking an adverb)
pi chissu, for that reason; therefore (strictly speaking a prepositional phrase)
pi chistu, for this reason; therefore (strictly speaking a prepositional phrase)
pirciò **or** perciò, so, therefore, as a consequence (strictly speaking an adverb)
picchì **or** pirchì, because
picchì **or** pirchì, so that, in order that (subjunctive)
prima chi, before (time) (subjunctive)
puru chi, although
puru si, even if
quannu **or** quannu chi, when
sarvu chi non, unless (subjunctive)

sebbeni, although, even though (subjunctive)

secunnu chi, according to, as, so (subjunctive)

senza chi, unless, without (subjunctive)

si[+] or siddu or su, if (sometimes requires the subjunctive)

siccomu, as, since

tuttavia, nevertheless; yet; still; however (strictly speaking an adverb)

unni, where, wherever

vistu chi, since; seen that

Examples

(1) U picciottu studia assai e perciò va a essiri (vâ siri) prumossu. The boy studies a lot; therefore, he's going to pass.

(2) Vaiu a fallu picchì aiu a vogghia. I'm going to do it because I feel like it.

(3) U giustu è difficili fari secunnu chi parrau u prufeta. The right thing is difficult to do; so spoke the prophet.

(4) Mentri chi u bebbè (u picciriddu) durmia, a mamma cci cantava na ninna nanna. While the baby was sleeping, the mother was singing a lullaby to it.

(5) Puru ca Eduardu parra sicilianu câ so famigghia e chî so parenti, parra talianu nnâ scola. Although Edward speaks Sicilian with his family and his relatives, he speaks Italian in school.

(6) Puru si me matri mi cumanna, nun û fazzu. Even if my mother commands me, I won't do it.

(7) Mi cedi a via a mia (or mi lassa passari) ca sugnu vecchiu. He yields me the right of way because I'm old.

(8) Iddu capisci ca avi tortu. He understands that he's wrong.

(9) Iu liggia u giurnali e ntantu me mugghieri mi stirava a cammisa. I was reading a newspaper; meanwhile, my wife was ironing my shirt.

(10) Giacchì era na picciotta bedda, si maritau prestu. Since she was a beautiful young woman, she married quickly. **Sicilian proverb:** Cu nasci bedda, nasci maritata. She who is born beautiful is born married.

(11) Picchì tu sì povira e non ai nudda dota, iddu non si marita cu tia. Because you are poor and have no dowry, he will not marry you.

(12) Dunca iddu capisci megghiu zoccu avi a fari. Therefore he understands better what he must do.

(13) Prima chi so patri trasiu nnâ stanza, i picciriddi iucavanu chî so giucattuli. Before their father entered the room, the children were playing with their toys.

(14) Nustanti ca Giorgiu avi i sordi, non avi spinnu d'accattarisi na machina nova. Although George has the money, he has no wish to buy a new car.

Vocabulary

Nouns

l'ancilu, angel

lu cappeddu, hat (p -a)

lu carvuni, coal

lu cavaleri, horseman; nobleman

la ciamma or la sciamma, flame

la coppula, cap

lu cristianu, Catholic; fellow, person

Verbs

addunarisi (m'addugnu) (di), to notice; become aware (of)

arricriari (arricriu), to please; amuse

arricriarisi (m'arricriu), to please oneself; amuse oneself

arriminari (arriminu), to stir, shake up

arrustiri (arrustu or arrustisciu), to roast

111

Nouns (cont.)

lu cunzigghiu, advice, counsel
lu debbitu, debt
lu diamanti, diamond
l'erruri (M), error
lu fattu, fact; deed
la fedda, slice
la forza, strength, force, power
lu fumeri, dung; filth
la gloria, glory
la guerra, war
lu medicu, doctor (p medici)
la mircanzia, goods, merchandise
lu munzeddu, heap, pile
lu muscu, moss
lu nasu, nose
l'incendiu (ncendiu), fire (destructive)
lu nessu, link; connection
lu nomu, name
la nuci, walnut
la nucidda, hazelnut; nut (in general)
lu paisi, village; town; country*
lu pani, bread
lu panuzzu, bread, dear bread (diminutive)
la panza, belly, stomach
lu piccatu, sin, trespass
lu pisci, fish
lu pulici, flea
lu raggiu, ray; beam (e.g., sun); radius
lu regnu, kingdom
lu riposu, rest, quiet
lu ritrattu, picture; portrait
la ruina, ruin; collapse; downfall
lu santu, saint
lu sarvaturi, savior
la scarpa, shoe
lu scutu, the shield
li scuti, money (especially paper money)
lu sonnu, sleep; dream
la spina, thorn; (fish) bone
la tintazzioni, temptation
lu turcu, non-Catholic†; Turk
la vampa, flame
lu vinu, wine
lu vizziu, vice, defect (moral)
la vuluntà or voluntà, will

Verbs (cont.)

brillari, to shine, sparkle
bruciari (bruciu) or abbruciari, to burn, scorch
cacciari, to hunt, chase
crisciri (crisciu), to grow, grow up
cumannari, to command
cunzari (conzu), to repair; set in order, adjust
cunzigghiari (cunzigghiu), to counsel, advise
ciusciari (ciusciu) or sciusciari, to blow
fici, I did, he did; I made, he made
(i)ncugnari (ncugnu), to press against, push;
    approach
pagari, to pay
piccari (peccu), to sin; trespass
pinzari (penzu), to think
pirdunari (pirdugnu or pirdunu), to pardon
pisciari, to urinate, piss
raccumannari, to recommend
riparari, to repair; protect (e.g., from something)
santificari (santificu), to make holy, sanctify
scantari, to frighten, scare
scantarisi, to be frightened
sviari (sviu), to lead stray
tussiri (sc), to cough
valiri, to be worth
vizziari (vizziu or vizziu), to spoil, corrupt

Adjectives

abbastanza, enough (invariable)
azzolu, blue
biancu or vrancu or iancu, white
blu, blue (invariable)
cristianu, Catholic
cuntenti, happy, content
cuntentu, happy, content
giarnu or giannu, yellow
libbiru, free
liggeru, light, slight
santu, holy, hallowed
tristu, sad; mean
turcu, non-Catholic†; Turkish
urtimu or ultimu, last
umili, humble; unpretentious
virdi, green

Adverbs

abbastanza, enough
vulinteri, willingly

* The meaning depends on the context.

† In general, the term refers to any non-Catholic, regardless of race, creed, or nationality. This includes unbaptized children. Specifically, it means a "Turk", or if an adjective "Turkish".

Exercises

Exercise #1: Translate these proverbs into English and discuss what they mean. Also say these sentences aloud.

(1) Di lu carvuni si scippa nu diamanti. (2) Chiddu arrusti u so pisci ntê ciammi d'incendiu. (3) Pri assai cunzigghi si perdi la guerra. (4) Pisciacci supra i ruini prima ca addiventanu muschi. (5) Pulici porta cu dormi cû cani. (6) Li guai di la pignata li sapi la cucchiara chi l'arrimina. (7) Vali cchiù un fattu di centu paroli. (Note the word order.) (8) L'abbaiari dû cani non fa scantari i nuvuli. (9) Cu nun voli focu, livassi* i ligna. (10) L'occhiu mancia cchiù di la panza.

* This is a subjunctive form of the 3rd person singular being used as a command. Translate it as "let him take away".

Exercise #2: Translate the Lord's Prayer into Sicilian. Use the *tu* pronoun for the deity.

(1) Our father, who art in heaven, (2) hallowed be thy name, (3) thy kingdom come, thy will be done on earth as it is in heaven. (4) Give us this day our daily bread, and forgive us our sins, (5) as we forgive those who do evil to us, (6) and let us not fall into temptation, (7) but save us from evil. (8) Amen.

Exercise #3: Translate Exercise #4 of Chapters 5, 6, 7, and 8.

Exercise #4: Read this poem aloud, translate it, and try to memorize it. The source of this poem is Carmelo Caracè, *Parlar siciliano* (Firenze: Edizione Del Riccio, 1980), p. 253.

Nesci, nesci, suli, suli*
pi lu santu Sarvaturi.
Etta un pugnu di dinari,
arricria li cristiani.
Etta un pugnu di nuciddi
arricria li picciriddi.
Etta un pugnu di fumeri
arricria li cavaleri.

* Here *nesciri* means "to rise" or "to come out".

11   Verbs: Past Time

Purpose of the Chapter
We've already taken up how Sicilian verbs form the present and future time. The chief purpose of this chapter is to present the different tenses used in Sicilian to convey past time. Past time in Sicilian is more complicated than present or future time because there are four tenses for past time, but they don't have exactly the same usage or meanings. In addition, two of these tenses are simple tenses, that is, they do not require an auxiliary, or helping, verb such as *aviri*, and two of them are compound tenses, that is, they do employ a helping verb, namely, *aviri*. The uses of the various past tenses are distinguished, and in addition, irregular preterites and past participles are given.

The tenses of the past are:

- Imperfect (simple tense);
- Preterite (simple tense);
- Present perfect (compound tense – present of *aviri* + past particle);
- Past perfect (compound tense – imperfect of *aviri* + past particle).

Imperfect
The imperfect tense is very regular in its formation. As with the present tense, add the verbal endings (indicated in italics) to the stem of the verb. **Note:** To simplify the presentation, only one translation into English has been given out of the several possibilities. The Examples below illustrate the several different ways to translate the imperfect.

Conjugation 1
parrari, to speak
iu parr*ava*, I spoke*
tu parr*avi*, you spoke
vossìa parr*ava*, you spoke
iddu parr*ava*, he spoke
nuiatri parr*avamu*, we spoke
vuiatri parr*avavu*, you spoke
iddi parr*avanu* **or** parr*avunu*, they spoke

Conjugation 2
rispunniri, to reply
iu rispunn*ia*, I replied[†]
tu rispunn*ivi*, you replied
vossìa rispunn*ia*, you replied
iddu rispunn*ia*, he replied
nuiatri rispunn*iamu*, we replied
vuiatri rispunn*iavu*, you replied
iddi rispunn*ianu*, they replied

Conjugation 2 (alternate forms)
iu rispunn*eva* **or** rispunn*iva*, I replied[‡]
tu rispunn*evi* **or** rispunn*ivi*, you replied
vossìa rispunn*eva* **or** rispunn*iva*, you replied
iddu rispunn*eva* **or** rispunn*iva*, he replied
nuiatri rispunn*evamu* **or** rispunn*ivamu*, we replied
vuiatri rispunn*evavu* **or** rispunn*ivavu*, you replied
iddi rispunn*evanu* **or** rispunn*ivanu*, they replied

* The form *parravu* is also found.
† The form *rispunniu* is also found. **Note:** This form can be confused with preterite forms.
‡ The forms *rispunnevu* and *rispunnivu* are also found.

Several verbs have an irregular imperfect: *essiri*, *diri* (it's regular if you remember that the old infinitive is *diciri*), *fari* (it's regular if you remember that the old infinitive is *faciri*), and *iri*, the latter having both regular forms and forms as if it were a Conjugation 1 verb.

Verbs Having an Irregular Imperfect	Imperfect Forms
essiri, to be	**Singular forms:** iu era, tu eri, vossìa era, iddu era **Plural forms:** nuiatri eramu, vuiatri eravu, iddi eranu **or** erunu
diri, to say, tell	**Singular forms:** iu dicia **or** diceva **or** diciva, tu dicivi **or** dicevi, vossìa dicia **or** diceva **or** diciva, iddu dicia **or** diceva **or** diciva **Plural forms:** nuiatri diciamu **or** dicevamu **or** dicivamu, vuiatri diciavu **or** dicevavu **or** dicivavu, iddi dicianu **or** dicevanu **or** dicivanu
fari, to do, make	**Singular forms:** iu facia **or** faceva **or** faciva, tu facivi **or** facevi, vossìa facia **or** faceva **or** faciva, iddu facia **or** faceva **or** faciva **Plural forms:** nuiatri faciamu **or** facevamu **or** facivamu, vuiatri faciavu **or** facevavu **or** facivavu, iddi facianu **or** facevanu **or** facivanu
iri, to go	**Singular forms:** iu ia **or** iava **or** eva /yeva/, tu ivi **or** iavi **or** evi /yevi/, vossìa ia **or** iava **or** eva /yeva/, iddu ia **or** iava **or** eva **Plural forms:** nuiatri iamu **or** iavamu **or** evamu /yevamu/, vuiatri iavu **or** iavavu **or** evavu /yevavu/, iddi ianu **or** iavanu **or** evanu /yevanu/

Note: The spelling rules pointed out above in Chapter 5 also affect verbs in their imperfect forms. In the imperfect, the accent in every case falls on the endings. Therefore, if a verb is a stem-changing verb, the theme vowel is in its unstressed form. **Examples:** purtava, I carried; ripitia, I repeated, liggia, I read; vulava, I flew, etc.

Uses and Meanings of the Imperfect
Several different meanings can be given for the imperfect tense. It refers to an indefinite block of time in which some action or event was taking place. Since this is the case, the imperfect can apply to several distinct kinds of activities in the past. Using *parrava* as a model, it can be translated as: I spoke, I was speaking, I used to speak, I (habitually) would speak, I kept on speaking, I continued to speak. The translation depends on the specific context. Very often if there is an adverb in the sentence, it will give a clue as to which meaning is intended.

- Habitual or repeated action in the past (often translated with "would" or "used to" in English). **Example:** Ogni matina Anna cci dicia «bon giornu» a so patri. Every morning Anne would say "good morning" to her father.

- A general action or state continuing in the past as opposed to a single point-action in the past. **Example:** U prufissuri liggia nnâ bibbliuteca. The professor was reading in the library.
- General description of events in the past (used as a general narrative tense in the past). **Example:** Cc'era na vota un picciriddu chi caminava nni so nanna. Once upon a time there was a little boy who was walking to his grandmother's.
- Two past actions going on simultaneously. **Example:** Mentri ca idda manciava, guardava â televisioni. While she was eating, she was looking at television.
- An action occurring in the background (imperfect) when a sudden action happens (preterite). **Example:** Quannu mi chiamau (preterite – see below), era nnô iardinu. When he called me, I was in the garden.
- An occasional replacement for the conditional. **Example:** Iu tû dicia si putissi. I would tell it to you if I could. **Better Sicilian:** Iu tû dicissi si puteva.

Examples
(1) Ogni iornu ia â bibbliuteca pi studiari i me lizzioni. Every day I used to go to the library to study my lessons. (habitual action)
(2) Na vota ô misi u picciriddu cci purtava un pumu grossu e russu â prufissurissa. Once a month the little boy would bring his teacher a big, red apple. (habitual action)
(3) U vecchiu ripitia a stissa parola varii voti. The old man kept repeating the same word over and over. (repeated action in the past)
(4) Nnê misi di innaru e frivaru u tempu facia veru bruttu e friddu. In January and February the weather was really ugly and cold. (general state in the past)
(5) Quannu era picciridda, a me famigghia abbitava nnâ Sicilia. When I was a little girl, my family lived in Sicily. (general state in the past)
(6) I Franchi avianu sempri sufficienti dinari ma nun era na famigghia filici. The Franchis always had enough money, but they weren't a happy family. (general condition in the past)
(7) L'oraturi parrava e parrava ma nun û sintia nuddu. The orator kept on talking and talking, but no one was listening to him. (habital action and general state in the past)
(8) Cc'era na vota nu cunigghiu chi s'immagginava d'essiri un picciriddu. Once upon a time there was a rabbit who thought he was a little boy. (general state in the past)
(9) Iu liggia u giurnali e me mogghi nni priparava a cena. I was reading the newspaper, and my wife was preparing the evening meal for us. (two past actions going on simultaneously)
(10) Mentri chi iu parrava (imperfect), l'omu chi gridava forti trasiu (preterite) subbitu e cu forza nnâ stanza. While I was speaking (background action), the man (who was) shouting (general state in the past) loudly suddenly burst into the room.
(11) Mentri chi iddu niscia (imperfect) dâ casa, a fimmina cci desi (preterite) na timpulata. While he was leaving the house (background action), the woman gave him a slap. (single point-action occurring in the past)
(12) U sabbatu ia ô cinima e doppu vidia a me zita. On Saturdays I used to go to the movies and afterwards I would see my fianceé. (one habitual action followed by another)

Imperfect of aviri a + infinitive

aviri a accattari, to have to buy

Literary	Literary and spoken	Spoken
iu avia a accattari	aviâ accattari	aviâ 'ccattari
tu avivi a accattari	avivâ accattari	avivâ 'ccattari
vossìa avia a accattari	aviâ accattari	aviâ 'ccattari
iddu avia a accattari	aviâ accattari	aviâ 'ccattari
nuiatri aviamu a accattari	aviamâ accattari	aviamâ 'ccattari
vuiatri aviavu a accattari	aviavâ accattari	aviavâ 'ccattari
iddi avianu a accattari	avianâ accattari	avianâ 'ccattari

Note: All the abbreviated forms are gemination-causing words: aviâ[+], avivâ[+], aviamâ[+], aviavâ[+], avianâ[+].

Preterite

The preterite tense is that of a single point-action in the past. **Caution:** In form the preterite resembles the Italian *passato remoto*, but it is not used in the same way. In fact, in much of Italy today the *passato remoto* is used only as a literary form much like the French *passé défini*. It has been replaced by the *passato prossimo*. This is not the case in Sicilian. The usage of the Sicilian preterite is more akin to the preterite in Spanish and Portuguese. It can refer to an action that occurred a split second ago or to one that occurred long ago in the distant past. The regular forms are given below for the two conjugations. As usual, the appropriate verbal endings (shown in italics) are added to the verb stem.

Conjugation 1
parrari, to speak
iu parr*ai*, I spoke*
tu parr*asti*, you spoke
vossìa parr*au* **or** parr*ò*, you spoke
iddu parr*au* **or** parr*ò*, he spoke
nuiatri parr*ammu* **or** parr*amu*, we spoke[‡]
vuiatri parr*astivu*, you spoke**
iddi parr*arunu* **or** parr*aru*, they spoke[††]

Conjugation 2
rispunniri, to reply
iu rispunn*ivi*, I replied[†]
tu rispunn*isti*, you replied
vossìa rispunn*iu*, you replied
iddu rispunn*iu*, he replied
nuiatri rispunn*emmu* **or** rispunn*emu*, we replied[‡]
vuiatri rispunn*istivu*, you replied**
iddi rispunn*erunu* **or** rispunn*eru*, they replied[††]

* The forms *parravi, parraiu* and *parravu* are also commonly found.
† The forms *rispunnii, rispunniu* and *rispunnivu* are also commonly found.
‡ The form with double *m* is more frequently found than formerly, probably because of the influence of Italian.
** The forms *parrastu* and *rispunnistu* are also found.
†† The forms *parraru* and *rispunneru* are abbreviations of the longer forms, but are common.

Note: Remember also that the spelling rules pointed out above in Chapter 5 affect verbs in their preterite forms. In the preterite, the accent in every case falls on the endings. Therefore, if a verb is a stem-changing verb, the theme vowel is in its unstressed form. **Examples:** purt*ai*, I carried; ripit*ivi*, I repeated, ligg*ivi*, I read; vul*ai*, I flew, etc.

Irregular Preterites

Some verbs have irregular preterites. The verbs in the table below are the most important ones that you are likely to encounter. Irregular forms are found for the following: 1st person singular, 3rd person singular, 1st person plural, and 3rd person plural. The 2nd person singular and the 2nd person plural are always regular. The infinitive will be given followed by its preterite forms.

Verbs Having an Irregular Preterite	Preterite Forms
aviri, to have	**Singular forms:** iu appi **or** ebbi, tu avisti, vossìa appi **or** ebbi, iddu appi **or** ebbi **Plural forms:** nuiatri **appimu or** ebbimu, vuiatri avistivu, iddi **appiru or** ebbiru
cridiri, to believe, think*	**Singular forms:** iu critti, tu cridisti, vossìa critti, iddu critti **Plural forms:** nuiatri crittimu, vuiatri cridistivu, iddi crittiru
dari, to give	**Singular forms:** iu detti **or** desi, tu dasti, vossìa detti **or** desi, iddu detti **or** desi **Plural forms:** nuiatri dettimu **or** desimu, vuiatri dastivu, iddi dettiru **or** desiru
diri, to say, tell	**Singular forms:** iu dissi, tu dicisti, vossìa dissi, iddu dissi **Plural forms:** nuiatri dissimu, vuiatri dicistivu, iddi dissiru
essiri, to be	**Singular forms:** iu fui, tu fusti, vossìa fu⁺, iddu fu⁺ **Plural forms:** nuiatri fomu, vuiatri fustivu, iddi foru
fari, to do, make	**Singular forms:** iu fici, tu facisti, vossìa fici, iddu fici **Plural forms:** nuiatri ficimu, vuiatri facistivu, iddi ficiru
grapiri, to open†	**Singular forms:** iu aprivi, tu apristi, vossìa apriu, iddu apriu **Plural forms:** nuiatri apremmu, vuiatri apristivu, iddi apreru
mettiri, to put	**Singular forms:** iu misi, tu mittisti, vossìa misi, iddu misi **Plural forms:** nuiatri misimu, vuiatri mittistivu, iddi misiru
ntenniri, to hear, understand	**Singular forms:** iu ntisi, tu ntinnisti, vossìa ntisi, iddu ntisi **Plural forms:** nuiatri ntisimu, vuiatri ntinnistivu, iddi ntisiru
pariri, to seem	**Singular forms:** iu parsi, tu paristi, vossìa parsi, iddu parsi **Plural forms:** nuiatri parsimu, vuiatri paristivu, iddi parsiru
perdiri, to lose‡	**Singular forms:** iu persi, tu pirdisti, vossìa persi, iddu persi **Plural forms:** nuiatri persimu, vuiatri pirdistivu, iddi persiru
poniri, to place, set	**Singular forms:** iu posi, tu punisti, vossìa posi, iddu posi **Plural forms:** nuiatri posimu, vuiatri punistivu, iddi posiru
putiri, to be able	**Singular forms:** iu potti, tu putisti, vossìa potti, iddu potti **Plural forms:** nuiatri pottimu, vuiatri putistivu, iddi pottiru

Verbs Having an Irregular Preterite (cont.)	Preterite Forms
rispunniri, to respond**	**Singular forms:** iu rispusi, tu rispunnisti, vossìa rispusi, iddu rispusi **Plural forms:** nuiatri rispusimu, vuiatri rispunnistivu, iddi rispusiru
sapiri, to know	**Singular forms:** iu sappi, tu sapisti, vossìa sappi, iddu sappi **Plural forms:** nuiatri sappimu, vuiatri sapistivu, iddi sappiru
scriviri, to write††	**Singular forms:** iu scrissi, tu scrivisti, vossìa scrissi, iddu scrissi **Plural forms:** nuiatri scrissimu, vuiatri scrivistivu, iddi scrissiru
stari, to stay, dwell	**Singular forms:** iu stetti **or** stesi, tu stasti, vossìa stetti **or** stesi, iddu stetti **or** stesi **Plural forms:** nuiatri stettimu **or** stesimu, vuiatri stastivu, iddi stettiru **or** stesiru
teniri, to hold, keep‡‡	**Singular forms:** iu tinni, tu tinisti, vossìa tinni, iddu tinni **Plural forms:** nuiatri tinnimu, vuiatri tinistivu, iddi tinniru
veniri, to come	**Singular forms:** iu vinni, tu vinisti, vossìa vinni, iddu vinni **Plural forms:** nuiatri vinnimu, vuiatri vinistivu, iddi vinniru
vidiri, to see	**Singular forms:** iu vitti **or** visti, tu vidisti, vossìa vitti **or** visti, iddu vitti **or** visti **Plural forms:** nuiatri vittimu **or** vistimu, vuitri vidistivu, iddi vittiru **or** vistiru
viviri, to live	**Singular forms:** iu vissi, tu vivisti, vossìa vissi, iddu vissi **Plural forms:** nuiatri vissimu, vuiatri vivistivu, iddi vissiru
viviri, to drink	**Singular forms:** iu vippi, tu vivisti, vossìa vippi, iddu vippi **Plural forms:** nuiatri vippimu, vuiatri vivistivu, iddi vippiru
vuliri, to want, wish	**Singular forms:** iu vosi, tu vulisti, vossìa vosi, iddu vosi **Plural forms:** nuiatri vosimu, vuiatri vulistivu, iddi vosiru

* Regular forms are also common: cridivi **or** cridiu, cridisti, cridiu, cridemmu, cridistivu, crideru.

† *grapiri* is used more frequently in the present, but the other tenses and verb forms follow *apriri*.

‡ Regular forms are also common: pirdivi **or** pirdiu, pirdisti, pirdiu, pirdemmu, pirdistivu, pirderu.

** Regular forms are also common: rispunnivi **or** rispunniu, rispunnisti, rispunniu, rispunnemmu, rispunnistivu, rispunneru.

†† Regular forms are also common: scrivivi **or** scriviu, scrivisti, scriviu, scrivemmu, scrivistivu, scriveru.

‡‡ Regular forms are also common: tinivi **or** tiniu, tinisti, tiniu, tinemmu, tinistivu, tineru.

Uses and Meanings of the Preterite
The Sicilian preterite is confined chiefly to several very distinct uses.

- Single point-action occurring in the past. **Example:** Ora ora vitti a me frati. I just saw my brother.
- A limited continued set of single-point actions in the past. **Example:** Cincu uri arrè chiuviu e ora ora chiuviu. Five hours ago it rained, and it just now rained.
- A state, activity, or condition lasting for a limited period but now is over. **Example:** Aieri liggivi tuttu u iornu. Yesterday I read the entire day.
- Restricted action over a block of time but now is over. **Example:** Me patri stesi nni stu paisi pi na durata di vinti anni. My father lived in this town for twenty years (but he doesn't live there now).

Some verbs have different meaning when used in the preterite. The most common are:

- canusciri, to know. **Preterite meaning:** to meet (to be introduced to). **Example:** Aieri canuscivi â zita dû me bon amicu Petru. Yesterday I met the fiancée of my good friend, Peter.
- sapiri, to know (a fact). **Preterite meaning:** to learn. **Example:** A simana passata Catarina sappi ca so soggira vinia a vidiri a idda e a so maritu. Last week Catherine learned that her mother-in-law was coming to see her and her husband.

Examples
(1) Mamma! Mi tagghiai u iditu. Ah! Puvireddu! Fammillu vidiri. Mama. I cut my finger (just now). (single point-action in the past) Ah! You poor child! Let me see it.
(2) Aieri m'accattai un bonu libbru. Yesterday I bought a good book. (single point-action in the past)
(3) Gnaziu, ti vitti aieri. Ignatius, I saw you yesterday. (single point-action in the past)
(4) A simana passata â canuscivi. I met her (was introduced to her) last week. (single point-action in the past)
(5) Sappi ca idda avia arrivatu n'ura arrè. I learned that she had arrived an hour ago. (single point-action in the past)
(6) Sta matina chiuviu tri voti. This morning it rained three times. (limited set of single point-actions)
(7) L'annu passatu so maritu travagghiau assai. Last year her husband worked a lot. (state, activity, or condition lasting for a limited period now complete)
(8) L'avvucatu ascutau a storia di l'omu pi aiutallu. The lawyer listened to the man's story in order to help him. (single point-action in the past)
(9) U re rignau deci anni. The king reigned ten years (but he isn't reigning now). (restricted action over a block of time now complete)
(10) Iddu cuminciau a aviri fami e perciò iu nnô frigurifiru pi pigghiari quarchiccosa di manciari. He became hungry, and therefore he went to the refrigerator to get something to eat. (single point-actions occurring in the past)
(11) Mentri chi travagghiava nnô labburatoriu, u chimicu fici na scuperta mpurtanti. While he was working in the laboratory, the chemist made an important discovery. (habitual action in the past + single point-action occurring in the past)

Preterite with Present Perfect Meaning

In Sicilian the preterite can be used with a present perfect meaning. Sometimes *già* (already) is added.

Examples
(1) Parramu cû prufissuri dû prubblema. We've spoken to the professor about the issue.
(2) Iddu vinniu a machina a nautra pirsuna. He's sold the car to someone else.
(3) Già vitti dda pillicula. I've seen that movie.
(4) S'accattaru a casa. They've bought the house.
(5) Iddu mi detti l'appunti dâ classi. He's given me the notes from the class.

Preterite of aviri a + infinitive

aviri a accattari, to have to buy

Literary	Literary and spoken	Spoken
iu appi a accattari	appâ accattari	appâ 'ccattari
tu avisti a accattari	avistâ accattari	avistâ 'ccattari
vossìa appi a accattari	appâ accattari	appâ 'ccattari
iddu appi a accattari	appâ accattari	appâ 'ccattari
nuiatri appimu a accattari	appimâ accattari	appimâ 'ccattari
vuiatri avistivu a accattari	avistivâ accattari	avistivâ 'ccattari
iddi appiru a accattari	appirâ accattari	appirâ 'ccattari

Note: All the abbreviated forms are gemination-causing words: appâ⁺, avistâ⁺, appimâ⁺, avistivâ⁺, appirâ⁺.

Past Participle

The past particle is an important verbal form. It is, strictly speaking, an adjective, exhibiting both gender and number. **Example:** vistu (masculine singular), vista (feminine singular), visti (common plural), seen. The past participle for regular verbs is formed by dropping the infinitive ending and adding *-atu* (Conjugation 1) **or** *-utu* (Conjugation 2). Hence, the past participles for *parrari* and *rispunniri* are:

Conjugation 1
parr*atu*, spoken

Conjugation 2
rispunn*utu*, replied

Irregular Past Participles

There are some verbs having irregular past participles. Probably all the irregular past participles that you might encounter in Sicilian are listed below. The infinitive is given followed by its past participle. Note that some of these verbs also have a regular past participle. For verbs having both an irregular past participle and a regular one, the irregular one is used as an adjective and the regular one is the one most frequently used in forming compound tenses with *aviri*. Even if a verb has an irregular past participle, its preterite may be completely regular.

arricogghiri, to gather up, reap	arricotu (irregular) **or** arricugghiutu (regular)
chiudiri, to close	chiusu (irregular) **or** chiudutu (regular)
cociri, to cook	cottu (irregular) **or** cuciutu (regular)

Irregular past participles (cont.)

cogghiri, to pick, gather — cotu (irregular) **or** cugghiutu (regular)

curreggiri, to correct — currettu (irregular) **or** curriggiutu (regular)

curriri, to run — cursu (irregular) **or** currutu (regular)

difenniri, to defend — difisu (irregular) **or** difinnutu (regular)

diri, to say, tell — dittu (irregular)

distrudiri, to destroy — distruttu (irregular) **or** distrudutu (regular)

dividiri, to divide — divisu (irregular) **or** dividutu (irregular)

essiri, to be — statu (irregular)

fari, to do, make — fattu (irregular)

grapiri **or** apriri, to open — apertu (irregular) **or** graputu (regular)

iri, to go — iutu (irregular insofar as an initial *i* must be added)

leggiri, to read — lettu (irregular) **or** liggiutu (regular)

mettiri, to put — misu (irregular)

moriri **or** muriri, to die — mortu (irregular)

nasciri, to be born — natu (irregular) **or** nasciutu (regular)

ntenniri, to hear, understand — ntisu (irregular)

ntroduciri, to introduce (e.g., a new idea)* — ntroduttu (irregular) **or** ntroduciutu (regular)

offenniri, to defend — offisu (irregular) **or** offinnutu (regular)

offriri **or** uffriri, to offer — offertu (irregular) **or** uffrutu (regular)

pariri, to seem — parsu (irregular) **or** parutu (regular)

perdiri, to lose — persu (irregular) **or** pirdutu (regular)

pinciri, to paint (e.g., a portrait) — pintu (irregular) **or** pinciutu (irregular)

poniri, to place† — postu (irregular)

proibbiri, to prohibit, forbid — proibbitu (irregular) **or** proibbutu (regular)

pruteggiri, to protect — prutettu (irregular) **or** prutiggiutu (regular)

punciri, to sting, goad — puntu (irregular) **or** punciutu (regular)

ridiri, to laugh — risu (irregular) **or** ridutu (regular)

rispunniri, to respond, answer — rispostu (irregular) **or** rispunnutu (regular)

rumpiri, to tear, break — ruttu (irregular) **or** rumputu (regular)

scegghiri, to choose — scetu (irregular) **or** scigghiutu (regular)

sciogghiri, to loosen, untie — sciotu (irregular) **or** sciugghiutu (regular)

scriviri, to write — scrittu (irregular) **or** scrivutu (regular)

spenniri, to spend — spisu (irregular) **or** spinnutu (regular)

stenniri, to spread out, stretch out — stisu (irregular) **or** stinnutu (regular)

storciri, to wring, twist — stortu (irregular) **or** sturciutu (regular)

strinciri, to squeeze, tighten — strittu (irregular) **or** strinciutu (regular)

torciri, to twist — tortu (irregular) **or** turciutu (regular)

vidiri, to see — vistu (irregular) **or** vidutu (regular)

vinciri, to conquer, win — vintu (irregular) **or** vinciutu (regular)

---

* Other verbs based on *duciri* have similar past participles. **Examples:** pruduciri, cunnuciri, etc.

† Other verbs based on *poniri* have similar past participles. **Examples:** pruponiri; supponiri, etc.

Uses of the Past Participle

The past participle has several distinct uses. These are:

Use #1: Functions as an adjective with a past meaning.

Use #2: Introduces a subordinate clause. In this case the relative pronoun is not expressed.

Use #3: Introduces a dependent clause in the past. The gerund (see **Gerund** in Chapter 12) of *aviri* may be used in conjunction with the past participle. However, the gerund is used for the present situation. See the Examples under **Gerund** in Chapter 12.

Use #4: Functions in forming compound tenses (see below).

Use #5: Functions in the formation of the passive voice (see Chapter 14).

Examples of Use #1 (past participle as adjective with a past meaning)

(1) A putia è chiusa. The shop is closed.

(2) U lignu stortu s'addrizza ntô focu. The twisted piece of wood is straightened in the fire.

(3) U picciottu si pigghia i so sordi sparagnati e cci accatta un rigalu a so mamma. The boy takes his saved money and buys a present for his mother.

Examples of Use #2 (past participle introducing a subordinate clause)

(1) A putia chiusa nna l'estati grapi di novu nna l'autunnu. The shop (which was) closed in the summer will open again in the fall.

(2) I ciuri arricoti nnâ vasciurata si siccaru nnâ sira. The flowers (which were) gathered up in the afternoon wilted by the evening.

(3) I libbra misi supra â tavula scumpareru. The books (which were) placed on the table disappeared.

Examples of Use #3 (past participle introducing a dependent clause)

(1) Avennu vistu l'omu, u picciottu si vutau e si misi a curriri. Having seen the man, the boy turned and started to run. **Note:** Vistu l'omu, ... This sentence is OK too.

(2) Avennu fattu esclusioni dî sti dui punti, era pussibbili fari na lista dî caratteristichi cchiù mpurtanti. Having excluded these two points, it was possible to make a list of the most important characteristics. **Note:** Fattu esclusioni dî sti dui punti, ... This sentence is OK too

(3) Avennu arrivatu a li diciadott'anni, so patri cci fici un matrimoniu bonu. Having turned eighteen, her father arranged a good marriage for her. **Note:** Arrivatu a li diciadott'anni, ... This sentence is OK too

Use #4 is treated directly below in **Present Perfect**, and Use #5 is treated in Chapter 14.

Present Perfect

There are two compound past tenses in Sicilian: the present perfect and the past perfect. The perfect tenses (present and past) are formed with *aviri* as the helping verb followed by the past participle of the verb in question. Note that *aviri* can have both long forms (the normal ones) and short forms (abbreviated). See below. **Caution:** Unlike Italian, Sicilian uses only one auxiliary verb, *aviri*. This is true for (1) reflexive verbs and (2) verbs of motion and intransitive verbs, that is, verbs that don't take an object.

The present perfect is chiefly restricted to the following use.

- An action begun in the past and extending into the present. **Example:** L'omu a persu u so riloggiu. The man's lost his watch (just recently and this fact is still affecting the present situation).

The use of the present perfect is dependent upon the speaker's perception of the situation. If he/she perceives that the action has relevance and still has a bearing on the present situation, then the present perfect is likely to be used. On the other hand, if the speaker believes the action to be completed and therefore having no more bearing on the present, he'd probably use the preterite. In the sentences below, the same sentences are given using the present perfect and the preterite. The preterite means that the action or condition expressed by the sentence is already over.

Conjugation 1
parrari, to speak
iu aiu parratu, I have spoken
tu ai parratu, you have spoken
vossìa avi parratu, you have spoken
iddu avi parratu, he has spoken
nuiatri avemu parratu, we have spoken
vuiatri aviti parratu, you have spoken
iddi annu parratu, they have spoken

Conjugation 2
rispunniri, to reply
iu aiu rispunnutu, I have replied
tu ai rispunnutu, you have replied
vossìa avi rispunnutu, you have replied
iddu avi rispunnutu, he has replied
nuiatri avemu rispunnutu, we have replied
vuiatri aviti rispunnutu, you have replied
iddi annu rispunnutu, they have replied

Long Forms of aviri + past participle
aiu parratu
ai parratu
avi parratu
avemu parratu
aviti parratu
annu parratu

Short Forms of aviri + past participle
ê parratu
a parratu
a parratu
amu parratu
ati parratu
annu parratu (same as long form)

Examples with the present perfect
(1) A statu veramenti friddu stu mmernu. It's been very cold this winter (and it still continues to be cold).
(2) A causa d'esami aiu studiatu ass**ai**. Because of exams I've studied a lot (and I'm still studying).
(3) Nun m'a vulutu sentiri mai. You have never wanted to hear me (and you still don't).
(4) Ti aiu vinutu a vidiri. **or** Aiu vinutu a vidiriti (**or** vidirti). I've come to see you. (The action isn't over yet, at least in my mind.)

Examples with the preterite
(1) Fu veramenti friddu stu mmernu. It was very cold this winter (but now it isn't).
(2) A causa d'esami studi**ai** ass**ai**. Because of exams I studied a lot (but now I'm not studying any longer).
(3) Nun mi vosi sentiri mai. You never wanted to hear me.
(4) Ti vinni a vidiri (**or** Ti vinni a vitti). I came to see you. (The action is over, at least in my mind.)

Present with Present Perfect Meaning
In the case of a person performing an act extending over a period of time, Sicilian, like the other Romance languages, utilizes the present tense. In this case the condition, activity, or state extends from the past into the present with no interruptions. This usage normally involves a fixed structure.

- avi + block of time + ca (that) + main verb (condition, activity, state) in the present

Examples
(1) Avi tri anni c'abbitu nna sta città (**or** nta sta città). I've been living in this city for three years (and I'm still living there).
(2) Ora avi du simani ca mi doli stu malidittu denti. For two weeks now this damn tooth's been hurting me (and it's still hurting me).
(3) Avi deci anni ca u re regna. It's been ten years that the king's reigned (and he's still reigning).
(4) Avi cincu misi chi staiu cu stu patruni e ntuttu nun m'a datu chi la prima misata. It's been five months that I've been with this employer, and all in all he has only paid me the first month's wages.

Note: If the time refers to a past time, *avia* is used with the main verb in the past perfect. See (12) in the Examples under the **Past Perfect** directly below.

Past Perfect
The past perfect tense refers to an action occurring before the action of the main verb, which in this case is also in the past. It is commonly used in a subordinate clause often introduced by the conjunction *doppu chi*, "after" or *chi* (**or** alternatively *ca*), "that". The main clause commonly contains a verb in a past tense (generally the preterite but sometimes the imperfect). In English, although we should, strictly speaking, employ the past perfect, we normally just use the past. In some of the examples below, first the sentence is given in the present tense followed by the same sentence transposed into the past. Carefully note the order of the activities.

Conjugation 1
parrari, to speak
iu avia parratu, I had spoken
tu avivi parratu, you had spoken
vossìa avia parratu, you had spoken
iddu avia parratu, he had spoken
nuiatri aviamu parratu, we had spoken
vuiatri aviavu parratu, you had spoken
iddi avianu parratu, they had spoken

Conjugation 2
rispunniri, to reply
iu avia rispunnutu, I had replied
tu avivi rispunnutu, you had replied
vossìa avia rispunnutu, you had replied
iddu avia rispunnutu, he had replied
nuiatri aviamu rispunnutu, we had replied
vuiatri aviavu rispunnutu, you had replied
iddi avianu rispunnutu, they had replied

Note: Like any other imperfect of Conjugation 2, *aviri* has alternate forms. See **Imperfect** above. **Examples:** iu avia, iu aveva, iu aviva, etc. Naturally, any of these acceptable alternate forms can also be used in forming the past perfect.

Examples

(1) Prima manciu a cena e doppu leggiu a rivista TIME. First I eat my dinner, and afterwards I read TIME magazine. (present/present)

(2) Doppu chi avia manciatu a cena, liggivi a rivista TIME. After I ate my dinner (had eaten my dinner), I read TIME magazine. (past perfect/preterite)

(3) Vaiu ô cinima e poi viu a me zita. I go to the movies, and afterwards I see my fiancée. (present/present)

(4) Doppu chi iu avia iutu ô cinima, vitti a me zita. After I went to the movies (had gone to the movies), I saw my fianceé. (past perfect/preterite)

(5) U prufissuri grapi a finestra e poi cci duna n'esami ê studenti. The professor opens the window, and then he gives an exam to the students. (present/present)

(6) Doppu chi avia apertu a finestra, u prufissuri cci detti n'esami ê studenti. After he opened the window (had opened the window), the professor gave an exam to the students. (past perfect/preterite)

(7) Prima a picciridda arricogghi i beddi ciuri e poi cci l'arrigala a so mamma. First the little girl gathers the pretty flowers, and then she gives them to her mother. (present/present)

(8) Doppu chi a picciridda avia arricugghiutu i beddi ciuri, cci l'arrigalau a so mamma. After the little girl gathered the pretty flowers (had gathered the pretty flowers), she gave them to her mother. (past perfect/preterite)

(9) Mi avia (or M'avia) spugghiatu e mi avia (or m'avia) misu u piggiama quannu sunau u campanellu. I took off my clothes and put on my pijamas when the bell rang. (past perfect/preterite)

(10) L'avvucatu Berti nun avia caputu nenti dû prubblema dâ signura Filippi e pi chissu idda cci scrissi na littra pi chiariri a quistioni. The lawyer Berti didn't understand Mrs. Filippi's problem at all, and therefore she wrote him a letter to explain the issue. (past perfect/preterite)

(11) Quannu avia sintutu a malanova, a fimmina si misi a chianciri. When she heard the bad news, the woman began to cry. (past perfect/preterite)

(12) Avia deci anni ca u re avia rignatu. It had been ten years that the king reigned (and he was still reigning).

Past Participle with a Preceding Conjunctive Pronoun

In Sicilian, the part participle in a perfect tense is considered part of the verb and doesn't have to agree with a preceding conjunctive pronoun.

Examples

(1) Doppu chi l'avia manciatu, liggivi a rivista TIME. After I ate it (that is, my dinner), I read TIME magazine.

(2) Doppu chi l'avia apertu, u prufissuri cci detti n'esami ê studenti. After he opened it (that is, the window), the professor gave an exam to the students.

(3) Doppu chi a picciridda l'avia arricugghiutu, cci l'arrigalau a so mamma. After the little girl gathered them (that is, the pretty flowers), she gave them to her mother.

However, due to the growing influence of Italian, the trend now exists in Sicilian to have the part participle agree with a preceding conjunctive pronoun.

Examples

(1) Doppu chi l'avia manciata, liggivi a rivista TIME. After I ate it (that is, my dinner), I read TIME magazine.

(2) Doppu chi l'avia aperta, u prufissuri cci detti n'esami ê studenti. After he opened it (that is, the window), the professor gave an exam to the students.

(3) Doppu chi a picciridda l'avia arricugghiuti, cci l'arrigalau a so mamma. After the little girl gathered them (that is, the pretty flowers), she gave them to her mother.

Future Perfect Tense — Not Used in Sicilian

The future perfect tense is not used in Sicilian. Strictly speaking, the future perfect tense refers to an action taking place before the action of the main verb, which occurs in the future. In others words, the action expressed by the future perfect tense occurs before the action expressed by the main verb, and hence occurs "in the past" before the action of the main verb. **Example:** I shall have seen my fiancée before I go to the movies. This tense is cumbersome, even in English. In Sicilian, this tense is replaced by the simple present (acting as a future) or one of the other devices for expressing future time in Sicilian. See **Future Time** in Chapter 6. Again, the context and the time adverb (in this case "before") clarifies who or what will be seen first (the fiancée) and what will be seen afterwards (the movies). **Example:** Viu a me zita prima chi vaiu ô cinima. I'll see my fiancée before I go to the movies.

Sicilian for Everyday Situations

In place of the Vocabulary and Exercises, this chapter has a set of phrases or sentences dealing with using Sicilian in everyday life. Since the meanings of all the expressions and situations are given in English, you should be able to figure out the meanings of any word based on the previous words that you've learned and on the meaning of the expression or situation in question. **Note:** In the expressions and sentences given below, to identify clearly the English translation, the symbol **E:** (E: = English translation of the Sicilian) is employed.

Basic Expressions/Greetings

- Sì. **E:** Yes.
- No. **E:** No.
- Pi favuri **or** Pi piaciri. **E:** Please.
- Grazzii. **E:** Thank you.
- Tanti grazzii. **E:** Thanks a lot.
- Milli grazzii. **E:** Thanks very much.
- Nun è nenti. **E:** You're welcome.
- Pregu. **E:** You're welcome.
- Bon giornu. **E:** Good morning; hello.
- Bona sira. **E:** Good everning (typically 6-9 pm).
- Bona notti. **E:** Good night (used after the sun has gone down). Used to say goodbye.
- Ciau. **E:** Hi, hello; goodbye.
- Addiu. **E:** Goodbye.
- Arrividerci. **E:** Goodbye. **Note:** This Italian expression is now widely used.
- Ntra pocu. **E:** See you soon.
- Comu sì? **or** Comu stai? **E:** How are you?* (familiar singular)
- Comu è? **or** Comu sta? **E:** How are you?* (polite singular)
- Comu siti? **or** Comu stati? **E:** How are you?* (plural)

- Sugnu bonu. **or** Staiu beni. **E:** I'm well; I feel good.* (masculine)
- Sugnu bona. **or** Staiu beni. **E:** I'm well; I feel good.* (feminine)
- Semu boni. **or** Stamu beni. **E:** We're well; we feel good.* (plural)
- Sugnu veramenti bonu. **or** Staiu veramenti beni. **E:** I'm very well.* (masculine)
- Sugnu veramenti bona. **or** Staiu veramenti beni. **E:** I'm very well.* (feminine)
- Semu veramenti boni. **or** Stamu veramenti beni. **E:** We're very well.* (plural)
- Mi sentu bonu. **E:** I feel good. (masculine)
- Mi sentu bona. **E:** I feel good. (feminine)
- Ni sintemu boni. **E:** We feel good. (plural)
- Comu è to mogghi? **E:** How's your wife? (familiar)
- Comu è so mogghi? **E:** How's your wife? (polite)
- Me mogghi è bona. **E:** My wife's well.
- Comu è a to famigghia? **E:** How's your family? (familiar)
- Comu è a so famigghia? **E:** How's your family? (polite)
- E tu ? **E:** And you? (familiar)
- E vossìa? **E:** And you? (polite)
- E lei? **E:** And you? (polite)
- E vuiatri? **E:** And you? (plural)
- Scusami. **E:** Excuse me. (familiar)
- Vossìa mi scusa. **E:** Excuse me. (polite)
- Mi scusassi. **E:** Excuse me. (formal polite)
- Scusatimi. **E:** Excuse me. (polite plural)

* Older Sicilian uses *essiri* with an appropriate adjective, e.g., *bonu/bona/boni*, whereas more recent Sicilian follows Italian and uses *stari* with an appropriate adverb, e.g. *beni*.

Asking Questions

- Cui **or** cu? **E:** Who?
- Cu sì? **E:** Who are you? (familiar)
- Cu è? **E:** Who are you? (polite)
- Cu siti? **E:** Who are you? (plural)
- Cu siti vuiatri? **E:** Who are you? (plural)
- E vuiautri cu siti? **E:** And who are you?
- Chi? **E:** What?
- Chi è? **E:** What is it?
- Chi è dda cosa? **E:** What's that there?
- Chi dici? **or** Chi sta dicennu? **E:** What are you saying? **or** What's he saying?
- Chi fai? **E:** What are you doing? (familiar singular) **or** What do you do (as a profession)?
- Chi fa? **E:** What are you doing? (polite singular) **or** What do you do (as a profession)?
- Chi faciti? **E:** What are you doing? (plural) **or** What do you do (as a profession)?
- Fazzu l'avvucatu. **or** Sugnu avvucatu. I'm a lawyer.
- Fazzu l'incigneri. **or** Sugnu ncigneri. I'm an engineer.
- Fazzu lu prufissuri. **or** Sugnu prufissuri. I'm a teacher.
- Fazzu lu prufissuri univirsitariu. **or** Sugnu un prufissuri univirsitariu. I'm a professor.
- Chi è chistu **or** Chi è chista? **E:** What is this?
- Unni? **E:** Where?

- Unni vai? **E:** Where are you going? (familiar singular)
- Unni va? **E:** Where are you going? (polite singular)
- Unni iti? **E:** Where are you going? (plural)
- Unni iti vuiatri? **E:** Where are you going? (plural)
- Unni è a banca? **E:** Where's the bank?
- Unni è a posta? **E:** Where's the post office?
- Unni è l'Albergu Casa Blanca? **E:** Where's the Casa Blanca Hotel?
- Unni cc'è un bonu risturanti? **E:** Where is there a good restaurant?
- Cc'è nu bonu risturanti ccà vicinu (**or** pagghiri ccà)? **E:** Is there a good restaurant near here?
- Comu? **E:** What? (Often used when asked a question which isn't understood.)
- Comu? **E:** How?
- Comu vaiu di ccà a ddà? **E:** How do I go from here to there?
- Comu mi pozzu accattari nu bigghiettu pi l'autobbussu? **E:** How can I purchase a ticket for the bus?
- Comu pozzu truvari u me albergu? **E:** How can I find my hotel?
- Quannu? **E:** When?
- Quannu arrivamu a Palermu? **E:** When do we arrive in Palermo?
- Quannu parti u trenu pi Catania? **E:** When does the train depart for Catania?
- Quannu parti l'autobbussu pû centru dâ città? **E:** When does the bus leave for downtown?
- Putissi...? **E:** May I...?
- Putissi iu vidiri l'urariu di l'autobbussu pi Missina? **E:** May I see the timetable for the bus for Messina?
- Mi putissi dari un giurnali? **E:** May I have a newspaper?
- Poi...? **E:** Can you...? (familiar singular)
- Pò...? **E:** Can you...? (polite singular)
- Putiti...? **E:** Can you...? (plural)
- Pi favuri, mi pò aiutari a truvari un tassì? **E:** Please, can you help me find a taxi?
- Mi pò diri unni è na sta mappa dâ città? **E:** Can you tell me where it is on this city map?
- Picchì? **E:** Why?
- Picchì vossìa nun avi u so passaportu? **E:** Why don't you have your passport?
- Picchì semu (i)n ritardu? **E:** Why are we late?
- Picchì è chi u picciottu arriva sempri pirtempu? **E:** Why is the boy always early?
- Mi vulissi accattari rigali pî me parenti nnê Stati Uniti. Pi favuri, mi pò diri unni cc'è na bona putia pî turisti? **E:** I'd like to buy some presents for relatives in the States. Please, can you tell me where there's a good shop for tourists?

Telling time

- Chi ura è? **E:** What time is it?
- È l'una. **E:** It's one o'clock.
- È l'una n puntu. **E:** It's one o'clock sharp.
- È l'una e chinnici. **E:** It's one fifteen.
- È l'una e un quartu. **E:** It's one fifteen.
- È l'una e trenta. **E:** It's one thirty.
- È l'una e menza. **E:** It's one thirty.
- È l'una e quarantacincu. **E:** It's one forty-five.

- Sunnu i dui menu un quartu. **E:** It's a quarter to two, that is, it's one forty-five.
- Manca nu quartu ê dui. **E:** It's a quarter to two. (**Literal meaning:** It lacks a quarter to two)
- Sunnu i dui. **E:** It's two o'clock.
- Sunnu i dui e menza. **E:** It's two thirty.
- Mancanu dudici ê tri. **E:** It's twelve to three. (**Literal meaning:** It lacks twelve to three)
- U me riloggiu avi i quattru e vinti. **E:** My watch shows twenty past four.
- È ura di fari culazzioni. **E:** It's time to have breakfast.
- È ura di pigghiari n'espressu. **E:** It's time to have an expresso.
- È ura di studiari. **E:** It's time to study.
- È ura di ripusari. **E:** It's time to rest.
- È ura di curcarisi. **E:** It's time to go to bed.
- È ura di addurmiscirisi. It's time to fall asleep.
- U me riloggiu è n ritardu (**or** in ritardu). **or** U me riloggiu è attrassatu. **E:** My watch's slow.
- U me riloggiu curri. **E:** My watch's fast.

Nationalities/Speaking Languages
Note how a person responds to a question. In the Romance languages, when asked a question, unless emphasis is required, they merely repeat the verb in the appropriate person.

Examples
Q.: Mi capisci bonu? **E:** Do you understand me well?
A.: Û (**or** â) capisciu **or** Sì, û (**or** â) capisciu. **E:** Yes or Yes, I do.
Q.: Parra vossìa (**or** parrati vuiatri) talianu? **E:** Do you speak Italian?*
A.: Sì, parru talianu. **E:** Yes, I speak Italian.

* The order verb/subject in a question can be inverted with the same meaning. **Example:**
Parra vossìa talianu? **or** Vossìa parra talianu? **E:** Do you speak Italian?

- Sugnu miricanu(a). **E:** I'm American.
- Semu miricani. **E:** We're American.
- Vegnu dî Stati Uniti. **E:** I come from the United States.
- Vinemu dî Stati Uniti. **E:** We come from the United States.
- Vegnu a vidiri parenti ccà nnâ Sicilia. **E:** I'm visiting relatives here in Sicily.
- Vinemu a vidiri parenti ccà nnâ Sicilia. **E:** We're visiting relatives here in Sicily.
- È a me prima visita nnâ Sicilia. **E:** It's my first visit to Sicily.
- È a nostra prima visita nnâ Sicilia. **E:** It's our first visit to Sicily.
- Parri nglisi? **E:** Do you speak English? (familiar singular)
- Parra nglisi? **E:** Do you speak English? (polite singular)
- Parrati nglisi? **E:** Do you speak English?
- Parru. **or** Sì, parru. **E:** Yes or Yes, I do.
- Sì sicilianu? **E:** Are you Sicilian? (familiar singular) **Note:** Here sì = you are.
- È sicilianu? **E:** Are you Sicilian? (polite singular)
- Siti siciliani? **E:** Are you Sicilian? (plural)
- Sugnu **or** Sì, sugnu. **E:** Yes **or** Yes, I am.
- Vuiatri siti siciliani? **E:** Are you Sicilian? (plural)
- Semu siciliani. **or** Sì, semu. **E:** We're Sicilians. **or** Yes, we are.

- Nun semu **or** No, nun semu. **E:** No **or** No, we are not.
- Parru bonu u sicilianu. **E:** I speak Sicilian well.
- Parrati u sicilianu accussì bonu ca nun criu ca siti veramenti miricani. **E:** You speak Sicilian so well that I don't believe you're really Americans.
- Parru picca u sicilianu. **E:** I speak Sicilian a little.
- Parru anticchia di sicilianu. **E:** I speak Sicilian very little.
- Nun sacciu parrari u sicilianu. **or** Nun sacciu u sicilianu. **E:** I don't know how to speak Sicilian.
- Nun parru u sicilianu. **E:** I don't speak Sicilian.
- Nun parru nè u sicilianu nè u talianu. **E:** I speak neither Sicilian nor Italian.
- Sacciu parrari u talianu ma nun sacciu u sicilianu. **E:** I know how to speak Italian but not Sicilian.
- Mi piacissi parrari u sicilianu megghiu chi û parru. **E:** I'd like to speak Sicilian better than I do.
- Pi favuri, nun sugnu di ccà. Parrati cchiù adaciu. **E:** Please, I'm not a native. Speak more slowly.
- Capisciu u sicilianu ma nun û parru. **E:** I understand Sicilian, but I don't speak it.
- Nun û capisciu bonu. **E:** I don't understand it very well.
- Capisciu sulu tanticchia. Pi piaciri, ripeti cchiù adaciu. **E:** I understand only a little. Please repeat more slowly.

Introductions

Sta parti parra di quattru siciliani chi si prisentanu l'unu a l'autru. **E:** This section involves four Sicilians introducing themselves: Giuvanni (Vanni) Suluzzu, Gaitanu (Tanu) Manfredi, Maria Bonfigghiu, Anna Tommi.

Giuvanni:	Mi chiamu Giuvanni Suluzzu. **E:** My name is John Suluzzu.
Maria:	Mi chiamu Maria Bonfigghiu e chista è a me bon'amica, Anna Tommi. **E:** My name is Mary Bonfigghiu, and this is my good friend, Anna Tommi.
Gaitanu:	Pirmittitimi di prisintarimi. (**or** Pirmittitimi di mi prisintari.) U me nomu è Tanu Manfredi. **E:** Permit me to introduce myself. My name is Tanu Manfredi.
Gaitanu:	Ti vogghiu prisintari u me bon amicu, Vanni Suluzzu. **E:** I want to present to you (familiar singular) my good friend, John Suluzzu.
Giuvanni:	Vi vulissi prisintari u me bon amicu, Tanu. **E:** I would like to present to you (plural) my good friend, Tano.
Maria:	Sugnu assai cuntenta di fari a to canuscenza. I'm very pleased to meet you (**or** to make your acquaintance)
Gaitanu:	Cu è dda signurina? Mi piacissi veramenti canuscilla. **E:** Who's that young lady over there? I'd really like to meet her.
Giuvanni:	Dda signurina è na bon'amica dâ me zita, Anna. **E:** That young lady over there is a good friend of my fiancée, Anna.

Sicilian last names are normally written in the Italian fashion, and have been for over one hundred years, especially by literate people. In public, the Italian name is used, especially if one doesn't know the person well. Among close friends or within the family circle, if the last name is used, the Sicilian version is found. The same is true of first, or Christian, names. Although many of these are similar to their Italian counterparts, there are some differences.

Below are some last names giving their Italianized spelling followed by how they would be written in Sicilian and their Sicilian pronunciation. In some cases, there is no difference. Two of the names in the dialogue above are included. In the above dialogue they are given in Sicilianized form since the young couples wish to be on a familiar basis with each other.

Written (Italian)	Written (Sicilianized)	Pronounced
Solozzo	Suluzzu	/suluttsu/
Bonfiglio	Bonfigghiu	/bŏnfiggyu/
Trombelli	Trummeddi	/ţrummedʼdʼi/
Abbandando	Abbannannu	/abbannannu/
Brasi	Brasi	/břasi **or** břazi/
Martoglio	Martogghiu	/mařtoggyu/
Andolini	Annulini	/annulini/
Provese	Pruvisi	/přuvisi **or** přuvizi/
Cipolla	Cipudda	/čipudʼdʼa/
Angilella	Anciledda	/ančiledʼdʼa/

12   Verbs: Nonfinite Forms

Purpose of the Chapter

The chief purpose of this chapter is to discuss two common verb forms that aren't conjugated like the verbs in Chapters 5 and 6. These forms are called the gerund and the infinitive. Since these forms don't show person, gender, or number, they are called nonfinite forms. In addition, the present participle is introduced.

Gerund

In Sicilian, as in the other Romance languages, the gerund is a common form resembling verbal forms in English ending in *–ing*. For example, *speaking* and *replying* if one uses the two verbs given in Chapter 5 above. The gerund is formed from a verb by dropping the infinitive ending and adding *-annu* (Conjugation 1) **or** *-ennu* (Conjugation 2) to the stem of the verb. Hence, the gerunds for *parrari* and *rispunniri* are:

Conjugation 1

parr*annu*, speaking

Conjugation 2

rispunn*ennu*, replying

Caution: As was said above, the gerund is a common form resembling verbal forms in English ending in *–ing*. However, gerunds in Sicilian are not used in the same way as in English. In English a gerund is a verbal noun. **Example:** The running in the competition was fierce. Also be cautious regarding the present participle. In English, these also end in *-ing* and are employed as verbal adjectives. **Example:** The running boy stumbled. Neither the gerund as it is used in English nor the English present participle corresponds to the Sicilian gerund, which is used chiefly to form the so-called progressive tenses. See **Progressive Tenses** below. The Sicilian gerund is invariable, and it is never used as an adjective.

The gerund in Sicilian can be used in an absolute sense to introduce a dependent clause referring back to the main clause. Generally, the dependent clause refers to the subject of the main clause, but not always. See Examples 4-6 below. The verb in the main clause may be in the present tense, or it may be in one of the past tenses. The sense of the sentence determines what tense is appropriate for the main clause. In addition, conjunctive pronouns can be added to the gerund following the same rules that were presented in Chapter 7. See **Spelling Rules – Conjunctive Pronouns Added to Verb Forms**. **Note:** Several different translations of the gerund-containing clauses are possible. See below.

Examples

(1) Vidennu l'omu, u picciottu si vota e sâ scappa. Upon seeing the man, the boy turns and runs away. **Note:** When he sees the man, … . This translation of the gerund-containing clause is also acceptable.

(2) Vidennu l'omu, u picciottu si vot**au** e sâ scapp**au**. Upon seeing the man, the boy turned and ran away. **Note:** When he saw the man, … . This translation of the gerund-containing clause is also acceptable.

(3) Vidennulu, u picciottu si vota e sâ scappa. Upon seeing him, the boy turns and runs away.

(4) Arrivannu a li diciadott'anni, lu patri di la picciotta cci fa un matrimoniu bonu. Having turned eighteen, the girl's father will arrange a good marriage for her. **Note:** When she turns eighteen, ... This translation of the gerund-containing clause is also acceptable.

(5) Arrivannu a li diciadott'anni, lu patri di la picciotta cci fici un matrimoniu bonu. Having turned eighteen, the girl's father arranged a good marriage for her. **Note:** When she turned eighteen, ... This translation of the gerund-containing clause is also acceptable.

(6) Arrivannu a li diciadott'anni, lu patri di la picciotta cci vulia fari un matrimoniu bonu. Having turned eighteen, the girl's father wanted to arrange a good marriage for her. **Note:** When she turned eighteen, ... This translation of the gerund-containing clause is also acceptable.

(7) Parrannu vasciu ô parrinu, l'omu cci cunfissa i so piccati. Speaking in a whisper to the priest, the man confesses his sins to him.

(8) Parrannu vasciu ô parrinu, l'omu cci cunfiss**au** i so piccati. Speaking in a whisper to the priest, the man confessed his sins to him.

(9) Parrannucci vasciu, l'omu cunfiss**au** i so piccati. Speaking to him in a whisper, the man confessed his sins.

The gerund of *aviri* (*avennu*) can also be used with the past participle to introduce a dependent clause. In this case, the verb in the main clause will generally be in one of the past tenses. See Chapter 11, especially **Uses of the Past Participle**, Use #3.

Gerunds of Stem-Changing Verbs and Verbs Showing Spelling Changes
Gerunds of stem-changing verbs and verbs showing spelling changes follow the same rules as outlined in Chapter 5. The gerund ending bears the stress, so the theme vowel is in its unstressed value.

<u>Examples</u>

<u>Infinitive</u>	<u>Gerund</u>
vulari, to fly	vulannu, flying
vestiri, to dress	vistennu, dressing
circari, to look for	circannu, looking for
manciari, to eat	manciannu, eating
cogghiri, to pick	cugghiennu, picking
danniggiari, to injure	danniggiannu, injuring
asciari, to find	asciannu, finding
vuscari, to earn a living	vuscannu, earning a living
taliari, to look at	taliannu, looking at

Progressive Tenses
In Sicilian, as in the other Romance languages, another important function of the gerund is to form the so-called progressive tenses. The progressive tenses don't exist in every Romance language. For example, they aren't found in French or Romanian. In Sicilian, several verbs function with the gerund to produce progressive verb forms with different shades of meaning. These are:

- *iri* (denotes continuous action);

- *stari* (denotes action starting or in progress);
- In addition to *stari* and *iri*, *veniri* is sometimes used to indicate a slow, and somewhat surreptitious, progressive movement towards the speaker.

Progressive Present
The progressive present is very common in Sicilian.

Examples
(1) Va parrannu e facennu signa chî manu. He keeps right on speaking and making signs with his hands.
(2) Giorgiu va gridannu strati strati di pura gioia. George keeps on shouting through the streets out of sheer joy. **Note:** strati strati = through the streets. Reduplication of a noun to indicate thoroughness and/or intensity is characteristically Sicilian.
(3) U picciottu sta studiannu u sicilianu p'imparari bonu ssa lingua. The boy is studying Sicilian to learn that language well.
(4) Ora ora mi staiu manciannu un bonu aranciu. Right now I'm eating a good orange.
(5) Na bedda picciotta si sta avvicinannu a mia. A pretty girl is approaching me.
(6) Dd'omu grassu mi va taliannu e nun mi piaci. That fat man keeps on looking at me, and I don't like it.
(7) A vecchia si sta avvicinannu a mia e mi sta uffrennu un pumu. Ora mû staiu pigghiannu e manciannu. Sapi bonu. The old woman is coming up to me and is offering me an apple. Now I'm taking it and eating. It tastes good.
(8) A vecchia si veni avvicinannu a mia. The old woman is slowly sneaking up on me.
(9) U vecchiu sta cuntannu na storia ê picciriddi. The old man's telling the children a story.
(10) Iu û sacciu chiddu chi stai pinzannu ma tu nun capisci comu sunnu i cosi. I know what you're thinking, but you don't understand how things are.
(11) U vecchiu sta cuntannu i picciriddi. The old man's counting the children.

Progressive Imperfect
The progressive imperfect can also be formed. This is also very commonly used.

Examples
(1) Ia parrannu e facennu signa chî manu. He kept right on speaking and making signs with his hands.
(2) Giorgiu iava gridannu strati strati di pura gioia. George kept on shouting through the streets out of sheer joy.
(3) U picciottu stava studiannu u sicilianu p'imparari bonu ssa lingua. The boy was studying Sicilian to learn that language well.
(4) Mi stava manciannu n'aranciu quannu me mugghieri mi chiamau pâ cena. I was eating an orange when my wife called me to dinner.
(5) U vecchiu stava cuntannu na storia ê picciriddi. The old man was telling the children a story.
(6) Na bedda picciotta si stava avvicinannu a mia. A pretty girl was approching me.
(7) Dd'omu grassu mi ia taliannu e nun mi piacia. That fat man kept on looking at me, and I didn't like it.
(8) Mentri chi a signura si stava vistennu, u so picciriddu si misi a chianciri. While the lady (married) was dressing herself, her child began to cry.

Present Participle

There are two participles in Sicilian, the present participle and the past participle; both can function as adjectives. The present participle is often translated by a verbal adjective or a verbal noun ending in -*ing*, but it is sometimes translated without an -*ing*. **Examples:** gridanti, shouting; siccanti, boring; abbitanti, inhabitant. **Caution:** In Sicilian, the present participle never functions as it does in English to introduce a subordinate clause. **Example:** I see a large man carrying a package. In Sicilian a relative pronoun introducing the subordinate clause would be required. **Example:** Viu a n'omu grossu chi porta nu pacchettu. I see a large man carrying a package.

Infinitive

Infinitives are used in a variety of situations in Sicilian. They are generally used after prepositions where English would employ the present participle. When they're translated into English, they will generally be translated as present particles.

Infinitive after Prepositions

At times Sicilian uses an infinitive after a preposition, but it's more common to use a subordinate clause. The verb in the main clause can be in the present tense or in one of the other tenses, depending on the meaning.

Examples

(1) Prima di manciari l'omu chiama a so mugghieri. Before eating the man calls his wife.
(2) Prima di manciari l'omu chiam**au** a so mugghieri. Before eating the man called his wife.
(3) Senza pinzari l'omu ridi ô picciottu. Without thinking the man laughs at the boy.
(4) Senza pinzari l'omu rid**iu** ô picciottu. Without thinking the man laughed at the boy.
(5) Doppu vidiri a so zita, u picciottu si senti cchiù cuntentu. After seeing his fiancée, the young man becomes very happy. **Note:** Doppu chi vidi a so zita, ... This is more common than the infinitive construction.
(6) Doppu vidiri a so zita, u picciottu si sintiu cchiù cuntentu. After seeing his fiancée, the young man became very happy. **Note:** See (5).
(7) A vidiri a l'omu, u picciottu si vota e sâ scappa. Upon seeing the man, the boy turns and runs away. **Note:** The part participle construction is more common. See Use #3 under **Uses of the Past Participle** in Chapter 11.
(8) A vidiri a l'omu, u picciottu si vut**au** e sâ scapp**au**. Upon seeing the man, the boy turned and ran away. **Note:** See (7).

Infinitive Used as a Noun

In English, as was pointed out above, the gerund performs the function of a verbal noun. **Example:** Speaking gives John great pleasure. In Sicilian, the infinitive is used instead. In this case, they're masculine singular and generally preceeded by the definite article. Since they function as nouns, they may be modified by an adjective. When translating them into English, translate them as (English) gerunds, normally without an article, either definite or indefinite.

Examples

(1) U parrari duna un grossu piaciri a Giuvanni. Speaking gives John great pleasure.
(2) U manciari bonu cci piaci a Peppi. Eating well is what Joe likes. **or** Joe likes to eat well.

(3) U vidiri è cridiri. **or** Vidiri è cridiri. Seeing is believing. **Note:** Infinitives used as nouns are likely to be unaccompanied by a definite article when used in a proverb.

Infinitive as a Substitute for a Subordinate Clause

If the same subject governs two verbs, instead of using a subordinate clause, the second verbal form is generally the infinitive. Such sentences can be translated into English either with a present or present perfect participle construction with some verbs, or with an infinitive construction with other verbs. In the case of the participle constructions, a subordinate clause is an alternative way of expressing the sentence. In other cases, the verb of the main clause governs an infinitive rather than a subordinate clause. In these cased, a pronoun is used as verbal object. See also **Common Verbs Governing the Infinitive** in Chapter 6. This is in contrast to cases where the subject of the main clause is different from the subject of the subordinate clause. Compare these sentences with the examples in Chapter 13, especially those of **Present Subjunctive** and the **Imperfect Subjunctive/Past Perfect Subjunctive**.

Examples

(1) Iddu nega di aviricci datu l'assegnu ô diritturi. He denies having given the check to the director. (present participle construction) **or** He denies that he gave the check to the director. (subordinate clause construction)

(2) Iddu nig**au** di aviricci datu l'assegnu ô diritturi. He denied having given the check to the director. (present perfect participle construction) **or** He denied that he gave the check to the director. (subordinate clause construction)

(3) Iu disiddiru fari chissu. I wish to do that. (infinitive construction)

(4) Iu disiddirava fari chissu ma non û fici. I wanted to do that but I didn't. (infinitive construction) **or** I wished I had done that but I didn't. (subordinate clause construction)

(5) Ti proibbisciu di iri ô cinima sta vasciurata. I forbid you to go to the movies this afternoon. (ti = verbal object)

(6) Ti proibbivi di iri ô cinima sta vasciurata. I forbade you to go to the movies this afternoon. (ti = verbal object)

Sicilian Dialogues

In place of the Vocabulary and Exercises, this chapter and the following chapter contain a short story about two Sicilian brothers who have come to the United States. Common phrases and sentences are set forth in Sicilian. Most of the necessary vocabulary has been covered in previous lessons. New words introduced in the **Sicilian Dialogues** (#1 and #2) can be found in the Sicilian-English Vocabulary in the back of the book.

Sicilian Dialogue #1

Prisintamu na sturiedda p'introduciri diversi dialoghi n sicilianu. Sta storia tratta di dui frati, Vitu e Marcu Terranostra, e l'avvinturi d'iddi nnê Stati Uniti. Ncumincia appena doppu a fini dâ secunna guerra munniali. Quannu finiu a guerra nnâ Sicilia, Vitu e Marcu pigghiaru un bastimentu pî Stati Uniti e arrivaru ntâ città di Baltimore nnô statu dû Maryland. Abbitanu nta na parti dâ città ca si chiama Piccola Italia a causa dû gran numiru d'immigranti taliani ca cci stannu. Vitu è u frati cchiù granni e lass**au** a so zita, Cecilia, n Sicilia cu l'intinzioni di farla veniri ê Stati Uniti quannu avi risparmiatu abbastanza sordi. Iddu travagghia nnôn furnu comu aiutanti ô furnaru. Marcu è senza travagghiu e cerca mpiegu. Oggi è duminica e i dui frati si vestunu pi gghiri a missa.

E: We present a little story to introduce several dialogues in Sicilian. This story deals with two brothers, Vito and Marco Terranostra, and their adventures in the United States. It begins shortly after the end of the Second World War. When the war ended in Sicily, Vito and Marco caught a freighter to the United States and arrived at the city of Baltimore in the state of Maryland. They live in a part of the city known as Little Italy because of the large number of Italian immigrants living there. Vito is the older brother and has left his fiancée, Cecilia, behind in Sicily with the intention of having her sent to the United States when he's saved enough money. He works as an assistant at a baker's shop. Marco doesn't have a job and is seeking employment. Today is Sunday and the two brothers are getting dressed to go to mass.

Vitu: (a Marcu)	Vestiti, Marcu, ca semu già n ritardu. Talia u riloggiu. Sunnu già i novi e cinquanta e a missa cumincia ê deci e menza. **E:** Get dressed, Marco. We're already late. Just look at the clock. It's nine fifty and mass starts at ten thirty.
Marcu:	Va beni, mi staiu priparannu cchiù prestu possìbbili. Proimi dda cammisa supra a seggia e mâ mettu. **E:** OK. I'm hurrying as fast as I can. Hand me that shirt on the chair and I'll put it on.
Vitu:	Quali cammisa? Unni è? Non â viu. **E:** What shirt? Where is it? I don't see it.
Marcu:	È ddà, supra a seggia, vicinu a finestra. Chidda bianca. Â vidi ora? **E:** It's there on the chair near the window. The white one. Do you see it now?
Vitu:	Ah, sì, ora â viu. (Va a pigghialla) Marcu, sta cammisa mi pari lorda. Chista non tâ poi mettiri pi gghiri â missa! **E:** Ah, yes, I see it now. (He goes to fetch it) Marco, this shirt seems dirty to me. You can't wear this to go to mass.
Marcu:	Sì sicuru ca voi iri â missa? Oggi fa na bedda iurnata e nni putissimu iri a caminari strati strati vicinu ô portu a taliari tutti ddi beddi picciotti chi portanu vistini eleganti. Oggi è duminica e tutti vonnu fari bedda fiura. **E:** Are you sure that you want to go to church? It's really great weather today, and we could walk along the streets to the port and look at all the attractive girls wearing their pretty dresses because it's Sunday and they want to make a good appearance.
Vitu:	Marcu, sai ca aiu n'anciledda n Sicilia ca m'aspetta cu pacenza finu a quannu aiu accumulatu abbastanza sordi pi farla veniri ccà ô me latu. **E:** Marco, you know that I have my little angel back there in Sicily who's patiently waiting for me until I've saved enough money to have her sent here at my side.
Marcu:	Va beni, Vitu, è bonu pi tia ca ai a to anciledda ma iu non aiu a nuddu. E mi piacissi truvarinni una pi mia. **E:** That's good, Vito, it's really good that you have your little angel, but I have no one. And I would like to find one for me.
Vitu:	No, non pozzu. U me patruni, Mastru Peppi, ogni duminica va sempri a missa e cci dissi ca cci ieva. **E:** No, I can't do. My boss, Mastru Peppi, always goes to mass every Sunday, and I told him I would go there.
Marcu:	Chistu è u to prubblema. Vaiu a fari na passiatedda ô portu. **E:** That's your problem. I'm going to take a little stroll down by the port.
Vitu:	Accumpagnami a sentiri a missa, Marcu. Fammi stu piaciri. Mastru Peppi avi na gran bedda figghia chi avi a essiri ddà. **E:** Come with me to church,

	Marco, do me this favor. Mastru Peppi has a very pretty daughter's who'll be there.
Marcu:	Ora capisciu! E comu si chiama? **E:** Now I understand! So, what's her name?
Vitu:	Si chiama Catarina. Avi i trizzi ncutti ncutti e niuri comu na notti senza luna e avi l'occhi niuri lucenti. È na siciliana bedda bedda. **E:** Her name's Catherine. She has very thick tresses black as the night and shining black eyes. She's a real Sicilian beauty.
Marcu:	Ora a missa mi pari cchiù ntirissanti. Va beni, t'accumpagnu. **E:** Now you make church sound more interesting. OK, I'll come along.

Ntâ chesa (At church)

Vitu e Marcu acchiananu a scalunata dâ chesa e trasunu. Arrivanu propiu n tempu giustu. S'assettanu ntôn bancu mentri u parrinu s'avvicina a l'artaru maggiuri e a missa cumincia.

E: Vito and Marco are climbing the steps of the church and enter. They arrive just in time. They sit down on a bench as the priest approaches the high alter and mass begins.

Marcu: (a Vitu)	Unni è sta bedda siciliana? Non â viu. **E:** Where is this Sicilian beauty? I don't see her.
Vitu:	Zittiti, Marcu. A missa sta cuminciannu. **E:** Shhh, Marco, the mass's starting.
Marcu:	Aah, criu ca ora â viu. Ddà, vicinu â culonna. È idda? (Cci ciuciulia na cosa a Vitu e poi cci duna na guvitata) **E:** Aah, I think I see her now. There, near the column. Is that she? (He whispers to Vito and then nudges him.)
Vitu:	Marcu, zittiti! **E:** Be quiet!
Marcu:	È idda? (Duna na taliata a na bedda giuvina ca non cci duna cuntu. Iddu duna nautra guvitata a Vitu.) Dimmi si è idda!. **E:** Is that she? (He glances at a beautiful young woman who isn't paying any attention to him. He nudges Vito again.) Tell me if that is the girl!
Vitu:	(Non cci dici nenti ma fa signu di sì. Marcu fa un gran surrisu a Vitu e cci ciuciulia nt'aricchia.) **E.** (He says nothing to Marco but nods. Marco gives him a broad smile and whispers in his ear.)
Marcu:	Sugnu nnamuratu di idda, daveru. Ai a prisintarimi a idda appena a missa finisci. OK? **E.** I'm really in love with her. You've got to introduce me to her as soon as mass's over. OK?

Ntâ scala dâ chesa (On the stairs of the church)

Doppu ca finisci a missa, a genti nesci dâ chesa e cumincia a scinniri dâ scalunata. Vitu e Marcu si avvicinanu a Mastru Peppi e a so figghia. Mastru Peppi è viduvu e Catarina è figghia unica. Catarina è assai orgugliusa d'essiri miricana, ma puru è orgugliusa dâ so eredità siciliana. Penza di essiri na picciotta cumpletamenti muderna, ma puru ama e rispetta i tradizzioni e i custumi antichi. Ora è studintissa ntô Colleggiu di Notre Dame dû Maryland, un culleggiu criatu specialmenti pî fimmini. Studia storia europea e avi ntiressi spiciali pâ storia dâ Sicilia.

E. After mass is over, the people are coming out of church and going down the steps. Vito and Marco approach Mastru Peppi and his daughter. Mastru Peppi is a widower, and Catherine is an only daughter. Catherine is very proud of being an American, but she is also proud of her Sicilian heritage. She thinks of herself as a thoroughly modern young woman, but she also loves and respects the old ways and traditions. She's presently a student at the College of Notre Dame of Maryland which is a college created specially for women. She studies European history and has a special interest in the history of Sicily.

Vitu:	Bon giornu, Mastru Peppi. Bon giornu, Catarina. Comu stati? **E.** Hello, Mastru Peppi. Hello, Catherine. How are you (plural)?
Mastru Peppi:	Ah, bon giornu, Vitu. Semu boni. E tu, comu sì? **E.** Ah, hello Vito. We are well. And you, how are you?
Vitu:	Chi bedda iurnata oggi, veru? Mi piaci assai u misi d'aprili. Vi piaci puru? **E.** It's really nice today, isn't it? I really like the month of April. Do you like it also?
Catarina:	Iu adoru u misi d'aprili. Criu ca è u misi cchiù beddu di l'annu. Tutti i ciuri sboccianu e i culuri dâ primavera sunnu na meravigghia. Finarmenti u mmernu accabbau, grazzii a Diu. **E.** I adore April. I think that it's the most beautiful month of the year. All the flowers are in bloom and the colors of spring are marvelous. Finally, winter's over, thank God.
Vitu:	Mastru Peppi e Catarina, vi vulissi prisintari a Marcu, me frati cchiù picciriddu. Mastru Peppi and Catherine, I'd like to present my younger brother, Marco.
Mastru Peppi:	Tantu piaciri. (Cci strinci a manu a Marcu.) **E.** I'm pleased to meet you. (He shakes hands with Marco.)
Catarina:	Sugnu cuntenta di fari a so canuscenza. (surridennu a Marcu.) So frati, Vitu, nni piaci assai a mia e a me patri. **E.** It gives me great pleasure to meet you. (She smiles at Marco.) Vito, my father and I like your brother a lot.
Marcu:	(Iddu sta ddà comu si un furmini l'avissi curputu. Finarmenti parra.) Ah, U piaciri è miu! **E.** (He stands there as if a bolt of lightening has struck him. Finally he speaks.) Ah, the pleasure is all mine.

Marcu avi un appuntamentu cu Catarina (Marco has a date with Catherine)
Marcu cci dumanna vinti dollari a Vitu pi purtari Catarina ô risturanti ntâ Piccola Italia. Ntô 1946 vinti dollari valevanu cchiossai di oggi. Vitu cci l'impresta.

E. Marco asks Vito for twenty dollars to take Catherine to a restaurant in Little Italy. In 1946 twenty dollars were worth a lot more than today. Vito lends it to him.

Vitu:	Nta quali risturanti â porti? **E:** What restaurant are taking her to?
Marcu:	Stamu iennu nni Giulianu. **E:** We're going to Giuliano's.
Vitu:	Non aiu statu mai ddà. È bonu? **E:** I've never been there. Is it good?
Marcu:	Canusciu unu dî cammareri. Si chiama Pitruzzu. **E:** I know one of the waiters. His name's Pete.
Vitu:	U manciari com'è, bonu? **E:** Is the food good there?
Marcu:	Dilizziusissimu. **E:** Very good.
Vitu:	Fratuzzu meu, divertiti stasira. **E:** Little brother, have a good time this evening.
Marcu:	Catarina e iu n'amu a divertiri assai. Ciau. **E:** Catherine and I are going to enjoy ourselves. Bye.

Vitu: Sì assai furtunatu ca semu ccà ntâ Merica e non ntâ Sicilia unni è ancora nicissariu essiri accumpagnati di tutta a famigghia. Ciau e salutami a Catarina. **E:** You're really lucky that we're here in America and not in Sicily where it's still necessary to be accompanied by the whole family. Bye and say a hello to Catherine from me.

Marcu: Sarai servitu! **E.** I certainly will.

13   Verbs: Subjunctive

Purpose of the Chapter
This chapter deals with the subjunctive, which is, strictly speaking, not a tense but a mood. The other two moods in Sicilian are the indicative and the imperative. These were discussed in previous chapters. The subjunctive refers to what is subjective and/or hypothetical: things the subject wishes, or supposes, or presumes, or thinks, or what might be, as opposed to the indicative which expressed certainty and statements of fact. Unlike English, in which the subjunctive has all but disappeared (we still have a few vestiges, for example, in the "were" of "if I were you"), it is still widely used in the Romance languages. The conditional is also introduced even though its occurrence is relatively rare.

Subjunctive
The subjunctive is generally used to indicate what may be the case as opposed to what is actually the case. It is used in several distinct ways. These are:

> **Use #1:** Hypothetical conditions in the past after certain verb types (see the list below);
> **Use #2:** After certain subordinating conjunctions if the verb in the main clause is in the past;
> **Use #3:** As a polite imperative, that is "Would you...";
> **Use #4:** The conditional in certain types of sentences.

Verb Types Triggering the Subjunctive
In the Romance languages, certain verb types in the principal clause trigger a verb in the subjunctive mood in the subordinate clause. In Sicilian, if the verb in the principal clause is in the past or suggests a situation or context that is more hypothetical (contrary-to-fact) than actual, the subjunctive is triggered. The imperfect or past perfect subjunctive is required in such circumstances. **Caution:** If the verb in the principal clause is in the present, Sicilian generally does not use the subjunctive, but again, if a situation or context is more hypothetical (contrary-to-fact) than actual, the subjunctive is triggered. Again, the imperfect or past perfect subjunctive is required in such circumstances. See **Present Subjunctive** below. The triggering verb types are:

- Verbs of desiring, wanting, or willing;
- Verbs of hoping or fearing;
- Verbs of commanding, ordering, or demanding;
- Verbs of thinking or supposing;
- Verbs of granting or permitting;
- Verbs of fearing or regretting;
- Many impersonal verbs;
- Verbs of denying (negation);
- Verbs of doubting (uncertainty);
- Also cases involving an indefinite someone or something (strictly speaking, not a verb type, but included here for completeness).

Present Subjunctive

In Sicilian, as in some of the other regional languages of Italy, the present subjunctive has practically disappeared. It has been replaced by the present indicative. Sicilian generally employs the present indicative in the subordinate clause if the verb of the main clause is in the present. However, as was pointed out above, if the speaker conceives the situation or context to be more hypothetical (contrary-to-fact) than actual, the subjunctive is triggered. Again, the imperfect or past perfect subjunctive is required in such circumstances. See the Examples below. When the verb of the main clause is in the past, the subjunctive is triggered if one of the uses cited above is applicable. See the examples in **Past Perfect Subjunctive** below.

Examples

(1) Iu vogghiu ca tu travagghi tuttu u iornu ê to studii. I want you to work all day on your studies.

(2) Iu speru ca vuiatri m'accumpagnati ô cinima. I hope that you'll accompany me to the movies.

(3) Iddu nega ca Rubertu avi u libbru mmanu (**or** in manu). He denies that Robert has the book in his hand.

(4) Iu dubbitu ca Marta avi i sordi p'accattarisi a machina ca voli. I doubt that Martha has the money to buy the car that she wants.

(5) Disiddiru ca Maria veni a vidiri a mia oggi. I want Mary to come see me today.

(6) È nicissariu ca Giuvanni studia a chimica p'essiri prumossu. It's necessary that John study chemistry to be promoted.

(7) Niatri ti cumannamu ca fai chistu ora ora. We command that you do this right now.

(8) Ti pari ca Maria veni oi? Do you think Mary'll come today?

(9) Mi pari ca idda è bedda assai. I think that she's very beautiful.

(10) Iddi si lamentanu (**or** A iddi cci dispiaci) ca to figghiu è n statu gravi. They regret that your son's in a grave state.

(11) Idda disiddira ca iddu cci addumanna a manu a so patri. She desires that he ask her father for her hand.

(12) Quannu chi crisci iddu, mi scantu ca ritorna ccà a ammazzarimi. When he grows up, I fear that he'll come back and kill me.

(13) Suppognu ca tu voi iri ô cinima sta vasciurata. I suppose that you want to go to the movies this afternoon.

(14) U prufissuri pirmetti ca i studenti usanu u computer duranti l'esami di fisica. The professor permits the students to use a computer during the physics examination.

(15) Niatri circamu na pirsuna ca parra nglisi. We're looking for someone who speaks English.

Note: In some of the Examples above, an imperfect subjunctive could also be used if the speaker conceives the situation or context to be more hypothetical (contrary-to-fact) than actual. Examples (4), (5), (8), (9), (12), (13), and (15) could be so construed.

Remnants of the Present Subjunctive

The present subjunctive is at times found in Literary Sicilian and is also sometimes found in some proverbs and sayings, and in a few imperatives of short, widely used verbs. See **Imperative of the Common Verbs** in Chapter 6.

Examples of the present subjunctive in proverbs and short imperatives

(1) … mai paci pozz'aviri a la so casa. … may he never be able to have peace in his house. See Caracè (1980), p. 144 (La Barunissa di Carini).

(2) Amici siamu e li vurzi si cummattanu. **Sicilian proverb.** Let's be friends, and let our purses fight. **Meaning:** We get along, but our economic interests clash.

(3) Vegna. Come. (2nd person singular polite imperative of *veniri*)

(4) Bon venga. /bom meña **or** bom veña/. Welcome.

(5) Vaia. Vaia. Get going! Come on! (2nd person singular polite imperative of *iri*)

(6) Iamu. Let's go. (1st person plural polite imperative of *iri*)

(7) Siati boni picciriddi. Be good children. (2nd person plural imperative of *essiri*)

(8) Sia gintili. Be nice. (2nd person singular familiar and polite imperative of *essiri*)

(9) Binidica. Bless. (A greeting showing respect to the person asked to bless.)

Present Subjunctive of essiri and aviri

The forms of the present subjunctive of *essiri* are still fairly frequently used, so you should familiarize yourself with them. **Note:** The word "that" is given in parentheses to remind you that subjunctive forms normally occur in a dependent clause. The subjunctive forms of *aviri* are given for reference.

essiri, to be	aviri, to have
iu sia, (that) I am	iu aia, (that) I have
tu sia, (that) you are	tu ai, (that) you have
vossìa sia, (that) you are	vossìa aia, (that) you have
iddu sia, (that) he is	iddu aia, (that) he has
nuiatri siamu, (that) we are	nuiatri aiamu, (that) we have
vuiatri siati, (that) you are	vuiatri aiati, (that) you have
iddi sianu, (that) they are	iddi aianu, (that) they have

Note: In reality, the English subjunctive forms of "to be" are: I be, you be, he/she be, we be, you be, they be. These forms aren't used in the translation since they sound very archaic.

Imperfect Subjunctive

Unlike the present subjunctive, the imperfect subjunctive is widely used in Sicilian, and this is one of the tenses whose usage and forms you must thoroughly master. Several different meanings can be given for the imperfect subjunctive. Using *parrassi* as a model, it can be translated as: I spoke, I was speaking, I could speak, I might speak, etc. The exact translation depends on the specific context. See the examples and the uses below.

Conjugation 1	**Conjugation 2**
parrari, to speak	rispunniri, to reply
iu par*rassi*, (that) I spoke	iu rispunn*issi*, (that) I replied
tu par*rassi*, (that) you spoke	tu rispunn*issi*, (that) you replied
vossìa par*rassi*, (that) you spoke	vossìa rispunn*issi*, (that) you replied
iddu par*rassi*, (that) he spoke	iddu rispunn*issi*, (that) he replied
nuiatri par*rassimu*, (that) we spoke	nuiatri rispunn*issimu*, (that) we replied
vuiatri par*rassivu*, (that) you spoke	vuiatri rispunn*issivu*, (that) you replied
iddi par*rassiru*, (that) they spoke	iddi rispunn*issiru*, (that) they replied
or iddi par*rassinu*, (that) they spoke	**or** iddi rispunn*issinu*, (that) they replied

Most verbs have a regular imperfect subjunctive, but several have an irregular one: *diri* (it's regular if you remember that the old infinitive is *diciri*), *essiri*, and *fari* (it's regular if you remember that the old infinitive is *faciri*).

Verbs Having an Irregular Imperfect Subjunctive	Imperfect Subjunctive Forms
diri, to say, tell	**Singular forms:** iu dicissi, tu dicissi, vossìa dicissi, iddu dicissi **Plural forms:** nuiatri dicissimu, vuiatri dicissivu, iddi dicissiru **or** dicissinu
essiri, to be	**Singular forms:** iu fussi, tu fussi, vossìa fussi, iddu fussi **Plural forms:** nuiatri fussimu, vuiatri fussivu, iddi fussiru **or** fussinu
fari, to do, make	**Singular forms:** iu facissi, tu facissi, vossìa facissi, iddu facissi **Plural forms:** nuiatri facissimu, vuiatri facissivu, iddi facissiru **or** facissinu

Imperfect Subjunctive of aviri a + infinitive

aviri a accattari, to have to buy

Literary	Literary and spoken	Spoken
iu avissi a accattari	avissâ accattari	avissâ 'ccattari
tu avissi a accattari	avissâ accattari	avissâ 'ccattari
vossìa avissi a accattari	avissâ accattari	avissâ 'ccattari
iddu avissi a accattari	avissâ accattari	avissâ 'ccattari
nuiatri avissimu a accattari	avissimâ accattari	avissimâ 'ccattari
vuiatri avissivu a accattari	avissivâ accattari	avissivâ 'ccattari
iddi avissiru a accattari	avissirâ accattari	avissirâ 'ccattari

Past Perfect Subjunctive

The auxiliary verb for the past perfect subjunctive is also *aviri*. In the examples above in **Present Subjunctive**, the verb of the main clause is in the present tense as is the verb in the subordinate clause. If the verb of the main clause were in one of the past tenses, the verb in the subordinate clause would also be in an appropriate past form, either the imperfect subjunctive or the past perfect subjunctive. The past perfect subjunctive must be used if the activity in the subordinate clause occurred before the activity of the main clause. The same examples are used below as used above in **Present Subjunctive**, but the tense of the verb of the main clause is in the past, triggering a subjunctive in the subordinate clause. Note carefully what subjunctive is used (imperfect subjunctive **versus** past perfect subjunctive) and the corresponding meaning of the sentence.

Conjugation 1
parrari, to speak
iu avissi parratu, I had spoken
tu avissi parratu, you had spoken
vossìa avissi parratu, you had spoken
iddu avissi parratu, he had spoken
nuiatri avissimu parratu, we had spoken
vuiatri avissivu parratu, you had spoken
iddi avissiru parratu, they had spoken
or iddi avissinu parratu, they had spoken

Conjugation 2
rispunniri, to reply
iu avissi rispunnutu, I had replied
tu avissi rispunnutu, you had replied
vossìa avissi rispunnutu, you had replied
iddu avissi rispunnutu, he had replied
nuiatri avissimu rispunnutu, we had replied
vuiatri avissivu rispunnutu, you had replied
iddi avissiru rispunnutu, they had replied
or iddi avissinu rispunnutu, they had replied

Examples

(1) Iu vulia ca tu travagghiassi tuttu u iornu ê to studii. I wanted you to work all day on your studies.

(2) Iu spirava ca vuiatri m'accumpagnassivu ô cinima. I was hoping that you could accompany me to the movies.

(3) Iu spirava ca vuiatri m'avissivu accumpagnatu ô cinima. I was hoping that you could have accompanied me to the movies.

(4) Iddu nig**au** ca Rubertu avissi u libbru mmanu (**or** in manu). He denied that Robert had the book in his hand.

(5) Iddu nig**au** ca Rubertu avissi avutu u libbru mmanu (**or** in manu). He denied that Robert had had the book in his hand.

(6) Iu dubbit**ai** ca Marta avissi i sordi p'accattarisi a machina ca vulia. I doubted that Martha had the money to buy the car that she wanted.

(7) Disiddir**ai** ca Maria vinissi a vidiri a mia oggi. I wanted Mary to come see me today.

(8) Disiddir**ai** ca Maria avissi vinutu a vidiri a mia oggi prima ca partivi. I wished that Mary had come to see me today before I left.

(9) Era nicissariu ca Giuvanni studiassi a chimica p'essiri prumossu. It was necessary that John study chemistry to be promoted.

(10) Niatri vi cumannammu ca facissivu chistu subbitu. We commanded that you (p) do this right away.

(11) Ti paria ca Maria vulissi veniri oggi? Did you think Mary would want to come today?

(12) Ti paria ca Maria avissi vinutu oggi? Did you think Mary would have come today?

(13) Mi paria ca idda fussi bedda assai. I thought that she was very beautiful.

(14) Mi paria ca idda avissi statu bedda ass**ai**. I thought that she had been very beautiful.

(15) A iddi cci dispiaciu ca to figghiu fussi malatu. They regretted that your son was ill.

(16) A iddi cci dispiaciu ca to figghiu avissi statu malatu. They regretted that your son had been ill.

(17) Idda disiddirava ca iddu cci addumannassi a manu a so patri. She desired that he would ask her father for her hand.

(18) Mi scantava ca quannu crisceva iddu, riturnassi ccà a ammazzarimi. I feared that when he grew up, he'd come back and kill me.

(19) Suppuneva ca tu avissi vulutu iri ô cinima sta vasciurata. I supposed that you had wanted to go to the movies this afternoon.

(20) U prufissuri pirmisi ca i studenti usassiru u computer duranti l'esami di fisica. The professor permitted the students to use a computer during the physics examination.

(21) Niatri circavamu na pirsuna ca parrassi nglisi. We were looking for someone who spoke English.

(22) Niatri circavamu dda picciotta c'avia parratu nglisi â festa. We were looking for that girl who had spoken English at the party. (Definite person; therefore, no subjunctive)

There are cases where the verb in the main clause is in the present, but the verb in the subordinate clause takes the subjunctive. This can happen when the subordinate clause is governed by a conjunction that triggers the subjunctive. See the next section.

Subjunctive after Subordinating Conjunctions

It was pointed out in Chapter 10 that various subordinating conjunctions require the verb in the subordinate clause to be in the subjunctive. If the verb in the main clause is in a present tense, the present indicative is generally used in the subordinate clause if a present meaning is intended. Conjunctions having the notation (subjunctive) following them take the subjunctive if the speaker conceives the situation or context to be more hypothetical (contrary-to-fact) than actual. If the verb in the main clause is in one of the past tenses, the verb in the subordinate clause will generally be in an appropriate past form, either the imperfect subjunctive or the past perfect subjunctive, depending on the meaning. Carefully examine the examples below. Other constructions are also possible, allowing one to avoid the subjunctive, e.g., (16) and (17) employing a *preposition + infinitive* instead.

Examples

(1) Puru chi avi i sordi, nun s'accatta a machina. Although he has the money, he won't buy the car.

(2) Puru chi avissi i sordi, nun s'accattassi a machina. Although he had the money, he wouldn't buy the car.

(3) Puru chi avissi avutu i sordi, nun s'avissi accattatu a machina. Although he had had the money, he would not have bought the car.

(4) Nesciu dâ casa puru si chiovi. I am going out even if it rains.

(5) Niscissi dâ casa puru si chiuvissi. I would go out even if it rained.

(6) Puru si è u cchiù spertu dâ classi, nun cci lassanu scriviri u saggiu pi vinciri u premiu. Even if he is the smartest in class, they're not going to let him compose the essay to win the prize.

(7) Puru si fussi u cchiù spertu dâ classi, nun cci lassassiru scriviri u saggiu pi vinciri u premiu. Even if he were the smartest in class, they wouldn't let him compose the essay to win the prize.

(8) Puru si avissi statu u cchiù spertu dâ classi, nun cci avissiru lassatu scriviri u saggiu pi vinciri u premiu. Even if he had been the smartest in class, they wouldn't have let him compose the essay to win the prize.

(9) Sebbeni ddu cristianu è riccu, avi sempri mala furtuna. Although that guy's rich, he always has bad luck.

(10) Sebbeni ddu cristianu fussi riccu, avia sempri mala furtuna. Although that guy was rich, he always had bad luck.

(11) Si nun mi duna idda i sordi, nun pozzu iri â festa. If she doesn't give me the money, I can't go to the party.

(12) Si nun mi dassi idda i sordi, nun putissi iri â festa. If she didn't give me the money, I couldn't go to the party.

(13) Si nun m'avissi datu idda i sordi, nun avissi pututu iri â festa. If she had not given me the money, I could not have gone to the party.

(14) Cci vaiu a parrari n modu ca tuttu si fa cu versu. I'm going to speak to her so that everything will get done properly.

(15) Cci ivi (**or** cci **iu**) a parrari n modu ca tuttu si facissi cu versu. I went to speak to her so that everything would get done properly.

(16) Pi putiri iri â festa, a mamma m'avissi a dari i sordi. So that I can go to the party, my mother should give me the money.

(17) Pi putiri iri â festa, a mamma m'appi a dari (**or** m'appâ dari) i sordi. So that I could go to the party, my mother had to give me the money.

If-sentences

There are certain types of sentences known as if-sentences. These are simply sentences using the subordinating conjunction *si* **or** *siddu*. They follow the same rules as given above for other subordinating conjunctions. If the if-sentence expresses a contrary-to-fact situation that would most likely never take place, the subjunctive is used. Note the examples below.

Examples

(1) Si aiu i sordi, m'accattu a machina. If I have the money, I'll buy the car. (You may indeed have it, and if you do, you'll buy it.)

(2) Si avissi i sordi, m'accattassi a machina. If I had the money, I would buy the car. (But I don't have it, so I can't buy it. – This is a contrary-to-fact situation.)

(3) Si avissi avutu i sordi, m'avissi accattatu a machina. If I had had the money, I would have bought the car. (But I didn't have it, so I didn't buy it. – This is a contrary-to-fact situation.)

(4) Si iu parru cu iddu, cci dicu a virità. If I speak with him, I'll tell him the truth. (You may indeed speak with him, and if you do, you'll tell him.)

(5) Si iu parrassi cu iddu, cci dicissi a virità. If I spoke with him, I'd tell him the truth. (But you may never speak with him, so you may never have the chance to tell him the truth. – This is a contrary-to-fact situation.)

(6) Si iu avissi parratu cu iddu, cci avissi dittu a virità. If I had spoken with him, I'd have told him the truth. (But you didn't speak with him, so you never had the chance to tell him the truth. – This is a contrary-to-fact situation.)

Subjunctive as a Polite Imperative or a Conditional

The imperfect subjunctive can often function as a polite form of the imperative, and it can also function in place of a conditional. In some of the examples directly above, the use of the subjunctive as a conditional is given. In general, the conditional is translated as "would … ".

Examples

(1) Vulissivu quarchiccosa di cchiù? Would you (p) like something else?

(2) Mi putissi favuriri di veniri a me casa pi manciari? Could you favor me at my house for dinner? (i.e., Would you come to my house for dinner?)

(3) Mi facissi stu piaciri e vinissi a manciari cu nuiatri n casa. Would you do me this favor and come to eat with us in our home.

(4) Vulissi iri ô cinima sta vasciurata, ma a mamma nun mû pirmetti. I'd like to go to the movies this afternoon, but my mother won't allow me.

(11) Sì, iu cci issi si fussi di tia. Yes, I'd go if I were you.

(12) Sì, iu cci avissi iutu si avissi statu di tia. Yes, I would have gone if I had been you.

(13) Mi facissi vidiri a casa chi voli vinniri. Show me the house that you want to sell.

(14) Mi dicissi a virità. Tell me the truth.

(15) Tû dicissi sû sapissi. I'd tell it to you if I knew it. (sû = si + û)

(16) Cci l'accattassi. Buy it for him.

(17) Ccî ddumanassi i sordi. Ask him for the money.

(18) Vulissi diri na cosa. I'd like to say a thing.

Conditional

Like the use of the simple future, the use of the conditional has increased in Sicilian, again probably due to the influence of Italian. So you should at least familiarize yourself with these forms because you may encounter them if you read any Sicilian, especially more recently written materials. The endings are very regular for the two conjugations. These forms aren't recommended. They are given so that you can recognize them when you encounter them. **Note:** It is recommended that you use an appropriate form of the subjunctive to express conditional meanings rather than the conditional.

Conjugation 1

iu parr*iria*, I would speak
tu parr*irissi*, you would speak
vossìa parr*iria*, you would speak
iddu parr*iria*, he would speak
nuiatri parr*iriamu*, we would speak
vuiatri parr*iriavu*, you would speak
iddi parr*irianu*, they would speak

Conjugation 2

iu rispunn*iria*, I would reply
tu rispunn*irissi*, you would reply
vossìa rispunn*iria*, you would reply
iddu rispunn*iria*, he would reply
nuiatri rispunn*iriamu*, we would reply
vuiatri rispunn*iriavu*, you would reply
iddi rispunn*irianu*, they would reply

The following verbs have an irregular conditional.

Verbs Having an Irregular Conditional	Conditional Forms
essiri, to be	**Singular forms:** iu saria, tu sarissi, vossìa saria, iddu saria **Plural forms:** nuiatri sariamu, vuiatri sariavu, iddi sarianu
fari, to do, make*	**Singular forms:** iu faria, tu farissi, vossìa faria, iddu faria **Plural forms:** nuiatri fariamu, vuiatri fariavu, iddi farianu
vuliri, to want, wish	**Singular forms:** iu vurria, tu vurrissi, vossìa vurria, iddu vurria **Plural forms:** nuiatri vurriamu, vuiatri vurriavu, iddi vurrianu

* The verbs *dari* and *stari* follow exactly the same pattern as *fari*.

Examples of the conditional in the literature

(1) Lu poviru omu cci aviria datu la so arma a lu diavulu pi du sordi. The poor man would have given his soul to the devil for two cents.

(2) Lu so primu figghiu aviria duvutu purtari ddu nomu gluriusu. His first son would have to bear that glorious name.

(3) Iu tû diria si tû putissi. I'd tell you if I could.

Examples of the conditional in the literature

(1) Lu poviru omu cci aviria datu la so arma a lu diavulu pi du sordi. The poor man would have given his soul to the devil for two cents.
(2) Lu so primu figghiu aviria duvutu purtari ddu nomu gluriusu. His first son would have to bear that glorious name.
(3) Iu tû diria si tû putissi. I'd tell you if I could.
(4) Ti manniria n galera pi calunnia, parola mia! I'd send you to jail for slander, upon my word!

All of the above examples can be rendered in better Sicilian using appropriate forms of the imperfect subjunctive.

Examples redone with the imperfect subjunctive

(1) Lu poviru omu cci avissi datu la so arma a lu diavulu pi du sordi. The poor man would have given his soul to the devil for two cents.
(2) Lu so primu figghiu avissi duvutu purtari ddu nomu gluriusu. His first son would have to bear that glorious name.
(3) Iu tû dicissi si tû putissi. I'd tell you if I could.
(4) Ti mannassi n galera pi calunnia, parola mia! I'd send you to jail for slander, upon my word!

Sicilian Dialogue #2

Sta parti cuntinua a storia di l'avvinturi di Vitu e Marcu Terranostra ntâ Merica.

E: This is a continuation of Vito and Marco Terranostras' adventures in America.

Nnô risturanti (At the restaurant)

Marcu e Catarina vannu ô risturanti ca si chiama Giulianu. Ddà si mancia bonu e a prezzi raggiunevuli e Marcu è amicu dû cammareri. U patruni, Don Micheli, è assittatu supra na seggia vicinu â porta e si sta surbennu un cafè espressu caudu di na tazzitta.

E: Marco and Catherine go to a restaurant called Giuliano's. The food's good there and is reasonably priced, and Marco is a friend of the waiter. The owner, Don Micheli, is seated on a chair near the door and is sipping a hot espresso from a demi-tasse.

Marcu:	Bona sira, Don Micheli. Semu dui. **E:** Good evening, Don Micheli. There are two of us.
Don Micheli:	È chiaru ca vi pozzu vidiri chî me stissi occhi. E comu siti vuiatri stasira? (Duna na taliata cu l'occhi aperti a Catarina.) **E:** That's clear since I can see you with my own two eyes. And how are you this evening? (He gives Catherine the once over.)
Marcu:	Stamu beni, Don Micheli. Grazzii. **E:** We're well, Don Micheli. Thanks.
Don Micheli:	Vulissivu na tavula vicinu a finestra o una ntô menzu dû risturanti? **E:** Would you like a table near the window or at the center of the restaurant?
Catarina:	Prifirisciu a tavula vicinu a finestra. Tu chi dici, Marcu? **E:** I prefer a table near the window. What do you think, Marcu?

Marcu:	Certamenti, vicinu a finestra! (sutta vuci a Catarina) Accussì stamu cchiù intimi. **E:** Certainly, near the window! (Turning to Catarina) This way we will be more to ourselves.
Don Micheli:	Benissimu, allura. Pi piaciri, siguitimi. **E:** Excellent, then. Please, follow me.

Marcu e Catarina accumpagnanu a Don Micheli e s'assettanu nta na tavula accantu na finestra larga. **E:** Marco and Catherine accompany Don Micheli and sit down at a table next to a wide window.

Catarina:	Ah, com'è rumanticu. A nostra tavuluzza avi na cannila e un mazzu di violi comu piacinu a mia. Sta tuvagghia e sti tuvagghioli sunnu elegantissimi e di linu puru. È propriu comu m'immagginava. Ti piaci, Marcu? **E:** Ah, how romantic. Our little table has a candle and a bunch of violets as I like them. This tablecloth and these napkins of pure linen are very elegant. It's just how I imagined it. Do you like it, Marco?
Marcu:	Certamenti, Catarina. Si sì cuntenta tu, sugnu cuntentu iu. **E:** Certainly, Catherine. If you're happy, I'm happy.
Catarina:	Marcu, tutti i me amici mi chiamanu Trina e tu puru m'ai a chiamari Trina. **E:** Marco, all my friends call me Trina (Cathy) and you should call me Trina too.
Cammareri: (a tutti dui)	Bona sira, signuri. Speru ca u nostru risturanti sia di vostru gradimentu. **E:** Good evening. I do hope you enjoy our restaurant.
Marcu:	Unni è Petru, u cammareri abbituali? **E:** Where's Peter, the regular waiter?
Cammareri:	Non potti veniri a travagghiari stasira. Iu pigghiaiu u so postu. **E:** He couldn't work this evening. I'm filling in for him.
Catarina:	Oh, bona sira. Chi postu simpaticu! Vulemu manciari a la siciliana stasira, comu si fussimu a Palermu. Chi nni raccumanna? **E:** Oh, good evening. What a nice spot. We want to eat Sicilian style, as if we were in Palermu. What would you recommend?
Cammareri:	Vi raccumannu comu primu un piattu di pasta chî sardi. È fatta câ sarsa di pumadoru cû finocchiu sarvaggiu, sardi frischi e tanti autri beddi cosi. E comu secunnu, na bedda bistecca a griglia cû cuntornu di patati ô furnu e ligumi. **E:** I'd recommend as the first dish a good pasta with sardines. It's made with tomato sauce, wild fennel, fresh sardines and many other good things. And as the second course, roast beef, baked potatoes, and vegetables.
Catarina:	I sardi non mi piacinu, pi diri a virità. Ma si ti piaci a tia, Marcu, tâ poi pigghiari tu. Forsi pi mia un piattu di pasta a la Norma, ca non è palermitana, ma è sempri siciliana! **E:** I really don't like sardines. But if you like them, Marcu, you can have it. Perhaps, for me a serving of pasta alla Norma. It's not from Palermo, but it's always from Sicily.
Marcu:	Si non è palermitana, di unni è? **E:** If it's not from Palermo, where is it from?
Catarina:	U me prufissuri all'università mi dissi ca â fannu a Catania in onuri di Vincenzu Bellini, un gran composituri d'opera. **E:** My professor at the University told me that they prepare it in Catania in honor of Vincenzu Bellini, the great opera composer.

Marcu:	(a Catarina) Va beni, poi mû cunti. (ô cammareri) Chi autru nni cunzigghia? **E:** (to Catherine) OK, later you will tell me about it. (to the waiter) What else would you recommend?

Mentri chi u cammareri parra, Marcu talia a lista. **E:** While the waiter's talking, Marco's looking at the menu.

Cammareri: (a Marcu)	Comu primu avemu na stupenna mulinciana (**or** milinciana) fritta cu caciu palermitanu. È na specialità dâ casa. Chistu è veramenti un piattu sicilianu. **E:** As the first dish, we have superb fried eggplant with Palermitan cheese. It's the house specialty. It's a real Sicilian dish.
Marcu: (ô cammareri)	Va beni, pâ signurina purtassi a pasta a la Norma pi primu. Pi mia, mi purtassi a pasta chî sardi. Comu pozzu rifiutari l'offertà!? Pi secunnu, purtassi u piscispata la griglia cû risu pâ signurina. (a Catarina) — Sugnu sicuru ca ti piaci!— e pi mia na bedda bistecca non troppu cotta. **E:** All right, for the young lady, please bring Pasta a la Norma as first dish. And the Pasta with Sardines for me. How can I refuse the offer?! For the second, bring the grilled Swordfish with Rice for the young lady. (to Catherine) — I am sure you will like it! — and a good steak for me, but not too cooked.
Catarina:	U pisci mi piaci. Sulu i sardi non mi piacinu! **E:** I like fish. Only sardines I don't like.
Cammareri:	Benissimu. Mentri u cocu pripara tuttu, vi portu un pocu di pani di casa e l'antipastu dâ casa. Pi viviri, vuliti vidiri a lista dî vini? **E:** Very well. While the cook prepares everything I will bring you some homemade bread and the antipasto of the house. Would you like to see the wine list?
Marcu:	Non cc'è bisognu, ni purtassi menza caraffa di vinu russu e menza di vinu biancu dâ casa. L'aiu assaggiatu autri voti e ha statu sempri bonu **E:** There is no need, bring us half a carafe of red and half of white wine of the house. I have tried it other times, and it has always been good.
Cammareri:	Avi raggiuni. U vinu dâ casa è bonissimu. Û fa Don Micheli ogni annu! Ottima silezzioni. **E:** You are right. Our wines are excellent. Don Micheli himself makes them every year. An excellent choice.

Doppu ca fineru di manciari. **E:** After they've eaten.

Catarina:	Vulissi nu passasapuri. Quacchicosa di duci. **E:** I'd like dessert. Something sweet.
Marcu:	Bona pinzata. Cammareri, purtassi, pi favuri, n pocu di frutta. Chi cc'è? **E:** Good thinking. Waiter, please bring us some fruit. What do you have?
Cammareri:	Ah, avemu frutta di staciuni, caci siciliani e comu cosa duci avemu torta di puma, di cioccolattu, cannoli, e poi gelati fatti comu ntâ Sicilia, surbetti di lumiuni. Sunnu na vera dilizzia. **E:** Ah, we have fresh fruits, an assortment of Sicilian cheeses and as desserts we have apple pie, chocolate cake, cannoli and ice cream as they make it in Sicily, lemon sherbet. They're true delights.
Catarina:	Mi pigghiu a frutta frisca. **E:** I'll take the fresh fruits.

Marcu:	E iu mi pigghiu un cannolu e naturalmenti doppu nni pigghiamu du cafè. **E:** And I'll take a cannolu, and of course we'll have two espressos.

Un pocu cchiù tardu. **E:** A little while later.

Marcu:	Cammareri, u cuntu, pi favuri. **E:** Waiter, the bill, please.
Cammareri:	Certu, signuri. Eccu a vui. **E:** Of course, sir. Here it is.

Marcu paga u cuntu e poi iddu e Catarina nesciunu dû risturanti. **E:** Marco pays the bill, and then he and Catherine leave the restaurant.

Na bona pinzata pi armari un cummerciu (A good idea to start a business)

U iornu siguenti Marcu vidi a Petru nnâ strata e si cci avvicina. **E:** The next day Marco sees Peter on the street and approaches him.

Marcu:	Petru, aieri sira iu e n'amica manciammu nni Giulianu, ma non ti vittimu. Picchì no? Comu ti senti? Sì malatu? **E:** Peter, last evening a friend of mine and I ate at Giuliano's, but we didn't see you there. Why not? Are you feeling OK? Are you ill?
Petru:	No, mi sentu bonu. Pigghiai na sirata libbira picchì vuleva riflettiri un pocu supra u futuru. Talè. Travagghiannu pi l'autri non si arriva mai a fari furtuna. Vinni in America pi dari un futuru cchiù bonu ê me figghi. Vulissi armari na pizzaria e vulissi ca tu ti mittissi cu mia comu sociu. **E:** No, I feel fine. I took a night off since I wanted to reflect on my future. Look. Working for others never made anyone rich. I came to America to give a better future to my children. I would like to set up a pizzeria, and I would like you to come in with me as a partner.
Marcu:	Iu non sugnu cocu. Comu ti putissi aiutari? **E:** I am not a cook. How could I help?
Petru:	T'inzignu iu comu si fa a megghiu pizza dû munnu! E t'assicuru ca i Miricani si mettunu a fari a fila davanti u nostru postu **E:** I will teach how to make the best pizza in the world. And I assure you that the Americans will wait on line in front of our pizza place.
Marcu:	Si û dici tu, cci cridu! Facemula sta pizzaria! **E:** If you say so, I believe you. Let's start this pizzeria!

Marcu e Petru si misiru d'accordu e dicideru di dumannari a Don Micheli d'impristaricci i sordi pi affittari u postu, pigghiari u furnu, e tuttu chiddu ca era nicissariu pi armari na bedda pizzaria ntô centru dâ cità. Don Micheli fu assai gentili cu iddi e cci mpristau abbastanza pi cuminciari a travagghiari. Doppu un pocu di tempu, a fama di sta nova pizzaria si sparsi in tutta a cità e veramenti a genti cuminciau a fari a fila davanti a porta. Marcu e Petru oramai non putevanu serviri a tutti e appiru bisognu di autri genti chi travagghiavanu ntê mumenti quannu cc'eranu cchiù clienti. Infini Marcu e Petru dumannarunu a Vitu di divintari sociu cu iddi e accussì fu.

In pocu tempu u sognu dî tri siciliani si avvirau. Vitu potti mannari a chiamari a so zita dâ Sicilia e si spusarunu prestu. Marcu dumannau a Catarina di maritarisi cu iddu e naturalmenti idda, ca ntô frattempu s'avia nnamurata d'iddu, cci dissi subbitu di sì. Petru ca già avia famigghia e figghi vitti u so sognu finalmenti curunatu. E tutti i tri vissiru cuntenti, pinzannu ca ntâ Merica i sogni si ponnu accattari cû travagghiu e câ serietà.

E: Marco and Peter agreed to do this and decided to ask Don Micheli to lend them the money to lease a place, get an oven, and all the other necessities to set up a fine pizzeria in a downtown location. Don Micheli was very kind to them, and loaned them enough to start up their business. After a little while, the reputation of this pizzeria spread throughout the entire city, and people really did wait in line in front of their door. By now Marco and Peter were not able to serve everyone, and they needed more people to help them when the pizzeria got really full. Finally they asked Vito to become a partner with them and so that's the way it was.

Within a short while the dream of the three Sicilians was realized. Vito was able to send for his fiancée from Sicily, and they got married almost as soon as she arrived. Marco asked Catherine to marry him, and because she's fallen in love with him in the meanwhile, immediately said yes. Peter, who already had a family and children, saw his dream finally come true. And all three lived happily, thinking that in America dreams can become reality through hard work and seriousness of purpose.

14   Verbs: Passive Voice

Purpose of the Chapter

The chief purpose of this chapter is to introduce the passive voice. The passive voice means that the subject of the sentence, rather than being the agent, is the patient, that is, the action is performed on the subject rather than the subject performing the action. Consider these examples in English.

Examples

- John shot the deer. This sentence is in the active voice. "John" is (1) the subject and (2) the agent since it is he performing the action. The "deer" is (1) the direct object and (2) the patient since it is the receiver of the action.
- The deer was shot by John. This sentence is in the passive voice. The "deer" is (1) the subject and (2) the patient since it is the receiver of the action. "John" is (1) the object of the preposition "by" and (2) the agent since it is he performing the action.

Passive Constructions in Sicilian

In Sicilian there are two ways of performing the passive. These are:

- Impersonal passive reflexive;
- Use of *e*ssiri, or sometimes veniri, as an auxiliary.

The first, the impersonal reflexive passive, is very commonly used. This construction was taken up in **Chapter 7**. See **Impersonal Reflexive Passive** in that chapter.

Essiri as an Auxiliary of the Passive

The other method for forming the passive in Sicilian is to use a construction involving *essiri* as an auxiliary verb with the past participle. If an agent is expressed, the preposition "by" is translated by *di* in Sicilian. The model of the passive construction is:

- patient (receives the action) + form of *e*ssiri + past participle (adjective)
  + *di* + agent (performs action)

In the passive construction, the past participle acts in the capacity of an adjective in all cases; therefore, it must receive an ending agreeing with its subject.

Examples

(1) A porta è chiusa dâ fimmina. The door is closed by the woman.
(2) I porti sunnu chiusi dî fimmini. The doors are closed by the women.
(3) I ciuri eranu coti dâ picciridda. The flowers were picked by the little girl.
(4) U picciriddu fu rimpruviratu di so mamma. The little boy was scolded by his mother.
(5) Iddu dubbit**au** chi l'assegnu avissi statu scrittu dû diritturi. He doubted that the check had been written by the director.
(6) A littra avi ad **e**ssiri scritta dû prisidenti dâ banca. The letter will be written (**or** should be written) by the president of the bank.
(7) Sâ (= si a) me machina avissi statu arrubbata dû latru, mala furtuna m'avissi succidutu. If my car had been robbed by the thief, bad luck would have befallen me.

Veniri as an Auxiliary of the Passive

When the agent isn't specified, it's fairly common to use *veniri* rather than *essiri* as the auxiliary verb. The use of *veniri* is found with 3rd person singular and plural.

Examples

(1) A porta è chiusa dâ fimmina. The door is closed by the woman. (She's in the act right now of closing it.)

(2) **versus** A porta veni chiusa. The door is shut. (It's in that state; no one's actively involved in doing it.)

(3) I ciuri eranu coti dâ picciridda. The flowers were picked by the little girl. (She was in the act of picking them.)

(4) **versus** I ciuri vinianu coti. The flowers were picked. (They're in that state; no one's actively involved in doing it.)

(5) A littra fu scritta dû prisidenti dâ banca. The letter was written by the president of the bank. (He wrote it.)

(6) **versus** A littra vinni scritta. The letter was written. (It was in that state, but the agent's unclear or unspecified.)

Avoidance of the Passive

In Sicilian, the passive isn't favored, and other syntactic constructions are often used to avoid it. The use of the impersonal reflexive passive is one such construction, especially if no specified agent is designated. Another is the use of the active voice in place of the passive.

(1) Passive construction

U giurnali è liggiutu ogni iornu. The newspaper's read every day.

Impersonal Reflexive Passive

Si leggi u giurnali ogni iornu. People read the newspaper every day.

(2) Passive construction

L'arvulu fu ittatu n terra dô ventu forti. The tree was thrown to the ground by the strong wind.

Active construction

L'arvulu û itt**au** n terra u ventu forti. **or** U ventu forti itt**au** l'arvulu n terra. The strong wind threw the tree to the ground.

Vocabulary

Nouns	Verbs
l'andatura **or** annatura, gait; pace	accurdari (accordu), to reconcile (people); tune up (an instrument)
l'assegnu, check (e.g., bank check)	addattari, to suckle, nurse
l'assenza, absence	addivintari (addiventu) **or** divintari (diventu), to become
l'attu (M), act; deed; action	
l'avu, grandfather; greatgrandfather; ancestor	addutari (addotu) [dd] **or** dutari (dotu), to endow, give in dowry, pass down
l'ava, grandmother; greatgrandmother	
la banca, bank	aggradiri **or** gradiri (sc), to like, please
lu bancu **or** vancu, bench (p -a)	arricchiri **or** ricchiri (sc), to enrich, make rich
la cacca, excrement, shit (human)	

156

Nouns (cont.)

la cadenza, cadence; modulation
la cammarera, waitress; maid
lu cammareri, waiter (p -a)
lu cantu, song; corner, angle (of a room)
la catina, chain
la chitarra, guitar
la cattiva, widow
lu centru, center; middle
lu centru cummerciali, shopping mall
   or shopping center
la corda, rope; cord
lu cumportamentu or cumpurtamentu, behavior
la dota, dowry, endowment
la fatica, fatigue; effort
lu fumu, smoke
la funtana, fountain
la furchetta, fork
la furmicula, ant
la gaggia, cage
la galera, jail, penitentiary
lu giuellu, jewel
lu gradimentu, pleasure, liking
lu gruppu, knot; set; group
lu gruppu di putii, shopping mall or
   shopping center
la lampa, lamp; light post
lu lampu, lightening, flash
lu mircatu, market
la minna, breast
l'innamurata (nnamurata), girl friend
l'innamuratu (nnamuratu), boy friend
mannari, to send; forward
la minna, breast (for nursing)
l'inciuria (nciuria), offense; insult
la nota, note; (musical) note
l'orfanu, orphan
lu passaportu, passport
la pezza, rag
lu pezzu, piece; bit
la pillicula, film, movie
lu populu, people
la prescia, haste, hurry
lu prufeta, prophet
lu prufissuri, teacher; professor (p -a)
la putia, shop, store
lu rigalu or rialu, present, gift
la soggira, mother-in-law
lu soggiru, father-in-law
lu sonu, sound
la sumigghianza, similarity; likeness
la tila, canvas; screen; curtain; cloth
la vidua or viduva, widow

Verbs (cont.)

arricchirisi or ricchirisi (sc), to become rich
arricurdarisi (m'arricordu) or ricurdarisi
   (mi ricordu), to remember
arrigalari (arrigalu) or rigalari (rigalu),
   to present, give as a gift
arripizzari (arripezzu), to mend, patch
arrubbari (arrobbu) or rubbari (robbu), to rob
attuppari (attuppu), to plug up, stop up
aviri a chi fari (cu), to concern, have to do (with)
caminari (caminu), to walk
castigari, to punish
cinari (cenu), to have dinner
cumunicari (cumunicu), to communicate
cumunicari (cumunicu) or cuminicari
   (cumenicu), to administer communion
   (i.e., the sacrament)
cumunicarisi or cuminicarisi, to receive
   communion
cunnannari, to condemn; convict
cunziddirari (cunziddiru), to consider
danniggiari (danneggiu), to damage, harm
dari corpa, to beat, thrash
dubbitari (dubbitu), to doubt
esibbiri (sc), to exhibit, show
farisi cena, to have dinner
inchiri (inchiu), to fill, fill up
lampiari (3s lampia), to lighten, flash
mustrari (mostru), to show
oddiari (oddiu), to hate, detest
partiri, to depart, leave
percepiri (percepu), to perceive
raggiunari (raggiunu), to discuss, debate
scanciari, to exchange; cash (e.g., a check)
spenniri, to spend
sputari (sputu), to spit
suffriri (soffru or suffrisciu), to suffer
sunari (sonu), to sound, ring (e.g., telephone),
   play (e.g., an instrument)
sunnarisi (mi sonnu), to dream; imagine
suppurtari (supportu), to support; endure
sustituiri (sc), to substitute, take the place of
tessiri, to weave
viviri, to live

Adjectives

camulutu, moth-eaten
diunu, deprived of food, fasting
giulivu, joyous, happy
putativu, reputed, supposed
sazziu, satiated, full
servu, servile
simili (a), similar (to), alike

Nouns (cont.)

lu viduu **or** viduvu, widower
la vucca, mouth
la zita, fiancée
lu zitu, fiancé

Adjectives (cont.)

strippa, sterile (adjective with two endings)
vasciu, low

Adverbs

a lu iornu **or** ô iornu, a day; per day
a la simana **or** â simana, a week; per week
di novu, again
mancu, any more, any longer (negative adverb)
(i)mprescia, hastily, hurredly
(i)nzemmula **or** (i)nzemi, together

Exercises

Exercise #1: Review the preterite of these verbs. Write out and practice the preterites of the following verbs. You must thoroughly master this important tense. Also note the differences between the regular and irregular preterite endings.

amari (regular preterite), to love
aviri (irregular preterite), to have
battiri (regular preterite) to beat
dari (irregular preterite), to give
diri (irregular preterite), to say, tell
essiri (irregular preterite), to be
finiri (regular preterite), to finish
iri (regular preterite), to go
irisinni (regular preterite), to go away
poniri (irregular preterite), to place, set
purtari (regular preterite), to carry; wear
putiri (irregular preterite), to be able

ripetiri (regular preterite), to repeat
sapiri (irregular preterite), to know (e.g., a fact)
scriviri (regular and irregular preterite), to write
scurdarisi (regular preterite), to forget
stari (irregular preterite), to stay, be, dwell, rest
sustituiri (regular preterite), to substitute
teniri (irregular preterite), to hold
veniri (irregular preterite), to come
vidiri (irregular preterite), to see
vistirisi (regular preterite), to dress oneself
viviri (irregular preterite), to drink
viviri (irregular preterite), to live

Exercise #2: Translate these sayings into English. Discuss what they mean. Also say these sentences aloud.

(1) A lu celu nun si va senza fatica. (2) Non si nni vidi nè fumu nè radica. (3) Vattinni Vanni c'un m'arricchisti, nenti mi purtasti e a casa inchisti. (4) Unu, pi nun sapiri nenti, pigghiau trent'anni di galera. (5) Diu non avi a scinniri di celu n terra pi castigarinni. (6) Cu amici e parenti avi non avi a chi fari cu nenti. (7) La fimmina è giuliva quannu è zita e quannu è cattiva. (8) Diu nni scanza di un malu vicinu. (9) Megghiu moriri sazziu ca diunu. (10) Parrau Seneca e dissi: « cacca ».*

* Famous Roman senator and orator (4 BCE?-65 CE). Do you think this still applies to many politicians today?

158

Exercise #3: Translate these sentences into Sicilian.

(1) The man couldn't come so he sent his son. (2) The housewife went shopping, bought a new dress, went home, and showed it to her mother-in-law. (3) Every month we'd go to gramma's house, and she'd give us all nice presents. (4) While I was writing a note to my girl friend in class, the teacher (M) caught me and gave me a lashing with his cane. (5) I won't stand for his bad behavior any longer. (6) Here's a check. Take it and go cash it at the bank. (7) Before going to the shopping mall, the whole family ate dinner. (8) Let's go to the movies tonight. There's a great film showing. (9) Do you want to see her again? No? Get out now. (10) Let the father take the son's place.

Sicilian Poem

Exercise: Read this poem aloud and translate it. Try to memorize it; the poem is a eulogy to the Sicilian language. It was written by the Sicilian poet, Ignazio Buttitta, or Gnaziu Buttitta (1899-1998). Buttitta was probably the greatest Sicilian poet of the twentieth century. Note how Buttitta describes the Italian language versus how he describes the Sicilian language. Why is Buttitta making such an impassioned plea for the Sicilian language? What do you think he's implying about the relation between Sicilian and Italian? The source of this poem is Caracè (1980), pp. 126-128. **Note:** A few of the words are spelled slightly differently than they appear in this book. The original spelling has been kept except that the circumflex accent has been added where appropriate.

Lingua e Dialettu

Un populu
mittitilu â catina
spugghiatilu
attuppatici a vucca,
è ancora libiru.

Livatici u travagghiu
u passaportu
a tavula unni mancia
u lettu unni dormi,
è ancora riccu.

Un populu
diventa poviru e servu,
quannu ci arrobbanu a lingua
addutata di patri:
è persu di sempri.

Diventa poviru e servu,
quannu i paroli non figghianu paroli
e si mancianu tra d'iddi.

Mi nn'addugnu ora,
mentri accordu a chitarra dû dialettu,
ca perdi na corda lu jornu.

Mentri arripezzu
a tila camuluta,
chi tisseru i nostri avi
cu lana di pecuri siciliani.

E sugnu poviru:
haiu i dinari,
e non li pozzu spenniri;
i giuelli,
e non li pozzu rigalari;
u cantu
ntâ gaggia
cu l'ali tagghiati.

Un poviru,
c'addatta ntê minni strippi
dâ matri putativa,
chi û chiama figghiu
pi nciuria.

Nuatri l'avevamu a matri,
nni l'arrubbaru;
aveva i minni a funtana di latti
e ci vippiru tutti,
ora ci sputanu.

Nni ristò a vuci d'idda,
a cadenza,
a nota vascia
dû sonu e dû lamentu:
chissi non nni ponnu rubbari.

Nni ristò a sumigghianza,
l'andatura,
i gesti,
i lampi nta l'occhi:
chissi non nni ponnu rubbari.

Non nni ponnu rubbari,
ma ristamu poviri
e orfani u stissu.

15   Diminutives/Augmentatives

Purpose of the Chapter

Sicilian, like the other Romance languages, makes frequent use of various endings that affect the meaning of the noun or adjective to which they are attached. These endings have been traditionally called diminutive and augmentative endings. The purpose of the chapter is to set forth these endings. They are added to various nouns, or adjectives, as suffixes. These endings can be added to past participles also since past participles are adjectives. They help to impart a particular shade of meaning to the word that is often difficult to convey in English. This is because such endings, for all practical purposes, no longer exist in English, although some did in earlier versions of the language (that is, in Old English and Middle English). How many English-speaking people today refer to a small lamb as a "lambykin" or to a small girl child as a "maidkin"?

Diminutives

Strictly speaking, a diminutive ending connotes smallness and renders this meaning to the noun (or adjective) to which it is suffixed. Since small things are often considered cute, or endearing, this meaning is also often imparted to the word. Some diminutive endings more frequently connote this meaning than others. Normally, when the ending is added to a particular noun, the gender is generally preserved. Also note that if an *e* or an *o* appears in a syllable that's stressed (generally the antepenult), then the diminutive ending shifts the accent further towards the back (the penult) and the vowels *e* or *o* change into an *i* or a *u* respectively, that is, the vowels revert to their unstressed value. The most frequent diminutive endings in Sicilian are these. The words formed in this fashion are nouns or adjectives (**Adjectives with Three Endings**) and function exactly the same way as the nouns and adjectives introduced in Chapter 3.

- -eddu(a) (often connotes "rather" or "somewhat" when used with an adjective)
- -ceddu(a) (often connotes "rather" or "somewhat" when used with an adjective)
- -teddu(a)
- -ettu(a) **or** ittu(a)
- -iddu(a)
- -liddu(a)
- -uddu(a)
- -uzzu(a) (definitely connotes endearing qualities; can often have a figurative meaning)

Examples

ammugghiatu, wrapped up	ammugghiateddu, sort of wrapped up
ammugghiatu, wrapped up	ammugghiatuzzu, nicely wrapped up
apa, bee	apuzza, dear little bee
biancu, white	bianculiddu, whitish
bonu, good	buniceddu, rather good
canzuna, song	canzunedda, little song
ciamma, flame	ciammuzza, dear little flame
ciuri, flower	ciuriddu, sweet little flower
cori, heart	curuzzu, dear, sweet heart

cuncumu, kettle	cuncumeddu, little kettle
facci, face	facciuzza, dear, sweet face
fedda, slice	fidduzza, sweet little slice
furnu, oven	furneddu, small oven; range (e.g., on an oven)
frati, brother	fratuzzu, dear brother (used to address one's brother)
giurnali, newspaper	giurnalettu, little newspaper; journal
gulutu, greedy	guluteddu, somewhat greedy
libbru, book	libbrettu, little book
monacu, monk	munacheddu, little monk
mortu, dead	murticeddu, dear little dead one*
pani, bread	panuzzu, sweet bread; roll
piattu, plate	piatticeddu, little plate (not a lot to eat)
pezzu, piece	pizzuddu, little piece
picciulu, little	picciuliddu, tiny
picciottu, boy	picciutteddu, young boy
picciulu, small	picciliddu **or** picciriddu, baby; little boy
pirsuna, person	pirsunedda, dear little person
poviru, poor fellow	puvireddu, poor little fellow
soru, sister	suruzza, dear sister (used to address one's sister)
tazza, cup (e.g. for coffee)	tazzitta, little cup, demi-tasse
tenniru, tender, delicate	tinnireddu, very delicate
varca, boat	varcuzza, dear little boat
ventu, wind	vinticeddu, little wind, i.e., a breeze

* This word also refers to presents given on All Souls' Day (November 2). In Sicily, as well as other Latin countries, this is an important feast day during which presents are exchanged and children receive gifts. N sicilianu si dici "u iornu dî morti".

Augmentatives

An augmentative ending connotes largeness and renders this meaning to the noun (or adjective) to which it is suffixed. Since large things are often seen as being clumsy, or even ugly, this meaning can also be imparted to the word. The augmentative ending *-azzu(a)* more frequently connotes this meaning than *-uni* (M)/*-una* (F) and *-azzu(a)* is often added to a noun, or adjective, to show contempt and dislike. When the ending *-azzu(a)* is added to a particular noun, the gender is generally preserved. The most frequent augmentative endings in Sicilian are these.

- -uni (M) and -una (F) (connotes the idea of "bigness")
- -azzu(a) (often connotes the idea of "ugliness","coarseness", or "meanness" in addition to "bigness")

Examples

arripizzatu, mended	arripizzatazzu, really badly mended
bruttu, ugly	bruttazzu, really ugly
crivu, sieve	crivazzu, big, coarse sieve
crivu, sieve	crivuni, big sieve
fimmina, woman	fimminuna, big (boned) woman
fimmina, woman	fimminazza, big, coarse woman

facci, face	facciazza, big ugly mug
omu, man	umazzu, big, mean man
spadda, shoulder	spaddazzi (common plural), big ugly shoulders
vucca, mouth	vuccazza, big ugly mouth

Words with a Diminutive or Augmentative Ending without That Meaning

Some words have a diminutive or an augmentative ending, but the ending has lost its force.
Example: scala (feminine), stairs; scaluni (masculine), step (of a stairway).

Vocative

When a person is addressing someone (the vocative) using a disjunctive personal pronoun, the preposition *a* is placed before the corresponding pronoun. In English, this *a* can be conveniently translated as "hey".

Examples
(1) A vui! You! Hey you!
(2) A vossìa! You! Hey you!

Vocabulary

Nouns
lu babbu, fool
la baccara, jar
la baccaredda, little jar (diminutive)
lu coddu, neck; (upper) back
lu curtigghiu, courtyard
li dinari, money; coins (p)
lu granu, copper coin; money (p -a)
lu issu, chalk, plaster
lu mariolu, rogue, scoundrel
la mazza, mallet
lu saccu, sack, bag
la statua, statue
la tila, canvas; screen; curtain; cloth

Adverbs
a lu mircatu **or** ô mircatu, cheaply*
(i)ncoddu, on the back
(i)ntantu, meanwhile

Conjunctions
già ca, since; now that

Verbs
allavancari, to topple
ammazzari, to kill
dari cuntu (a), pay attention (to); heed
fari vidiri, to show
mazziari (mazziu), to hit (with an object)
(i)nfilari (m'infilu) (nni **or** nta), to work into,
    thread into; end up (in)
stenniri, to spread, stretch out
vanniari (vanniu), to proclaim, cry aloud

Adjectives
a lu mircatu **or** ô mircatu, cheap*
babbu, foolish, stupid
caru, expensive; dear
grossu, big, large
lagnusu, lazy
loccu, stupid, dumb
luntanu, distant, far away
mariolu, roguish
spertu, clever, smart

* This is a prepositional phrase functioning as either an adjective or an adverb depending on the context.

163

Sicilian Short Story

Exercise: Read the Sicilian short story aloud and translate it.

To facilitate your reading skills, a brief short story is included in this chapter. It deals with a character named Giufà. This character is found throughout world literature, the universal fool. In some ways, he also represents Everyman. There exists a number of Sicilian stories in which Giufà appears as the main character. This story has been normalized in the general Sicilian set forth in this book, but originally it was recorded in the dialect of Central Sicily (CS-2). **Note:** The present tense can function as a past tense in story situations (historical present). This is fairly common in the Romance languages. The source of this story is Giuseppe Pitrè, *Fiabe, novelle e racconti popolare siciliani*, Vol. III, Reprinted (Clio: S.G. La Punta/CT, 1993), pp. 353-354.

Giufà e a statua di gghissu

Si cunta ca cc'era na mamma e avia un figghiu chiamatu Giufà. Sta mamma di Giufà campava povira. Stu Giufà era babbu, e lagnusu e mariolu. So matri avia na pocu di tila e cci dissi a Giufà:
— Pigghiati nu pocu di tila e â va' a vinni ntôn paisi luntanu e l'a' a vinniri a ddi pirsuni chi parranu picca.
Giufà si partiu câ tila ncoddu e si nni iu a vinniri. Arrivatu ntôn paisi accuminciau a vanniari:
— Cu voli a tila!?
Û chiamavanu i genti e accuminciavanu a parrari assai, a cu cci paria grossa e a cu cci paria cara. A Giufà cci paria ca parravanu assai e nun cci nni vulia dari. Dunca camina di ccà e camina di ddà e finarmenti s'infila ntôn curtigghiu. Ddà nun cc'era nuddu e cci truvau na statua di gghissu e cci dissi Giufà:
— Â vuliti accattari a tila? — E a statua nun cci dava cuntu; ntantu vitti ca parrava picca.
— Ora a vui, ca parrati picca, v'aiu a vinniri a tila. — Pigghia a tila e cciâ stenni di supra.
— Ora dumani vegnu pî grana. — E si nni iu.
Quannu agghiurnau, cci iu pî grana e a tila nun nni truvau e accussì cci dicia:
— Dunami i grana dâ tila. — E a statua nun cci dicia nenti.
— Già ca 'un mi vo' dari i grana, ti fazzu vidiri cu sugnu iu.
S'impresta un zappuni e va a mazzia a statua finu ca l'allavancau, e nnâ panza cci trova na baccaredda di dinari. Si metti i dinari nni nu saccu e si nni va nni so mà. Arrivannu, a so mà cci dissi:
— Â vinnivi a tila ad unu chi nun parrava e i grana â sira 'un mi nni detti; poi cci ivi a matina cû zappuni e l'ammazzai e û ittai n terra e mi detti sti dinari.
A mamma, ca era sperta, cci dissi:
— 'Un diri nenti ca a pocu a pocu ni emu manciannu sti dinari.

16   Model Verb Paradigms

Purpose of the Chapter

This chapter sets forth the verb paradigms, or patterns, covered in previous chapters for quick reference to consult the forms. The major paradigms are given for the two regular conjugations. Since you should know the pattern, only the English meanings of the infinitives will be given, and the endings will no longer be italicized since you should be able to recognize them by now. The personal pronouns are shown so that you may more easily identify the correct person and number of the various verb forms. **Note:** The names of the various tenses in Sicilian are given in parentheses.

The three verbs used in these paradigms will be these.

Conjugation 1	**Conjugation 2**	**Conjugation 2 (sc)**
parrari, to speak	rispunniri, to reply	finiri, to finish

Note: Except for the present tense and the imperative, the remaining tenses of *finiri* are identical to *rispunniri*. Hence, only the present and the imperative of *finiri* will be given.

Present
(lu prisenti indicativu)

Conjugation 1	**Conjugation 2**	**Conjugation 2 (sc)**
iu parru	iu rispunnu	iu finisciu
tu parri	tu rispunni	tu finisci
vossìa parra	vossìa rispunni	vossìa finisci
iddu parra	iddu rispunni	iddu finisci
nuiatri parramu	nuiatri rispunnemu	nuiatri finemu
vuiatri parrati	vuiatri rispunniti	vuiatri finiti
iddi parranu	iddi rispunninu	iddi finiscinu
or iddi parrunu	**or** iddi rispunnunu	**or** iddi finisciunu

The following verbs show irregularities in the present. Except for *diri**, *essiri*, and *fari*† all of them have regular 1st and 2nd person plural forms.

* The infinitive used to be *diciri*. All of the forms of the present tense are regular for this form. The imperfect, imperfect subjunctive, and the two regular forms of the preterite (2nd person singular and 2nd person plural) are formed from *diciri*.

† The infinitive used to be *faciri*. The 1st person and 2nd person plurals are regular for this form. The imperfect, imperfect subjunctive, and the two regular forms of the preterite (2nd person singular and 2nd person plural) are formed from *faciri*.

Verbs Having an Irregular Present	Present Forms
aviri, to have	**Singular forms:** iu aiu, tu ai, vossìa avi, iddu avi **Plural forms:** nuiatri avemu, vuiatri aviti, iddi annu
dari, to give	**Singular forms:** iu dugnu, tu duni, vossìa duna, iddu duna **Plural forms:** nuiatri damu, vuiatri dati, iddi dunanu **or** dununu
diri, to say, tell	**Singular forms:** iu dicu, tu dici, vossìa dici, iddu dici **Plural forms:** nuiatri dicemu, vuiatri diciti, iddi dicinu **or** diciunu
essiri, to be	**Singular forms:** iu sugnu, tu sì, vossìa è, iddu è **Plural forms:** nuiatri semu, vuiatri siti, iddi sunnu
fari, to do, make	**Singular forms:** iu fazzu, tu fai, vossìa fa, iddu fa **Plural forms:** nuiatri facemu, vuiatri faciti, iddi fannu
iri, to go	**Singular forms:** iu vaiu, tu vai, vossìa va, iddu va **Plural forms:** nuiatri emu /yemu/, vuiatri iti /yiti/, iddi vannu
putiri, to be able	**Singular forms:** iu pozzu, tu poi, vossìa pò, iddu pò **Plural forms:** nuiatri putemu, vuiatri putiti, iddi ponnu
sapiri, to know	**Singular forms:** iu sacciu, tu sai, vossìa sapi, iddu sapi **Plural forms:** nuiatri sapemu, vuiatri sapiti, iddi sannu
stari, to stay, dwell	**Singular forms:** iu staiu, tu stai, vossìa sta, iddu sta **Plural forms:** nuiatri stamu, vuiatri stati, iddi stannu
vuliri, to want, wish	**Singular forms:** iu vogghiu, tu voi, vossìa voli, iddu voli **Plural forms:** nuiatri vulemu, vuiatri vuliti, iddi vonnu

The following verbs have an irregular 1st person singular. Three of them also show a regular 1st person singular.

Verbs Having an Irregular 1st Person Singular Present	Present Forms
chiudiri, to close	**Singular form:** iu chiuiu **or** iu chiudu
cridiri, to believe, hold an opinion, think	**Singular form:** iu criu **or** iu cridu
poniri, to place, set	**Singular form:** iu pognu
teniri, to hold, keep	**Singular form:** iu tegnu
veniri, to come	**Singular form:** iu vegnu
vidiri, to see	**Singular form:** iu viu **or** iu vidu

Imperative
(l'imperativu)
Strictly speaking, the imperative is a mood, not a tense.

Conjugation 1
(tu) parra
(vossìa) parrassi
(iddu) parrassi
(nuiatri) parramu
(vuiatri) parrati
(iddi) parrassiru

Conjugation 2
(tu) rispunni
(vossìa) rispunnissi
(iddu) rispunnissi
(nuiatri) rispunnemu
(vuiatri) rispunniti
(iddi) rispunnissiru

Conjugation 2 (sc)
(tu) finisci
(vossìa) finissi
(iddu) finissi
(nuiatri) finemu
(vuiatri) finiti
(iddi) finissiru

Imperfect
(l'impirfettu or l'imperfettu indicativu)

Conjugation 1
iu parrava*
tu parravi
vossìa parrava
iddu parrava
nuiatri parravamu
vuiatri parravavu
iddi parravanu **or** parravunu

Conjugation 2
iu rispunnia **or** rispunneva **or** rispunniva[†]
tu rispunnivi **or** rispunnevi
vossìa rispunnia **or** rispunneva **or** rispunniva
iddu rispunnia **or** rispunneva **or** rispunniva
nuiatri rispunniamu **or** rispunnevamu **or** rispunnivamu
vuiatri rispunniavu **or** rispunnevavu **or** rispunnivavu
iddi rispunnianu **or** rispunnevanu **or** rispunnivanu

* The form *parravu* is also found.
† The forms *rispunniu*, *rispunnevu*, and *rispunnivu* are also found.

Several verbs have an irregular imperfect: *diri* (*diciri*), *essiri*, *fari* (*faciri*), and *iri*, the latter having both regular forms and forms as if it were a Conjugation 1 verb.

Verbs Having an Irregular Imperfect	Imperfect Forms
diri, to say, tell	**Singular forms:** iu dicia **or** diceva **or** diciva, tu dicivi **or** dicevi, vossìa dicia **or** diceva **or** diciva, iddu dicia **or** diceva **or** diciva **Plural forms:** nuiatri diciamu **or** dicevamu **or** dicivamu, vuiatri diciavu **or** dicevavu **or** dicivavu, iddi dicianu **or** dicevanu **or** dicivanu
essiri, to be	**Singular forms:** iu era, tu eri, vossìa era, iddu era **Plural forms:** nuiatri eramu, vuiatri eravu, iddi eranu **or** erunu

Verbs Having an Irregular Imperfect (cont.)	Imperfect Forms
fari, to do, make	**Singular forms:** iu facia **or** faceva **or** faciva, tu facivi **or** facevi, vossìa facia **or** faceva **or** faciva, iddu facia **or** faceva **or** faciva **Plural forms:** nuiatri faciamu **or** facevamu **or** facivamu, vuiatri faciavu **or** facevavu **or** facivavu, iddi facianu **or** facevanu **or** facivanu
iri, to go	**Singular forms:** iu ia **or** iava **or** eva /yeva/, tu ivi **or** iavi **or** evi /yevi/, vossìa ia **or** iava **or** eva /yeva/, iddu ia **or** iava **or** eva **Plural forms:** nuiatri iamu **or** iavamu **or** evamu /yevamu/, vuiatri iavu **or** iavavu **or** evavu /yevavu/, iddi ianu **or** iavanu **or** evanu /yevanu/

Preterite
(lu priteritu)

Conjugation 1
iu parrai*
tu parrasti
vossìa parrau **or** parrò
iddu parrau **or** parrò
nuiatri parrammu **or** parramu‡
vuiatri parrastivu**
iddi parrarunu **or** parraru††

Conjugation 2
iu rispunnivi†
tu rispunnisti
vossìa rispunniu
iddu rispunniu
nuiatri rispunnemmu **or** rispunnemu‡
vuiatri rispunnistivu**
iddi rispunnerunu **or** rispunneru††

* The forms *parravi*, *parraiu* and *parravu* are also commonly found.
† The forms *rispunnii*, *rispunniu* and *rispunnivu* are also commonly found.
‡ The form with double *m* is more frequently found than formerly, probably because of the influence of Italian.
** The forms *parrastu* and *rispunnistu* are also found.
†† The forms *parraru* and *rispunneru* are abbreviations of the longer forms, but are common.

Past Participle
(lu participiu passatu)

Conjugation 1
parratu

Conjugation 2
rispunnutu

Gerund
(lu gerundiu)

Conjugation 1
parrannu

Conjugation 2
rispunnennu

Imperfect Subjunctive
(l'impirfettu cungiuntivu or l'imperfettu congiuntivu)
Strictly speaking, the subjunctive is a mood, not a tense.

Conjugation 1
iu parrassi
tu parrassi
vossìa parrassi
iddu parrassi
nuiatri parrassimu
vuiatri parrassivu
iddi parrassiru **or** iddi parrassinu

Conjugation 2
iu rispunnissi
tu rispunnissi
vossìa rispunnissi
iddu rispunnissi
nuiatri rispunnissimu
vuiatri rispunnissivu
iddi rispunnissiru **or** iddi rispunnissinu

Several verbs have an irregular imperfect subjunctive: *diri* (*diciri*), *essiri*, and *fari* (*faciri*).

Verbs Having an Irregular Imperfect Subjunctive	Imperfect Subjunctive Forms
diri, to say, tell	**Singular forms:** iu dicissi, tu dicissi, vossìa dicissi, iddu dicissi **Plural forms:** nuiatri dicissimu, vuiatri dicissivu, iddi dicissiru **or** dicissinu
essiri, to be	**Singular forms:** iu fussi, tu fussi, vossìa fussi, iddu fussi **Plural forms:** nuiatri fussimu, vuiatri fussivu, iddi fussiru **or** fussinu
fari, to do, make	**Singular forms:** iu facissi, tu facissi, vossìa facissi, iddu facissi **Plural forms:** nuiatri facissimu, vuiatri facissivu, iddi facissiru **or** facissinu

Future
(lu futuru)

Conjugation 1
iu parrirò
tu parrirai
vossìa parrirà
iddu parrirà
nuiatri parriremu
vuiatri parririti
iddi parrirannu

Conjugation 2
iu rispunnirò
tu rispunnirai
vossìa rispunnirà
iddu rispunnirà
nuiatri rispunniremu
vuiatri rispunniriti
iddi rispunnirannu

The following verbs have an irregular future.

Verbs Having an Irregular Future	Future Forms
essiri, to be	**Singular forms:** iu sarò, tu sar**ai**, vossìa sarà, iddu sarà **Plural forms:** nuiatri saremu, vuiatri sariti, iddi sarannu
fari, to do, make*	**Singular forms:** iu farò, tu far**ai**, vossìa farà, iddu farà **Plural forms:** nuiatri faremu, vuiatri fariti, iddi farannu
vuliri, to want, wish	**Singular forms:** iu vurrò, tu vurr**ai**, vossìa vurrà, iddu vurrà **Plural forms:** nuiatri vurremu, vuiatri vurriti, iddi vurrannu

* The verbs *dari* and *stari* follow exactly the same pattern as *fari*.

Conditional
(lu cundizziunali or lu condizziunali)

Conjugation 1
iu parriria
tu parririssi
vossìa parriria
iddu parriria
nuiatri parririamu
vuiatri parririavu
iddi parririanu

Conjugation 2
iu rispunniria
tu rispunnirissi
vossìa rispunniria
iddu rispunniria
nuiatri rispunniriamu
vuiatri rispunniriavu
iddi rispunnirianu

The following verbs have an irregular conditional.

Verbs Having an Irregular Conditional	Conditional Forms
essiri, to be	**Singular forms:** iu saria, tu sarissi, vossìa saria, iddu saria **Plural forms:** nuiatri sariamu, vuiatri sariavu, iddi sarianu
fari, to do, make*	**Singular forms:** iu faria, tu farissi, vossìa faria, iddu faria **Plural forms:** nuiatri fariamu, vuiatri fariavu, iddi farianu
vuliri, to want, wish	**Singular forms:** iu vurria, tu vurrissi, vossìa vurria, iddu vurria **Plural forms:** nuiatri vurriamu, vuiatri vurriavu, iddi vurrianu

* The verbs *dari* and *stari* follow exactly the same pattern as *fari*.

Present Perfect
(lu pirfettu or lu perfettu indicativu)

Conjugation 1

iu aiu parratu
tu ai parratu
vossìa avi parratu
iddu avi parratu
nuiatri avemu parratu
vuiatri aviti parratu
iddi annu parratu

Conjugation 2

iu aiu rispunnutu
tu ai rispunnutu
vossìa avi rispunnutu
iddu avi rispunnutu
nuiatri avemu rispunnutu
vuiatri aviti rispunnutu
iddi annu rispunnutu

Long Forms of aviri

iu aiu parratu
tu ai parratu
iddu avi parratu
nuiatri avemu parratu
vuiatri aviti parratu
iddi annu parratu

Short Forms of aviri

ê parratu
a parratu
a parratu
amu parratu
ati parratu
annu parratu (same as long form)

Past Perfect
(lu cchiù-chi-pirfettu or lu cchiù-chi-perfettu indicativu)

Conjugation 1

iu avia parratu
tu avivi parratu
vossìa avia parratu
iddu avia parratu
nuiatri aviamu parratu
vuiatri aviavu parratu
iddi avianu parratu

Conjugation 2

iu avia rispunnutu
tu avivi rispunnutu
vossìa avia rispunnutu
iddu avia rispunnutu
nuiatri aviamu rispunnutu
vuiatri aviavu rispunnutu
iddi avianu rispunnutu

Note: Like any other imperfect of Conjugation 2, *aviri* has alternate forms. See **Imperfect** above. **Examples:** iu avia, iu aveva, iu aviva, etc. Naturally, any of these acceptable alternate forms can also be used in forming the past perfect.

Past Perfect Subjunctive
(lu cchiù-chi-pirfettu cungiuntivu or lu cchiù-chi-perfettu congiuntivu)

Conjugation 1

iu avissi parratu
tu avissi parratu
vossìa avissi parratu
iddu avissi parratu
nuiatri avissimu parratu
vuiatri avissivu parratu
iddi avissiru parratu

Conjugation 2

iu avissi rispunnutu
tu avissi rispunnutu
vossìa avissi rispunnutu
iddu avissi rispunnutu
nuiatri avissimu rispunnutu
vuiatri avissivu rispunnutu
iddi avissiru rispunnutu

Irregular Preterites

Irregular forms are found for the following: 1st person singular, 3rd person singular, 1st person plural, and 3rd person plural. The 2nd person singular and the 2nd person plural are always regular. The infinitive will be given followed by its preterite forms.

Verbs Having an Irregular Preterite	Preterite Forms
aviri, to have	**Singular forms:** iu appi **or** ebbi, tu avisti, vossìa appi **or** ebbi, iddu appi **or** ebbi **Plural forms:** nuiatri appimu **or** ebbimu, vuiatri avistivu, iddi appiru **or** ebbiru
cridiri, to believe, think*	**Singular forms:** iu critti, tu cridisti, vossìa critti, iddu critti **Plural forms:** nuiatri crittimu, vuiatri cridistivu, iddi crittiru
dari, to give	**Singular forms:** iu detti **or** desi, tu dasti, vossìa detti **or** desi, iddu detti **or** desi **Plural forms:** nuiatri dettimu **or** desimu, vuiatri dastivu, iddi dettiru **or** desiru
diri, to say, tell	**Singular forms:** iu dissi, tu dicisti, vossìa dissi, iddu dissi **Plural forms:** nuiatri dissimu, vuiatri dicistivu, iddi dissiru
essiri, to be	**Singular forms:** iu fui, tu fusti, vossìa fu⁺, iddu fu⁺ **Plural forms:** nuiatri fomu, vuiatri fustivu, iddi foru
fari, to do, make	**Singular forms:** iu fici, tu facisti, vossìa fici, iddu fici **Plural forms:** nuiatri ficimu, vuiatri facistivu, iddi ficiru
grapiri, to open[†]	**Singular forms:** iu aprivi, tu apristi, vossìa apriu, iddu apriu **Plural forms:** nuiatri apremmu, vuiatri apristivu, iddi apreru
mettiri, to put	**Singular forms:** iu misi, tu mittisti, vossìa misi, iddu misi **Plural forms:** nuiatri misimu, vuiatri mittistivu, iddi misiru
ntenniri, to hear, understand	**Singular forms:** iu ntisi, tu ntinnisti, vossìa ntisi, iddu ntisi **Plural forms:** nuiatri ntisimu, vuiatri ntinnistivu, iddi ntisiru
pariri, to seem	**Singular forms:** iu parsi, tu paristi, vossìa parsi, iddu parsi **Plural forms:** nuiatri parsimu, vuiatri paristivu, iddi parsiru
perdiri, to lose[‡]	**Singular forms:** iu persi, tu pirdisti, vossìa persi, iddu persi **Plural forms:** nuiatri persimu, vuiatri pirdistivu, iddi persiru
poniri, to place, set	**Singular forms:** iu posi, tu punisti, vossìa posi, iddu posi **Plural forms:** nuiatri posimu, vuiatri punistivu, iddi posiru
putiri, to be able	**Singular forms:** iu potti, tu putisti, vossìa potti, iddu potti **Plural forms:** nuiatri pottimu, vuiatri putistivu, iddi pottiru

Verbs Having an Irregular Preterite (cont.)	Preterite Forms
rispunniri, to respond**	**Singular forms:** iu rispusi, tu rispunnisti, vossìa rispusi, iddu rispusi **Plural forms:** nuiatri rispusimu, vuiatri rispunnistivu, iddi rispusiru
sapiri, to know	**Singular forms:** iu sappi, tu sapisti, vossìa sappi, iddu sappi **Plural forms:** nuiatri sappimu, vuiatri sapistivu, iddi sappiru
scriviri, to write††	**Singular forms:** iu scrissi, tu scrivisti, vossìa scrissi, iddu scrissi **Plural forms:** nuiatri scrissimu, vuiatri scrivistivu, iddi scrissiru
stari, to stay, dwell	**Singular forms:** iu stetti **or** stesi, tu stasti, vossìa stetti **or** stesi, iddu stetti **or** stesi **Plural forms:** nuiatri stettimu **or** stesimu, vuiatri stastivu, iddi stettiru **or** stesiru
teniri, to hold, keep‡‡	**Singular forms:** iu tinni, tu tinisti, vossìa tinni, iddu tinni **Plural forms:** nuiatri tinnimu, vuiatri tinistivu, iddi tinniru
veniri, to come	**Singular forms:** iu vinni, tu vinisti, vossìa vinni, iddu vinni **Plural forms:** nuiatri vinnimu, vuiatri vinistivu, iddi vinniru
vidiri, to see	**Singular forms:** iu vitti **or** visti, tu vidisti, vossìa vitti **or** visti, iddu vitti **or** visti **Plural forms:** nuiatri vittimu **or** vistimu, vuitri vidistivu, iddi vittiru **or** vistiru
viviri, to live	**Singular forms:** iu vissi, tu vivisti, vossìa vissi, iddu vissi **Plural forms:** nuiatri vissimu, vuiatri vivistivu, iddi vissiru
viviri, to drink	**Singular forms:** iu vippi, tu vivisti, vossìa vippi, iddu vippi **Plural forms:** nuiatri vippimu, vuiatri vivistivu, iddi vippiru
vuliri, to want, wish	**Singular forms:** iu vosi, tu vulisti, vossìa vosi, iddu vosi **Plural forms:** nuiatri vosimu, vuiatri vulistivu, iddi vosiru

*   Regular forms are also common: cridivi **or** cridiu, cridisti, cridiu, cridemmu, cridistivu, crideru.

†   *grapiri* is used more frequently in the present, but the other tenses and verb forms follow *apriri*.

‡   Regular forms are also common: pirdivi **or** pirdiu, pirdisti, pirdiu, pirdemmu, pirdistivu, pirderu.

**   Regular forms are also common: rispunnivi **or** rispunniu, rispunnisti, rispunniu, rispunnemmu, rispunnistivu, rispunneru.

††   Regular forms are also common: scrivivi **or** scriviu, scrivisti, scriviu, scrivemmu, scrivistivu, scriveru.

‡‡   Regular forms are also common: tinivi **or** tiniu, tinisti, tiniu, tinemmu, tinistivu, tineru.

Irregular Past Participles

The infinitive is given followed by its past participle. Note that some of these verbs also have a regular past participle. For verbs having both an irregular past participle and a regular one, the irregular one is used as an adjective and the regular one is the one most frequently used in forming compound tenses with *aviri*.

arricogghiri, to gather up, reap — arricotu (irregular) **or** arricugghiutu (regular)

chiudiri, to close — chiusu (irregular) **or** chiudutu (regular)

cociri, to cook — cottu (irregular) **or** cuciutu (regular)

cogghiri, to pick, gather — cotu (irregular) **or** cugghiutu (regular)

curreggiri, to correct — currettu (irregular) **or** curriggiutu (regular)

curriri, to run — cursu (irregular) **or** currutu (regular)

difenniri, to defend — difisu (irregular) **or** difinnutu (regular)

diri, to say, tell — dittu (irregular)

distrudiri, to destroy — distruttu (irregular) **or** distrudutu (regular)

dividiri, to divide — divisu (irregular) **or** dividutu (irregular)

essiri, to be — statu (irregular)

fari, to do, make — fattu (irregular)

grapiri **or** apriri, to open — apertu (irregular) **or** graputu (regular)

iri, to go — iutu (irregular insofar as an initial *i* must be added)

leggiri, to read — lettu (irregular) **or** liggiutu (regular)

mettiri, to put — misu (irregular)

moriri **or** muriri, to die — mortu (irregular)

nasciri, to be born — natu (irregular) **or** nasciutu (regular)

ntenniri, to hear, understand — ntisu (irregular)

ntroduciri, to introduce (e.g., a new idea) — ntroduttu (irregular) **or** ntroduciutu (regular)

offenniri, to defend — offisu (irregular) **or** offinnutu (regular)

offriri **or** uffriri, to offer — offertu (irregular) **or** uffrutu (regular)

pariri, to seem — parsu (irregular) **or** parutu (regular)

perdiri, to lose — persu (irregular) **or** pirdutu (regular)

pinciri, to paint (e.g., a portrait) — pintu (irregular) **or** pinciutu (irregular)

poniri, to place — postu (irregular)

proibbiri, to prohibit, forbid — proibbitu (irregular) **or** proibbutu (regular)

pruteggiri, to protect — prutettu (irregular) **or** prutiggiutu (regular)

punciri, to sting, goad — puntu (irregular) **or** punciutu (regular)

ridiri, to laugh — risu (irregular) **or** ridutu (regular)

rispunniri, to respond, answer — rispostu (irregular) **or** rispunnutu (regular)

rumpiri, to tear, break — ruttu (irregular) **or** rumputu (regular)

scegghiri, to choose — scetu (irregular) **or** scigghiutu (regular)

sciogghiri, to loosen, untie — sciotu (irregular) **or** sciugghiutu (regular)

scriviri, to write — scrittu (irregular) **or** scrivutu (regular)

spenniri, to spend — spisu (irregular) **or** spinnutu (regular)

stenniri, to spread out, stretch out — stisu (irregular) **or** stinnutu (regular)

storciri, to wring, twist — stortu (irregular) **or** sturciutu (regular)

strinciri, to squeeze, tighten — strittu (irregular) **or** strinciutu (regular)

torciri, to twist — tortu (irregular) **or** turciutu (regular)

vidiri, to see — vistu (irregular) **or** vidutu (regular)

vinciri, to conquer, win — vintu (irregular) **or** vinciutu (regular)

174

Key to the Exercises

Key to Chapter 4

Exercise #2

(1) oils of Sicily (2) near the city (3) at the beginning (4) next to the desk (5) far from the city (6) under the bed (7) on top of the table (8) during the week (9) after dinner (10) behind the door (11) in front of the chair (12) as far as the river (13) in front of the children (14) inside the box (15) for (the sake of) love (16) in Sicily (17) towards home (18) outside the house (19) with the oil (20) with regard to the bill (21) in the magazines (22) like the president (23) among the peoples of the world (24) instead of the brother (25) in the corner of the bedroom (26) with (by means of) the hammer (27) because of the rain (28) with the bait on the hook (29) against the elements of nature (30) by means of the telephone (31) before lunch (32) with regard to the lesson of this grammar (33) around the tree (34) at the airport (35) except the boy (36) except the girl (37) facing the professor (38) for (the sake of) the cat (39) in the midst of wild woods (40) by means of the letter of the professor (F) or by means of the professor's letter (41) by means of the letters of the professors **or** by means of the professors' letters (42) besides John (43) on the wall (44) regarding the serious problem (45) close to the telephone booth (46) in the letter (47) near the town square (i.e., piazza) (48) the Italians against the Germans (49) the red versus the green (50) in the heavens

Key to Chapter 5

Exercise #1

(1) Love hides every defect. **Meaning:** The meaning is clear. (2) Time is money. **Meaning:** The meaning is clear. (3) The years pass and the days fly. **Meaning:** Time flies. (4) Jealousy is the moth of love. **Meaning:** Jealousy eats away (figuratively speaking) love. (5) A man isn't measured by the breadth of a hand. **Meaning:** There's more to a human being that physical stature. (6) Jealousy poisons the heart, spilling hatred into sweet love. **Meaning:** The meaning is clear. (7) With or without a rooster, God makes the day. **Meaning:** Physical events take place regardless of our actions. (8) A house isn't climbed without a ladder. **Meaning:** A person doesn't accomplish his task without the proper tools. (9) We keep an eye out for scorpions and serpents, but we don't look for the millipede. **Meaning:** Pay attention even to the smallest details. The devil's in the details. (10) The twisted piece of wood is straightened in the fire. **Meaning:** Adversity helps correct our faults.

Exercise #2

(1) The man carries the books into the study. (2) The little boy repeats his mother's words. (3) The peasant sells the eggs in the town square. (4) True love is a gift of God. (5) The woman washes the laundry in the basin. (6) The little boys (**or** children) finish the work. (7) The mother scolds her son, and the little boy cries. (8) The sun is in the sky. (9) The moon is beautiful; I love the moon. (10) In the mornings the rooster always crows.

Exercise #3

(1) U figghiu ama a so matri. (2) U viddanu porta un gaddu. (3) Mmenzu dâ chiazza a fìmmina chianci. (4) L'omini misuranu i ligna. (5) U donu di l'omu è beddu. (6) U figghiu di l'omu acchiana a scala. (7) U scurpiuni avvilena u gaddu. (8) I picciriddi non teninu d'occhiu ê sirpenti. (9) L'omu ammuccia sempri l'ova cû difettu. (10) A donna di casa guarda i libbra ntô studiu.

Key to Chapter 6

Exercise #1

(1) See Palermo and enjoy; see Naples and then die. **Meaning:** There was a strong rivalry between Naples and Palermo as the two capitals of the Kingdom of Two Sicilies. (2) Water having passed no longer grinds. [This literally refers to a mill run by a water wheel.] **Meaning:** Don't hold onto the past; it doesn't do any good. (3) Love is like a cucumber; it starts out sweet and ends up bitter. **Meaning:** The meaning is clear. (4) The tongue strikes where the tooth hurts. **Meaning:** Our actions often make something bad grow worse. (5) To wish is to be able. **Meaning:** Where there's a will, there's a way. (6) A lady without love is like a rose without a scent. **Meaning:** The meaning is clear. (7) A living person who's absent is like a dead person. **Meaning:** If a person isn't present to represent his interests, they aren't going to be heeded. (8) One cannot have meat without bones. **Meaning:** Even good things have their drawbacks. (9) A stone offered by a friend is like an apple. **Meaning:** We should value what a friend offers us regardless of its true value. (10) Quarrels within a family are like a fire in straw. **Meaning:** Family quarrels are virulent but they die out quickly.

Exercise #2

(1) The man's friend wants to sell his car. (2) The little boy is ready to go to school. (3) The old man always smokes a cigarette after dinner. (4) On Sundays we go to church. (5) I see a fat man at the window. (6) I should give (**or** I will give) my mother a bouquet of pretty flowers. (7) Tomorrow I'll carry Joan's books to school. (8) The sun gives energy and light to the earth. (9) The mother loves her children. (10) Dina is going to learn to drive the car.

Exercise #3

(1) Oggi u figghiu duna i puma russi a so matri. (2) Dumani vinnu a machina a l'amicu. (3) Mmenzu dâ casa u picciriddu accumincia a chianciri (**or** cianciri) pi so mamma. (4) A fìmmina duna corpa a l'omu e cci fa mali. (5) L'oduri dî ciuri è bonu. (6) U picciriddu offri a so manu â picciridda. (7) A manu avi cincu idita e i dui manu annu deci idita. (8) I finestri dâ casa sunnu granni e vecchi. (9) U picciriddu voli sapiri unni è so matri. (10) A vecchia macina u denti nna un pistuni (**or** nnôn pistuni).

Exercise #1

(1) What one sows, one reaps. **Meaning:** You reap what you sow. (2) Only believe a little of what you see; don't believe anything you hear. **Meaning:** Don't be credulous about things. Since Sicily was invaded many times, Sicilians are a cautious people. Can you blame them? (3) Don't bother a sleeping dog. **Meaning:** Let sleeping dogs lie. Don't stir things up because they may have an outcome that you're not expecting. (4) When the cat washes her face, it's a sign that it's going to rain. **Meaning:** Folklore regarding predicting the weather. Probably just about as good as any other way. (5) Every friend that one loses is a step that one descends. **Meaning:** The more friends you lose, the worse off you are. In a society where people depend more on friends to get things done rather than on an impersonal bureaucracy, losing a good friend is a serious matter. (6) The true friend is one who doesn't talk poorly about you. **Meaning:** The meaning is clear. (7) An old tree doesn't bend. **Meaning:** As you grow older, you become less flexible, physically and intellectually. (8) The earth is made for the peasant. **Meaning:** Refers to the old social order in Sicily where people who were born into a particular station generally could never get out of it. (9) Scratch your friend where he itches. **Meaning:** Help your friend in the way that'll help him best, (and of course he's expected to scratch you where you itch.) (10) A false friend is a bad neighbor; he throws a stone and (then) hides his hand. **Meaning:** Beware of false friends. When you're nor aware, they stab you in the back and then pretend that they've done nothing.

Exercise #2

(1) I give money to my friends and hatred to my enemies. (2) That older (granni = adult, older person) woman who's looking at me in the street is my aunt. (3) Whosoever loves me is blessed. (4) I don't understand a thing you're telling me. (5) Don't say anything to anybody. (6) He can take whatever he finds here. (7) The woman is chatting with her neighbor who's wearing a red dress. (8) I thank you for your great patience that you have. (9) Give me one (of them) and you'll be happy you did. (10) The window is open, and I can hear the noises of the cars in the street.

Exercise #3

(1) U picciriddu pigghia a manu di so mamma. (2) Dumani aiu a iri nnô me amicu e a daricci nu donu di me soru. (3) Tegnu d'occhiu ê vostri sordi chi sunnu supra a tavula. (4) A manu mi doli. I manu mi dolinu (**or** dolunu). (5) Chiddu chi disia aggiri accussì pò irisinni (**or** si nni pò gghiri). (6) Oggi mi nni pigghiu dui di chiddi ca vecchia vinni. (7) L'accattu e cciû dugnu. (8) Û vidu ca ora ora nesci dâ casa. (9) Bonu! Chi è ca vuliti fari oggi? (10) Non mi battiri cû to vastuni.

Key to Chapter 8

Exercise #1

(1) A relative who doesn't give you (anything), a friend who doesn't lend you (anything), run from them like the plague. **Meaning:** If your friends and relatives won't help you, you'd

better go somewhere else. (2) He who sits down on two chairs will bump his ass on the ground. **Meaning:** You can't please two people at once. You can't serve two masters. (3) He who has a pretty wife is always singing; he who has a little money is always counting (it). **Meaning:** The meaning is clear. (4) What you do for others you do it for yourself. **Meaning:** Helping others will make you a better person. The Golden Rule. (5) Prisons, illnesses, and necessities reveal the hearts of friends. **Meaning:** Adversity brings out the best in friends. Also you'll find out who your true friends are. (6) A drinking buddy'll leave you in a flash. **Meaning:** "Good time" friends will abandon you when you get in a jam, so don't depend on them. (7) To a true friend speak clearly. **Meaning:** You should tell the truth to a true friend. (8) He who lives all year sees every festival. **Meaning:** The longer you live, the more experiences you accumulate. (9) A tree which doesn't bear fruit, cut it at its roots. **Meaning:** Get rid of someone (or something) that's no good. (10) Let the wicked man fry in his own oil. **Meaning:** Let someone bad who's gotten into trouble pay the consequences.

Exercise #2

(1) Tell me what you want, and I'll give it to you at once. (2) Today I'll buy two books, and tomorrow I'll read both (of them). (3) I'll go away tomorrow, and you'll never see me again. (4) What you (p) want to do, you (p) can do. (5) The old woman takes the oil and puts it in the frying pan to fry the fish. (6) The boys are working as hard as they can. (7) The little girl's afraid of the dog who's barking loudly at her, and she calls out for her mom with a frightened voice. (8) Take the check and cash it. (9) Where are they living now? I haven't seen them in a long time. (10) I like to read interesting books and meet people who travel all over.

Exercise #3

(1) Tu sì u megghiu e non ti vidu mai cchiù. (2) Fammi vidiriti nautra vota e sugnu cuntenti. (3) Ti pari ca chistu è un lettu commudu? (4) Sta fimmina è nica e vecchia e non pò vidiri beni. (5) Accattatilla ora o dumani qualchi autru cristianu l'accatta. (6) Dimmi chiaru chi voi ca fazzu e û fazzu subbitu. (7) A famigghia dû viddanu abbita (**or** sta) nta na nica casa (**or** nna na nica casa) vicinu a nuiatri. (8) Criu ca iddu è riccu ma Giorgiu è cchiù riccu d'iddu. (9) M'assettu propiu ccà e m'addumu a pipa. (10) U vecchiu gintilomu trasi nnâ stanza e iu nesciu.

Key to Chapter 9

Exercise #1

(1) Every saint has his feast. **Meaning:** There's a time and place for everything. (2) Every rooster crows in his own rubbish heap. **Meaning:** Every man is king in his own house. (3) August rains produce oil, honey, and must. **Meaning:** Early rains help the harvest. (4) January is half sweet and half bitter. **Meaning:** There's often a respite in the cold weather in January, but it doesn't last long. (5) When heat and dryness prevail in September, the earth is prepared for the (sowing of) seed. **Meaning:** The meaning is clear. (6) November is the month of the dear dead ones. **Meaning:** November 2 is All Souls' Day in the feast days of the Roman Catholic Church, and a very important holiday in Sicily. Presents (murticeddi) are given to children. (7) A hot and dry September causes every fruit to ripen. **Meaning:** The meaning is clear. (8) February is short, but it's the worse of all. **Meaning:** In the Northern Hemisphere

February is known for its nasty weather. (9) April brings forth the flowers and everything beautiful, but the month of May gets all the applause. **Meaning:** The meaning is clear. Have you ever done something and someone else got all the credit? (10) The calm weather lasts up to the end of autumn. **Meaning:** The calm always precedes the storm. (11) The one never says what he does, and the other never does what he says. **Meaning:** The meaning is clear. Do you know two people who match this description? Who doesn't. (12) When winter doesn't have a head, it has a tail. **Meaning:** If winter gets a late start, it lingers a long time. (13) The gardens dry up, and the dung heaps flower. **Meaning:** There's a dearth of talented people, but plenty of fools. Probably refers to politics. (14) Wednesday's in the middle of the week. **Meaning:** The meaning is clear. (15) He who knows how to pretend knows how to win. **Meaning:** Playing dead can increase your chances of survival, and pretending can also increase your chances of survival in lots of areas. (16) Fortune is a wheel; it comes and goes. **Meaning:** The meaning is clear. (17) My days must come. **Meaning:** Sooner or later I've got to get lucky. (18) Plant trees in your vineyard. If you don't pick fruit, you'll gather pieces of wood. **Meaning:** Make a good plan and carry it through. If the results aren't exactly what you expected, you'll still benefit in some way. (19) If a tree doesn't bloom in April, it won't in another season either. **Meaning:** If something doesn't take place when it's supposed to, it isn't going to happen later either. (20) Little by little love works its way in. **Meaning:** The meaning is clear. (21) A house without sunshine, and the doctor enters at all hours. **Meaning:** Lack of sunshine can mean that the inhabitants are leading unhealthy lives. Getting exposure to some sun is healthy, but today we know that too much exposure to the sun isn't healthy for you. It may also mean that the inhabitants are depressed and thus prone to illnesses. Of course, the days when doctors made house calls are long past. (22) One ought to iron while the iron is hot. **Meaning:** Strike while the iron's hot. (23) A foreseen misfortune isn't felt as badly. **Meaning:** The meaning is clear. (24) The sheep which gives up its wool is bitter. **Meaning:** We don't like having to give up things that we'd like to keep. Do taxes come to mind? (25) He who loves you makes you weep, and he who hates you makes you laugh. **Meaning:** People we love can hurt us deeply; people we hate we laugh at. (26) Fools build their houses; prudent people buy them. **Meaning:** If you can buy something already made, it's better. A sure sign that the industrial revolution caught on in Sicily. (27) The sacristan's money comes singing and leaves singing. **Meaning:** Easy come; easy go. (28) One knows how a love affair starts, but no one knows how it will end. **Meaning:** The meaning is clear. (29) In love I take you, and in anger I leave you. **Meaning:** Similar to the last sentence in meaning. A love affair begins well, but often ends in anger and a lot of hurt feelings. (30) He who has cold hands is in love; he who has warm hands has taken a mistress. **Meaning:** Cold hands means a person is nervous, as we often are beginning a love affair. Warm hands means the person has a lot of passion and is experienced in life. (31) Throw a bone to a barking dog. **Meaning:** Oil the squeaking wheel. (32) Woe unto that house where the hen crows and the rooster's silent. **Meaning:** It's the house of a henpecked man. (33) Save the chaff and squander the flour. **Meaning:** Spendthrifts waste what's useful, and pile up a lot of worthless and useless stuff. (34) Eat the bait and defecate the hook. **Meaning:** If you swallow the bait (the sales line), you'll regret the consequences. If it looks too good to be true, it probably is. (35) He has a long arm and a short one. **Meaning:** He takes with the long arm and holds back with the short one, that is, a user. (36) He speaks as much as a judge. **Meaning:** Judges tend to be longwinded (well, they're lawyers too, aren't they?) and typically not easy to understand. (37) A judge must have two ears. **Meaning:** He must listen carefully to both sides (one ear for each side) to make a just decision. (38) Judges, presidents, and lawyers aren't found in heaven. **Meaning:** The meaning is clear. They aren't esteemed any more even now.

179

(39) He who eats makes crumbs. **Meaning:** Every activity makes some scrap. Every effort produces unwanted or unexpected effects. (40) To him who has (good) fortune everything goes well for him. **Meaning:** Everything typically goes great for someone who already has good luck.

Exercise #2

(1) He who's in a rush makes mistakes. **Meaning:** Haste makes waste. (2) It hurts me to stay with you; it hurts me more to leave you. (3) The twentieth century was a terrible one. Will the twentyfirst century be a better one for humanity? (4) Love is better than hatred. (5) In one hand I hold a sword, and in the other I hold the branch of peace.

Key to Chapter 10

Exercise #1

(1) From the (piece of) coal one extracts a diamond. **Meaning:** In what at first appears of little value, something of great value is found. (2) That one roasts his fish in the flames of the fire (e.g., of someone's house). **Meaning:** Refers to a person who takes advantage of another's misfortune. (3) The war is lost through too much advice (being given). **Meaning:** Too many cooks spoil the broth. (4) Piss on the ruins before they turn into moss. **Meaning:** Take advantage of the situation now before it's too late. (5) He who sleeps with dogs has fleas. **Meaning:** You're known by the company you keep. (6) The ladle knows the troubles of the pot that it stirs. **Meaning:** Someone who knows you well, or intimately, knows your deepest problems, and what's worrying you. (7) A deed is worth more than a hundred words. **Meaning:** Action is worth more than words. (8) The barking of a dog doesn't frighten the clouds. **Meaning:** Don't waste your efforts in vain. (9) He who doesn't want a fire, let him take away the wood. **Meaning:** Remove things which could lead to disputes or cause problems. (10) The eye eats more than the stomach. **Meaning:** The eye is bigger than the stomach.

Exercise #2

Lu Patri Nostru

(1) Patri nostru, chi sì n celu, (2) santificatu sia (**or** è) lu to nomu, (3) vegna (**or** veni) lu to regnu e sia (**or** è) fatta la to vuluntà n terra comu è n celu. (4) Dunannillu oggi lu nostru pani cutiddianu e pirduna a nuiautri li nostri piccati (5) comu pirdunamu a chiddi chi nni fannu mali a nuiautri (6) e non farinni cadiri nta la tintazzioni (7) ma scanzanni di lu mali. (8) Amen.

Note: This assumes God is addressed using *tu*. In older Sicilian, God was addressed with *vui*. See the remarks made in Examples 9-10 of **Relative Pronouns**, Chapter 7, **Pronouns**.

Exercise #3

Exercise #4, Chapter 5

(1) I'm here. (2) That's the way it's done. (3) I have a sister. (4) This is Johnny's house. (5) It's as heavy as lead. (6) Don't fall! (7) The milk here's for the cat. (8) Listen. They're knocking at the door. (9) Give me a drop of water. I'm dying of thirst. (10) Well! Good heavens!

Exercise #4, Chapter 6

(1) This morning the old man leaves the house. (2) A beautiful woman'll vist us next week. (3) We speak in this fashion, but over there they speak in that fashion. (4) I'm going to bed (**Literal meaning:** I'm going to lie down). (5) The little boy's big. (6) He's right. (7) The dog gnaws the bone. (8) Take time and live. (9) Peter says to Charles: "I'm angry at you, and I'll give you a fist in your face." (10) Later, crying, Charles says to his mother: "Peter gave me a bloody nose."

Exercise #4, Chapter 7

(1) We're selling that portrait (over there). (2) You (polite) take that one, and I'll take this one. (3) Tell it to me. (4) Don't you see that you're as old as me (**or** as I)? (5) Don't blow in his face! (6) I can't find your shoes. (7) Today it's going to rain. (8) I'm right. There's only two hundred dollars under my hat. (9) Tomorrow I'll send the money and finally pay this debt. (10) I'm your father who loves you very much.

Exercise #4, Chapter 8

(1) Go off to hunt. (2) Wine gives me a headache. (3) I'm going to bed because I'm sleepy. (4) That hat of his is large. (5) When my mother commands (me), I do it. (6) This is the house that he wants to sell me. (7) I'm sorry but I can't eat this slice of burnt meat. Take it away. (8) The little girl hides (herself) under the bed, and the little boy can't find her. (9) Tomorrow we're leaving the village for the United States where we have relatives who live in New York City. (10) The old man is coughing and speaking so softly that we can't understand him clearly.

Exercise #4

> Rise, rise, sun, sun
> For (the sake of) the holy savior.
> Throw a fistful of coins
> to please everybody.
> Throw a fistful of nuts
> to please the little children.
> Throw a fistful of dung
> to please the noblemen.

Key to Chapter 14

Exercise #2

(1) One doesn't go to heaven without an effort. **Meaning:** The meaning is clear. (2) One sees neither the smoke nor the root of him. **Meaning:** He vanished into thin air. (3) Go away, Johnny, because you didn't make me rich, you didn't bring me anything, and you (just) filled up the house. **Meaning:** Sounds like an unwanted guest or a relative who overextended his stay. (4) One, for not knowing anything, got thirty years in jail. **Meaning:** The criminal code of silence wasn't broken even if so-and-so (unu) had to spend thirty years in the penitentiary. (5) God doesn't have to come down from heaven to the earth to punish us. **Meaning:** The meaning is clear. He can do that right where he's at. (6) He who has friends and relatives doesn't have to be concerned about anything. **Meaning:** The meaning is clear. You can see by now that the friendship structure and the family structure are very important items in Sicilian society. (7) A woman is joyous when she gets engaged and when she becomes a widow. **Meaning:** The meaning is clear. This certainly says something about matrimony. (8) God spare us from a bad neighbor. **Meaning:** The meaning is clear. See Chapter 7, **Exercise 1**, (10). (9) Better to die full than hungry. **Meaning:** The meaning is clear. (10) Seneca spoke, and he said: "Shit." **Meaning:** The meaning is clear. Know any politicians that you could still say this about?

Exercise #3

(1) L'omu non putìa veniri accussì mannau a so figghiu. (2) A donna di casa fici a spisa e s'accattau na vistina nova e poi iu a casa e cciâ mostrau â soggira. (3) Ogni misi iamu (or iavamu) nnâ nanna e nni dava beddi rigali a tutti. (4) Mentri chi scrivìa na nota â me nnamurata n classi, u prufissuri s'addunau di mia e mi detti corpa cû so vastuni. (5) Nun supportu cchiù u so malu cumportamentu. (6) Eccu n'assegnu. Pigghiatillu e va' a scanciallu â banca. (7) Prima di iri ô centru cummerciali tutta a famigghia manciau a cena. (8) Iamu ô cinima stasira. Ê na pillicula stupenna. (9) Voi vidirla arrè? No? Vattinni ora! (10) Faciticci pigghiari ô patri u postu dû figghiu.

Sicilian Poem

Language and Dialect

You can place
A people in chains;
You can despoil them
Stop up their mouths
And still they're free.

Take away their work
Their passports
The table where they eat
The bed where they sleep,
And still they're wealthy.

A people
Become poor and servile
When their language is robbed from them
Which was passed down from their fathers:
They are lost forever.

They become poor and servile,
When words no longer beget words
And devour one another.

I just now noticed this,
While tuning the instrument of my dialect,
Which loses a cord a day.

While I was mending
The moth-eaten tapestry,
Which our forefathers wove
From the wool of Sicilian sheep.

And I am poor:
I have money
And I can't spend it;
And jewels
And I can't give them away.
The song
In its cage
with its wings clipped.

I am a poor man
Who suckles at the barren breasts
Of his supposed mother,
Who calls him a son
insultingly.

We had a mother,
And they've taken her from us
She had breasts that were fountains of milk
And all drank from them;
Now they spit on her.

Her voice has stayed with us:
The cadence,
The low note
Of sound and of lament;
These they couldn't take from us.

Her likeness has stayed with us:
The pace,
The gestures,
The flashes in our eyes;
These they couldn't take from us.

They couldn't take (these) from us,
But we are impoverished
And orphans all the same.

Key to Chapter 15

Sicilian Short Story

Giufà and the Plaster Statue

It's told that once there was a mother, and she had a son called Giufà. This mother of Giufà lived in a poor fashion. Giufà was foolish, lazy, and roguish. His mother had a bit of cloth, and she said to Giufà :
"Take some of this cloth and go sell it in a distant village, and you must sell it to those persons who don't speak a lot."
Giufà left with the cloth on his back and set out to sell it. Having arrived at a village, he began to call out:
"Who wants (some) cloth?"
Some people called him and began to speak a lot. There were those who thought it was too thick, and those who thought it was too expensive. It seemed to Giufà that they spoke too much, and he didn't want to give them any. Therefore he walked all about, and finally he wound up in a courtyard. There wasn't anybody there, but he found a plaster statue, and Giufà said to it:
"Do you want to buy the cloth?" And the statue paid no attention to him; meanwhile, he noted that it spoke very little.
" Listen you. I've got to sell you the cloth since you speak very little." He took the cloth and spread it over it (the statue).
" Listen. Tomorrow I'll come for the money." And he left.
When the next day came, he went there for the money and he didn't find the cloth, so he said to it.
" Give me the money for the cloth." And the statue said nothing to him.
" Since you don't want to give me the money, I'll make you see who I am."
Someone lent him a mattock, and he went and hit the statue until he toppled it, and in its belly he found a little jar of coins. He placed the coins in a sack and went back to his mother. When he arrived, he said to his mother:
"I sold the cloth to one who didn't speak, and in the evening he didn't give me the money, so the next morning I went there with a mattock and killed him and threw him to the ground, and he gave me these coins."
The mother, who was clever, said to him:
"Say nothing, and little by little we'll eat up these coins."

References

Purpose of the Section

This brief section covers the references used in the process of creating this book. Many of the works dealing with Sicilian are written in Italian. The ones written in Italian have Italian titles. Serious research on the Sicilian language demands a good working knowledge of Italian.

Attanasio, S. (1989) *Parole di Sicilia*. Milano: Mursia Editore. A compendium of Sicilian proverbs. The orthography is a little different from what is presented in this book, but still very understandable. In Sicilian and Italian. If you enjoy proverbs, this book is very worthwhile.

Avolio, C. (1984) *Introduzione allo studio del dialetto siciliano*. Bologna: Arnaldo Forni Editore. This is a reissue of the edition of Noto (1882). A bit old fashioned. It traces the etymology of numerous Sicilian words, showing especially the influence of Greek, Arabic, Provençal, Catalan, and Spanish on the Sicilian vocabulary.

Bellestri, J. (1985) *Basic Sicilian-English Dictionary*. Ann Arbor, MI. A very useful work in English for those who don't read Italian.

Bellestri, J. (1988) *English-Sicilian Dictionary*. Ann Arbor, MI. Ditto.

Bentley, D. (1997) "Language and dialect in modern Sicily." *The Italianist*, **17**, 204-230. A careful, and very well done, study of how Italian affects Sicilian and also how Sicilian also influences the Regional Italian spoken in Sicily. It contains many examples of Sicilian and contrasts it both with Regional Italian and with Standard Italian. This paper is especially useful since it's in English.

Bonner, K. (1998) "Some Principal Differences among Sicilian Dialects." *Arba Sicula*, **19**, Nos. 1&2, 96-121. A useful study of some of the principle phonological and grammatical changes among the different Sicilian dialects (the Sicilian *parrati*).

Caracè, C. (1980) *Parlar siciliano*. Firenze: Edizione Del Riccio. This work gives a good review of the historical development of Sicilian. In addition, it contains a number of brief works written in some of the various Sicilian dialects. It is very weak on the grammar though. In Sicilian and Italian.

Castagnola, M. (1980) *Dizionario fraseologico siciliano-italiano*. Palermo: Vito Cavallotto Editore. This work originally appeared in the nineteenth century, and is largely a compendium of sayings and expressions in Sicilian. It also contains a large anthology of Sicilian poetry. It is not really a dictionary in the modern sense, regardless of what the title claims, but still it covers many expressions. In Sicilian and Italian.

Copani, I. (1990) *Il siciliano ieri e oggi: Etimologia dei vocaboli tipici*. Catania: c.u.e.c.m. Kind of a short dictionary. Contains many useful Sicilian words. In Sicilian and Italian.

Cronin, C. (1970) *The Sting of Change: Sicilians in Sicily and Australia*. Chicago: The University of Chicago. This is an excellent recent sociological/anthropological study of Sicilians both in Sicily and in Australia.

Di Pietro, R.J. (1960) "The Structural Description of an Alcamese Sicilian Dialect in America." Ph.D. Dissertation. Cornell University. A very useful work showing the principal grammatical and phonological features of Alcamese Sicilian. This book utilizes a lot of linguistic symbolism in presenting its material and is aimed at the professional linguist.

Ducibella, J.W. (1934) "The Phonology of the Sicilian Dialects." Ph.D. Dissertation. The Catholic University of America. Very abstruse. It bristles with linguistic symbolism. If you're not into an excruciatingly painstaking work written in difficult symbolism, then this work is not for you. Di Pietro's work, although not so broad, is much more readable.

Fodale, P. (1964) "The Sicilian Dialects as a Diasystem: A Study in Structural Dialectology." Ph.D. Dissertation. The University of Michigan. Fodale compares the phonology and some of the grammatical aspects of six separate dialects of Sicilian. The six dialects are drawn from Eastern, Western, and Central Sicilian.

Fulci, I. (1855) *Lezioni filologiche sulla lingua siciliana.* Catania: V. Dondice. A difficult work written in the pedantic style so characteristic of the nineteenth century. Still it is useful since Fulci captures many of the essential grammatical features of Sicilian before it was exposed to the onslaught of Italian.

Gower-Chapman, C. (1971) *Milocca: A Sicilian Village.* Cambridge, MA: Schenkman Publishing Co. This excellent anthropological study was done in 1928-29 by Ms. Gower as field work towards her Ph.D. from the University of Chicago. Ms. Gower learned Sicilian on her own from Sicilian immigrants in Chicago, and then proceeded to go to Sicily to study firsthand Sicilian customs and habits. Milocca is a small village in the mountainous region of the province of Caltanissetta. Although it doesn't directly address the Sicilian language, it contains many references to linguistic expressions exposing their sociolinguistic meanings, as one would expect in an anthropological work. One has to admire the stamina and determination of Ms. Gower since it was very bold indeed for a young unmarried woman to do what she did at that time and in a small, remote village.

Hall, R.A., Jr. (1974) *Descriptive Italian Grammar.* Westport, CT: Greenwood Press. This is a reprint of the 1948 Cornell University Press *Descriptive Italian Grammar.* This book is a thorough linguistic description of the Italian language. It is not an easy read.

Leone, A. (1995) *Profilo di sintassi siciliana.* Palermo: Centro di Studi filologici e linguistici siciliani. This excellent work is the result of a detailed questionnaire sent to various people within Sicily, and contains much very useful information on Sicilian and its syntax. There are many concrete examples of Sicilian presented in this work.

Lepschy, A.L./Lepschy, G. (1994) *The Italian Language Today,* 2nd ed. London and New York: Routledge. A good update on the principal changes occurring in modern Italian. Not much on Sicilian in it though.

Lo Piparo, F., ed. (1990) *La Sicilia linguistica oggi.* Palermo: Centro di Studi filologici e linguistici siciliani. This book is full of statistics on the state of Sicilian in Sicily. Useful from a sociolinguistic point of view, but it contains no examples of Sicilian.

Maiden, M./Mair, P., eds. (1997) *The Dialects of Italy.* London and New York: Routledge. Very technical. For those into the complex linguistic changes occurring within the various languages of Italy, it is a must-have. The article by Ruffino on Sicilian cited below comes from this book.

Mazzola, M.L. (1976) *Proto-Romance and Sicilian.* Lisse: The Peter de Ridder Press. It displays a comparison of a number of words in three separate Sicilian dialects, a Sardinian dialect, and Italian. It also discusses the phonology of the dialects presented, including the Sardinian dialect. A discussion of the Sicilian vowel system and its derivation from Latin is included.

Mortillaro, V. (1997) *Nuovo Dizionario Siciliano-Italiano.* Bologna: Arnaldo Forni Editore. This is a reissue of Palermo: Edizione Forte Anelli (1876-81). Useful but of course doesn't contain more modern words.

Piccitto, G. (1947) *Elementi di ortografia siciliana.* Catania: Dott. G. Crisafulli. Although irritatingly short on concrete examples, this book helped establish firm orthographic principles for Sicilian.

Piccitto, G., ed. (1977) *Vocabolario siciliano A-E*, Vol. I. Palermo e Catania: Centro di Studi Filologici e Linguistici Siciliani. The *Vocabolario siciliano*, all four volumes (the fifth and last is expected to appear sometime in 2001), is an absolute must for anyone doing, or planning to do, serious work in Sicilian.

Piccitto, G./Tropea, G., ed. (1985) *Vocabolario siciliano F-M*, Vol. II. Palermo e Catania: Centro di Studi Filologici e Linguistici Siciliani.*

Piccitto, G./Tropea, G., ed. (1990) *Vocabolario siciliano N-Q*, Vol. III. Palermo e Catania: Centro di Studi Filologici e Linguistici Siciliani.*

Piccitto, G./Tropea, G., ed. (1997) *Vocabolario siciliano R-Sg, Vol. IV.* Palermo e Catania: Centro di Studi Filologici e Linguistici Siciliani.*

Pitrè, G./Wentrup, C.F. (1995) *Grammatica siciliana del dialetto e delle parlate.* Palermo: Flaccovio Editor. This is a reissue of the edition of Palermo (1875). An interesting and useful work by one of Sicily's greatest dialectologists. Giovanni Ruffino has written an Introduction and updated the work in the form of notes. Most of the book however is devoted to Sicilian dialectology; it is very short on the grammar.

Privitera, J.F./Privitera, B. (1995) *Language as Historical Determinant: The Normans in Sicily (1061-1200).* Washington, DC: American International Book Development Council. An interesting study carefully documenting the influence of French and Northern Italian on the dialect of San Fratello. This influence was so strong that the San Fratellan dialect was incomprehensible to the rest of Sicily.

Ruffino, G. (1997) "Sicily" in Maiden and Mair, *op. cit.*, Chapter 43, pp. 365-375.

Simeti, M.T. (1986) *On Persephone's Island: A Sicilian Journal.* New York: Vintage Books. Not much on the Sicilian language in this book, but it's marvelously written and contains a wealth of insight into late twentieth century Sicilian customs and habits. The only comment she does make indicates that she is very familiar with Italian, but Sicilian is really not her cup of tea. However, unlike Ms. Gower's (Gower Chapman above) work, Mrs. Simeti writes of her experiences more in the form of a novel and not from an anthropological perspective. Whether you find this approach more palatable depends on your tastes and inclinations. Of course, Sicily itself changed quite a bit from when Ms. Gower was living there to when Mrs. Simeti was, and still is, living there.

---

* Volumes II, III, and IV under the direction of Prof. Giovanni Tropea after Dr. Piccitto passed away.

Sicilian-English Vocabulary

This vocabulary gives the words found in the Vocabularies of Chapters 5-10 and Chapters 14-15 plus some of the basic words. It would make the book inordinately long to include every Sicilian word listed in all the chapters. Consult the Contents or the Index for more information. **Note:** Remember that masculine (M) nouns end in *-u* and feminine (F) nouns end in *-a*. Also remember that nouns ending in *-zzioni* and *-tà* are feminine. Nouns not conforming to this rule are gender-marked in the vocabulary below. The abbreviation 3s = 3rd person singular. See also the abbreviations given in the introductory paragraph in the English-Sicilian Vocabulary. **Note:** Although every attempt has been made to make this vocabulary as complete as possible, it simply was not feasible to include every word contained within all the chapters of this book.

A

a la simana **or** â simana, a week; per week
a lu iornu **or** ô iornu, a day; per day
a bon mircatu, cheap **or** cheaply
a, at, to, for, by means of, from, in
a picca prezzu, cheap **or** cheaply
abbaiari, to bark
abbannunari (abbannunu), to abandon, leave
abbastanza, enough (inv. adj. **or** adv.)
abbastari (3s abbasta), to be enough, suffice
abbisugnari (abbisognu), to need, require; be necessary (impers.)
abbitari (abbitu), to live (in a place), inhabit
abbitutini (F), custom, habit
abbituali, habitual, usual
abbruciari, to burn, scorch
accabbari (accabbu), to finish, end
accattari, to buy
acchianari, to climb; climb into (nni **or** nna), (e.g., a car)
accuminciari (accuminciu **or** accumenciu) **or** accuminzari (accumenzu), to begin
accumpagnari (accumpagnu), to accompany
accumulari (accumulu), to accumulate
accurdari (accordu), to reconcile (people); tune up (an instrument)
accussì, thus, so
aceddu, bird (p -a **or** -i)
acitu, vinegar
acqua, water; rain
addattari, to suckle, nurse
addisiari (addisiu), to desire, wish
addisiddirari (addisiddiru), to desire, wish
addivintari (addiventu), to become
addivirtirisi (m'addivertu), to amuse oneself, have fun, have a good time
addrizzari (addrizzu), to straighten
addumannari, to ask

addumari (addumu), to light up; turn on (e.g. a light)
addunarisi (m'addugnu) (di), to notice; become aware (of)
addurmisciri (addurmisciu), to fall asleep
addutari (addotu), to endow, give in dowry, pass down
adurari (adoru), to adore
aduri **or** oduri (M), odor, smell (not pejorative)
affamatu, hungry
affumari (affumu), to smoke (e.g., meat)
agghiu, garlic
agghiurnari (agghiornu), to start a new day; dawn (impersonal) (3s agghiorna)
aggiri, to act (in a certain way), behave
aggradiri (sc), to like, please
agneddu, lamb (p -a **or** -i)
aieri, yesterday
aiutu, help
ala, wing
aliva **or** oliva, olive
allatu, beside, at the side of
allavancari, to topple
amari, to love
amaru, bitter
amica, friend (p -chi)
amicu, friend (p -ci)
ammazzari, to kill
ammuccari (ammuccu), to put in the mouth; bite
ammucciari (ammucciu), to hide
amu, hook
amuri (M), love
ancilu, angel
andatura **or** annatura, gait; pace
angulu, corner
annu, year

anticu, old, ancient
antinatu, ancestor
anuri **or** onuri (M), honor
apa, bee
aranciu, orange
arba, dawn
argentu, silver
aricchia **or** oricchia, ear
arma, soul
armali (M), animal
armari, to arm; set up (e.g., a business), furnish
arraggia, anger, rage; rabies
arraggiarisi (m'arraggiu) (cu), to be angry (at), irritated (at)
arraggiatu (cu), agitated, bothered (with), angry (at)
arraspari, to scratch, grate
arrassu, far off
arrè **or** arreri, behind; again
arricchiri (sc), to enrich, make rich
arricchirisi (sc), to become rich
arricogghiri (arricogghiu), to gather up, reap
arricriari (arricriu), to please; amuse
arricriarisi (m'arricriu), to please oneself; amuse oneself
arricurdarisi (m'arricordu), to remember
arrifarisi (m'arrifazzu), to make oneself over again; recover (e.g., one's health)
arrigalari (arrigalu), to present, give as a gift
arriminari (arriminu), to stir, shake up
arrinesciri (arrinesciu), to succeed at
arrinisciutu, successful
arripizzari (arripezzu), to mend, patch
arristari (arrestu), to remain, stay
arrubbari (arrobbu), to rob
arrusicari (arrusicu), to gnaw
arrustiri (arrustu **or** arrustisciu), to roast
artaru **or** alturu, alter
arvulu **or** arburu, tree
asciuttu, dry; skinny
asciuttu, dryness, drought
ascutari (ascutu), to listen to (takes DO)
assaggiari, to try, taste
assegnu, check (e.g., bank check)
assenti, absent
assenza, absence
assicurari (assicuru), to assure
assittarisi (m'assettu), to sit down
astutari, to turn off (e.g., a light); estinguish (e.g., a light, a fire, etc.)
attu, act; deed; action
attuppari (attuppu), to plug up, stop up
autru, other

autunnu, autumn
ava, grandmother; greatgrandmother
avanzari, to advance; surpass
aviri (aiu), to have
aviri a (ê), to have to
aviri a chi fari (cu), to concern, have to do (with)
aviri disidderiu (di), to have a desire (for), have an urge (to)
aviri fami, to be hungry
aviri ficatu, be courageous (see essiri curaggiusu)
aviri siti, to be thirsty
aviri spinnu (di), to have a desire (for), have an urge (to)
avu, grandfather; greatgrandfather; ancestor
avvicinarisi (m'avvicinu) **or** abbicinarisi (m'abbicinu), to approach
avvilinari (avvilenu) **or** abbilinari (abbilenu), to poison
avvirarisi (3s s'avvera), to become true, be realized
avvucatu **or** abbucatu, lawyer
azzaru, steel (p -a)
azzolu, blue

B

babbu, fool
babbu, foolish, stupid
baccara, jar
baccaredda, little jar (dim.)
banca, bank
bancu, bench; bank (e.g., sand) (p -a)
banna, place
bannera, flag
barbaru, barbarian
bastari (3s basta), to be enough, suffice
bastibbili, enough, sufficient
battiri, to beat, strike, hit
beddu **or** bellu, beautiful, good-looking, handsome, pretty
bestia, animal; beast
biancaria, linens; laundry; underwear
biancu, white
biatu **or** beatu, blessed; happy; fortunate
biccheri (p -a), drinking glass
biddizza, beauty
binzina, gasoline
bippita, drink (see vippita)
bisognu, need; requirement
bistecca, beefsteak, meat
bisugnari (bisognu), to need, require; be necessary (impers.)

biunnu, blond
biviri, to drink (see viviri)
blu, blue (inv.)
blussa **or** brussa, blouse
bonu! well! just imagine!
bonu, good
bottu, explosion; noise
brillari, to shine, sparkle
bruciari (bruciu), to burn, scorch
bruttu, ugly, bad (weather)
bunazza, calm (of the sea), tranquility (of the
    sea)
buttigghia, bottle

C

cacari, to defecate, shit
cacca, excrement, shit (human)
cacciari, to hunt, chase
caciu, cheese
cadenza, cadence; modulation
cadiri, to fall
calma, calm, tranquility
calmu, calm, tranquil, peaceful
caminari (caminu), to walk
cammara, bedroom
cammarera, waitress; maid
cammareri, waiter (p -a)
cammisa, shirt
campagna, country
campari, to live
camula, moth
camulutu, moth-eaten
canciari, to change, alter; exchange
cani (M), dog
canigghia, bran, chaff
cannarozza (p) **or** cannarozzi (p), throat
cannila, candle
cantari, to sing; crow
cantu, song; corner, angle (of a room)
canuscenza, acquaintance
canusciri (canusciu), to know (a person)
canzuna, song
capiddu, hair (of the head)
capiri (sc), to understand
capitulu, chapter
cappeddu, hat (p -a)
carciri (M), jail
carnaciumi **or** carnaciuni (F), complexion
carnaciumi **or** carnaciuni chiara, fair
    complexion
carnaciumi **or** carnaciuni scura, dark
    complexion
carni (F), flesh, meat

carta, paper
caru, expensive; dear
carusa, girl
carusu, boy
carvuni (M), coal
casa, house; home
caspita! good heavens! wow!
cassetta, box
castigari (castigu), to punish
catina, chain
catolicu, Catholic
cattidrali (F), cathedral
cattiva, widow
caudu, heat
caudu, hot
causi (p), pants
cavaddu, horse
cavaleri (M), horseman; nobleman
cc'è, there is
ccà, here
cchiù, more
cci sunnu **or** cci su', there are
cecu, blind
celesti **or** cilesti, (sky) blue
celu, sky, heavens (p -a **or** -i)
cena, supper, dinner, evening meal
centru cummerciali, shopping center **or**
    shopping mall
centru, center; middle
cersa, oak tree
cervu, deer
chesa **or** chiesa **or** clesia **or** cresia, church
chi, what
chiacchiara **or** chiacchira, chatter, gossip
chiacchiariari (chiacchiariu), to chatter, gossip
chiamari, to call, call out
chiamarisi, to be called, be named
chianciri (chianciu) **or** cianciri, to cry, weep
chiantari, to plant
chianu, plain, level, flat, smooth
chiariri (sc), to clarify; explain
chiaru, clear; evident; light (e.g., of a color –
    see *virdi* below); light-completed
chiattu, plump, stout
chiavi (F), key
chiazza, square (e.g., of a town), piazza
chinu, full
chioviri (3s chiovi), to rain (impers.)
chitarra, guitar
chiudiri (chiuiu **or** chiudu), to close
chiummu, lead (the metal)
ciamma **or** sciamma, flame
ciatari **or** sciatari, to breathe

ciatu **or** sciatu, breath
ciciru, chickpea
cinari (cenu), to have dinner
cintu, belt
circa, about, approximately
circari (cercu) (di), to seek, look for; try (to)
cità, city
citari, to quote
citrolu, cucumber
ciuciuliari (ciuciuliu), to whisper, murmur;
   chirp
ciumi **or** sciumi (M), river
ciuri **or** sciuri (M), flower
ciuriri **or** sciuriri (sc), to flower
ciusciari (ciusciu) **or** sciusciari, to blow
cocciu di racina, grape (individual)
cocciu, kernel; berry; grain (individual) (p -a)
cociri (cociu), to cook (takes an object)
cocu, cook (p -a **or** -i)
coddu, neck; (upper) back
cogghiri (cogghiu), to pick; gather
commudu, comfortable; convenient
comu, like, as
contra, against, opposite, versus
coppula, cap
corda, rope; cord
cori, heart
cosa, thing
costu, cost, price
cravatta, tie
criari (criu), to create
cridiri (criu **or** cridu), to believe, think
crisciri (crisciu), to grow, grow up
cristianu, Catholic (see turcu); fellow, person
cu, with, by means of
cucchiara, (large) spoon; ladle
cucchiaredda, teaspoon
cucchiariari (cucchiariu), to serve; ladle
cucchiaru, spoon (p -a)
cucina, cousin (F)
cucina, kitchen
cucinari (cucinu), to cook (in a general sense)
cucinu, cousin (M)
cuda, tail
cui **or** cu, who
culleggiu **or** colleggiu, college
cultu, cultured
culu, rear end, ass   (posterior)
culuri (M), color
cumannari, to command
cuminciari (cuminciu **or** cumenciu), to begin
cummerciu, business, commerce

cummigghiari (cummogghiu), to cover;
   protect; hide
cumportamentu **or** cumpurtamentu, behavior
cumpurtarisi (mi cumportu), to behave
cumuni, common
cumunicari (cumunicu), to communicate
cumunicari **or** cuminicari (cumenicu), to
   administer communion (i.e., the sacrament)
cumunicarisi (mi cumunicu) **or** cuminicarisi
   (mi cumenicu), to receive communion
cunfurtibbili, comfortable
cungratulari (cungratulu), to congratulate
cunigghiu, rabbit
cunnannari, to condemn; convict
cunnuciri (cunnuciu), to conduct
cuntanti, cash, money (ready-at-hand)
cuntari (cuntu), to count; tell (e.g., a story)
cuntenti, happy, content
cuntentu, happy, content
cuntornu, side dish
cuntu, bill (e.g., at a shop); story
cunzari (conzu), to repair; set in order, adjust
cunziddirari (cunziddiru), to consider
cunzigghiari (cunzigghiu), to counsel; advise
cunzigghiu, advice; counsel
cura, care
curaggiu, courage
curaggiusu, courageous
curcarisi (mi curcu), to lie down, go to bed
curpa, fault, blame
currenti, stream; ordinary; current
curriri (curru), to run
currumpiri **or** corrumpiri, to corrupt
curtigghiu, courtyard
curtu, short
curunatu, crowned, fulfilled
cuscinu, pillow
cusiri **or** cusiri (cusu), to sew, stitch
custari (3s costa), to cost
custumi, custom, habit, behavior
cuteddu, knife (p -a)
cutiddianu, daily
cutra, blanket
cuttuni, cotton

D

danniggiari (danneggiu), to damage, harm
danniggiu, injury, damage
dannu, injury, damage
dari (dugnu), to give
dari corpa, to beat, thrash
dari cuntu (a), pay attention (to); heed
darrè **or** darreri, behind

191

davanti, before, in front of
debbitu, debt
debbuli, weak; feeble
denti (M), tooth
di novu, again
di, of, from, by, about
dia, goddess
dialettu, dialect (often used to refer to Sicilian,
   as in *n dialettu*, that is, in Sicilian)
diamanti (M), diamond
diavulu, devil
dicidiri (dicidu), to decide
difettu, defect
difficili, difficult, hard
dilizzia, delicacy, delicious thing
dilizziu, delicacy, delicious thing
dilizziusu, delicious
dinaru or dinari (p more common), money
diri (dicu), to say, tell
diri minzogni, to tell lies
diritturi, director
discursu, discourse, talk
disgrazzia, misfortune, bad luck
disiari (disiu), to desire, wish
disidderiu, desire, wish
disiddirari (disiddiru), to desire, wish
disiu, desire, wish
distanti, distant
distinu, destiny
ditistari (ditestu), to detest
diu, god (p dei or dii)
diunu, deprived of food, fasting
divintari (diventu), to become
divirtimentu, fun
divirtirisi (mi divertu), to amuse oneself, have
   fun, have a good time
doliri or duliri (mi doli), to hurt (impersonal)
donna, lady; woman (Italianism; see fimmina)
donu, gift (p -a)
doppu, after (time)
doppupranzu, afternoon
dormiri or durmiri (dormu), to sleep
dota or doti, dowry, endowment
dubbitari (dubbitu), to doubt
dubbiu, doubt, uncertainty
duci, sweet
duluri (M), pain; sorrow; affliction
dumani, tomorrow
dumanna or dimanna, question
dumannari (dumannu), to ask
duminari (dominu), to dominate
duminica or duminicaddì or duminicaddìa,
   Sunday

duranti, during
dutari (dotu), to endow, give in dowry, pass
   down
duviri (devu or divu), to ought to; owe

E

e, and
ebbica or epica or epuca, epoch, period of time
eccettu, except for, save for, but for
eccu, here is, here are, look, behold
ecunomicu, economical
eleganti or liganti, elegant
energia, energy
ennaru or iennaru, son-in-law (p -a)
eredità, heritage
erruri (M), error
esattu, exact
esibbiri, to exhibit, show
esplodiri, to explode
esplosioni (F), explosion
essiri (sugnu) or siri, to be
essiri capaci (di), to be able (to)
essiri curaggiusu, to be courageous
essiri (i)nnamuratu (di), to be in love (with)
essiri chiaru di peddi, to have a light
   completion
essiri scuru di peddi, to have a dark completion
europeu, European

F

fabbricari (fabbricu) or frabbicari (frabbicu),
   to build
facci (F), face
facili, easy
fami (F), hunger
famigghia, family
fari (fazzu), to make; do
fari chiaru, to clarify; explain
fari dumanni (a), to question, ask questions
fari na passiata, to stroll
fari risposta (a), to respond (to), answer
fari vidiri (a), to show
farina, flour
fari cena, to have dinner
farmacia, pharmacy, drug store
fatica, fatigue; effort
fattu, fact; deed
fausu, false
favuriri (sc), favor
fedda, slice
feli (M), bile; hatred
ferru, iron
festa, party; festival

fibbia, buckle
ficatu, liver; courage (p -a)
ficcari (ficcu), to thrust; push
ficcarisi (mi ficcu), to insinuate oneself
ficu (F), fig (p ficu)
figghi fimmini, daughters
figghi masculi, sons
figghia, daughter
figghiu, son
figura or fiura, figure, shape
fila, line, queue
filu, thread, wire (p -a)
fimmina, woman (more common than *donna*)
finarmenti, finally
finciri (finciu), to pretend; feign
finestra, window
fini (F), end
fini (M), purpose, goal, aim
fini dâ simana, end of the week
finiri (sc), to finish, end, bring to completion
finocchiu, fennel
firiri (sc), to wound, injure
firita, wound
focu, fire (p –a)
foddi, crazy, insane
fodira di cuscinu, pillow case
fodira, lining
fogghia, leaf
forti, strong; heavy; intense; severe
forza, strength, force, power
francisi (M), francisa (F), French
frati, brother
frattempu, meanwhile
friddu, cold
friiri, to fry
friscu, fresh
frumaggiu or furmaggiu, cheese
frumentu or furmentu, grain
fruttu, fruit (p -a or -i)
fudda, crowd
fuiri, to flee
fumari (fumu), to smoke (e.g., a cigarette)
fumeri (M), dung; filth
fumu, smoke
funnu, bottom
funtana, fountain
furchetta, fork
furmicula, ant
furmini or fulmini (M), lightning bolt
furneddu, kitchen stove (dim.)
furnu, oven
furtuna, fortune
furtunatu, fortunate

G

gaddina or iaddina, hen
gaddinaru or iaddinaru, chicken coop (p -a)
gaddu or iaddu, rooster
gaggia, cage
galera, jail, penitentiary
garzuni [dz], helper; apprentice (p -a)
gatta or iatta, cat
gattareddu, kitten (dim.)
gattu or iattu, cat
genti (F), people (collective n.)
gergu, slang
gessu, chalk, plaster (see issu)
ghiacciu, ice
già, already
giacca, jacket
giarnu or giannu, yellow
gilatu or gelatu, icy; ice cream
gilusia, jealousy
ginituri or genituri, parents
gintili, polite, courteous, kind
gioveddì or giuviddì or giuviddìa or iuviddì or
    iuviddìa or iovidi, Thursday
girari, to tour
giru, tour
giucattulu, toy
giuellu, jewel
giulivu, joyous, happy
giustizzia, justice
giustu or iustu, fair; right
giuvini (M), giuvina (F), young
gloria, glory
gluriusu, glorious
(i)gnuranti, ignorant
godiri or gudiri (godu), to enjoy
gonna, skirt
gottu, goblet, mug
gradimentu, pleasure, liking
gradiri (sc), to like, please
granni, great; older; adult; very
granu, copper coin; money (p -a)
grassu, fat
grazzia, grace, charm
grazzii, thanks, thank you
grossu, big, large
gruppu di putii, shopping center or shopping
    mall
gruppu, knot; set; group
guadagnari or vadagnari, to earn (e.g., money)
guaiu, woe, trouble, misfortune (p guai)
guardari or vardari, to notice; to look out for;
    look at

guccia, drop
guerra , war
gula, throat
guvitu, elbow

I

iamma **or** amma, leg
iancu, white
iardinu, garden (p -a **or** -i)
icari (icu), to bend
idda, she; it
iddi, they
iddu, he; it
iditu, finger (p -a)
inchiri (inchiu), to fill, fill up
intimu, intimate
iocu, game (p -ura)
iornu, day (p -a)
iri (vaiu), to go
iri a finiri, to end up
iri di corpu, to defecate
irisinni (mi nni vaiu), to go away, leave (e.g, a place)
isari (isu) **or** aisari, to lift up, raise
isca, bait
issu, chalk, plaster (see gessu)
ittari (ettu **or** iettu), to throw
iu **or** eu **or** io, I
iucari (iocu), to play
iudici (M), judge
iurnata, day (duration of)

L

lacu **or** lagu, lake
ladiu **or** lariu, ugly
lagnusu, lazy
lamintarisi (mi lamentu), to regret
lampa, lamp; light post
lampadina (elettrica), light bulb
lampiari (3s lampia), to lighten, flash
lampu, lightning, flash
lana, wool
lanna, can (for packaging)
lanzari, to vomit, puke, throw up
lanzu, vomit
largu, broad, wide
lassari, to allow, let; leave (alone)
latti, milk
lavari, to wash
leggiri (leggiu), to read
lei, you (pol. s)
lestu, quick, fast
lettu, bed

letu, glad, pleased, delighted
libbiru, free
libbru, book (p -a)
liganti **or** eleganti, elegant
ligari (legu), to tie, bind; connect
liggeru, light, slight
lignu, piece of wood (p -a)
ligumi (p), vegetables
limitari (limitu), to limit
lingua, tongue; language
linu, linen
linzolu, sheet (p -a)
lira, Lira
lista, list
lista, list, menu
liti (F), quarrel, fight
littra, letter
liuni (p -a), lion
liunissa, lioness
livari (levu), to take away, remove
livarisi (mi levu), to take off (e.g., a shirt)
loccu, stupid, dumb
longu, tall, long
luci (F), light
lumi (M), lamp; light (artificial)
luna, moon
lunghizza, length
luneddì **or** luniddì **or** luniddìa **or** lunidi, Monday
luntanu, distant, far away
lupu, wolf (p -a)
lustru, shiny

M

mà (F), mother; mamma; mom
ma, but
macari, also, even
machina, machine; car
macinari (macinu), to crush, grind
magru, thin
mai cchiù, never again
mala sorti, bad luck
malanova, bad news
malatia, disease, illness
malatu, ill, sick
mali (M), evil; trouble; illness, disease
malidiciri (malidiciu), to curse, damn
malidittu, cursed, damned
malu, bad, wicked, evil
mamma, mother; mamma; mom
manciari, to eat; itch (e.g., from an irritation)
mancu, any more, any longer (neg. adv.)

maniari (maniu), to handle (e.g., by hand); touch; manage; drive (e.g., a car)

mannari, to send; forward

manu (F), hand (p manu)

maravigghia or meravigghia, marvel, amazement

maravigghiusu or meravigghiusu, marvellous, astounding

marazzu, embarrassment

mari, sea, ocean

mariolu, rogue, scoundrel

mariolu, roguish

marmu, marble

marruni or marrò, brown

marteddì or martiddì or martiddìa or martidi, Tuesday

matina, morning

matita, pencil

matri (F), mother

matri granni, grandmother

matrici (F), church (the chief one in the town)

maturari (maturu), to mature; ripen

mazza, mallet

mazziari (mazziu), to hit (with an object)

mazzu, bouquet; bunch (p -a)

medicu, physician (p -ci)

megghiu (adj. or adv.), better

meli (M), honey

menu, less

meravigghia (see maravigghia)

mercoleddì or merculiddì or merculiddìa or mercuddì or mercuddìa or mercudi, Wednesday

merda, shit

mettiri, to put, start

migghiurari (migghiuru), to improve, better

millipedi, millipede (poisonous)

minna, breast

minzogna, lie (untruth)

mircanti, merchant, business person

mircanzia, goods, merchandise

mircatu, market

miricanu, American

miscari, to mix

misi, month

missa, mass

misurari (misuru), to measure; gauge

mitallicu or metallicu, metallic

mitallu or metallu, metal

mittìrisi (mi mettu), put on (e.g., a shirt)

(i)mmagginarisi (m'immagginu), to imagine

(i)mmernu or (i)nvernu, winter

(i)mmitari or (i)nvitari, to invite

(i)mmriacu or (i)mpriacu, drunk

(i)mmurtali, immortal

mobbili (M), furniture (individual piece)

mogghi (F), wife

monaca, nun (p -chi)

monacu, monk (p -ci)

moriri or muriri (moru), to die

morti (F), death

mortu, dead

mortu, dead man

moru, person with a dark-complexion; Moor

(i)mparari, to learn

(i)mpastari, to knead dough

(i)mpidiri (sc), to hinder

(i)mpiegatu, employee

(i)mpiegu, employment

(i)mprescia, hastily, hurredly

(i)mpristari (mprestu), to loan, lend

mubbilia, furniture (in general)

muddica, crumb; soft part of bread

mugghieri (F), wife

munita, money; coin

munnizza, trash, garbage

munnizzaru, dung heap; rubbish pile (p -a)

munniali, world (adj.)

munnu, world

muntagna, mountain

munzeddu di fumeri, dungheap

munzeddu, heap, pile

murmuriari (murmuriu), to murmur

murtali, mortal; deadly

murticeddu, dear little dead one (dim.)

muru, wall (p -a or -i)

musca, fly

muscu, moss

musica, music

mustrari (mostru), to show; exhibit

mustu, must (juice extracted from grapes)

mutivu or motivu, purpose; reason

N

(i)n fatti, in fact

(i)n fretta, in a rush

nanna or nonna, grandmother

nannu or nonnu, grandfather

nasciri (nasciu), to be born

nascita, birth

nasu, nose

natura, nature

navi (F), ship

(i)ncapu, on, on top of

(i)ncazzarisi (m'incazzu) (cu), to become angry (at), fly off the handle (at)

(i)ncendiu, fire (destructive)
(i)nchianari, to climb; climb into (nni or nna),
  (e.g., a car)
(i)nchiudiri (nchiuiu or nchiudu), enclose
(i)ncigneri (M or F), engineer
(i)nciuria, offense; insult; nickname
(i)ncoddu, on the back
(i)ncontru, meeting, encounter
(i)ncugnari (ncugnu), to press against, push;
  approach
(i)ncuminzari (ncumenzu), to begin
(i)ncuntrari (ncontru), to encounter; meet
(i)ncuttu, very close, thick
nervu, nerve; strength; switch (to whip with)
nesciri (nesciu) (di), to go out (of); exit; leave
  from (e.g., a place)
nessu, link; connection
nevula or neula, cloud (large)
(i)nfacci, facing
(i)nfilari (m'infilu) (nni or nta), to work into,
  thread into; wind up (in)
(i)ngannari, to cheat
(i)ngarzari [dz], to take a mistress
(i)nglisi (M), (i)nglisa (F), English
nicissità, necessity
nicissitati, necessity (older form)
nicu, little, small; young
nigozziu, business; shop
nimicu, enemy (p -ci)
niputi (M or F), nephew/niece; grandchild
niuru or niru, black; dark; gloomy
nivi (F), snow
(i)nnamurarisi (m'innamuru) (di), to fall in love
  (with), be in love (with)
(i)nnamurata, girl friend
(i)nnamuratu, boy friend
(i)nnuccenti, innocent
nni or nna, in, at (the place of or the house of)
(i)ntirissari (ntiressu), to interest
(i)ntirissari (m'intiressu) (nna or nta), to
  become interested (in), be interested (in)
no, no
nomu, name
non or nun or un or nn' (before a vowel), not
nora, daughter-in-law
nota, note; (musical) note
notti, night
novu, new
(i)n ritardu, late (**Literal meaning:** in delay)
nta, within, in
(i)ntantu, meanwhile
(i)ntenniri, to hear, understand

(i)ntilliggenti or (i)ntelliggenti, intelligent,
  smart
(i)ntinzioni or (i)ntenzioni, purpose; reason
(i)ntiressu or (i)ntiressi, interest
(i)ntirissanti or (i)nterissanti, interesting
ntra, within
(i)ntricanti, scheming, plotting
nuci (F), walnut
nucidda, hazelnut; nut (in general)
nui, we
nuiatri or niatri or nuiautri or niautri, we
nutari (notu), to record; note
nuttata, night (duration of)
nuvula, cloud
(i)nzemmula or (i)nzemi, together
(i)nzignari (nzignu), to teach

O

occhiu, eye
oddiari (oddiu), to hate, detest
oddiu, hatred
oduri or aduri (M), odor, smell (not pejorative)
offertà, offer
offriri or uffriri (offru), to offer
ogghiu, oil (p -a)
ogni, each, every (inv. – precedes noun)
oi or oggi, today
oliva or aliva, olive
omu, man (p omini)
onuri or anuri (M), honor
opinioni, opinion, belief
ordinariu or urdinariu, ordinary
orfanu, orphan
orgugliusu, proud
oricchia or aricchia, ear
oru, gold
orvu or orbu, blind
ossu, bone (p -a)
ovu, egg (p -a)

P

pà (M), father; dad, pop
pacchettu, package
pacenza or pacenzia, patience; forbearance
paci, peace
padedda, frying pan
pagari, to pay
pagghia, straw
pagghiri, towards, in the vicinity of, around
paisi (M), village, town, country
paletta di munnizza, dust pan
pani (M), bread
panna, cream

panuzzu, bread, dear sweet bread (dim.)

panza, belly, stomach

paradisu, paradise

pardu, leopard

parenti (M or F), relative

pariri (mi pari), to seem to; think (impers.)

pariri, opinion, judgment

pariri, to appear

parmu, span, breath of a hand (lit. palm)

paru, pair (p -a)

parola or palora, word

parrari, to speak; discuss

parrata, subdialect

partiri, to leave, depart

passaportu, passport; free movement

passari, to pass (time, etc.); pass over to
  (e.g., a house)

passiari (passiu), to stroll

passiata, stroll

pastu, food; meal

patata, potato

patri (M), father

patri granni, grandfather

patruni, master; owner; boss; landlord

pattu, pact, agreement

pavimentu, floor

pazzu, crazy, insane; foolish

pazzu, fool

pecura, sheep

peddi (F), skin; hide (of an animal)

pedi (M), foot

peiu or peggiu, worse

percepiri (percepu), to perceive

perdiri (perdu), to lose

pesta, pest, disease, plague

petra, stone

pettu, chest (of body), breast

pezza, rag

pezzu, piece; bit

pi or pri, for, by, to, through, for the sake of

piaciri (M), pleasure

piaciri (mi piaci), to please (impers.)

piattu, plate (p -a or -i)

piccari (peccu), to sin; trespass

piccatu, sin

picciotta, girl (adolescent), young woman

picciottu, boy (adolescent), young man

picciridda or piccilidda, baby; child; little girl

picciriddu or picciliddu, baby; child; little boy

picciuli (p), money; small change

picciulu, small (*nicu* is more common)

pigghiari (pigghiu), to take; seize; catch

pignata, pot, sauce pan

pignatedda, little pot, little sauce pan (dim.)

pillicula, film, movie

pilu, hair (of the body) (p -a)

pinna, feather; pen

pinzari (penzu), to think

pipa, pipe

pipi, pepper

pirdunari (pirdugnu or pirdunu), to pardon

pirsuna, person

pisanti, heavy (weighty)

pisci (M), fish

pisciari, to urinate, piss

pitittu, appetite

piu, pious, religious

plausu, applause; thanks

poi, then, afterwards

poniri (pognu), to place, to set

populu, people

porcu, pig (p -ci)

porta, door

postu, place

poviru, poor man

poviru, poor; unfortunate

pregu, you're welcome

prescia, haste, hurry

prestu, soon; early

pricisu, precise; exact

primavera, spring (season)

primu (piattu), first dish (in a restaurant)

principiu, beginning

priparari (priparu), to prepare

prisenti, present

prisidenti, president

prividiri (prividu), to foresee

prividutu or privistu, foreseen

prizziusu, precious; lovely

proiri (proiu) (a), to hand (to), hand over (to),
  give (to)

propiu or propriu (adj.), proper; exact;
  accurate; own

propiu or propriu (adv.), exactly; just; right

prudenti, prudent, cautious

prudenza or prudenzia, prudence, caution

prufeta (M), prophet

prufissuri (M), professor; teacher (p -a)

prufissurissa, professor; teacher

prupositu or propositu, purpose; reason

pugnu, fist (p -a)

pulici (M), flea

pulizziari (pulizziu), to clean; polish

pumu, apple (p -a)

puntu, dot; period (of punctuation)

purtari (portu), to carry

puru, also, even
puru, pure
pusari (posu), to put down, lay down, place
pussìbbili **or** possìbbili, possible
putativu, reputed, supposed
putìa, shop, store
putiri (pozzu), to be able
puvireddu, little poor one (dim.)

Q

qualità, quality
quannu, when
quarchi **or** qualchi **or** cacchi, some
quarchi vota **or** qualchi vota, sometimes
quari **or** quali, which
quasetta **or** causetta, sock, stocking
quaternu **or** quadernu, notebook (p -a **or** -i)
quatrari, to satisfy
quatratu, square
quatratu, square (geometric form)
quatru, picture; painting
quattrini (p), money; small change
quistioni (F), topic

R

raccumannari, to recommend
raccuntari (raccuntu), to narrate, tell (e.g., a story)
racina, grapes
radica, root; origin; source
raggia, anger, rage; rabies
raggiatu (cu), agitated, bothered (with), angry (at)
raggiu, ray; beam (e.g., sun); radius
raggiunari (raggiunu), to discuss, debate
raggiunevuli, reasonable, rational
raggiuni, reason (e.g., man's reason)
rama, branch
ramu, copper
raru, unusual
regnu, kingdom
ribbillarisi (mi ribbellu), to rebel
ricchiri (sc), to enrich, make rich
ricchirisi (sc), to become rich
riccu, rich
riciviri (ricivu), to receive
ricurdarisi (mi ricordu), to remember
ridiri (riu **or** ridu), to laugh
rifiutari (rifiutu), to refuse
riflettiri (riflettu), to reflect, ponder
rigalari (rigalu), to present, give as a gift
rigalu **or** rialu, present, gift
riliggioni **or** religgioni, religion

riliggiusu **or** religgiusu, religious
riloggiu, clock, watch
rimpruvirari (rimproviru), to scold
ringrazziari (ringrazziu), to thank
riparari, to repair; protect (e.g., from something)
ripetiri (ripetu), to repeat
riposu, rest, quiet
ripusari (riposu), to rest
risparmiari (risparmiu), to save, economize
risposta, response, answer
rispunniri (rispunnu), to reply, answer, respond
ristari (restu) to remain, stay
risu, rice
rispettu, respect
ritardu, delay
ritrattu, picture; portrait
riturnari (ritornu), return, come back
robba, clothes, stuff
rosa, rose
rota, wheel
rubbari (robbu), to rob
ruina, ruin; collapse; downfall
rumanticu, romantic
rumpiri (rumpu), to break; tear
russu, red; Russian

S

sabbatu **or** sabbatuddì **or** sabbatuddìa, Saturday
saccu, sack, bag
sali, salt
saluti (F), health, well-being
sangu, blood
santificari (santificu), to make holy, sanctify
santu, holy, hallowed
santu, saint
sapiri (sacciu), to know (a fact); to know how
sapiri, to taste, have a determinate taste
sapuni (M), soap
sapuri (M), flavor, taste
sapurusu, tasty, delicious
sarda, sardine
sarvaggiu, wild; savage; primitive
sarvaturi, savior
saviu, wise person
saviu, wise, prudent
sazziu, satiated, full
sbagghiu, mistake, error
sbattiri, to bang; bump
sbucciari (sbocciu), to blossom, be in bloom
scala, ladder; stairs; staircase
scalunata, a (series) of steps

scaluni, step (of a staircase) (p -a)
scancia, instead of
scanciari, to exchange; to cash (e.g., a check)
scantari, to freighten, scare
scantarisi (mi scantu), to be frightened
scantu, fear; fright
scantusu, frightened, scared
scanzari, to avoid, shun; save, rescue
scappari, to run away, flee; run off
scarpa, shoe
scattari, to burst, explode; break out
scatula, box
sceccu, donkey
scena, scene
schiavu, slave
sciarra or scerra, quarrel, argument, fight
sciarriarisi (mi sciarriu) (cu), to argue, fight
    (with)
scinniri (scinnu) (di), to go or come down
    (from), descend; climb out of (e.g., a car)
scioccu, silly, foolish, stupid
scippari (scippu), to extract, pull out
scola, school
scopu, effect
scriviri (scrivu), to write
scrusciu, noise
scummigghiari (scummogghiu), to uncover; reveal
scumpariri, to disappear
scuncicari (sconcicu or scuncicu), to provoke; incite;
scuntrari (scontru), to encounter; meet; run
    into; collide head on
scupa, broom
scupitta, brush
scurdarisi (mi scordu), to forget
scurpiuni or scorpiuni, scorpion
scurriri, to flow
scuru, dark, dim; dark (e.g., of a color – see
    virdi below); dark-completed
scusari (scusu), to excuse
scuti (p), money (especially paper money)
scutu, shield
seculu, century
secunnu or sacunnu, according to
secunnu (piattu), second dish (in a restaurant)
seggia, chair
sempri, always
sentiri (sentu), to hear
senza, without
senzu, sense, feeling
serviri (servu), to serve; be of use (mi servi)
servu, servile
sforzu, effort
sfragari, to waste, to squander

sfurtunatu, unfortunate
sì, yes
sicaretta, cigarette
siccari (siccu), to dry up, wither away
siccu, thin, skinny; weak
sicilianu, Sicilian
siculu, Sicilian
sicuru, sure, certain
signu, sign; proof (p -a)
signura, madam, missus (abbr. Mrs.); lady
signuri, sir, mister (abbr. Mr.)
signurina, miss, Miss (abbr. Ms.)
siguenti, following
simana, week
simenza, seed
simili (a), similar (to), alike
siminari (siminu or seminu), to sow
simpaticu, nice
simplici, simple; common
sintirisi (mi sentu), to feel
sipariu, curtain
sira, evening
sirata, evening (duration of)
sirpenti or serpenti, serpent
siti (F), thirst
soggira, mother-in-law
soggiru, father-in-law
sognu, dream
sonnu, sleep; dream
sonu, sound
sordi (p), money
soru (F), sister (p soru)
spaddi (p), back
spanniri, to spill; leak
sparagnari, to save up; spare (e.g., a life)
spariri (sc), to disappear
sparrari, to talk poorly about
sparti, moreover, besides, not including
spata, sword
spenniri, to spend
sperdiri (sperdu), to scatter, disperse, spread
spersu or sparsu or spirdutu, scattered,
    dispersed
spertu, clever, smart
spiari (spiu), to ask, inquire
spicchiu, fruitstone
spiciali, special
spicialità, specialty
spidiri (sc), to send; dispatch
spiegari, to explain, clarify; unfold
spina, thorn; (fish) bone
spinnu, desire, longing (for)
spiranza, hope

199

spirari (speru), to hope
spiritu, spirit; mind; wit
spisa, expense
spissu, often
spugghiari (spogghiu), to deprive, strip
spugghiarisi (mi spogghiu), to undress
spusarisi (mi sposu) (cu), to marry
sputari (sputu), to spit
stabbiliri (sc), to establish
staciuni **or** stagiuni, season
stancarisi (mi stancu), to be tired, become tired
stanza, room
stari (staiu), to stay, dwell
stari pi, to be ready to + infinitive
stati **or** estati (F), summer
statua, statue
stenniri, to spread, stretch out
stidda, star
stinnicchiari (stinnicchiu), to streach out,
    spread out
stirari (stiru), to stretch out; iron
stissu, same; very; own
stomacu, stomach
stoffa, cloth
storia, story; history
stortu, twisted
stranu, strange
stranutari (stranutu), to sneeze
stranutu, sneeze
strata, street
strippa, sterile (adj. with two endings)
strittu, narrow; tight
struzzu, ostrich
studiari, to study
studiu, study
stuiari (stuiu), to wipe
stunatu, out-of-touch, out-of-it
stupennu, stupendous
stupitu, stupid, dumb
su, on
succediri (3s succedi), to happen, take place
suffittu, ceiling
suffriri (soffru **or** suffrisciu), to suffer
suggettu, subject
suli, sun
suliri (sogghiu), to be accustomed to
sulu, alone; only
sumigghianza, similarity; likeness
sunari (sonu), to sound, ring (e.g., telephone),
    play (e.g., an instrument)
sunnarisi (mi sonnu), to dream; imagine
supirari (supiru), to surpass; exceed
suppurtari (supportu), to support; endure

supra, on, on top of (more common than *su*),
    over
surbiri (sc), to sip
surci (M), rat; mouse
surridiri, to smile
surrisu **or** sorrisu, smile
sustituiri (sc) , to substitute, take the place of
sutta, under
sviari (sviu), to lead stray

T

taciri (taciu), to be silent, remain silent
tagghiari (tagghiu), to cut
tali, such
talianu, Italian
taliari (taliu), to look at
tanti voti, many times, often
tantu, so much
tappitu, rug, carpet
tardu, late (see *n ritardu*)
tastari, to taste
tata (M), dad
tauru, bull
tavula, table
tazza, cup (e.g., coffee)
telefunari (telefunu), to telephone
telefunu, telephone
televisioni (F), television
tema (M), theme, subject; topic
tempu, time (p -ura)
teniri (tegnu), to hold, keep
teniri d'occhiu (a), to keep an eye out (for **or**
    on)
tenna, shade (window); tent
terra, earth, land
tessiri, to weave
testa, head
tettu, roof
tigri (F), tiger
tigri masculu, tiger (male)
tila, canvas; screen; curtain; cloth
timpuliari (timpuliu), to slap, smack
tinaci, stubborn, tenacious
tinciri (tinciu), to dye; cheat
tintazzioni, temptation
tintu, bad, wicked, evil; dyed
tirribbili, terrible
togghiri, to take away, remove
tradizzioni, tradition
tranni, except for, save for, but for
tranquillità, calm, tranquility
tranquillu, calm, tranquil, peaceful
trasiri (trasu) (ntra **or** nna), to enter

travagghiari (travagghiu), to work
travagghiu, work; job
tristu, sad; mean
trizza, tress
truvari (trovu), to find
tu, you (fam.)
tuccari (toccu), to touch
tumazzu, cheese
tunnu, round
tuppuliari (tuppuliu), to knock
turcu, non-Catholic (of any creed or religion);
  Turk
turmintari (turmentu), to torment; torture
tussiri (sc), to cough
tuttavia, still; yet; nevertheless; however
tuvagghia, tablecloth
tuvagghiolu, napkin

U

ugnu, nail (e.g., of a finger or toe) (p -a)
umili, humble; unpretentious
ummira, shadow
unicu, sole, only
univirsità or università, university (n.)
univirsitariu or universitariu, university (adj.)
unni, where
ura, hour
ursu, bear
urtimu or ultimu, last

V

vacca, cow
valiri, to be worth
vampa, flame
vancu, bench (p -a)
vanniari (vanniu), to proclaim, cry aloud
vapuri, steam
variu, various
vasari, to kiss
vasca, basin, tub
vasciu, low; soft (e.g., voice)
vasciurata, afternoon
vastuni, cane; stick (p -a)
vasu, vase; kiss
vasuni, kiss (more common than *vasu*) (p -a)
vecchiu, old
veniri (vegnu), to come
veniri a vidiri, to come to see, visit
venneddì or vinniddì or vinniddìa or vennadi,
  Friday
ventu, wind
veramenti or viramenti, truly, very
veru, true

vespa, wasp
vestiri (vestu), to dress
viaggiari, to travel
viaggiu, trip
vicinu (M), vicina (F), neighbor
vicinu, close to, near
vicinu, living nearby
viddanu, peasant; for-hire farm laborer
vidiri or viiri (viu or vidu), to see
vidua or viduva, widow
viduta, sight, view
viduu or viduvu, widower
viggilari (viggilu), to watch over, keep watch
viggilia, vigil, watch
vigna, vineyard
vigurusu, vigorous; hard (e.g. by exertion)
vilenu, poison
vina, vein
vinciri (vinciu) to conquer, win
vinirisinni (mi nni vegnu), to come from (a
    place); have an orgasm, climax
vinniri (vinnu), to sell
vinniceddu, breeze (dim.)
vintura, fortune, destiny, fate
vinu, wine
vippita, drink
virdi chiaru, light green
virdi scuru, dark green
virdi, green
virdura, vegetable
virità, truth
visita, visit
visitari (visitu), to visit, call on
vista, sight, view
vistina, dress
vistirisi (mi vestu), to dress oneself; get
    dressed
vistiti (p), clothes
vistitu, suit (man's)
vita, life
viviri, to drink
viviri, to live
vivu, alive, living; alert
vizziari (vizziu or vizziu), to spoil, corrupt
vizziu, vice, defect (moral)
voscu, woods, forest (p -ura)
vossìa or vussìa, you (pol. s)
vota, turn; time
votu, vote
vrancu, white
vrazzu, arm (p -a)
vrigogna, shame
vucca, mouth

vuci (F), voice
vugghiri (vugghiu), to boil
vui, you (pol. s)
vuiatri **or** vuatri **or** vuiautri **or** vuautri, you (p)
vulari (volu), to fly
vulinteri, willingly
vuliri (vogghiu), to want
vuliri beni, to love
vuliri mali, to hate
vuluntà **or** voluntà, will
vuscari (vuscu), to earn (e.g., a living)
vutari (votu), to vote; turn

Z
zagara [dz], orange blossom

zampa, paw
zappa, hoe
zappuni, mattock (p -a)
zefiru [dz], breeze
zeru [dz], zero
zia **or** za, aunt
zingaru, gypsy
zita, fiancée
zittirisi (mi zittu), be quiet, keep one's mouth
  shut
zitu, fiancé
ziu **or** zu, uncle
zona [dz], zone
zuccaru, sugar

English-Sicilian Vocabulary

This section gives only the English correspondent for those words found in the Sicilian-English vocabulary in the previous section. Different versions of the same word are separated by an **or**. Synonyms are separated by a semicolon. **Note:** All parts of speech are marked for your convenience using these abbreviations: adj. = adjective; adv. = adverb; aug. = augmentative; DO = direct object; dim. = diminutive; interj. = interjection; impers. = impersonal; inv. = invariable; n. = noun; p = plural; pol. = polite; prep. = preposition; pron. = pronoun; s = singular; v. = verb.

A

a day (per day), a lu iornu **or** ô iornu
a week (per week), a la simana **or** â simana
abandon (v.), abbannunari (abbannunu)
able (be) (v.), putiri (pozzu); essiri capaci di
about (prep.), circa; di
absence (n.), assenza
absent (adj.), assenti
accompany (v.), accumpagnari (accumpagnu)
according to (prep.), secunnu **or** sacunnu
accumulate (v.), accumulari (accumulu)
accurate (adj.), propiu **or** propriu
accustomed to (v.), suliri (sogghiu)
acquaintance (n.), canuscenza
act (n.), attu
act (in a certain way) (v.), aggiri
action (n.), attu
adjust (v.), cunzari (conzu)
administer communion (i.e., the sacrament) (v.), cumunicari **or** cuminicari (cumenicu)
adore (v.), adurari (adoru)
adult (adj.), granni
advance (v.), avanzari
advice (n.), cunzigghiu
advise (v.), cunzigghiari (cunzigghiu)
affliction (n.), duluri (M)
after (time) (adv. **or** prep.), doppu
afternoon (n.), vasciurata; doppupranzu
afterwards (adv.), poi
again (adv.), arrè **or** arreri; di novu
against (prep.), contra
agitated (with) (adj.), arraggiatu (cu) **or** raggiatu (cu)
agreement (n.), pattu
aim (n.), fini (M)
alert (adj.), vivu
alike (adj.), simili (a)
alive (adj.), vivu
allow (v.), lassari
alone (adj.), sulu
already (adv.), già

also (adv.), macari, puru
alter (n.), artaru **or** altaru
alter (v.), canciari
always (adv.), sempri
amazement (n.), maravigghia **or** meravigghia
American (n. **or** adj.), miricanu
amuse (v.), arricriari (arricriu)
amuse oneself (v.), arricriarisi (m'arricriu); addivirtirisi (m'addivertu) **or** divirtirisi (mi divertu)
ancestor (n.), antinatu; avu
ancient (adj.), anticu
and (conj.), e
angel (n.), ancilu
anger (n.), arraggia
anger (n.), raggia
angle (of a room) (n.), cantu
angry (at) (adj.), arraggiatu (cu) **or** raggiatu (cu)
animal (n.), bestia; armali
answer (n.), risposta
answer (v.), rispunniri (rispunnu); fari risposta (a)
ant (n.), furmicula
any longer (neg. adv.), mancu
any more (neg. adv.), mancu
appear (v.), pariri
appetite (n.), pitittu
applause (n.), plausu
apple (n.), pumu (p -a)
apprentice (n.), garzuni [dz]
approach (v.), avvicinarisi (m'avvicinu) **or** abbicinarisi (m'abbicinu); (i)ncugnari (ncugnu)
approximately (prep. **or** adv.), circa
argue (with) (v.), sciarriarisi (mi sciarriu) (cu)
argument (n.), sciarra **or** scerra
arm (n.), vrazzu (p -a)
arm (v.), armari
around (prep. **or** adv.), pagghiri
as (adv.), comu

203

ask (v.), addumannari **or** dumannari
ask (v.), spiari (spiu)
ask questions (v.), fari dumanni (a)
ass (posterior) (n.), culu
assure (v.), assicurari (assicuru)
astounding (adj.), maravigghiusu **or**
   meravigghiusu
at (prep.), a
at (the place of **or** the house of) (prep.), nni **or**
   nna
at the side of (prep.), allatu
aunt (n.), zia **or** za
autumn (n.), autunnu
avoid (v.), scanzari

B

baby (n.), picciriddu **or** picciliddu (M),
   picciridda **or** piccilidda (F)
back (n.), spaddi (p)
back (upper) (n.), coddu
bad (adj.), malu; tintu
bad (weather) (adj.), bruttu **or** malu
bad luck (n.), disgrazzia
bad news (n.), malanova
bag (n.), saccu
bait (n.), isca
bang (v.), sbattiri
bank (e.g., sand) (n.), bancu
bank (n.), banca
barbarian (n. **or** adj.), barbaru
bark (v.), abbaiari
basin (n.), vasca
be (v.), essiri (sugnu) **or** siri
be angry (at) (v.), arraggiarisi (m'arraggiu)
   (cu)
be in bloom (v.), sbucciari (sbocciu)
be in love (with) (v.), essiri (i)nnamuratu (di)
be interested (in) (v.), (i)ntirissari (m'intiressu)
   (nna **or** nta)
be irritated (at) (v.), arraggiarisi (m'arraggiu)
   (cu)
be necessary (impers.) (v.), abbisugnari
   (abbisognu) **or** bisugnari (bisognu)
be of use (v.), serviri (mi servi) (impers.)
be realized (v.), avvirarisi (3s s'avvera)
beam (e.g., sun) (n.), raggiu
bear (n.), ursu
beast (n.), bestia
beat (v.), battiri; dari corpa
beautiful (adj.), beddu **or** bellu
beauty (n.), biddizza
become (v.), addivintari (addiventu) **or**
   divintari (diventu)

become angry (at) (v.), ncazzarisi (m'incazzu)
   (cu)
become aware (of) (v.), addunarisi
   (m'addugnu) (di)
become interested (in) (v.), (i)ntirissari
   (m'intiressu) (nna **or** nta)
become rich (v.), arricchirisi (sc) **or**
   ricchirisi (sc)
become tired (v.), stancarisi (mi stancu)
become true (v.), avvirarisi (3s s'avvera)
bed (n.), lettu
bedroom (n.), cammara
bee (n.), apa
beefsteak (n.), bistecca
before (prep. **or** adv.), davanti
begin (v.), accuminciari (accuminciu **or**
   accumenciu) **or** accuminzari (accumenzu)
   or cuminciari (cuminciu **or** cumenciu) **or**
   ncuminzari (ncumenzu)
beginning (n.), principiu
behave (v.), cumpurtarisi (mi cumportu), aggiri
behavior (n.), cumportamentu **or**
   cumpurtamentu
behavior (n.), custumi
behind (prep. **or** adv.), arrè **or** arreri; darrè **or**
   darreri
behold (interj.), eccu
belief (n.), opinioni
believe (v.), cridiri (criu **or** cridu)
belly (n.), panza
belt (n.), cintu
bench (n.), bancu
bench (n.), vancu (p -a)
bend (v.), icari (icu)
berry (n.), cocciu
beside (prep.), allatu
besides (adv. **or** prep.), sparti
better (adj. **or** adv.), megghiu
better (v.), migghiurari (migghiuru)
big (adj.), grossu
bile (n.), feli (M)
bill (e.g., at a shop) (n.),
bind (v.), ligari (legu)
bird (n.), aceddu (p -a **or** -i)
birth (n.), nascita
bit (n.), pezzu
bite (v.), ammuccari (ammuccu)
bitter (adj.), amaru
black (adj.), niuru **or** niru
blame (n.), curpa
blanket (n.), cutra
blessed (adj.), biatu **or** beatu
blind (adj.), cecu

blind (adj.), cecu; orvu **or** orbu
blond (adj. **or** n.), biunnu
blood (n.), sangu
blossom (v.), sbucciari (sbocciu)
blouse (n.), blussa **or** brussa
blow (v.), ciusciari (ciusciu) **or** sciusciari
blue (adj.), azzolu; blu (inv.); (sky blue) celesti **or** cilesti
boil (v.), vugghiri (vugghiu)
bone (fish) (n.), spina
bone (n.), ossu (p -a)
book (n.), libbru (p -a)
born (be) (v.), nasciri (nasciu)
boss (n.), patruni
bothered (with) (adj.), arraggiatu (cu) **or** raggiatu (cu)
bottle (n.), buttigghia
bottom (n.), funnu
bouquet (n.), mazzu (p -a)
box (n.), cassetta; scatula
boy (n.), picciottu (adolescent); carusu
boy friend (n.), (i)nnamuratu
bran (n.), canigghia
branch (n.), rama
bread (n.), pani (M); panuzzu (dim.)
break (v.), rumpiri (rumpu)
break out (v.), scattari
breast (for nursing) (n.), minna
breast (n.), pettu
breath (n.), ciatu **or** sciatu
breath of a hand (lit. palm) (n.), parmu
breathe (v.), ciatari **or** sciatari
breeze (n.), zefiru [dz]; vinticeddu (dim.)
bring to completion (v.), finiri (sc)
broad (adj.), largu
broom (n.), scupa
brother (n.), frati
brown (adj.), marruni **or** marrò
brush (n.), scupitta
buckle (n.), fibbia
build (v.), fabbricari (fabbricu) **or** frabbicari (frabbicu)
bull (n.), tauru
bump (v.), sbattiri
bunch (n.), mazzu (p -a)
burn (v.), bruciari (bruciu) **or** abbruciari
burst (v.), scattari
business (n.), cummerciu
business (n.), nigozziu
business person (n.), mircanti
but (conj.), ma
but for (prep.), eccettu; tranni
buy (v.), accattari

by (prep.), di; pi **or** pri
by means of (prep.), a; cu; pi menzu di
by the way (adv.), a prupositu **or** a proposìtu

C

cadence (n.), cadenza
cage (n.), gaggia
call (v.), chiamari
call on (v.), visitari (visitu)
call out (v.), chiamari
called (be) (v.), chiamarisi
calm (adj.), calmu; tranquillu
calm (n.), calma; tranquillità
calm (n.), bunazza (of the sea)
can (for packaging) (n.), lanna
candle (n.), cannila
cane (n.), vastuni
canvas (n.), tila
cap (n.), coppula
car (n.), machina
care (n.), cura
carpet (n.), tappitu
carry (v.), purtari (portu)
cash (e.g., a check) (v.), scanciari
cash (n.), cuntanti
cat (n.), gatta **or** iatta (F), gattu **or** iattu (M)
catch (v.), pigghiari (pigghiu)
cathedral (n.), cattidrali (F)
Catholic (n. **or** adj.), cristianu (see turcu); catolicu
caution (n.), prudenza **or** prudenzia
cautious (adj.), prudenti
ceiling (n.), suffittu
center (n.), centru
century (n.), seculu
certain (adj.), sicuru
chaff (n.), canigghia
chain (n.), catina
chair (n.), seggia
chalk (n.), issu **or** gessu
change (v.), canciari
chapter (n.), capitulu
charm (n.), grazzia
chase (v.), cacciari
chatter (n.), chiacchiara **or** chiacchira
chatter (v.), chiacchiariari (chiacchiariu)
cheap (adj.) **or** cheaply (adv.), a bon mircatu; a picca prezzu
cheat (v.), (i)ngannari; tinciri (tinciu)
check (e.g., bank check) (n.), assegnu
cheese (n.), caciu; frumaggiu **or** furmaggiu; tumazzu
chest (of body) (n.), pettu

chicken coop (n.), gaddinaru or iaddinaru
  (p –a)
chickpea (n.), ciciru
child (n.), picciriddu or picciliddu (M),
  picciridda or piccilidda (F)
chirp (e.g., a bird) (v.), ciuciuliari (ciuciuliu)
church (n.), chesa or chiesa or clesia or cresia;
  church (n.), (the chief one in the town),
  matrici (F)
cigarette (n.), sicaretta
city (n.), città
clarify (v.), chiariri (sc); spiegari
clean (v.), pulizziari (pulizziu)
clear (adj.), chiaru
clever (adj.), spertu
climax (sexually) (v.), vinirisinni (mi nni
  vegnu)
climb (v.), acchianari; (i)nchianari
climb into (e.g., a car) (v.), acchianari (nna);
  (i)nchianari (nna)
climb out of (e.g., a car) (v.), scinniri (scinnu)
  (di)
clock (n.), riloggiu
close (v.), chiudiri (chiuiu or chiudu)
cloth (n.), tila; stoffa
clothes (n.), vistiti (p); robbi (p)
cloud (n.), nuvula
cloud (large) (n.), nevula or neula
coal (n.), carvuni (M)
coin (n.), munita
cold (n. or adj.), friddu
collapse (n.), ruina
college (n.), culleggiu or colleggiu
collide (head on) (v.), scuntrari (scontru)
color (n.), culuri (M)
come (v.), veniri (vegnu)
come back (v.), riturnari (ritornu)
come from (a place) (v.), vinirisinni (mi nni
  vegnu)
come to see (v.), veniri a vidiri; visitari (visitu)
comfortable (adj.), commudu; cunfurtibbili
command (v.), cumannari
commerce (n.), cummerciu
common (adj.), simplici; cumuni
communicate (v.), cumunicari (cumunicu)
complexion (n.), carnaciumi or carnaciuni (F)
complexion (dark) (n.), carnaciumi or
  carnaciuni scura
complexion (fair) (n.), carnaciumi or
  carnaciuni chiara
concern (v.), aviri a chi fari (cu)
condemn (v.), cunnannari
conduct (v.), cunnuciri (cunnuciu)

congratulate (v.), cungratulari (cungratulu)
connect (v.), ligari (legu)
connection (n.), nessu
conquer (v.), vinciri (vinciu)
consider (v.), cunziddirari (cunziddiru)
content (adj.), cuntenti; cuntentu
convenient (adj.), commudu; cumminienti
convict (v.), cunnannari
cook (n.), cocu (p -a or -i)
cook (in a general sense) (v.), cucinari (cucinu)
cook (v.), cociri (cociu) (takes an object)
copper (n.), ramu
copper coin (n.), granu (p -a)
cord (n.), corda
corner (n.), angulu; cantu
corrupt (v.), currumpiri or corrumpiri; vizziari
  (vizziu or vizziu)
cost (n.), costu
cost (v.), custari (3s costa)
cotton (n.), cuttuni
cough (v.), tussiri (sc)
counsel (n.), cunzigghiu
counsel (v.), cunzigghiari (cunzigghiu)
count (v.), cuntari (cuntu)
country (n.), paisi (M); campagna
courage (n.), curaggiu; ficatu (p -a)
courageous (adj.), curaggiusu
courageous, be (v.), essiri curaggiusu; aviri
  ficatu
courteous (adj.), gintili
courtyard (n.), curtigghiu
cousin (n.), cucina (F), cucinu (M)
cover (v.), cummigghiari (cummogghiu)
cow (n.), vacca
crazy (adj.), pazzu; foddi
cream (n.), panna
create (v.), criari (criu)
crow (v.), cantari
crowd (n.), fudda
crowned (adj.), curunatu
crumb (n.), muddica
crush (v.), macinari (macinu)
cry (v.), chianciri (chianciu) or cianciri
cry aloud (v.), vanniari (vanniu)
cucumber (n.), citrolu
cultured (adj.), cultu
cup (e.g., coffee) (n.), tazza
current (n. or adj.), currenti
curse (v.), malidiciri (malidiciu)
cursed (adj.), malidittu
curtain (n.), tila; sipariu
custom (n.), custumi; abbitutini (F)
cut (v.), tagghiari (tagghiu)

D

dad (n.), pà (M); tata (M)
daily (adj.), cutiddianu
damage (n.), dannu **or** danniggiu
damage (v.), danniggiari (danneggiu)
damn (v.) malidiciri (malidiciu)
damned (adj.) malidittu
dark (adj.), niuru; scuru
dark (e.g., of a color) (adj.), scuru (e.g., virdi scuru)
dark-completed (adj.), scuru, di peddi scura
daughter (n.), figghia
daughter-in-law (n.), nora
daughters (n. p), figghi fimmini
dawn (impers.) (v.), agghiurnari (3s agghiorna)
dawn (n.), arba
day (n.), iornu (p -a); iurnata (duration of)
dead (adj.), mortu
dead man (n.), mortu
dead one (n.), murticeddu (dim.)
deadly (adj.), murtali
dear (adj.), caru
death (n.), morti
debate (v.), raggiunari (raggiunu)
debt (n.), debbitu
decide (v.), dicidiri (dicidu)
deed (n.), fattu; attu
deer (n.), cervu
defecate (v.), cacari; iri di corpu
defect (moral) (n.), vizziu
defect (n.), difettu
delay (n.), ritardu
delicacy (n.), diliziu **or** dilizzia
delicious (adj.), dilizziusu; sapurusu
delicious thing (n.), dilizziu
delighted (adj.), letu
depart (v.), partiri
deprive (v.), spugghiari (spogghiu)
deprived (of food) (adj.), diunu
descend (v.), scinniri (scinnu) (di)
desire (n.), disiu **or** disidderiu; spinnu
desire (v.), addisiari (addisiu) **or** disiari (disiu) **or** addisiddirari (addisiddiru) **or** disiddirari (disiddiru)
destiny (n.), vintura; distinu
detest (v.), oddiari (oddiu); ditistari (ditestu)
devil (n.), diavulu
dialect (n.), dialettu (often used to refer to Sicilian, as in *n dialettu*, that is, in Sicilian)
diamond (n.), diamanti (M)
die (v.), moriri **or** muriri (moru)
difficult (adj.), difficili

dim (adj.), scuru
dinner (n.), cena
director (n.), diritturi
disappear (v.), scumpariri; spariri (sc)
discourse (n.), discursu
discuss (v.), raggiunari (raggiunu); parrari
disease (n.), malatia; mali (M); pesta
dispatch (v.), spidiri (sc)
disperse (v.), sperdiri (sperdu)
dispersed (adj.), spersu **or** sparsu **or** spirdutu
distant (adj.), luntanu; distanti
do (v.), fari (fazzu)
dog (n.), cani (M)
dominate (v.), duminari (dominu)
donkey (n.), sceccu
door (n.), porta
dot (n.), puntu
doubt (n.), dubbiu
doubt (v.), dubbitari (dubbitu)
downfall (n.), ruina
dowry (n.), dota **or** doti
dream (v.), sunnarisi (mi sonnu)
dream (n.), sonnu **or** sognu
dress (n.), vistina
dress (v.), vestiri (vestu)
dress oneself (v.), vistirisi (mi vestu)
drink (n.), vippita **or** bippita
drink (v.), viviri **or** biviri
drinking glass (n.), biccheri (p -a)
drive (e.g., a car) (v.), maniari (maniu)
drop (n.), guccia
drought (n.), asciuttu
drug store (n.), farmacia
drunk (adj.), (i)mmriacu **or** (i)mpriacu
dry (adj.), asciuttu
dry up (v.), siccari (siccu)
dryness (n.), asciuttu
dumb (adj.), loccu; stupitu
dung (n.), fumeri (M)
dung heap (n.), munnizzaru (p -a); munzeddu di fumeri
during (prep. **or** adv.), duranti
dust pan (n.), paletta di munnizza
dwell (v.), stari (staiu)
dye (v.), tinciri (tinciu)
dyed (adj.), tintu

E

each (precedes noun) (inv. adj.), ogni
ear (n.), oricchia **or** aricchia
early (adv.), prestu
earn (e.g. money) (v.), guadagnari **or** vadagnari

earn (e.g., a living) (v.), vuscari (vuscu)
earth (n.), terra
easy (adj.), facili
eat (v.), manciari
economical (adj.), ecunomicu
economize (v.), risparmiari (risparmiu)
effect (n.), scopu
effort (n.), fatica; sforzu
egg (n.), ovu (p -a)
elbow (n.), guvitu
elegant (adj.), eleganti or liganti
embarrassment (v.), marazzu
employee (n.), (i)mpiegatu
employment (n.), (i)mpiegu
enclose (v.), nchiudiri (nchiuiu or nchiudu)
encounter (n.), ncontru
encounter (v.), (i)ncuntrari (ncontru); scuntrari
   (scontru)
end (n.), fini (F)
end (v.), accabbari (accabbu); finiri (sc)
end of the week (n.), fini dâ simana
end up (v.), iri a finiri
endow (v.), addutari (addotu) or dutari (dotu)
endowment (n.), dota or doti
endure (v.), suppurtari (supportu)
enemy (n.), nimicu (p -ci)
energy (n.), energia
engineer (n.), (i)ncigneri (M or F)
English (n. or adj.), (i)nglisi (M), (i)nglisa (F)
enjoy (v.), godiri or gudiri (godu)
enough (adj.), bastibbili, abbastanza (inv.)
enough (adv.), abbastanza
enough, be (v.), abbastari (3s abbasta) or
   bastari (3s basta)
enrich (v.), arricchiri (sc) or ricchiri (sc)
enter (v.), trasiri (trasu) (ntra or nna)
epoch (n.), ebbica or epica or epuca
error (n.), erruri (M); sbagghiu
establish (v.), stabbiliri (sc)
estinguish (e.g., a light, a fire, etc.) (v.),
   astutari
European (n. or adj.), europeu
even (adv.), macari, puru
evening (n.), sira; sirata (duration of)
evening meal (n.), cena
every (precedes noun) (inv. adj.), ogni
evident (adj.), chiaru
evil (adj.), malu; tintu
evil (n.), mali (M)
exact (adj.), esattu; pricisu; propiu or propriu
exactly (adv.) propiu or propriu
exceed (v.), supirari (supiru)
except for (prep.), eccettu; tranni

exchange (v.), scanciari; canciari
excrement (n.), cacca
excuse (v.), scusari (scusu)
exhibit (v.), esibbiri (sc); mustrari (mostru)
exit (v.), nesciri (nesciu) (di)
expense (n.), spisa
expensive (adj.), caru
explain (v.), spiegari; chiariri (sc)
explode (v.), esplodiri; scattari
explosion (n.), esplosioni (F); bottu
extract (v.), scippari (scippu)
eye (n.), occhiu

F

face (n.), facci (F)
facing (prep. or adv.), (i)nfacci
fact (n.), fattu
fair (just) (adj.), giustu or iustu
fall (v.), cadiri
fall asleep (v.), addurmisciri (addurmisciu)
fall in love (with) (v.), (i)nnamurarisi
   (m'innamuru) (di)
false (adj.), fausu
family (n.), famigghia
far away (adj.), luntanu
far off (adv.), arrassu
farm laborer (n.), viddanu
fast (adj.), lestu
fasting (adj.), diunu
fat (adj.), grassu
fate (n.), vintura
father (n.), pà (M); patri (M)
father-in-law (n.), soggiru
fatigue (n.), fatica
fault (n.), curpa
favor (v.), favuriri (sc)
fear (n.), scantu
feather (n.), pinna
feeble (adj.), debbuli
feel (v.), sintirisi (mi sentu)
feeling (n.), senzu
feign (v.), finciri (finciu)
fellow (n.), cristianu
fennel (n.), finocchiu
festival (n.), festa
fiancé (n.), zitu
fiancée (n.), zita
fig (n.), ficu (F) (p ficu)
fight (n.), sciarra or scerra; liti
fight (with) (v.), sciarriarisi (mi sciarriu) (cu)
figure (n.), figura or fiura
fill (v.), inchiri (inchiu)
fill up (v.), inchiri (inchiu)

film (n.), pillicula
filth (n.), fumeri (M)
finally (adv.), finarmenti
find (v.), truvari (trovu)
finger (n.), iditu (p -a)
finish (v.), finiri (sc); accabbari (accabbu)
fire (destructive) (n.), (i)ncendiu
fire (n.), focu (p -a)
first dish (in a restaurant) (n.), primu (piattu)
fish (n.), pisci (M)
fist (n.), pugnu (p -a)
flag (n.), bannera
flame (n.), ciamma or sciamma; vampa
flash (n.), lampu
flash (v.), lampiari (3s lampia)
flat (adj.), chianu
flatten (v.), stirari (stiru)
flavor (n.), sapuri (M)
flea (n.), pulici (M)
flee (v.), fuiri; scappari
flesh (n.), carni (F)
floor (n.), pavimentu
flour (n.), farina
flow (v.), scurriri
flower (n.), ciuri or sciuri (M)
flower (v.), ciuriri or sciuriri (sc)
fly (n.), musca
fly (v.), vulari (volu)
fly off the handle (at) (v.), ncazzarisi
    (m'incazzu) (cu)
following (adj.), siguenti
food (n.), pastu
fool (n.), pazzu (lit. crazy); babbu
foolish (adj.), pazzu; scioccu; babbu
foot (n.), pedi (M)
for (prep.), a; pi or pri
for the sake of (prep.), pi or pri
forbearance (n.), pacenza or pacenzia
force (n.), forza
foresee (v.), prividiri (prividu)
foreseen (adj.), prividutu or privistu
forest (n.), voscu (p -ura)
forget (v.), scurdarisi (mi scordu)
fork (n.), furchetta
fortunate (adj.), biatu or beatu; furtunatu
fortune (n.), furtuna; vintura
forward (v.), mannari
fountain (n.), funtana
free (adj.), libbiru
free movement (n.), passaportu
French (n. or adj.), francisi (M), francisa (F)
fresh (adj.), friscu

Friday (n.), venneddì or vinniddì or vinniddìa
    or vennadi
friend (F) (n.), amica (p -chi)
friend (M) (n.), amicu (p -ci)
fright (n.), scantu
frighten (v.), scantari
frightened (adj.), scantusu
frightened (be) (v.), scantarisi (mi scantu)
from (prep.), a; di
fruit (n.), fruttu (p -a or -i)
fruitstone (n.), spicchiu
fry (v.), friiri
frying pan (n.), padedda
fulfilled (adj.), curunatu
full (adj.), sazziu (satiated); chinu
fun (have) (v.), addivirtirisi (m'addivertu) or
    divirtirisi (mi divertu)
fun (n.), divirtimentu
furnish (v.), armari
furniture (in general) (n.), mubbilia
furniture (individual piece) (n.), mobbili (M)

G

gait (n.), andatura or annatura
game (n.), iocu (p -ura)
garbage (n.), munnizza
garden (n.), iardinu (p -a or -i)
garlic (n.), agghiu
gasoline (n.), binzina
gather (v.), cogghiri (cogghiu)
gather up (v.), arricogghiri (arricogghiu)
gauge (v.), misurari (misuru)
get dressed (v.), vistirisi (mi vestu)
gift (n.), donu (p -a); rigalu or rialu
girl (n.), picciotta (adolescent); carusa
girl friend (n.), (i)nnamurata
give (as a gift) (v.), arrigalari (arrigalu) or
    rigalari (rigalu)
give (v.), dari (dugnu); proiri (proiu) (a)
give in dowry, (v.), addutari (addotu) or dutari
    (dotu)
glad (adj.), letu
gloomy (adj.), niuru
glorious (adj.), gluriusu
glory (n.), gloria
gnaw (v.), arrusicari (arrusicu)
go (v.), iri (vaiu)
go away (v.), irisinni (mi nni vaiu)
go or come down (from), (v.), scinniri (scinnu)
    (di)
go out (of) (v.), nesciri (nesciu) (di)
go to bed (v.), curcarisi (mi curcu)
goal (n.), fini (M)

goblet (n.), gottu

god (n.), diu (p dei **or** dii)

goddess (n.), dia

gold (n.), oru

good (adj.), bonu

good heavens! (interj.), caspita!

good-looking (adj.), beddu **or** bellu

goods (n.), mircanzia

gossip (n.), chiacchiara **or** chiacchira

gossip (v.), chiacchiariari (chiacchiariu)

grace (n.), grazzia

grain (individual) (n.), (p -a), cocciu

grain (n.), frumentu **or** furmentu

grandchild (n.), niputi (M **or** F)

grandfather (n.), nannu **or** nonnu; patri granni; avu

grandmother (n.), nanna **or** nonna; matri granni; ava

grape (individual) (n.), cocciu di racina

grapes (p) (n.), racina

grate (v.), arraspari

great (adj.), granni

greatgrandfather (n.), avu

greatgrandmother (n.), ava

green (adj.), virdi

grind (v.), macinari (macinu)

group (n.), gruppu

grow (v.), crisciri (crisciu)

grow up (v.), crisciri (crisciu)

gypsy (n.), zingaru

H

habit (n.), custumi; abbittutini (F)

habitual (adj.), abbituali

hair (of the body) (n.), pilu (p -a)

hair (of the head) (n.), capiddu

hallowed (adj.), santu

hand (n.), manu (F) (p manu)

hand (to) (v.), proiri (proiu) (a)

hand over (to) (v.), proiri (proiu) (a)

handle (e.g., by hand) (v.), maniari (maniu)

handsome (adj.), beddu **or** bellu

happen (v.), succediri (3s succedi)

happy (adj.), biatu **or** beatu; cuntenti; cuntentu; giulivu

hard (e.g. by exertion) (adj.), vigurusu

hard (to do) (adj.), difficili

harm (v.), danniggiari (danneggiu)

haste (n.), prescia

hastily (adv.), (i)mprescia

hat (n.), cappeddu (p -a)

hate (v.), vuliri mali; oddiari (oddiu)

hatred (n.), feli (M); oddiu

have (v.), aviri (aiu)

have a dark complexion (v.), **essiri scuru di peddi**

have a desire (for) (v.), aviri disidderiu (di); aviri spinnu (di)

have dinner (v.), cinari (cenu); fari cena

have fun (v.), addivirtirisi (m'addivertu) **or** divirtirisi (mi divertu)

have a good time (v.), addivirtirisi (m'addivertu) **or** divirtirisi (mi divertu)

have a light complexion (v.), **essiri chiaru di peddi**

have an orgasm (v.), vinirisinni (mi nni vegnu)

have an urge (to) (v.), aviri disidderiu (di); aviri spinnu (di); aviri vogghia (di)

have to (v.), aviri a (ê)

have to do (with) (v.), aviri a chi fari (cu)

hazelnut (n.), nucidda

he (pron.), iddu

head (n.), testa

health (n.), saluti (F)

heap (n.), munzeddu

hear (v.), (i)ntenniri (ntennu); sentiri (sentu)

heart (n.), cori

heat (n.), caudu

heavens (n.), celu (p -a **or** -i)

heavy (strong) (adj.), forti

heavy (weighty) (adj.), pisanti

heed (v.), dari cuntu (a)

help (n.), aiutu

helper (n.), garzuni [dz]

hen (n.), gaddina **or** iaddina

here (adv.), ccà

here are (adv.), eccu

here is (adv.), eccu

heritage (n.), eredità

hide (of an animal) (n.), peddi (F)

hide (v.), ammucciari (ammucciu); cummigghiari (cummogghiu)

hinder (v.), (i)mpidiri (sc)

history (n.), storia

hit (v.), battiri

hit (with an object) (v.), mazziari (mazziu)

hoe (n.), zappa

hold (v.), teniri (tegnu)

holy (adj.), santu

home (n.), casa

honey (n.), meli (M)

honor (n.), onuri **or** anuri

hook (n.), amu

hope (n.), spiranza

hope (v.), spirari (speru)

horse (n.), cavaddu

horseman (n.), cavaleri (M)
hot (adj.), caudu
hour (n.), ura
house (n.), casa
however (adv.), tuttavia
humble (adj.), umili
hunger (n.), fami (F)
hungry (adj.), affamatu
hungry, be (v.), aviri fami
hunt (v.), cacciari
hurredly (adv.), (i)mprescia
hurry (n.), prescia
hurt (impers.) (v.), doliri or duliri (mi doli)

I

I (pron.), iu or eu or io
ice (n.), ghiacciu
ice cream (n.), gilatu or gelatu
icy (adj,), gilatu or gelatu
ignorant (adj.), (i)gnuranti
ill (adj.), malatu
illness (n.), malatia; mali (M)
imagine (v.), (i)mmagginarisi (m'immagginu);
    sunnarisi (mi sonnu)
immortal (adj.), (i)mmurtali
improve (v.), migghiurari (migghiuru)
in front of (prep. or adv.), davanti
in (prep.), a; nni or nna; nta
in a rush (adv.), (i)n fretta; (i)n prescia
in fact (adv.), (i)n fatti
in the vicinity of (prep. or adv.), pagghiri
incite (v.), scuncicari (sconcicu or scuncicu)
inhabit (v.), abbitari (abbitu)
injure (v.), firiri (sc)
injury (n.), dannu or danniggiu
innocent (adj.), (i)nnuccenti
inquire (v.), spiari (spiu)
insane (adj.), pazzu; foddi
insinuate oneself (v.), ficcarisi (mi ficcu)
instead of (prep.), scancia
insult (n.), (i)nciuria
intelligent (adj.), ntilliggenti or ntelliggenti
intense (adj.), forti
interest (n.), (i)ntiressu or (i)ntiressi
interest (v.), (i)ntirissari (ntiressu)
interesting (adj.), (i)ntirissanti or (i)nterissanti
intimate (adj.), intimu
invite (v.), (i)mmitari or (i)nvitari
iron (n.), ferru
iron (v.), stirari (stiru)
it (pron.), idda (F); iddu (M)
Italian (n. or adj.), talianu
itch (e.g., from an irritation) (v.), manciari

J

jacket (n.), giacca
jail (n.), carciri (M); galera
jar (n.), baccara; baccaredda (dim.)
jealousy (n.), gilusia
jewel (n.), giuellu
job (n.), travagghiu
joyous (adj.), giulivu
judge (n.), iudici (M)
judgment (n.), pariri
just (adv.) propiu or propriu
just imagine! (interj.), bonu!
justice (n.), giustizzia

K

keep (v.), teniri (tegnu)
keep an eye out (for or on) (v.), teniri d'occhiu
    (a)
keep one's mouth shut (v.), zittirisi (mi zittu)
keep watch (v.), viggilari (viggilu)
kernel (n.), cocciu
key (n.), chiavi (F)
kill (v.), ammazzari
kind (adj.), gintili
kingdom (n.), regnu
kiss (n.), vasuni
kiss (v.), vasari
kitchen (n.), cucina
kitchen stove (n.), furneddu (dim.)
kitten (n.), gattareddu (dim.)
knead dough (v.), (i)mpastari
knife (n.), cuteddu (p -a)
knock (v.), tuppuliari (tuppuliu)
knot (n.), gruppu
know (a fact) (v.), sapiri (sacciu)
know (a person) (v.), canusciri (canusciu)
know how (v.), sapiri (sacciu)

L

ladder (n.), scala
ladle (n.), cucchiara
ladle (v.), cucchiariari (cucchiariu)
lady (n.), donna; signura
lake (n.), lacu or lagu
lamb (n.), agneddu (p -a or -i)
lamp (n.), lampa; lumi
land (n.), terra
landlord (n.), patruni
language (n.), lingua
large (adj.), granni; grossu
last (adj.), urtimu or ultimu
late (adj.), tardu; (i)n ritardu

laugh (v.), ridiri (riu **or** ridu)

laundry (n.), biancaria

lawyer (n.), avvucatu **or** abbucatu

lay down (v.), pusari (posu)

lazy (adj.), lagnusu

lead (the metal) (n.), chiummu

lead stray (v.), sviari (sviu)

leaf (n.), fogghia

leak (v.), spanniri

learn (v.), (i)mparari

leave (alone) (v.), lassari

leave (v.), irisinni (mi nni vaiu); partiri;
   abbannunari (abbannunu)

leave from (v.), nesciri (nesciu) (di)

leg (n.), iamma **or** amma

lend (v.), (i)mpristari (mprestu)

length (n.), lunghizza

leopard (n.), pardu

less (pron. **or** adv.), menu

let (v.), lassari

letter (n.), littra

level (adj.), chianu

lie (untruth) (n.), minzogna

lie down (v.), curcarisi (mi curcu)

life (n.), vita

lift up (v.), isari (isu) **or** aisari

light (adj.), liggeru

light (e.g., of a color) (adj.), chiaru (e.g., virdi
   chiaru)

light (n.), luci (F)

light (artificial) (n.), lumi (M)

light bulb (n.), lampadina (elettrica)

ligth-completed (adj.), chiaru, di peddi chiara

light post (n.), lampa

light up (v.), addumari (addumu)

lighten (v.), lampiari (3s lampia)

lightning (n.), lampu

lightning bolt (n.), furmini **or** fulmini (M)

like (adv.), comu

like (v.), aggradiri (sc) **or** gradiri (sc); piaciri

likeness (n.), sumigghianza

liking (n.), gradimentu

limit (v.), limitari (limitu)

line (n.), fila

linen (n.), linu

linens (n.), biancaria

lining (n.), fodira

link (n.), nessu

lion (n.), liuni (p -a)

lioness (n.), liunissa

Lira (n.), lira

list (n.), lista

listen to (takes DO) (v.), ascutari (ascutu)

list (n.), lista

little (adj.), nicu

little boy (n.), picciriddu **or** picciliddu (M)

little girl (n.), picciridda **or** piccilidda (F)

live (in a place) (v.), abbitari (abbitu); stari

live (v.), campari; viviri

liver (n.), ficatu

living (adj.), vivu

living nearby (adj.), vicinu

loan (v.), (i)mpristari (mprestu)

long (adj.), longu

longing (for) (n.), spinnu

look (interj.), eccu

look at (v.), taliari (taliu); guardari **or** vardari

look for (v.), circari (cercu)

look out for (v.), guardari **or** vardari

lose (v.), perdiri (perdu)

love (n.), amuri (M)

love (v.), amari; vuliri beni

lovely (adj.), prizziusu

low (adj.), vasciu

luck (n.), furtuna

luck (bad) (n.), mala sorti

M

machine (n.), machina

madam (n.), signura

maid (n.), cammarera

make (v.), fari (fazzu)

make holy (v.), santificari (santificu)

make oneself over again (v.), arrifarisi
   (m'arrifazzu)

make rich (v.), arricchiri (sc) **or** ricchiri (sc)

mallet (n.), mazza

man (n.), omu (p omini)

manage (v.), maniari (maniu)

many times (adv.), tanti voti

marble (n.), marmu

market (n.), mircatu

marry (v.), spusarisi (mi sposu) (cu)

marvel (n.), maravigghia **or** meravigghia

marvellous (adj.), maravigghiusu **or**
   meravigghiusu

mass (n.), missa

master (n.), patruni

mattock (n.), zappuni (p -a)

mature (v.), maturari (maturu)

meal (n.), pastu

mean (adj.), tristu

meanwhile (adv.), (i)ntantu

meanwhile (n.), frattempu

measure (v.), misurari (misuru)

meat (n.), carni (F); bistecca

meet (v.), (i)ncuntrari (ncontru); scuntrari (scontru)

meeting (n.), ncontru

mend (v.), arripizzari (arripezzu)

menu (n.), lista

merchandise (n.), mircanzia

merchant (n.), mircanti

metal (n.), mitallu or metallu

metallic (adj.), mitallicu or metallicu

middle (n.), centru

milk (n.), latti

millipede (poisonous) (n.), millipedi

mind (n.), spìritu

misfortune (n.), disgrazzia; guaiu (p guai)

miss (abbr. Ms.), signurina

missus (abbr. Mrs.) (n.), signura

mistake (n.), sbagghiu

mister (abbr. Mr.) (n.), signuri

mix (v.), miscari

modulation (n.), cadenza

momma (n.), mà; mamma

Monday (n.), luneddì or luniddì or luniddìa or lunidi

money (n.), sordi (p); dinaru or dinari (p more common); liri (p); quattrini (p); munita; picciuli (p); scuti (p); grana (p)

money (ready-at-hand) (n.), cuntanti

monk (n.), monacu (p -ci)

month (n.), misi

moon (n.), luna

Moor (n.), moru

more (pron. or adv.), cchiù

moreover (adv.), sparti

morning (n.), matina

mortal (adj.), murtali

moss (n.), muscu

moth (n.), camula

moth-eaten (adj.), camulutu

mother (n.), mà; matri; mamma

mother-in-law (n.), soggira

mountain (n.), muntagna

mouse (n.), surci (M)

mouth (n.), vucca

movie (n.), pillicula

mug (n.), gottu

murmur (v.), ciuciuliari (ciuciuliu); murmuriari (murmuriu)

music (n.), musica

must (juice extracted from grapes) (n.), mustu

N

nail (e.g., of a finger or toe) (n.), ugnu (p -a)

name (n.), nomu

named (be) (v.), chiamarisi

napkin (n.), tuvagghiolu

narrate (v.), raccuntari (raccuntu)

narrow (adj.), strittu

nature (n.), natura

necessity (n.), nicissità or nicissitati (older form)

neck (n.), coddu

need (n.), bisognu

need (v.), abbisugnari (abbisognu) or bisugnari (bisognu)

neighbor (n.), vicina (F), vicinu (M)

nephew (n.), niputi (M)

nerve (n.), nervu

never again (adv.), mai cchiù

nevertheless (adv.), tuttavia

new (adj.), novu

news (bad) (n.), malanova

nice (adj.), simpaticu; bonu

nickname (n.), (i)nciuria

niece (n.), niputi (F)

night (n.), notti; nuttata (duration of)

no (adv.), no

nobleman (n.), cavaleri (M)

noise (n.), scrusciu; bottu

non-Catholic (regardless of race or creed) (n. or adj.), turcu

nose (n.), nasu

not (adv.), non or nun or un or nn' (before a vowel)

not including (adv. or prep.), sparti

note (musical) (n.), nota

note (n.), nota

note (v.), nutari (notu)

notebook (p -a or -i) (n.), quaternu or quadernu

notice (v.), guardari or vardari; addunarisi (m'addugnu) (di)

nun (n.), monaca (p -chi)

nurse (v.), addattari

nut (in general) (n.), nucidda

O

oak tree (n.), cersa

ocean (n.), mari

odor (n.), oduri or aduri

of (prep.), di

offense (n.), (i)nciuria

offer (n.), offertà

offer (v.), offriri or uffriri (offru)

often (adv.), tanti voti; spissu

oil (n.), ogghiu (p -a)

old (adj.), vecchiu; anticu

older (adj.), granni
olive (n.), aliva **or** oliva
on (prep.), ncapu; su; supra (more common
   than *su*)
on the back (adv.), (i)ncoddu
on top of (prep.), supra; (i)ncapu
once (adv.), na vota
only (adj.), unicu
only (adv.), sulu
opinion (n.), opinioni; pariri
opposite (prep.), contra
orange (n.), aranciu
orange blossom (n.), zagara [dz]
ordinary (adj.), ordinariu **or** urdinariu; currenti
origin (n.), radica
orphan (n.), orfanu
ostrich (n.), struzzu
other (pron. **or** adj.), autru
ought to (v.), duviri (devu **or** divu)
out-of-it (adj.), stunatu
out-of-touch (adj.), stunatu
oven (n.), furnu
over (prep. **or** adv.), supra
owe (v.), duviri (devu **or** divu)
own (adj.), propiu **or** propriu; stissu
owner (n.), patruni

P

pace (n.), andatura **or** annatura
package (n.), pacchettu
pact (n.), pattu
pain (n.), duluri (M)
painting (n.), quatru
pair (n.), paru (-a)
pants (n.), causi (p)
paper (n.), carta
paradise (n.), paradisu
pardon (v.), pirdunari (pirdugnu **or** pirdunu)
parents (p) (n.), ginituri **or** genituri
party (n.), festa
pass (time, etc.) (v.), passari
pass over to (e.g., a house) (v.), passari
pass down (v.), addutari (addotu) **or** dutari
   (dotu)
passport (n.), passaportu
patch (v.), arripizzari (arripezzu)
patience (n.), pacenza **or** pacenzia
paw (n.), zampa
pay (v.), pagari
pay attention (to) (v.), dari cuntu (a)
peace (n.), paci
peaceful (adj.), calmu; tranquillu
peasant (n.), viddanu

pen (n.), pinna
pencil (n.), matita
penitentiary (n.), galera
people (n.), genti (F) (collective n.); populu
pepper (n.), pipi
perceive (v.), percepiri (percepu)
period (of time) (n.), ebbica **or** epica **or** epuca
period (of punctuation) (n.), puntu
person (n.), cristianu; pirsuna
pest (n.), pesta
pharmacy (n.), farmacia
physician (n.), medicu (p -ci)
piazza (n.), chiazza
pick (v.), cogghiri (cogghiu)
picture (n.), quatru; ritrattu
piece (n.), pezzu
pig (n.), porcu (p -ci)
pile (n.), munzeddu
pillow (n.), cuscinu
pillow case (n.), fodira di cuscinu
pious (adj.), piu
pipe (n.), pipa
piss (v.), pisciari
place (n.), banna
place (n.), postu
place (v.), poniri (pognu); pusari (posu)
plague (n.), pesta
plain (flat) (adj.), chianu
plant (v.), chiantari
plaster (n.), issu **or** gessu
plate (n.), piattu (p -a **or** -i)
play (e.g., an instrument) (v.), sunari (sonu)
play (v.), iucari (iocu)
please (impers.) (v.), piaciri (mi piaci)
please (v.), aggradiri (sc) **or** gradiri (sc);
   arricriari (arricriu)
please oneself (v.), arricriarisi (m'arricriu)
pleased (adj.), letu
pleasure (n.), piaciri (M); gradimentu
plotting (adj.), (i)ntricanti
plug up (v.), attuppari (attuppu)
plump (adj.), chiattu
poison (n.), vilenu
poison (v.), avvilinari (avvilenu) **or** abbilinari
   (abbilenu)
polish (v.), pulizziari (pulizziu)
polite (adj.), gintili
ponder (v.), riflettiri (riflettu)
poor (adj.), poviru
poor man (n.), poviru
poor one (n.), puvireddu (dim.)
pop (father) (n.), pà (M); tata
portrait (n.), ritrattu

possible (adj.), pussibbili **or** possibbili
pot (little) (n.), pignatedda (dim.)
pot (n.), pignata
potato (n.), patata
power (n.), forza
precious (adj.), prizziusu
precise (adj.), pricisu
prepare (v.), priparari (priparu)
present (adj.), prisenti
present (n.), donu (p -a); rigalu **or** rialu
present (v.), arrigalari (arrigalu) **or** rigalari
    (rigalu)
president (n.), prisidenti
press against (v.), (i)ncugnari (ncugnu)
pretend (v.), finciri (finciu)
pretty (adj.), beddu **or** bellu
price (n.), costu
primitive (adj.), sarvaggiu
proclaim (v.), vanniari (vanniu)
professor (n.), prufissuri (M) (p -a),
    prufissurissa (F)
proof (n.), signu (p -a)
proper (adj.), propiu **or** propriu
prophet (n.), prufeta (M)
protect (v.), cummigghiari (cummogghiu);
    riparari
proud (adj.), orgugliusu
provoke (v.), scuncicari (sconcicu **or** scuncicu)
prudence (n.), prudenza **or** prudenzia
prudent (adj.), saviu; prudenti
puke (v.), lanzari
pull out (v.), scippari (scippu)
punish (v.), castigari (castigu)
pure (adj.), puru
purpose (n.), fini (M); prupositu **or** propositu
push (v.), ficcari (ficcu); (i)ncugnari (ncugnu)
put (in the mouth) (v.), ammuccari (ammuccu)
put (v.), mettiri
put down (v.), pusari (posu)
put on (e.g., a shirt) (v.), mittirisi (mi mettu)

Q

quality (n.), qualità
quarrel (n.), sciarra **or** scerra; liti
question (n.), dumanna **or** dimanna
question (v.), fari dumanni (a)
queue (n.), fila
quick (adj.), lestu
quiet (n.), riposu
quiet, be (v.), zittirisi (mi zittu)
quote (v.), citari

R

rabbit (n.), cunigghiu
rabies (n.), arraggia **or** raggia
radius (n.), raggiu
rag (n.), pezza
rage (n.), arraggia **or** raggia
rain (impers.) (v.), chioviri (3s chiovi)
rain (n.), acqua
raise (v.), isari (isu) **or** aisari
rare (adj.), raru
rat (n.), surci (M)
rational (adj.), raggiunevuli
ray (n.), raggiu
read (v.), leggiri (leggiu)
ready to + infinitive (v.), stari pi
reap (v.), arricogghiri (arricogghiu)
rear end (n.), culu
reason (e.g., man's reason) (n.), raggiuni
reason (purpose) (n.), mutivu **or** motivu;
    prupositu **or** propositu; (i)ntinzioni
reasonable (adj.), raggiunevuli
rebel (v.), ribbillarisi (mi ribbellu)
receive (v.), riciviri (ricivu)
receive communion (v.), cumunicarisi (mi
    cumunicu) **or** cuminicarisi (mi cumenicu)
recommend (v.), racumannari
reconcile (people) (v.), accurdari (accordu)
record (v.), nutari
recover (e.g., one's health) (v.), arrifarisi
    (m'arrifazzu)
red (adj.), russu
reflect (v.), riflettiri (riflettu)
refuse (v.), rifiutari (rifiutu)
regret (v.), lamintarisi (mi lamentu)
relative (n.), parenti (M **or** F)
religion (n.), riliggioni **or** religgioni
religious (adj.), piu; riliggiusu **or** religgiusu
remain (v.), arristari (arrestu) **or** ristari (restu)
remember (v.), arricurdarisi (m'arricordu) **or**
    ricurdarisi (mi ricordu)
remove (v.), livari (levu); togghiri
repair (v.), riparari; cunzari (conzu)
repeat (v.), ripetiri (ripetu)
reply (v.), rispunniri (rispunnu); fari risposta
    (a)
reputed (adj.), putativu
require (v.), abbisugnari (abbisognu) **or**
    bisugnari (bisognu)
requirement (n.), bisognu
rescue (v.), scanzari
respect (n.), rispettu
respond (v.), rispunniri (rispunnu);
response (n.), risposta

215

rest (n.), riposu
rest (v.), ripusari (riposu)
return (v.), riturnari (ritornu)
reveal (v.), scummigghiari (scummogghiu)
rice (n.), risu
rich (adj.), riccu
right (adj.), giustu **or** iustu
right (adv.) propiu **or** propriu
ring (e.g., telephone) (v.), sunari (sonu)
ripen (v.), maturari (maturu)
river (n.), ciumi **or** sciumi (M)
roast (v.), arrustiri (arrustu **or** arrustisciu)
rob (v.), arrubbari (arrobbu) **or** rubbari (robbu)
rogue (n.), mariolu
roguish (adj.), mariolu
romantic (adj.), rumanticu
roof (n.), tettu
room (n.), stanza
rooster (n.), gaddu **or** iaddu
root (n.), radica
rope (n.), corda
rose (n.), rosa
round, tunnu (adj.),
rubbish pile (n.), munnizzaru (p -a)
rug (n.), tappitu
ruin (n.), ruina
run (v.), curriri (curru)
run away **or** run off (v.), scappari
run into (v.), scuntrari (scontru)
Russian (n. **or** adj.), russu

S

sack (n.), saccu
sad (adj.), tristu
saint (n.), santu
salt (n.), sali (M)
same (adj.), stissu
sanctify (v.), santificari (santificu)
sardine (n.), sarda
satiated (adj.), sazziu
satisfy (v.), quatrari
Saturday (n.), sabbatu **or** sabbatuddì **or** sabbatuddìa
sauce pan (little) (n.), pignatedda (dim.)
sauce pan (n.), pignata
savage (adj.), sarvaggiu
save for (prep.), eccettu
save for (prep.), tranni
save **or** save up (v.), sparagnari; risparmiari (risparmiu)
save (rescue from) (v.), scanzari
savior (n.), sarvaturi
say (v.), diri (dicu)

scare (v.), scantari
scared (adj.), scantusu
scatter (v.), sperdiri (sperdu)
scattered (adj.), spersu **or** sparsu
scene (n.), scena
scheming (adj.), (i)ntricanti
school (n.), scola
scold (v.), rimpruvirari (rimproviru)
scorch (v.), bruciari (bruciu) **or** abbruciari
scorpion (n.), scurpiuni **or** scorpiuni
scoundrel (n.), mariolu
scratch (v.), arraspari
screen (n.), tila
sea (n.), mari
season, (n.), staciuni **or** stagiuni
second dish (in a restaurant) (n.), secunnu (piattu)
see (v.), vidiri **or** vidiri (viu **or** vidu)
seed (n.), simenza
seek (v.), circari (cercu)
seem (v.), pariri (mi pari)
seize (v.), pigghiari (pigghiu)
sell (v.), vinniri (vinnu)
send (v.), spidiri (sc); mannari
sense (n.), senzu
serpent (n.), sirpenti **or** serpenti
serve (esp. liquid food) (v.), cucchiariari (cucchiariu) serve (v.), serviri (servu)
servile (adj.), servu
set (n.), gruppu
set (v.), poniri (pognu)
set in order (v.), cunzari (conzu)
set up (e.g., a business) (v.), armari
severe (adj.), forti
sew (v.), cusiri **or** cusiri (cusu)
shade (window) (n.), tenna
shadow (n.), ummira
shake up (v.), arriminari (arriminu)
shame (v.), vrigogna
shape (n.), figura **or** fiura
she (pron.), idda
sheep (n.), pecura
sheet (n.), linzolu (p -a)
shield (n.), scutu
shine (v.), brillari
shiny (adj.), lustru
ship (n.), navi (F)
shirt (n.), cammisa
shit (n.), cacca; merda
shit (v.), cacari
shoe (n.), scarpa
shop (n.), putia, nigozziu

shopping center **or** shopping mall (n.), gruppu di putii; centru cummerciali

short (adj.), curtu

show (v.), esibbiri (sc); mustrari (mostru); fari vidiri (a)

shun (v.), scanzari

Sicilian (n. **or** adj.), sicilianu; siculu

sick (adj.), malatu

side dish (n.), cuntornu

sight (n.), vista **or** viduta

sign (n.), signu (p -a)

silent (be **or** remain) (v.), taciri (taciu)

silly (adj.), scioccu

silver (n.), argentu

similar (to) (adj.), simili (a)

similarity (n.), sumigghianza

simple (adj.), simplici

sin (n.), piccatu

sin (v.), piccari (peccu)

sing (v.), cantari

sip (v.), surbiri (sc)

sir (n.), signuri

sister (n.), soru (F) (p soru)

sit down (v.), assittarisi (m'assettu)

skin (n.), peddi (F)

skinny (adj.), asciuttu; magru; siccu

skirt (n.), gonna

sky (n.), celu (p -a **or** -i)

slang (n.), gergu

slap (v.), timpuliari (timpuliu)

slave (n.), schiavu

sleep (n.), sonnu

sleep (v.), dormiri **or** durmiri (dormu)

slice (n.), fedda

slight (adj.), liggeru

smack (v.), timpuliari (timpuliu)

small (adj.), picciulu; nicu

small change (n.), picciuli (p); quattrini (p)

smart (adj.), (i)ntilliggenti **or** (i)ntelliggenti; spertu

smell (not pejorative) (n.), oduri **or** aduri

smile (n.), surrisu **or** sorrisu

smile (v.), surridiri

smoke (e.g., a cigarette) (v.), fumari (fumu)

smoke (e.g., meat) (v.), affumari (affumu)

smoke (n.), fumu

smooth (adj.), chianu

sneeze (n.), stranutu

sneeze (v.), stranutari (stranutu)

snow (n.), nivi (F)

so (adv.), accussì **or** cussì

so much (adj. **or** pron.), tantu

soap (n.), sapuni (M)

sock (n.), quasetta **or** causetta

soft part of bread (n.), muddica

soft (e.g., voice) (adj.), vasciu

sole (adj.), unicu

some (pron. **or** adj.), quarchi **or** qualchi **or** cacchi

sometimes (adv.), quarchi vota **or** qualchi vota

son (n.), figghiu

song (n.), cantu; canzuna

son-in-law (p -a) (n.), ennaru **or** iennaru

sons (n. p), figghi masculi

soon (adv.), prestu

sorrow (n.), duluri (M)

soul (n.), arma

sound (n.), sonu

sound (v.), sunari (sonu)

source (n.), radica

sow (v.), siminari (siminu **or** seminu)

span (n.), parmu

spare (e.g., a life) (v.), sparagnari

sparkle (v.), brillari

speak (v.), parrari

special (adj.), spiciali

specialty (n.), spicialità

spend (v.), spenniri

spill (v.), spanniri

spirit (n.), spiritu

spit (v.), sputari (sputu)

spoil (v.), vizziari (vizziu **or** vizziu)

spoon (large) (n.), cucchiara

spoon (n.), cucchiaru (p -a)

spread (v.), stenniri; sperdiri (sperdu)

spread out (v.), stinnicchiari (stinnicchiu)

spring (n.), primavera

squander (v.), sfragari

square (adj.), quatratu

square (e.g., of a town) (n.), chiazza

square (geometric form) (n.), quatratu

staircase (n.), scala

stairs (n.), scala

star (n.), stidda

start (a new day) (v.), agghiurnari (agghiornu)

start (v.), mettiri

statue (n.), statua

stay (v.), stari (staiu); arristari (arrestu) **or** ristari (restu)

steam (n.), vapuri

steel (n.), azzaru (p -a)

step (of a staircase) (n.), scaluni (p -a)

steps (a series of) (n.), scalunata

sterile (adj. with two endings), strippa

stick (n.), vastuni

still (adv.), tuttavia

stir (v.), arriminari (arriminu)

stitch (v.), cusiri **or** cusiri (cusu)

stocking (n.), quasetta **or** causetta

stomach (n.), stomacu, panza

stone (n.), petra

stop up (v.), attuppari (attuppu)

store (n.), putia

story (n.), cuntu; storia

stout (adj.), chiattu

straighten (v.), addrizzari (addrizzu)

strange (adj.), stranu

straw (n.), pagghia

stream (n.), currenti

street (n.), strata

strength (n.), forza; nervu

stretch out (v.), stinnicchiari (stinnicchiu);
   stirari (stiru); stenniri

strike (v.), battiri

strip(v.), spugghiari (spogghiu)

stroll (n.), passiata

stroll (v.), passiari (passiu); fari na passiata

strong (adj.), forti

stubborn (adj.), tinaci

study (n.), studiu

study (v.), studiari

stuff (n.), robba

stupendous (adj.), stupennu

stupid (adj.), loccu; scioccu; babbu; stupitu

subdialect (n.), parrata

subject (n.), suggettu; tema (M)

substitute (v.), sustituiri (sc)

succeed at (v.), arrinesciri (arrinesciu)

successful (adj.), arrinisciutu

such (adj.), tali

suckle (v.), addattari

suffer (v.), suffriri (soffru **or** suffrisciu)

suffice (v.), abbastari (3s abbasta) **or** bastari
   (3s basta)

sufficient (adj.), bastibbili, abbastanza (inv.)

sugar (n.), zuccaru

suit (man's) (n.), vistitu

summer (n.), stati **or** estati (F)

sun (n.), suli

Sunday (n.), duminica **or** duminicaddì **or**
   duminicaddìa

supper (n.), cena

support (v.), suppurtari (supportu)

supposed (adj.), putativu

sure (adj.), sicuru

surpass (v.), avanzari; supirari (supiru)

sweet (adj.), duci

switch (to whip with) (n.), nervu

sword (n.), spata

T

table (n.), tavula

tablecloth (n.), tuvagghia

tail (n.), cuda

take (the place of) (v.), sustituiri (sc)

take (v.), pigghiari (pigghiu)

take a mistress (v.), (i)ngarzari [dz]

take away (v.), livari (levu); togghiri

take note (v.), addunarisi (m'addugnu)

take off (e.g., a shirt) (v.), livarisi (mi levu)

take place (v.), succediri (3s succedi)

talk (n.), discursu

talk poorly about (v.), sparrari

tall (adj.), longu

taste (n.), sapuri (M)

taste (v.), tastari; sapiri (have a determinate
   taste); assaggiari

tasty (adj.) sapurusu

teach (v.), (i)nzignari (nzignu)

teacher (n.), prufissuri (M) (p -a);
   prufissurissa (F)

tear (v.), rumpiri

teaspoon (n.), cucchiaredda (dim.)

telephone (n.), telefunu

telephone (v.), telefunari (telefunu)

television (n.), televisioni (F)

tell (e.g., a story) (v.), cuntari (cuntu);
   raccuntari (raccuntu)

tell (v.), diri (dicu)

tell lies (v.), diri minzogni

temptation (n.), tintazzioni

tenacious (adj.), tinaci

tent (n.), tenna

terrible (adj.), tirribbili

thank (v.), ringrazziari (ringrazziu)

thank you, grazzii

thanks (n.), plausu; grazzii

theme (n.), tema (M)

then (adv.), poi

there are (adv. + v.), cci sunnu **or** cci su'

there is (adv. + v.), cc'è

they (pron.), iddi

thick (adj.), (i)ncuttu

thief (n.), latru

thin (adj.), magru; siccu

thing (n.), cosa

think (impers.) (v.), pariri (mi pari)

think (v.), cridiri (criu **or** cridu); pinzari
   (penzu)

thirst (n.), siti (F)

thirsty, be (v.), aviri siti

thorn (n.), spina

thrash (v.), dari corpa
thread (n.), filu (p -a)
thread into (v.), (i)nfilari (m'infilu) (nni **or** nta)
throat (n.), cannarozza (p) **or** cannarozzi (p); gula
through (prep.), pi **or** pri
throw (v.), ittari (ettu **or** iettu)
throw up (v.), lanzari
thrust (v.), ficcari (ficcu)
Thursday (n.), gioveddì **or** giuviddì **or** giuviddìa **or** iuviddì **or** iuviddìa **or** iovidi
thus (adv.), accussì **or** cussì
tie (n.), cravatta
tie (v.), ligari (legu)
tiger (male) (n.), tigri masculu
tiger (n.), tigri (F)
tight (adj.), strittu
time (n.), tempu (p -ura)
time (period of time) (n.), vota
tired, be (v.), stancarisi (mi stancu)
to (prep.), a; pi **or** pri
today (adv.), oi **or** oggi
together (adv.), (i)nzemmula **or** (i)nzemi
tomorrow (adv.), dumani
tongue (n.), lingua
tooth (n.), denti (M)
topic (n.), tema (M); quistioni
topple (v.), allavancari
torment (v.), turmintari (turmentu)
torture (v.), turmintari (turmentu)
touch (v.), maniari (maniu); tuccari (toccu)
tour (n.), giru
tour (v.), girari
towards (prep. **or** adv.), pagghiri
town (n.), paisi (M)
toy (n.), giucattulu
tradition (n.), tradizzioni
tranquility (n.), calma; tranquillità
tranquility (of the sea) (n.), bunazza
tranquil (adj.), calmu; tranquillu
trash (n.), munnizza
travel (v.), viaggiari
tree (n.), **arvulu or** arburu
trespass (v.), piccari (peccu)
tress (n.), trizza
trip (n.), viaggiu
trouble (n.), mali (M); guaiu (p guai)
true (adj.), veru
truly (adv.), veramenti **or** viramenti
truth (n.), virità
try (sample) (v.), assaggiari
try (v.), circari (cercu)
tub (n.), vasca

Tuesday (n.), marteddì **or** martiddì **or** martiddìa **or** martidi
tune up (an instrument) (v.), accurdari (accordu)
Turk (n. **or** adj.), turcu
turn (n.), vota
turn (v.), vutari (votu)
turn off (e.g. a light) (v.), astutari
turn on (e.g. a light) (v.), addumari (addumu)
twisted (adj.), stortu

U

ugly (adj.), bruttu; ladiu **or** lariu
uncertainty (n.), dubbiu
uncle (n.), ziu **or** zu
uncover (v.), scummigghiari (scummogghiu)
under (prep.), sutta
understand, capiri (sc); (i)ntenniri (ntennu)
underwear (n.), biancaria
undress (v.), spugghiarisi (mi spogghiu)
unfold (v.), spiegari
unfortunate (adj.), **poviru**; sfurtunatu
university (adj.), univirsitariu **or** universitariu
university (n.), univirsità **or** università
unpretentious (adj.), **umili**
unusual (adj.), raru
urinate (v.), pisciari
usual (adj.), abbituali

V

various (adj.), variu
vegetable (n.), virdura
vegetables (n.), ligumi (p)
vein (n.), vina
versus (prep.), contra
very (adv.), assai; granni; veru; veramenti **or** viramenti
very close (adj.), (i)ncuttu
vex (v.), scuncicari (sconcicu **or** scuncicu)
vice (n.), vizziu
view (n.), vista **or** viduta
vigil (n.), viggilia
vigorous (adj.), vigurusu
village (n.), paisi (M)
vinegar (n.), acitu
vineyard (n.), vigna
visit (n.), visita
visit (v.), **veniri a vidiri**; visitari (visitu)
voice (n.), vuci (F)
vomit (n.), lanzu
vomit (v.), lanzari
vote (n.), votu
vote (v.), vutari (votu)

W

waiter (n.), cammareri (p -a)
waitress (n.), cammarera
walk (v.), caminari (caminu)
wall (n.), muru (p -a or -i)
walnut (n.), nuci (F)
want (v.), vuliri (vogghiu)
war (n.), guerra
wash (v.), lavari
wasp (n.), vespa
waste (v.), sfragari
watch (n.), riloggiu
watch (n.), viggilia
watch over (v.), viggilari (viggilu)
water (n.), acqua
we (pron.), nuiatri or niatri or nuiautri or
    niautri; nui
weak (adj.), debbuli; siccu
weave (v.), tessiri
Wednesday (n.), mercoleddì or merculiddì or
    merculiddìa or mercuddì or mercuddìa or
    mercudi
week (n.), simana
weep (v.), chianciri (chianciu) or cianciri
well! (interj.), bonu!
well-being (n.), saluti (F)
what (pron.), chi
wheel (n.), rota
when (adv.), quannu
where (adv.), unni
which (pron.), quari or quali
whisper (v.), ciuciuliari (ciuciuliu)
white (adj.), biancu or iancu or vrancu
who (pron.), cui or cu
wicked (adj.), malu; tintu
wide (adj.), largu
widow (n.), cattiva; vidua or viduva
widower (n.), viduu or viduvu
wife (n.), mogghi (F) or mugghieri (F)
wild (adj.), sarvaggiu
will (n.), vuluntà or voluntà
willingly (adv.), vulinteri
win (v.), vinciri (vinciu)
wind (n.), ventu
wind up (in) (v.), (i)nfilari (m'infilu) (nni or
    nta)
window (n.), finestra
wine (n.), vinu
wing (n.), ala
winter (n.), (i)mmernu or (i)nvernu
wipe (v.), stuiari (stuiu)

wire (n.), filu (p -a)
wise (adj.), saviu
wise person (n.), saviu
wish (n.), disiu or disidderiu
wish (v.), addisiari (addisiu), addisiddirari
    (addisiddiru), disiari (disiu), disiddirari
    (disiddiru)
wit (n.), spiritu
with (prep.), cu
wither away (v.), siccari (siccu)
within (prep.), nta; ntra; dintra
without (prep.), senza
woe (n.), guaiu (p guai)
wolf (n.), lupu (p -a)
woman (n.), fimmina; donna (Italianism)
wood (n.), lignu (p -a)
woods (n.), voscu (p –ura)
wool (n.), lana
word (n.), parola or palora
work (n.), travagghiu
work (v.), travagghiari (travagghiu)
work into (v.), (i)nfilari (m'infilu) (nni or nta)
world (n.), munnu
world (adj.), munniali
worse (adj. or adv.), peiu or peggiu
worth (be) (v.), valiri
wound (n.), firita
wound (v.), firiri (sc)
wow! (interj.), caspita!
write (v.), scriviri (scrivu)

Y

year (n.), annu
yellow (adj.), giarnu or giannu
yes (adv.), sì
yesterday (adv.), aieri
yet (adv.), tuttavia
you (fam.) (pron.), tu
you (p) (pron.), vuiatri or vuatri or vuiautri or
    vuautri; vui
you (pol. s) (pron.), vussìa or vossìa; vui; lei
young (adj.), giuvina (F), giuvini (M); nicu
young man (n.), picciottu
young woman (n.), picciotta
you're welcome, pregu

Z

zero (n.), zeru [dz]
zone (n.), zona [dz]

Index

Please consult also the Table of Contents in the front since it contains a listing of topics considered in this book.